Educational

Measurements

and their

Interpretation

EDUCATIONAL

MEASUREMENTS

and their

INTERPRETATION

Frederick B. Davis

University of Pennsylvania

Wadsworth Publishing Company, Inc.

Belmont, California

L.C. Cat. Card No.: 64 – 18138
Printed in the United States of America
Second printing: August 1965

Preface

This book is intended as a basic text for courses in psychological and educational measurement and as a handbook for clinical and school psychologists, counselors, and school administrators. It emphasizes the practical uses of tests and other evaluative instruments in schools and clinics. As a school psychologist and consultant in measurement, I discovered that most of the questions about testing and the uses of tests posed by teachers, counselors, and school administrators were not answered in standard texts in the field. Therefore, in chapters 8, 9, 10, 11, and 13 I have formulated many of these questions, presented techniques for answering them, and illustrated these techniques with actual test scores. Appendix M provides information about many tests in common use; it makes computation unnecessary when one is using the techniques for interpreting individual scores given in chapter 8.

Since, like most texts, this book includes more material than can be covered in some courses, it has been organized to serve students with widely different backgrounds and interests. In an introductory undergraduate course in psychological testing or educational measurement, the needs of some students can best be met by covering only chapters 1 through 8, 12, and appendix M. A course so organized omits all computation of the basic statistics given in appendixes A through G.

An elective course for typical college seniors or beginning graduate students might perhaps cover chapters 1 through 8, 12, and 13, plus appendixes A through G, and M. Other parts of the book are then conveniently available for special assignments or independent reading. Instructors of graduate courses in which the students have already taken beginning courses in statistics or in psychological and educational measurement may wish to use chapters 1 through 7 and appendixes A through G mainly as review material and to concentrate on chapters 8 through 13 and appendixes H, I, and M. The material in these chapters, together with the readings in the lists of selected references, will usually challenge the best graduate students, including those who have had good mathematical training.

The inclusion of material not readily available elsewhere on the interpretation of individual and group scores, the measurement of change, the measurement of over- and underachievement, and school marking procedures

vii

makes this book particularly suitable for graduate courses in educational measurement, psychological testing, and measurement in guidance. Students who have used traditional textbooks in these areas will find that much of the content of this book supplements rather than duplicates what they have already learned.

The types of tests and test interpretations discussed in this book are limited to those that can appropriately be used by psychologists, counselors, teachers, and other school personnel who do not have extensive clinical experience involving approved supervised training in clinical practice. For this reason, descriptions of personality inventories and projective techniques have been omitted. Accumulated data point more and more to the conclusion that these inventories and techniques lack useful validity, especially when they are administered to examinees who want to make the best possible impression.

The statistical symbols used in this book reflect modern practice and will facilitate the students' progression to more advanced texts. It will be noted that an estimate of the population standard deviation, denoted s, is ordinarily employed instead of the sample standard deviation—denoted S in this book—which is commonly used in introductory texts in educational or psychological measurement. The computation of both statistics is given in appendix C.

Learning exercises are not included in this book because they will be available in a self-teaching workbook to accompany this text.

I am grateful to Arthur P. Coladarci, Lee J. Cronbach, Leonard S. Feldt, Eric F. Gardner, Donald M. Medley, Marion F. Shaycoft, and Robert E. Stake for helpful comments about the manuscript and to Charlotte Croon Davis for her many suggestions, especially with respect to chapter 12.

Frederick B. Davis

ACKNOWLEDGMENT

I am indebted to the late Professor Sir Ronald A. Fisher, F.R.S., Cambridge, to Dr. Frank Yates, F.R.S., Rothamsted, and to Messrs. Oliver & Boyd, Edinburgh, for permission to reprint, in abridged form, Table No. III from their book "Statistical Tables for Biological, Agricultural and Medical Research."

TABLE OF CONTENTS

Chapter One

MEASUREMENT AND ITS USES IN SCHOOLS

THE NATURE OF MEASUREMENT

When most people think of *measurement* in education, they think only of written examinations or tests. While the latter are indeed used, they provide only a small part of the necessary information. Assigning an object or a person to one of two or more groups or ranking one object or person as better or worse in some respect than another is just as much a part of measurement as obtaining a test score for a pupil or his strength of grip. For example, a teacher who says, "John is a fine boy," is measuring John in two respects: first, she assigns him to a category of people that she labels *fine* (rather than to categories that she might label *ordinary* or *disagreeable*), and, second, she assigns him to the male sex.

In the same way, a teacher who describes Helen as a "better speller than May" has, on the basis of some kind of information, measured the spelling status of both girls and compared their rank orders in spelling status. The information may have been the teacher's impression of the correctness with which the girls spelled words in their written compositions or it may have consisted of objectively determined scores on a carefully constructed spelling test. Measurements of one sort or another are constantly being made by anyone professionally involved in education. If formal or informal tests are not used, other data that lead to judging pupils are employed. It is, therefore, desirable for all educators to understand the fundamental nature of measurement, how it can be useful in schools, how to employ measurements effectively and fairly, and how to interpret the data obtained in the process.

Defining what is to be measured. A basic requirement for measurement is defining the property or the characteristic to be measured. If this property

1

or characteristic can be defined, it can (however imperfectly) be measured. Since a person or an object ordinarily has many observable properties, the property to be measured should be defined as precisely as possible. *Length*, for example, is the property possessed by a line, but not by a point (which has only *position*). *Area* is possessed by every surface, and *volume* by every three-dimensional object. When units of measurement (such as inches, acres, cubic centimeters) are agreed upon, the properties of length, area, and volume can be expressed as numerical quantities.

Measurement by grouping. The crudest sort of measurement consists simply of defining a property carefully and judging whether a person or an object possesses any of it or none of it. The amount possessed, if any, is not specified. In schools, measurement by grouping is used in many ways—for example, when we separate pupils into two groups, boys and girls, and provide curricula that differ, especially in physical education, for the two groups.

A somewhat more refined type of measurement is represented by defining a property and setting up categories representing degrees or amounts of it. A teacher may rate the posture of the pupils in his class according to five categories:

Category	Description
5	Very good; erect carriage at all times.
4	Good; moderately erect carriage at all times.
3	Mediocre; carriage generally not erect.
2	Poor; carriage tends to be slouched.
1	Very poor; slouches badly most of the time.

When pupils are grouped in this way, a distinction can be made between the posture of any pupil in one category and that of another pupil in a different category, but no distinctions can be made among the postures of the pupils in any one category.

None of the distinctions among pupils in the five categories indicate *how much* better one pupil's posture is than another's. This measurement by grouping merely indicates that pupils in category 5 are judged superior in some degree to those in category 4; that those in category 4 are judged superior in some degree to those in category 3; and so on. There is no reason to believe that the improvement in posture represented by the difference between categories 4 and 5 is the same as that represented by the difference between categories 3 and 4, or any other two categories.

Measurement by ranking. Carried to its limit, grouping pupils into categories that represent degree or amount of a defined property or characteristic means setting up as many categories as there are pupils. The pupils are placed in rank order according to the amount of the property each is judged to possess.   The pupil judged to exhibit the property to the highest degree may be assigned rank 1, the pupil judged to exhibit the property to the next highest degree may be assigned rank 2, and so on.

The advantages of ranking are clear.   If there are no ties (pupils judged to exhibit the defined property to the same degree), each individual can be differentiated from every other.   No claim need be made that the differences between successive ranks represent equal increments of the property measured.   For example, if pupils were ranked on the basis of posture, the pupil ranked 5 might have markedly better posture than the pupil ranked 6, whereas the pupil ranked 1 might have only the tiniest bit better posture than the pupil ranked 2.

However, measurement by rankings has certain grave limitations.   The rank order assigned to one or more of the pupils in a group may be changed if one or more pupils drop out or if new pupils enter the group.   In other words, there is nothing fixed or absolute about ranks.   They are relative only to the particular persons or objects ranked.   Furthermore, the fact that the differences between successive ranks may represent varying increments in the property on which the rankings are based affects the meaningfulness of ordinary mathematical operations applied to them.   Adding, subtracting, multiplying, and dividing ranks may produce misleading results.   This severely limits the usefulness of ranks for many purposes.

Another fundamental weakness in ranking is that, if the number of pupils to be ranked is large, the fine distinctions required to assign a different rank to each pupil simply cannot be made with a reasonable degree of accuracy for most of the properties or characteristics of importance in schools.   Certain physical measurements, such as height and weight, could probably be measured in exceedingly fine units if special instruments were employed.   But ordinary stadiometers (calibrated in eighths of an inch) or scales (calibrated in quarter pounds) cannot yield measurements fine enough to prevent many ties from occurring in a large group of pupils.

Measurement by fixed values.   To avoid some of the limitations of ranking, most measurement in schools is accomplished by assigning certain tasks for all pupils to perform.   A numerical value is attached by one means or another to the outcome of each task performed; the sum of these values is usually taken as the total score for each pupil.   For example, a typical objective test comprises sixty tasks; each task is called an *item*.   The property or characteristic to be measured by the test is carefully defined in advance, and items are devised to cause the examinees to perform tasks that make up elements or aspects of that property or characteristic.

It is often conveniently assumed that each task represented by an item is of equal importance in the property being measured and that the same numerical value can be assigned to a successful performance of each item.

Successful performance is ordinarily defined as the choice of an answer given in the scoring key as correct; all other answers are considered incorrect. Each incorrect response is usually assigned the same numerical value, which is often zero. The scoring of a test is thus made very easy and almost free from differences among scorers. Anyone who scores the test carefully will get the same result.

The assumption that the task required by each item is equally important in determining the property or characteristic that the test is intended to measure is rarely, if ever, completely justified. However, in a well-constructed test it is often satisfied well enough for practical purposes.

Some tests, especially those used informally by teachers in their own classes, are made up of items that do not include responses from which a choice is to be made. Instead, the pupil may be asked to respond in a word, a sentence, a paragraph, or even an essay; items of this kind can be called *open-end* items.

Open-end items are chiefly useful for teaching purposes. Paragraphs or essays constitute a record of a pupil's thinking processes as he wrote his response. As such, it may be rated by his teacher for completeness and accuracy of content and adequacy of written expression. When it is returned to the pupil, it should be discussed with him and used as a basis for further study and rewriting; otherwise, much of its unique value will be lost.

Measurement by fixed values has the merit of obtaining scores that, at least for objectively scored items, are independent of the nature of the group tested. A pupil who takes an objectively scored test will get the same score whether he is a member of a below-average or an above-average group. The scoring is easy, quick, and consistent from pupil to pupil. With ingenious and well-constructed items, a wide variety of factual knowledge, work skills, reasoning processes, understandings, attitudes, and opinions can be measured.

It is, nonetheless, true that each increase of one point in total score does not represent the same increment in the property measured by a fixed-value test; to help overcome this defect, test scores are sometimes converted to derived scores (see chapter 2). However, the correspondence of fixed-value scores and increments in the property measured by these tests is usually considered sufficiently close to permit performing ordinary mathematical operations (such as addition, subtraction, multiplication, and division) with the scores.

USES OF TESTS IN SCHOOLS

Measurement has always played an important role in education; teachers have used examinations to guide their teaching and to determine how much their pupils have learned.   However, it is only since the end of the nineteenth century that a concerted and systematic effort has been made to develop and refine examinations and to apply them in a scientific way.

Examinations and tests of one sort or another, formal or informal, are used by conscientious teachers for several purposes:

1. To find out at the beginning of a school year or other teaching period what knowledge, skills, and understandings their pupils already possess in the subject matter to be taught.   Examinations given for this purpose are often called *pretests*.   Ideally, the program of study for each pupil should be planned on the basis of his pretest scores and other relevant information about him.   In practice, the best that can be done in most schools is to form, within each class, groups that have different assignments adjusted to the level of their average pretest scores.   At the very least, pretest scores indicate to the teacher the general level and range of knowledge or skill in the class.

2. To determine periodically the extent to which pupils have learned the subject matter taught.   Most of the examinations used for this purpose must be constructed by the teacher to cover the specific knowledge, skills, and understandings that he has taught.   Properly constructed and used, these examinations provide intermediate goals for pupils, motivate them to carry out their assignments, and indicate the need for and the content of reviews.   Their results often lead to the regrouping of pupils within the classroom and serve as one of the bases on which marks or grades may be determined.

3. To compare the achievement of an individual pupil with the achievement levels of pupils in his own class or at his grade level in the school, the community, or the nation.   Comparisons of this kind often provide a meaningful framework or perspective by which an individual's performance can be evaluated.

4. To compare the achievement level of a pupil in one subject-matter field with his achievement in another field or in several other fields. Elementary school teachers, for example, often make comparisons of this kind to identify the strengths and weaknesses of an individual pupil. This kind of information enables them to capitalize on his strengths and build up his areas of weakness.

5. To identify pupils who are exceptionally gifted or unusually poor in their attainments.   Special assignments and opportunities can be pro-vided for gifted pupils, and provisions for remedial instruction can be made for those whose achievement in basic subjects, such as reading or arithmetic, is outstandingly low.

6. To compare the current subject-matter achievement of a pupil with his previous or future achievement in the same field.   This type of comparison permits conclusions regarding his progress in learning.

7. To estimate a pupil's potential or aptitude for learning.   Esti-mates of this kind are often made by means of the assumption that the individual pupil has had roughly the same opportunity to learn the material tested as have average pupils of his age or grade group.   Next, his level of attainment is compared with that of pupils of his age or grade

group; then, it is inferred that he will maintain his relative standing in the group as he learns more of the material tested, or material fairly similar to it in terms of the mental and physical abilities employed.

8. To estimate whether a pupil has learned as much in a given sub-ject-matter area as his potential or aptitude for learning in the area would lead one to expect. This sort of comparison is basic to a judgment of the degree of achievement displayed by a pupil. For obvious reasons, teachers are usually more interested in identifying underachievers than overachievers.

All these uses of tests, plus some other uses, are discussed in this book. Practical examples are given, and the basic principles underlying them are outlined so that teachers can understand what they are doing and can generalize from the specific applications discussed.

A teacher needs to know how to use tests to solve practical problems in planning instruction and understanding pupils; a teacher also needs to know how to build adequate examinations to measure what his pupils have learned. He must be familiar with the procedures for combining test scores, ratings of classroom and laboratory performance, and other factors to obtain valid, fair, and reasonably accurate marks.

A teacher must also know how to select standardized tests from the large number in print. He must be able to talk intelligently with parents, school administrators, guidance counselors, and school psychologists about the achievement and aptitudes of his pupils. If he is going to read educa-tional journals and reports, he needs a minimal knowledge and understanding of measuring instruments in the schools; otherwise, the terms used will make the reports nearly meaningless to him.

School administrators and guidance counselors need to know how teachers can profitably use examinations. They also have occasion to compare groups of pupils with one another and with representative samples of pupils of various types. They must be especially skilled in selecting tests for school use and in discussing test results with parents and pupils. Coun-selors, of course, have a special need for test scores to predict a pupil's performance in subsequent schooling and in various occupational fields for which he may want to prepare.

Education in the 1960s is clearly moving toward a closer association between measurement and teaching practices. Nowhere is this more appa-rent than in the individualization of instruction through the use of care-fully programmed instructional materials; repeated checks on attainment are characteristic of these. The increasing desire for high standards and quality in educational institutions and the recognition that more generous social and financial support must be provided to attain and maintain these goals mean, inevitably, an ever-increasing use of the appropriate measuring instruments.

Summary

Measurement in education can be accomplished in various ways: by grouping, by ranking, or by fixed values.

The first step in measurement consists of defining with great precision the property to be measured. The crudest sort of measurement by grouping involves simply determining whether an object or person possesses any of this property or none of it. A more refined type of measurement by grouping consists of setting up categories representing different degrees or amounts of the property being measured and assigning an object or a person to the category most nearly representative of the amount of the property possessed by it or him.

If there are as many categories as there are objects or persons, measurement by grouping becomes measurement by ranking.

To overcome limitations of measurement by grouping or ranking, most educational measurement is accomplished by assigning fixed values to performance on tasks assigned uniformly to all pupils being measured.

Knowledge of the principles, procedures, and materials of educational measurement is fundamental for teachers, counselors, school psychologists, and school administrators. Increasing emphasis on individualization of instruction and instructional materials and on maintenance of high standards makes the need for this knowledge more and more apparent.

Selected References

Chauncey, Henry, and Norman Frederiksen, "The Functions of Measurement in Educational Placement," in Lindquist, E. F., ed., *Educational Measurement*, Chapter 4. Washington: American Council on Education, 1951.

Cook, Walter W., "The Functions of Measurement in the Facilitation of Learning," in Lindquist, E. F., ed., *Educational Measurement*, Chapter 1. Washington: American Council on Education, 1951.

Dailey, John T., and Isadore Goldberg, "The Uses of Tests in Public Senior High Schools," in Flanagan, John C., *et al.*, *Studies of the American High School*. Washington: Project TALENT Office, University of Pittsburgh, 1962.

Darley, John G., and Gordon V. Anderson, "The Functions of Measurement in Counseling," in Lindquist, E. F., ed., *Educational Measurement*, Chapter 3. Washington: American Council on Education, 1951.

Findley, Warren G., "Purposes of School Testing Programs and Their Efficient Development," in Findley, Warren G., ed., *The Impact and*

Improvement of School Testing Programs, Chapter 1.   Sixty-second Year-book of the National Society for the Study of Education, Part II.   Chicago, 1963.

Lorge, Irving D., "The Fundamental Nature of Measurement," in Lindquist, E. F., ed., *Educational Measurement*, Chapter 14.   Washington: American Council on Education, 1951.

Stevens, S. Smith, "On the Theory of Scales of Measurement," *Science*, CIII (1946), 345–382.

Tyler, Ralph W., "The Functions of Measurement in Improving Instruction," in Lindquist, E. F., ed., *Educational Measurement*, Chapter 2.   Washington: American Council on Education, 1951.

Chapter Two

BASIC CHARACTERISTICS OF TEST SCORES

Before it is possible to discuss the principles involved in selecting, constructing, administering, and scoring tests as well as interpreting and using test scores, it is necessary to be familiar with their most important characteristics:

1. Their accuracy of measurement.
2. Their relative precision of measurement.
3. Their validity.
4. Their types and the types of norms used with them.

ACCURACY OF MEASUREMENT

Definitions

The accuracy of measurement of a set of scores is indicated by the extent to which the scores obtained by the examinees approach their *true scores*. The true score of each examinee is defined as his average score on an indefinitely large number of equivalent forms of a test given under identical favorable conditions while he is well motivated and remains the same in all relevant respects throughout the testing. It is obvious that an examinee can remain well motivated and unchanged in other respects for only a limited time—perhaps while he takes two or three forms of a test. In practice, he cannot be given an indefinitely large number of equivalent forms; therefore, his true score is a hypothetical concept and cannot be computed. However, it is a valuable concept, and there are many occasions to use it. To estimate

9

the true score of an individual or the true average of a group is the real objective in giving a test. We customarily use an individual's obtained score as the estimate of his true score and a group's obtained average as the estimate of the group's true average; it is easy to forget that the obtained score is only an imperfect substitute for our real objective, the true score.

The difference between an examinee's obtained score and his true score is defined as an *error of measurement*. Thus, we can represent the relationship of his true score, his obtained score, and the error of measurement by equations 2.1, 2.2, and 2.3, as follows:

$$Xo = Xt + Xe, \tag{2.1}$$

$$Xt = Xo - Xe, \tag{2.2}$$

$$Xe = Xo - Xt, \tag{2.3}$$

where Xo = an obtained score,
$\quad Xt$ = the corresponding true score, and
$\quad Xe$ = the error of measurement in Xo.

In the definition of true score at the beginning of this section, *equivalent* forms of a test were mentioned; although the general meaning of this term is self-evident, it should be defined and distinguished from *parallel* forms. Two or more test forms are *parallel* if each one consists of a set of items drawn in the same way from a single large supply of items. Parallel forms yield scores that, in an indefinitely large sample of examinees at an appropriate age or grade level, are measures of the same mental or physical characteristics; however, these scores do not necessarily have the same averages, distributions, or accuracy of measurement. Two or more forms are *equivalent* if, in addition to having the properties of parallel forms, they yield scores in an indefinitely large sample of examinees that have identical averages and distribute themselves around their averages in the same way. In other words, the distributions of their scores are identical. Consequently, their accuracy of measurement is the same.

At this point, it is appropriate to define *comparable* tests. These are tests of *different* mental or physical characteristics that, like equivalent forms, yield scores in an indefinitely large sample of examinees at an appropriate age or grade level that have identical averages, distributions, and accuracy of measurement.

In practice, equivalent *tests* or comparable *tests* are rarely found. However, we can derive equivalent *scores* from the actual scores (usually called *raw scores*) yielded by parallel tests and comparable *scores* from the raw scores yielded by nonparallel tests. In a defined sample of examinees, these equivalent or comparable scores have means and distributions that are alike. Their accuracy of measurement, however, is not necessarily the same.

Sources of Errors of Measurement

If an examinee obtained a score identical to his true score (when both scores were rounded to the nearest whole number), the error of measurement in his obtained score would be zero. Why does this rarely happen? What causes errors of measurement?

The main sources of errors of measurement are listed in Table 2.1. The *first* one is variation in the sets of items that make up equivalent forms. An examinee's *true* score is the average of his scores on an indefinitely large number of equivalent forms under the conditions specified. Any differences between his true score and his scores on the forms that he took are by definition errors of measurement. Such differences occur partly because some forms happen to be made up of items that are easier on the whole for that particular examinee (though not for examinees in general) than the items that make up other forms. These variations are chance effects of the assignment of items to the various equivalent forms.

TABLE 2.1

Important Sources of Errors of Measurement

Source	Attributable to:
I. Variations in groups of items that make up equivalent tests	Test
II. Variations in: (1). Manner and correctness of test administration (giving directions properly, keeping time limits accurately, etc.) (2). Conditions during the test administration (distractions, lighting, ventilation, weather etc.)	Test administrator and environment
III. Variations in: (1). Physical condition (2). Emotional status (3). Motivation (4). Rate of work (5). Mental set on specific test items	Examinee
IV. Guessing	Examinee

Most people realize that you cannot be sure how *all* the voters in an election will cast their ballots by finding out how a small part, or sample, of them will vote. In the same way, you cannot be sure of an examinee's level of knowledge or skill by testing him with a tiny sample of the total. Yet that is all that even a fairly long test can include from any field. For example, the forty-eight items in the *Stanford Intermediate-II Word Meaning Test* constitute only a small fraction of the words commonly encountered by pupils in grades 5 and 6, for whom the test is intended. They constitute an even smaller fraction of the hundreds of thousands of words in an unabridged dictionary.

The *second* major source of errors of measurement is variation in the conditions of test administration. For example, the administrator misreads his watch in giving one form and unknowingly allows an extra two minutes; an examinee's score on this particular form would probably be higher than his true score, thus producing an error of measurement. Differences in the environment may also produce errors of measurement. Fire engines passing the testing room may distract the examinee during one session, slowing him down or causing him to make mistakes; as a result, his score on the form he is taking at this time may be lower than his true score. Unusually good weather, with ideal temperature and humidity, may increase an examinee's efficiency so that he scores higher than his true score.

A *third* source of errors of measurement consists of variations within the examinee himself. Headaches, stomach aches, and extreme fatigue are examples of physical conditions that may affect his performance. His emotional state, reflecting his relationships with members of his family and with his schoolmates, may lead to day-to-day variations in performance. The attitude of the examinee not only may affect his rate of work and atten- tion to the task at hand but may even completely alter the property or characteristic measured by the second of two equivalent forms from that measured by the first one. For example, one examinee tried to answer *correctly* the items in Form 1 of a perception test and to answer *incorrectly* those in Form 2; since his perception skill was excellent, he got a high score on Form 1 and a low score on Form 2. This sort of behavior, which is evidence of poor motivation, may render test results meaningless and certainly produces gross differences between the obtained scores and the true scores of some examinees. These differences may be treated as errors of measurement.

If an examinee gets a poor mental set toward a particular item at the beginning of a test and is thereby greatly delayed in answering this item, the time lost may prevent his trying as many items as he otherwise would and cause his score to be lower than his true score.

The *fourth* major source of errors of measurement listed in Table 2.1 is guessing by the examinee. If he guesses at random among the five choices of an item, he has one chance in five of marking it correctly. If he knows that three of the choices are not correct, he has one chance in two of marking it correctly, provided that he guesses between the two remaining choices. In one form of a test, he may be lucky in his guesses; in another form, he may be unlucky. Thus, guessing may produce variations in test scores.

THE INFLUENCE OF ERRORS
OF MEASUREMENT ON
OBTAINED SCORES

Let us consider the influence of errors of measurement on the scores obtained by a seventh grade pupil, Harold Jones. Harold took Form W of the *Stanford Advanced Spelling Test* on September 16. He marked twenty-seven items correctly and got a grade score of 74. How close 74 is to his true score we do not know, but we are naturally more interested in his true level of skill in spelling than we are in his obtained score on Form W, which contains only fifty-eight items.

For purposes of illustration, let us imagine that there are a tremendously large number of equivalent forms of the *Stanford Advanced Spelling Test* and that Harold takes all of them, each time under similar conditions, each time trying to do his best, and each time having the same true level of skill in spelling. Under these circumstances (impossible in real life), his obtained scores would vary quite a bit from form to form because of differences among the samples of fifty-eight items in each form and would produce the bell-shaped distribution shown in Figure 2.1.

The center strip of this distribution represents obtained scores that are identical with Harold's true score in spelling skill. This strip is labeled 0 because each of the obtained grade scores in it differs by less than half a point from his true grade score, the exact position of which is shown by the dotted line at the center of the distribution. Grade scores that are .5 up to 1.5 points higher than Harold's true score are in the strip labeled +1. Similarly, each obtained score in the strip labeled +2 is 1.5 up to 2.5 points higher than Harold's true grade score, and so on up to the strip labeled +14. The percentages superimposed on the distribution indicate the approximate percentage of Harold's obtained scores that would fall in each strip. For example, about four out of every hundred of Harold's obtained scores on this test would be 5.5 up to 6.5 points *above* his true grade score. Although the distribution curve continues past the strips labeled +14 and −14, no strips have been drawn beyond these points because only a few times in every thousand testings would Harold obtain scores so different from his true grade score.

Notice that the distribution of obtained grade scores is symmetrical around the center; each half is a mirrored image of the other. Thus, about four out of every hundred of Harold's obtained grade scores will be 5.5 up to 6.5 points *below* his true grade score. The graph provides an estimate of

FIGURE 2.1

Hypothetical Distribution of Obtained Scores around the True Score of Harold Jones.

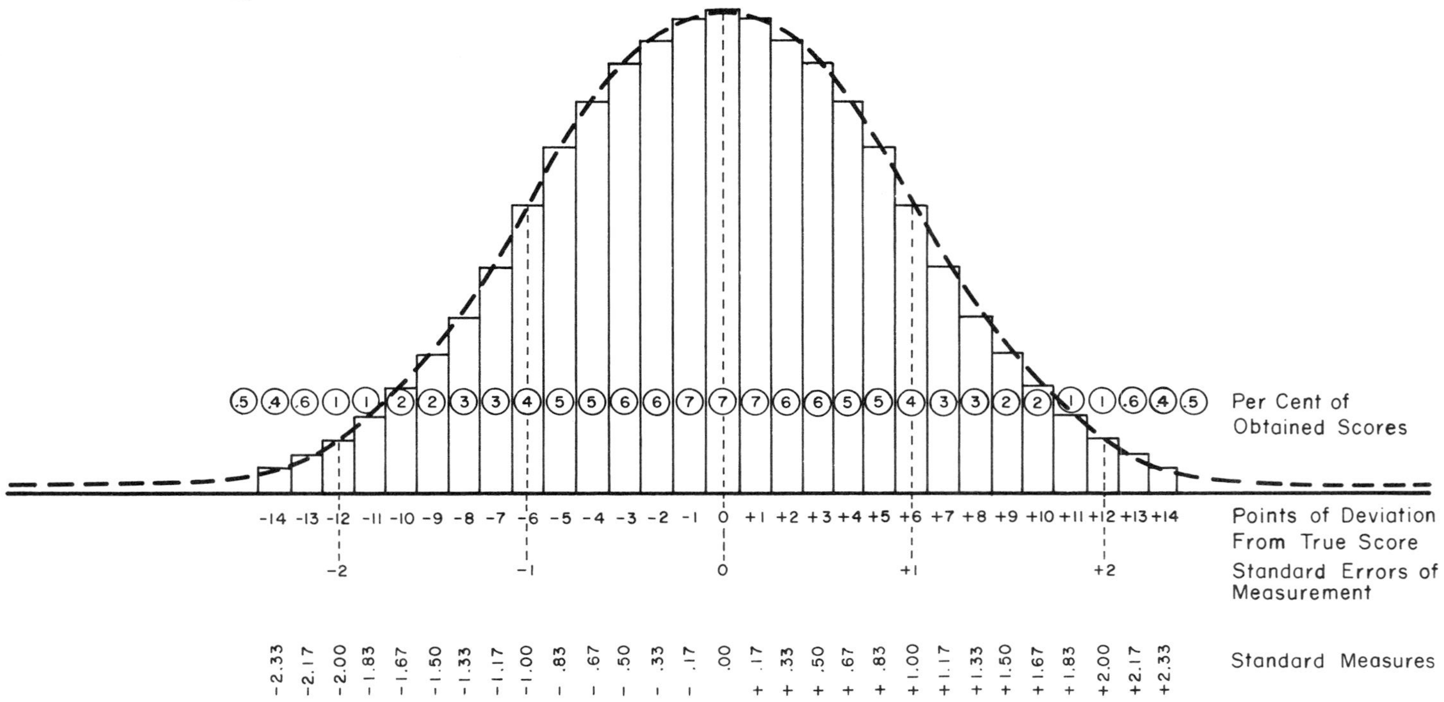

how often Harold would obtain a score within half a point of his true grade score. This would occur about seven times out of every one hundred testings, as shown by the percentage superimposed on the center strip. The small size of this percentage indicates the importance of estimating a range of obtained scores that is likely to include a pupil's true score. First, we must learn how a distribution of scores like the one in Figure 2.1 can be obtained in actual practice.

THE DISTRIBUTION OF ERRORS
OF MEASUREMENT

As stated in the previous section, if Harold could be tested over and over again with equivalent forms of the test of spelling, with both his true ability and his effort remaining the same throughout the testings, his successive scores would form a normal distribution centered around his true score. The difficulty is that we cannot actually test Harold, or any other pupil, in this way to build up such a distribution of scores. Therefore, instead of testing only one pupil many times, we test many pupils only twice. In fact, if the test allows enough time for every pupil to try every item, we may administer only one form, divide the items in it into two equivalent sets, and score each set separately. If the two sets of items are equivalent, they must measure the same skills and be of the same level of difficulty; each pupil's true score will then be the same on the two sets. For example, we may represent Harold's scores on the total set of items and on sets 1 and 2 as follows:

Total Set Obtained Score = Set 1 Obtained Score + Set 2 Obtained Score;
Set 1 Obtained Score = Set 1 True Score + Set 1 Error Score;
Set 2 Obtained Score = Set 2 True Score + Set 2 Error Score.

Suppose that we subtract Harold's *Set 2 Obtained Score* from his *Set 1 Obtained Score*. The result is not likely to be zero because, as we know, a pupil's scores vary from testing to testing. Next, suppose that we subtract his *Set 2 True Score + Set 2 Error Score* from his *Set 1 True Score + Set 1 Error Score*. Note that this is equivalent to subtracting his *Set 2 Obtained Score* from his *Set 1 Obtained Score*. Remember that under the testing conditions his *Set 1 True Score* must be the same as his *Set 2 True Score*. Consequently, the subtraction comes out as follows:

$$\begin{array}{l} \quad Set\ 1\ True\ Score\ +\ Set\ 1\ Error\ Score \\ -Set\ 2\ True\ Score\ -\ Set\ 2\ Error\ Score \\ \hline \quad\quad 0 \quad\quad\quad +\ Set\ 1\ Error\ Score\ -\ Set\ 2\ Error\ Score \end{array}$$

We can see that if we have scores for each pupil on the equivalent halves of an unspeeded test, the difference between these two half scores will be made up wholly of errors of measurement. These errors of measurement are the amounts by which the two scores of each pupil on the equivalent halves differ from his identical true scores on the two halves.

Now let us suppose that we test a large number of representative classes of pupils at the beginning of grade 7 with an unspeeded test, divide the test

FIGURE 2.2

Actual Differences between Half-Test Scores Obtained by 692 Examinees Compared with the Normal Distribution.

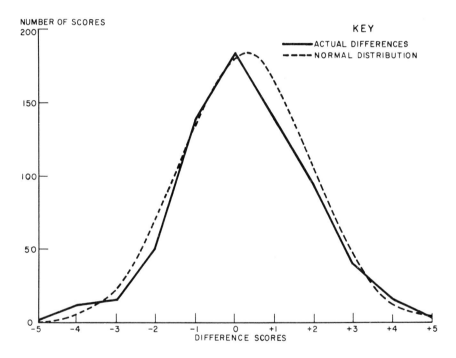

into two equivalent sets of items, and obtain the scores of all the pupils on both sets of items. We may now subtract each pupil's score on the second set from his score on the first set. The result will be a difference score for each pupil made up entirely of errors of measurement. Since these difference scores vary in size from pupil to pupil only because of errors of measurement, their distribution will approach that of a normal distribution as the number of pupils is increased and will center closely around zero. Interestingly enough, the spread of these differences, obtained by *subtracting* each pupil's *Set 2 Error Score* from his *Set 1 Error Score*, will be the same as the spread of scores obtained by *adding* each pupil's *Set* 1 *Error Score* to his *Set* 2 *Error Score*. Since this sum of the two error scores constitutes each pupil's *Total Set Error Score*, we may regard the distribution of differences between obtained half scores as the distribution of errors of measurement around the true total scores of the large number of pupils tested. This is how we obtain in practice a distribution of error scores like the one shown in Figure 2.1.

If all the seventh grade pupils we tested had the same true score as Harold and were tested under similar conditions, we would be justified in considering the distribution of differences between their half scores as identical with the distribution of obtained scores that we would get if we could give a

FIGURE 2.3

Actual Differences between Half-Test Scores Obtained by 1,043 Examinees Compared with the Normal Distribution.

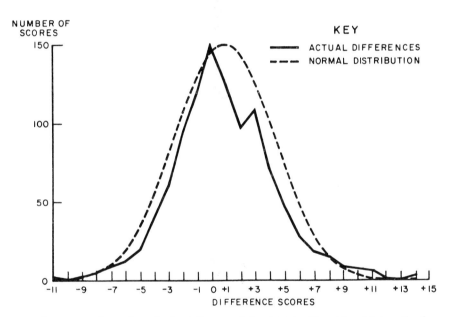

very large number of equivalent forms of the test to Harold. Naturally, in real life the true scores of the seventh grade pupils would vary considerably, but if their average true score is reasonably close to Harold's, we are on safe ground if we use the distribution of the differences between their half scores as if it were the distribution of Harold's error scores on a very large number of testings around his particular true score. This is exactly what we often do; the distribution in Figure 2.1 was obtained in this way.

To show how closely actual distributions of errors of measurement approach the normal distribution, two practical examples are presented in

Figures 2.2 and 2.3. In Figure 2.2, the distribution of differences between scores on two sets of seven items each in a fourteen-item test is given. This test was administered to 692 examinees. The differences between their scores on the two sets of items were obtained and plotted as a solid line in Figure 2.2. Note that for 184 examinees the difference between their half scores was actually zero. Yet three examinees had differences of five points. The broken line shows the shape of a normal distribution centered at the mean of the actual difference scores. It is remarkable how closely the actual distribution of error scores for the 692 examinees approaches the normal distribution.

Another illustration of the distribution of differences between half-test scores is shown in Figure 2.3. A long test of eighty-four items was divided into two sets of forty-two items each; the differences between the half-test scores of 1,043 examinees are plotted as a solid line. The broken line, as in Figure 2.2, shows a normal distribution centered at the mean of the actual difference scores. Again, the actual distribution of difference scores closely approaches the normal distribution. These two illustrations reassure us that errors of measurement do tend to form normal distributions, as our interpretive procedures assume.

The Standard Error of Measurement

We now need some "measuring rod" by which we can describe in a single number the spread of errors of measurement around an individual's true score. This single number ought to state in score points the distance on either side of the center of any distribution that includes a designated percentage of all the errors of measurement in the distribution. It might vary in magnitude from one distribution to another, but it should always define a distance on either side of the center that includes the same percentage of all the errors of measurement in the distribution. These requirements are met by the standard deviation of the distribution of errors of measurement, which we call the *standard error of measurement*. Hence, we use it for our "measuring rod" to indicate the spread of errors of measurement around a true score. It will be represented in this book as s_{meas}.* The

---

* In this book, the symbol s is used to represent an estimate of the standard deviation in the population of which the sample used for computation is representative. The Greek lower-case letter sigma, σ, is used to represent the standard deviation in that population. Thus, s is an estimate of σ. The symbol S is used to represent the standard deviation in the sample itself. The difference between s and S is shown clearly by their computations in appendix C.

To avoid unnecessary repetition, s_{meas} is referred to throughout the book as the standard error of measurement. More precisely, it is an estimate of the population standard error of measurement.

computation of any standard deviation is explained and illustrated in appendix C, and that of the standard error of measurement is given in appendix E. Here we shall simply explain how it is used as a *measuring rod* for errors of measurement.

In a normal distribution, like the distribution of Harold's obtained scores in Figure 2.1, about 68.26 per cent of the scores in the distribution are within one standard error of measurement of Harold's true score at the center of the distribution. According to the test publisher, the standard error of measurement for this test is approximately six grade-score points. Therefore, a vertical dotted line has been drawn through the distribution on each side of the center at a distance of six points from the latter. Between these vertical dotted lines would be about 68.26 per cent of the scores that Harold would have obtained on the tremendously large number of equivalent forms of the test that we imagined him taking. It naturally follows that, of the remaining 31.74 per cent of his scores, half (15.87 per cent) would lie more than one standard error of measurement above his true score at the center of the distribution and half would lie more than one standard error of measurement below his true score. Since the standard error of measurement is six points, each of the score points must represent one-sixth (or about .17) of a standard error of measurement. The center of each score range in Figure 2.1 has been labeled on the third line below the diagram to show its equivalent as a standard measure, or distance from the center in terms of sixths of a standard error of measurement of the distribution. Each score range (of one point) has superimposed on it, as noted before, the percentage of the total number of scores in the distribution that lie in it. These percentages were obtained by using Table K.1, and the method is explained and illustrated in appendix K. For convenience, the percentages in Figure 2.1 have been rounded off to the nearest whole numbers. Each strip is treated as though it represented a range that is one grade-score point, or .17 of a standard measure, wide. For example, the middle strip, corresponding to Harold's true score, is regarded as a range of standard measures from $-.085$ to $+.085$. Standard measures are defined and their computation is illustrated in appendix D.

Whatever the value of Harold's true grade score, we can be fairly sure that his obtained grade score of 74 on Form W is within about six points, or one standard error of measurement, of his true score. We draw this conclusion since we know that about 68 per cent of his scores on an indefinitely large number of equivalent forms of the *Stanford Advanced Spelling Test* given to him under the conditions postulated would be within one standard error of measurement of his true score.

Some tests have larger standard errors of measurement than others; the smaller the standard error of measurement, the more accurate the scores in the sense that the more closely do they distribute themselves around the examinee's true score. For practical purposes in the interpretation of test scores, therefore, the standard error of measurement plays an invaluable role. This point is made abundantly clear in chapters 8, 9, 10, and 11. For judging the relative precision of measurement of different tests, however, another indicator is employed—the test *reliability coefficient*, discussed in the next section.

RELATIVE PRECISION OF MEASUREMENT

The Reliability Coefficient

The degree of relative precision of measurement of a set of test scores is defined as test reliability.   It is represented by the *reliability coefficient*, which may be expressed as follows:

$$r_{XX'} = \frac{s^2_{Xt}}{s^2_{Xo}}, \tag{2.4}$$

where $r_{XX'}$ = the reliability coefficient of a set of scores derived from test X;

s^2_{Xt} = the square of the standard deviation of true scores on test X; and

s^2_{Xo} = the square of the standard deviation of obtained scores on test X.

Earlier in this chapter, it was stated that an examinee's obtained score is equal to his true score plus the error of measurement in his obtained score; that is, as given in equation 2.1, $Xo = Xt + Xe$.

If we make the reasonable assumption that there is no relationship* between the true scores of a group of examinees and the errors of measurement in their obtained scores it can easily be shown that

$$s^2_{Xo} = s^2_{Xt} + s^2_{Xe}. \tag{2.5}$$

The symbols s^2_{Xo} and s^2_{Xt} have just been defined with equation 2.4; s^2_{Xe} is the square of the standard deviation of errors of measurement, which means that it is the square of the standard error of measurement and may be denoted as $s^2_{\text{meas } X}$.   Therefore, equation 2.5 may be rewritten as:

$$s^2_{Xo} = s^2_{Xt} + s^2_{\text{meas } X}, \tag{2.6}$$

or, $$s^2_{Xt} = s^2_{Xo} - s^2_{\text{meas } X}. \tag{2.7}$$

* Expressed as a product-moment correlation coefficient between true scores and errors of measurement with their algebraic signs (plus and minus) attached.

If we substitute the right-hand side of equation 2.7 for its equivalent, s^2_{Xt}, in equation 2.4, we get:

$$r_{XX'} = \frac{s^2_{Xo} - s^2_{\text{meas } X}}{s^2_{Xo}}. \tag{2.8}$$

Putting each term in the numerator over the denominator separately, we find that:

$$r_{XX'} = \frac{s^2_{Xo}}{s^2_{Xo}} - \frac{s^2_{\text{meas } X}}{s^2_{Xo}},$$

or,

$$r_{XX'} = 1 - \frac{s^2_{\text{meas } X}}{s^2_{Xo}}. \tag{2.9}$$

To find the reliability coefficient of a set of test scores, we can use equation 2.9. This process is illustrated in appendix F. Inspection of equation 2.9 shows that, other things being equal, reliability *increases* as the standard error of measurement of obtained scores ($s_{\text{meas } x}$) *decreases* and as the standard deviation of obtained scores (s_{Xo}) *increases*. The relationships among these three statistics may be expressed in different ways by rearranging the terms in equation 2.9 as follows:

$$1 - r_{XX'} = \frac{s^2_{\text{meas } X}}{s^2_{Xo}},$$

or,

$$s^2_{\text{meas } X} = s^2_{Xo}(1 - r_{XX'}). \tag{2.10}$$

Taking the square root of both sides of equation 2.10 gives us:

$$s_{\text{meas } X} = s_{Xo}\sqrt{1 - r_{XX'}}. \tag{2.11}$$

Equation 2.11 often provides a convenient way of estimating the standard error of measurement.

Use of the reliability coefficient for judging the relative precision of measurement of two tests that differ greatly in length may be illustrated by comparing the reliability coefficients of the fourteen-item test and the eighty-four-item test for which distributions of obtained scores are shown in Figures 2.2 and 2.3, respectively.

For the fourteen-item test, the standard error of measurement is 1.63 and the standard deviation is 3.36. Equation 2.9 becomes:

$$r_{(14)(14)'} = 1 - \frac{2.66}{11.29} = .76.$$

For the eighty-four-item test, the standard error of measurement is 3.42 and the standard deviation is 15.29. Equation 2.9 becomes:

$$r_{(84)(84)'} = 1 - \frac{11.70}{233.78} = .95.$$

These reliability coefficients show that the eighty-four-item test measures with far greater precision than does the fourteen-item test despite the fact that the latter has a much smaller standard error of measurement.

Reliability coefficients have the same possible range as other correlation coefficients (-1.00 to $+1.00$), but in practice we hardly expect them to take negative values since the two sets of scores correlated presumably measure the same functions and ought to be positively related.

Comparisons of the standard errors of measurement and of the reliability coefficients of the fourteen-item and eighty-four-item tests emphasize two points that have already been made in this chapter:

1. For interpreting the scores of individual pupils, use the standard error of measurement.
2. For judging the relative precision of measurement of two or more tests, use the reliability coefficient.

Factors That Affect the Reliability Coefficient

The size of a reliability coefficient is affected by many factors, including:

1. The spread of errors of measurement around the true scores of the examinees.
2. The number of items in the test.
3. The degree to which the items measure the same mental functions.
4. The range of talent among the examinees.
5. The difficulty of the items for the examinees.

Of these five factors, the effect of the first has already been discussed. The effect of the second has been illustrated by the data pertaining to the fourteen-item and eighty-four-item tests. The general rule is that, other things being equal, test reliability increases with test length. This rule is expressed by a well-known equation called the Spearman-Brown Formula:

$$r_{NN'} = \frac{nr_{AA'}}{1 + (n - 1)r_{AA'}}, \qquad (2.12)$$

where $r_{NN'}$ = the reliability coefficient of a test n times as long as test A, and
$r_{AA'}$ = the reliability coefficient of test A.

Equation 2.12 has been found to operate very effectively if all of the n tests measure the same skills and have standard deviations of about the same size. For example, the eighty-four-item test for which the reliability coefficient was found to be .95 is exactly six times as long as the fourteen-item test for which the reliability coefficient was found to be .76. Applying the

Spearman-Brown Formula to the data for the fourteen-item test, we may estimate the reliability coefficient of the eighty-four-item test as follows:

$$r_{(84)(84)'} = \frac{6(.76)}{1 + (6 - 1)(.76)} = \frac{4.56}{4.80} = .95.$$

Thus, the Spearman-Brown Formula yields an estimate of the reliability coefficient of the eighty-four-item test that is exactly equal (to the second decimal place) to the reliability coefficient actually obtained by administering the eighty-four-item test and computing its reliability coefficient by equation 2.9.

A full discussion of the effects of the remaining three factors on the reliability coefficient lies outside the scope of this book. However, the more nearly the items in a test measure the same mental functions, the higher its reliability coefficient will tend to be. Likewise, the wider the spread of ability or skill in the property measured among the examinees, the higher the reliability coefficient will tend to be. To control this factor, it is best to estimate any reliability coefficient in a sample drawn from a single age group or a single grade group. Finally, the more nearly all the items in a test approach median difficulty among the examinees, the higher its reliability coefficient is likely to be. An item of median difficulty is one that is answered correctly by 50 per cent of the examinees. Thus, a test may yield rather reliable scores for one group of examinees and rather unreliable scores for another group. Since the examinees at a single age or grade level differ greatly in ability, the scores on a test of suitable difficulty for the examinees of average ability may be highly reliable for those examinees and rather unreliable for the examinees of very superior or very inferior ability. The implication to be drawn from these facts is that a test user should employ tests of median difficulty for the group of examinees he is most interested in measuring.

How High Must Reliability Coefficients Be?

This question is a little like "How high is up?" No satisfactory answer can be given. Naturally, among tests of equal validity, the most reliable are preferred. But, in practice, the test user can adapt his procedures for interpreting the scores of individuals and groups to the degree of reliability of these scores. Chapters 8, 9, 10, and 11 explain how to do this. The basic principle underlying the techniques described in these chapters is that the test user draws firm conclusions about the meaning of test scores only when his chances of making errors in these conclusions are less than a designated number out of every 100. The test user designates this number in advance. The procedures permit firm conclusions to be drawn regarding the scores of more examinees when tests of high reliability are used than when tests of low reliability are used.

Experience has shown that for measuring characteristics of individuals, scores with reliability coefficients below .75 are rather inefficient. For measuring the average characteristics of groups of the size of many classes, say twenty-five to fifty, scores with reliability coefficients as low as .50 may often be highly serviceable. With average scores in larger groups, even lower reliability coefficients are frequently useful. In general, then, it is most fruitful to select among equally valid tests those of highest reliability and to use procedures for interpreting scores that take into account their varying reliabilities.

VALIDITY

Validity is the extent to which the rank order of the scores of examinees for whom a test is appropriate is the same as the rank order of the same examinees in the property or characteristic that the test is being used to measure. This property or characteristic is called the *criterion*. Since any test may be used for many different purposes, it follows that it may have many validities, one corresponding to each criterion.

To determine the extent to which the rank orders of examinees in the test scores and the criterion are alike, the most straightforward and satisfactory procedure is to compute an appropriate measure of relationship, such as the product-moment correlation coefficient, between the examinees' test scores and their criterion scores. The correlation coefficient takes a numerical value between −1.00 and +1.00. A value of +1.00 indicates a perfect positive relationship between the two sets of scores correlated. The rank order of the examinees' scores is the same in both sets. A correlation coefficient of zero indicates complete lack of systematic relationship between the two sets of scores; no more than chance association is thereby shown to exist. A negative correlation coefficient indicates an inverse relationship between the sets of scores. A negative validity coefficient, therefore, means that pupils with low test scores tend to have high criterion scores and those with high test scores tend to have low criterion scores. The computation of two common types of correlation coefficients is explained and illustrated in appendix G.

Unfortunately, it is often impossible to estimate test validity by computing a correlation coefficient between test scores and criterion scores for the simple reason that criterion scores are not available. In fact, they are

TABLE 2.2

Types of Test Validity and Bases for Their Estimation

	Empirical Validity				Judgmental Validity			Empirical-Judgmental Validity	
	Predictive Validity	Concurrent Validity	Congruent Validity	Self-Defining Validity	Constructor Validity	User Validity	Face Validity	Inferential Validity	Factorial Validity
Bases for Estimation of Test Validity	Correlation with criterion data gathered at a later date	Correlation with criterion data gathered at about the same time	Correlation with test scores obtained at about the same time	Correlation with an equivalent form of the test	Comparison of content with test *constructor's* criterion Evaluation of test scoring procedures Evaluation of test directions Evaluation of examinee motivation	Comparison of content with test *user's* criterion	Comparison of apparent content of items with *layman's* criterion	Inferences about test validity from relevant data about a priori hypotheses	Inferences about relationships between test scores and factors previously identified

often not only unavailable but unobtainable. Under these circumstances, we must estimate test validity by judgmental procedures.

Table 2.2 presents a classification of the most common types of validity and the bases for estimating them. They will be described and illustrated in the remainder of this section.

Empirical Validity

Predictive validity. A predictive validity coefficient is obtained by computing an appropriate coefficient of correlation between scores on a test and criterion scores obtained at a later date. The predictor test scores should be kept strictly confidential until after the criterion scores have been obtained to prevent the latter from being influenced by them in any way. When predictive validity coefficients are reported, it is essential to specify the time interval elapsing between administration of the predictor tests and the gathering of the criterion data. In general, the greater the time elapsing between these two events, the less accurate will be prediction of criterion status from test score—that is, the lower the test's predictive validity will be.

A classic example of the estimation of predictive validity is that for the *Aviation Cadet Qualifying Examination,* Form I. This test was used in the summer and fall of 1943 for preliminary selection of men for aviation-cadet training in the U.S. Army Air Forces. Thousands of young men took this form of the examination and only about 58 per cent of them passed with scores of 180 points or more. A random sample of 1,305 applicants was selected for experimental purposes and allowed to proceed through classification and into training regardless of their scores on the *Qualifying Examination.* Of these, 265 ultimately graduated from Advanced Pilot Schools and received their wings. The remaining 1,040 were eliminated for a variety of reasons. The predictive validity coefficient of the *Aviation Cadet Qualifying Examination* in the group of 1,003 applicants who either graduated or were eliminated because of deficiency in learning to fly, fear of flying, or their own request was .50.

To show what a predictive validity coefficient of .50 means in practical terms, Figure 2.4 has been prepared.* Each bar in this figure shows the percentage of men who obtained scores in the range given at the left-hand end of the bar and who were eliminated for the reasons given above. Note that in the top group of thirty-nine men, who obtained scores of 272 or above, only 30.8 per cent were eliminated. In the bottom group of thirty-six men, who obtained scores of 0 to 122, 94.4 per cent were eliminated. As one glances from the top bar down to the bottom bar in the figure, he sees that a

---

* P. H. Du Bois, ed., *The Classification Program.* Army Air Forces Aviation Psychology Program Research Reports, No. 2 (Washington: Government Printing Office, 1947), figure 5.44, p. 242.

larger and larger percentage of the men were eliminated. In other words, there was a tendency for high-scoring men to succeed in flying training and for low-scoring men to fail. This tendency, which causes the bars to lengthen from top to bottom, is represented by the predictive validity coefficient of .50.

How effective this or any other test can be in weeding out men who would fail during the long process of pilot training depends on the passing mark that is set. The greater the proportion of applicants who are allowed to

FIGURE 2.4

Percentage of Aviation Cadets Eliminated from Pilot
Training in Each of Nine Stanine Groups.

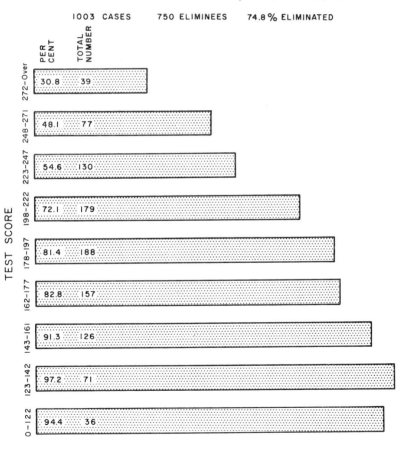

AVIATION CADET QUALIFYING EXAMINATION
AC121
PREFLIGHT THROUGH ADVANCED
ELIMINATION FOR FLYING DEFICIENCY, FEAR OR OWN REQUEST

1003 CASES   750 ELIMINEES   74.8% ELIMINATED

pass, the less effective the test can be in eliminating those likely to fail.   It is obvious that if this proportion were increased to 1.00 (and everybody was allowed to pass), the test would have accomplished nothing and might as well not have been given.   In the case of the *Aviation Cadet Qualifying Examination*, its function was simply to screen out the applicants most likely to fail; those who passed it were given a more elaborate set of classification tests.   For this reason, the passing mark was set at 180, allowing about 58 per cent of the applicants to pass.   Of these, about 65 per cent were eliminated in pilot training, whereas about 88 per cent of those who failed the *Qualifying Examination* also failed in pilot training.

If the passing mark on the examination had been raised to 240 so that only about 15 per cent of the applicants had passed, about 46 per cent of these would have been eliminated in pilot training.   This means that to have obtained 100 graduates of pilot training, only about 185 applicants with scores of 240 or more on the *Qualifying Examination* would have had to be started in pilot training.   But if no tests had been used, about 397 applicants would have had to begin training to obtain 100 graduates.   The saving in time, manpower, costs, and frustration achieved by using a simple three-hour test like the *Qualifying Examination* is at once obvious.   In practice, even greater savings were made by using more elaborate classification tests following the *Qualifying Examination*.

The catch is that, if only 15 per cent of the applicants had been accepted for pilot training, a large number of applicants would have to have been available because, to get 100 acceptable applicants, about 667 would have to have been tested.   Since there were plenty of applicants, this would have posed no serious problem.   In general, however, it must be remembered that the practical usefulness represented by a predictive validity coefficient depends not only on the size of the coefficient (the larger the better) but also on the percentage of applicants who can be rejected (the larger the better).

The selection tests used by the College Entrance Examination Board and the American College Testing Program have predictive validity coefficients of about .50 to .60 for the criterion of individual grade-point average in the freshman year.   If a college has many more candidates seeking admission than it can accommodate in its freshman class, tests of this kind can be of great value in reducing the percentage of failures among the students admitted. The greater the proportion of its applicants a college must accept in order to fill its freshman class, the less effective its admissions tests are likely to be.   In the limiting case where all applicants were admitted, the only value of the tests would lie in sectioning students on the basis of their knowledge and in identifying those freshmen most likely to need help in passing their courses.   These possibilities would still justify giving the examinations in many institutions that were adequately prepared to interpret and use the scores.

Concurrent validity. When criterion data are gathered at approximately the same time that predictor tests are administered, the techniques for ascertaining validity are the same as those used when the criterion data are gathered at a later date. But since the test scores are not used to *predict* (in the layman's sense of that word) the criterion scores, the result is called a concurrent validity coefficient.

Information about the concurrent validity of the *Cooperative Reading Comprehension Test*, Form Y, was obtained by administering this test to 106 eleventh grade boys on October 20, 1950.* A few days later their English teachers (who did not know their test scores) were asked to rate them on how well they read material connected with their classwork. The concurrent validity coefficient obtained by correlating the reading test scores in level of comprehension with the teachers' ratings was .52. This may not seem like a high coefficient if one is not familiar with the usual range of validity coefficients; compared with these, it is highly satisfactory. Teachers' ratings and marks are ordinarily not sufficiently reliable to permit their having high correlations with other variables. The relationship of .52 can be expressed in the same way as the predictive validity coefficient of .50 for the *Aviation Cadet Qualifying Examination*. Figure 2.5 shows the corresponding bar diagram. Another way of portraying the same data in practical terms is to make an expectancy table like that shown in Table 2.3. This indicates the percentage of boys at each of five score levels who were assigned

FIGURE 2.5

Average Comprehension Rating of Eleventh Grade Boys
in Each of Five Test-Score Intervals.

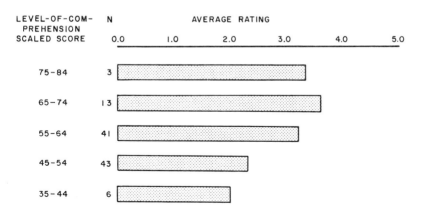

* A. E. Traxler, "Intercorrelations and Validity of Scores on Three Reading Tests," in *Educational Records Bulletin*, No. 56 (New York: Educational Records Bureau, 1951).

ratings of 1 to 5.   The pupils judged by their teachers to comprehend least well were given ratings of 1; those judged best able to comprehend were given ratings of 5.   Table 2.3 shows that pupils who obtained test scores of 35–44 were assigned low ratings.   None of these six pupils was given a rating higher than 3.   Conversely, pupils who had test scores of 75–84 tended to receive high ratings.

TABLE 2.3

Percentage of Eleventh Grade Boys in Each of Five
Test-Score Intervals Who Were Assigned Each of
Five Ratings*
($N = 106$)

Level-of-Comprehension Scaled Score	Percentage of Boys with Rating of					Number of Boys
	1	2	3	4	5	
75–84	0	0	67	33	0	3
65–74	0	8	46	15	31	13
55–64	5	12	39	37	7	41
45–54	12	35	46	7	0	43
35–44	33	33	34	0	0	6

   * Data from A. E. Traxler, *loc. cit.*   The Level-of-Comprehension scores were from the *Cooperative Reading Comprehension Test*, Higher Level, Form Y.

   Because teachers' ratings of the extent to which pupils can understand what they read are apt to be considerably less reliable than reading-test scores and to be affected by the pupils' abilities to express orally or in writing what they have read, these ratings may be a less satisfactory measure of the pupils' true abilities to comprehend what they have read than the scores from a test as carefully designed to yield level-of-comprehension scores as Form Y of the *Cooperative Reading Comprehension Test*.   Thus, the interpretation of the concurrent validity coefficient of .52 poses something of a dilemma. It can be conventionally considered as the validity coefficient of the test scores or, probably with equal justification, as the validity coefficient of teachers' ratings of their pupils' levels of comprehension.   This point stresses the importance of considering carefully the nature and basic merit of the criterion variable in any validity study.

   The criterion in empirical studies of validity.   The technique of establishing the empirical validity of test scores is straightforward once an appropriate coefficient to express the degree of relationship between the predictor and criterion scores has been agreed upon.   The real difficulty in making and interpreting such validity studies is to obtain a set of criterion scores that represents adequately the fundamental property or characteristic to be measured.

To select pilots for the U.S. Air Force, a test that places applicants in rank order according to their skill in piloting various types of aircraft in combat and in their capacity to lead other men in training and in combat should be used.   This rank order may be called our *ultimate criterion*.   At the same time, no one can become a pilot who cannot complete successfully the program of flying training.   Therefore, the selection test must place men in rank order according to their likelihood of completing advanced pilot training without discriminating against men who will later exhibit skill in leadership and combat.   This rank order may be called our *immediate criterion*.   Since it is impossible in peacetime and exceedingly difficult in wartime to obtain data pertaining to a pilot's skill or leadership in actual combat, our ultimate criterion cannot be used and some immediate criterion like graduation or elimination from the pilot-training course must be used.

There are several factors to consider in judging the adequacy of an immediate criterion for measuring the ultimate criterion:

1. To what extent the immediate criterion duplicates the traits that constitute the ultimate criterion.
2. To what extent the immediate criterion provides equal opportunity for all individuals to display the traits that constitute the ultimate criterion (in World War II, for example, pilots on escort duty over the English Channel had very different kinds of opportunities to exercise combat skill and leadership from those pilots on daylight bombing missions of German targets).
3. To what extent the immediate criterion is measured reliably (freshman grades given by a single instructor on one semester's work are not likely to be as reliable as honor-point ratios based on grades given by several instructors on the work of two semesters).

Congruent validity.   If test scores are correlated with a criterion measure that consists of scores from a test of established validity, the resulting coefficient is called a congruent validity coefficient.   It differs from a concurrent validity coefficient only in that the criterion measures for the latter are not test scores, whereas for the former they are.

An interesting example of a congruent validity coefficient is that obtained by Davis and Fifer* in correlating scores on a multiple-choice test of arithmetic reasoning with a parallel form of the test given without choices as a free-response test.   Most teachers and laymen regard the latter as a more

* F. B. Davis and G. Fifer, "The Effect of Test Reliability and Validity of Scoring Aptitude and Achievement Tests with Weights for Every Choice," *Educational and Psychological Measurement*, XVII (1959), 159–170.

valid measure of arithmetic-reasoning ability than the former. The congruent validity coefficient of the multiple-choice test proved to be .69. Since the reliability coefficients of the two sets of test scores were close to .69, the data provide no evidence that the two types of tests measure different reasoning skills. Apparently, a well-constructed multiple-choice test of arithmetic reasoning may be substituted without substantial loss of validity for a free-response test.

Self-defining validity. If the items in a test are perfectly representative of the ultimate criterion, the correlation coefficient between two equivalent forms of the test may be regarded as the self-defining validity coefficient of either one of them. This is a somewhat unconventional way to think of this coefficient, which is widely recognized as their parallel-forms reliability coefficient. Nonetheless, for tests like Form Y of the *Cooperative Reading Comprehension Tests*, it is quite possible that it represents both the most meaningful reliability coefficient and the most meaningful validity coefficient.

Judgmental Validity

When scores in the criterion variable or even a reasonably satisfactory approximation to them cannot be obtained, the validity of a test cannot be estimated by empirical methods. Subjective judgment of the extent to which the content of the test measures the weighted combination of information, skills, traits, and abilities that the test constructor or the test user wants to measure must then be employed. But the fact that a test does measure what the constructor or user wants it to measure does not mean that it will yield scores that have high validity unless it is properly administered to well-motivated examinees and scored by procedures that minimize opportunities for the examinees to increase their scores by using information, skills, traits, or abilities irrelevant to those it is intended to measure. The scoring system must also be such as to minimize subjective judgment and clerical errors on the part of the scorers.

Empirical validity coefficients by their very nature include the effects of test administration, examinee motivation, and scoring procedures along with the effects produced by the test content; all of these must be considered in estimating validity by judgmental procedures.

Constructor validity. The *first* step in estimating the constructor validity of a test is to study carefully the constructor's purpose and his definition of the ultimate criterion he built it to measure. This definition ordinarily takes the form of an outline of the information, skills, traits, and abilities that make up the criterion and should include an indication of the weight, or importance, of each of these.

The *second* step is to study the items carefully to determine the information, skills, traits, and abilities that are actually employed in answering them correctly. With these data, an outline of the kinds of information, skills, traits, and abilities that appear to be measured should be constructed.

The *third* step is to compare the two outlines and judge the extent to which they are alike. Since this process (like the identification of the information, skills, traits, and abilities that the items actually measure) is highly subjective, equally competent judges may differ somewhat in their appraisals. For this reason, independent appraisals are sometimes obtained from several judges and then combined.

The *fourth* step is to make sure that the scoring procedures are appropriate. If the test is speeded, some examinees will not have time to try every item and some of them may mark answers at random to all items they have not had time to read. To minimize the probability of their benefiting from this practice and thus reducing the constructor validity of the test, the scoring procedures should include correction for chance success. (This correction and the reasons for its use are fully discussed in chapter 4.)

For a power test on which almost every examinee has time to try every item, it is likewise best for the scoring procedures to include the correction for chance success. Most examinees are likely to find many items near the end so difficult that they cannot answer them on the basis of their knowledge or skill. Some may omit these and others may mark responses to them almost at random. To minimize the possibility that the latter will benefit, the scoring procedures should include correction for chance success.

The scoring procedures should also be examined to make sure that they yield consistent scores. That is, the rank order of the examinees' scores should be the same when the tests are scored by any qualified scorer. To the extent that this condition is *not* met, the reliability and constructor validity of the scores decrease. This means that scores from most essay examinations are not likely to have strikingly high constructor validity coefficients unless the procedures used in scoring them specify the points to be credited in so much detail that they might almost as well have been measured with objective items.

The *fifth* step in judging the constructor validity of a test is to examine the test directions to make sure that they set a clear purpose and allow the examinees to plan their rate of work properly. The method of scoring should be stated plainly and appropriate advice should be given about when to mark answers about which examinees do not feel sure.

The *sixth* step should be to judge whether the nature of the test items and the circumstances under which the tests are to be used are likely to motivate the examinees to answer the items honestly and to do as well as they can. Many personality questionnaires, for example, are likely to be answered honestly only when they are used for rather specialized research purposes. A young lady applying for a position as a secretary, for example, is not likely to answer "yes" to questions like "Do you frequently have severe headaches?" if she really wants to be considered for the position. The constructor validity of questionnaires and other tests given under practical conditions is apt to be poor if the examinees do not respond honestly during the testing.

User validity. The property or characteristic that a *test constructor* wants to measure and tries hard to measure in a test that he writes or assembles is not necessarily the property or characteristic that any given *test user* may want to measure. The *first* step in estimating the user validity of a test is, therefore, to formulate a clear statement of the purpose for which it is to be employed. This statement should be accompanied by a detailed outline of the information, skills, traits, and abilities that the test user wants to measure. An indication of the weight, or importance, of each of these should be provided. The *remaining five* steps in estimating the user validity of a test are the same as those employed in estimating the constructor validity.

Sometimes, a teacher is unable to find a standardized test that has user validity sufficiently high to satisfy him. In that case, he may want to construct a test especially for his own needs. The advantages of building a special test are obvious, but the labor and cost often make the undertaking impractical. Furthermore, a test constructed by a teacher for use in his own classes will not have been used in other classes or schools so he will not be able to compare the achievement of his pupils with that of others. The construction of tests for local use is discussed and illustrated in chapter 12.

Face validity. Face validity indicates the extent to which a test appears on casual inspection, especially by examinees or laymen, to measure what it is intended to measure. Suppose, for example, that a supermarket tests applicants for stockboy jobs to determine, among other characteristics, their accuracy and speed of visual perception. Items that require the applicant

FIGURE 2.6

Two Sample Items from Tests of Speed and Accuracy
of Visual Perception.

Directions: Underline the two syllables that are exactly alike.

1. mone   mono   mone   mine   mime
   ::::   ::::   ::::   ::::   ::::

Directions: Underline the two cans that are exactly alike.

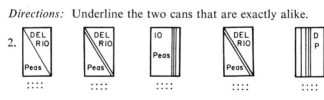

   ::::   ::::   ::::   ::::   ::::

to find in each item the two nonsense syllables among five that are exactly alike might be used for this purpose. Item 1 in Figure 2.6 is of this kind. Another kind of item that might be used for the same purpose is illustrated by item 2 in Figure 2.6. This requires the applicant to find the two cans out of the five that are exactly alike. Although the two types of items measure the same visual and mental functions, the one made up of pictures of canned foods has far greater face validity for selecting stockboys. The one made up of nonsense syllables has greater face validity for selecting proofreaders. The importance of face validity lies mainly in the fact that it affects the acceptance of tests by examinees and by the general public. Constructors of civil service examinations must pay particular attention to it.

Empirical-Judgmental Validity

Inferential validity. When suitable criterion scores are not available with which to correlate test scores, their *inferential validity* may be estimated by obtaining corroborative evidence. Suppose that a test thought to measure "industriousness" is given to a large group of college freshmen in September. The test constructor postulates that among students of equal scholastic aptitude and knowledge of world history in September, those in the highest quarter of the group in their world-history marks at the end of the semester will have a significantly higher average score on the "industriousness" test than will those in the lowest quarter with respect to the same marks. If this turns out to be so, the test constructor may properly infer that the data support the validity of his "industriousness" test. Inferential validity, then, is based on the formulation of hypotheses by subjective judgment and their testing by empirical means.

Factorial validity. Factorial validity indicates the extent to which test scores measure certain basic mental skills, often described as factors, that underlie performance on a variety of tests. It calls for the exercise of subjective judgment in identifying the factors and the use of experimental data for relating test scores and factor scores. The process is beset with many subtle opportunities for making undetected errors of judgment and inference; it falls beyond the scope of an introductory textbook in measurement.

TYPES OF SCORES OR NORMS

Raw Scores

The term *raw score* is used to describe the sum of the points earned by an examinee on a test. In some objective tests, one point is given for a correct response to each multiple-choice item, true-false item, or matching item.   The sum of these points represents an examinee's raw score.   For other objective tests, each examinee's raw score consists of the number of items he marks correctly minus a fraction of the number he marks incorrectly.   Essay tests ordinarily have a certain number of points assigned to each question and the sum of these earned by an examinee constitutes his raw score.   Only rarely does a raw score have meaning by itself.   For example, a free-response test measures the 100 fundamental addition facts in arithmetic; if an examinee gets a score of 50, we may estimate that he knows half of these fundamental operations.   In this case, the raw score is meaningful in itself.

Derived Scores

When more than one form of a test is constructed by selecting items for the various forms from a large supply of available items, efforts are made to produce forms that will measure the same mental and physical operations, that will be equally difficult, and that will yield scores having identical distributions.   However, minor variations in item difficulty usually prevent identical raw scores on all of the forms from being equivalent, or from representing the same level of ability or skill.   In order to have scores that

TABLE 2.4

Conversion of Raw Scores to Scaled Scores, *Davis Reading Test,*
Series 2*

Level of Comprehension Raw Scores				Scaled Scores	Speed of Comprehension Raw Scores			
Form 2A	Form 2B	Form 2C	Form 2D		Form 2A	Form 2B	Form 2C	Form 2D
40	40	40	40	96	80	80	80	80
—	—	—	—	95	79	79	79	79
—	—	—	—	94	78	78	78	78
39	39	39	39	93	77	77	—	77
—	—	—	—	92	76	76	77	—
—	—	—	—	91	—	75	—	76
—	38	38	38	90	75	74	76	75
38	—	—	—	89	74	73	75	74
—	—	—	—	88	73	—	74	73
—	37	37	—	87	—	72	73	72
—	—	—	37	86	72	71	72	71
37	—	—	—	85	71	70	71	70
—	36	36	—	84	70	69	70	69
—	—	—	36	83	69	68	69	68
36	35	35	—	82	68	67	68	67

TABLE 2.4 (*continued*)

Level of Comprehension Raw Scores				Scaled Scores	Speed of Comprehension Raw Scores			
Form 2A	Form 2B	Form 2C	Form 2D		Form 2A	Form 2B	Form 2C	Form 2D
—	—	—	35	81	67	66	67	66
35	34	34	—	80	66	65	66	65
—	—	—	34	79	65	63–64	64–65	64
34	33	33	—	78	63–64	61–62	62–63	62–63
—	32	32	33	77	61–62	59–60	60–61	60–61
33	31	31	32	76	59–60	57–58	58–59	58–59
32	30	30	—	75	57–58	55–56	56–57	56–57
—	29	29	31	74	55–56	53–54	54–55	54–55
31	28	28	30	73	53–54	50–52	51–53	52–53
30	27	27	29	72	50–52	48–49	48–50	49–51
29	26	26	28	71	48–49	45–47	46–47	47–48
28	25	25	27	70	46–47	43–44	44–45	45–46
27	24	24	26	69	44–45	41–42	42–43	43–44
26	23	23	25	68	41–43	38–40	39–41	40–42
25	21–22	21–22	23–24	67	38–40	35–37	35–38	37–39
23–24	20	20	22	66	35–37	32–34	32–34	34–36
22	18–19	18–19	20–21	65	32–34	28–31	29–31	31–33
19–21	17	16–17	18–19	64	28–31	25–27	25–28	27–30
17–18	14–16	14–15	16–17	63	24–27	21–24	20–24	22–26
15–16	12–13	11–13	12–15	62	19–23	17–20	16–19	18–21
13–14	10–11	9–10	11	61	16–18	14–16	13–15	15–17
11–12	9	8	9–10	60	14–15	12–13	11–12	13–14
10	8	7	8	59	11–13	10–11	10	10–12
8–9	7	6	7	58	10	8–9	8–9	9
7	6	5	6	57	8–9	7	6–7	7–8
5–6	5	4	5	56	6–7	6	5	6
—	4	3	4	55	5	5	4	5
4	3	2	3	54	4	4	3	4
3	2	—	2	53	3	3	2	3
2	—	1	—	52	2	2	1	2
1	1	—	1	51	1	1	—	1
—	—	—	—	50	—	—	—	—
0	0	0	0	49	0	0	0	0

are equivalent from form to form, many test constructors and publishers provide sets of *derived scores* for their tests.   Table 2.4 shows the raw scores in Level of Comprehension and Speed of Comprehension on the *Davis Reading Test*, Series 2, that correspond to a set of derived scores called scaled scores.   Note that raw scores in Level of Comprehension that correspond to a scaled score of 68 are 26, 23, 23, and 25 for Forms 2A, 2B, 2C, and 2D, respectively.   In Speed of Comprehension (for which the maximum possible raw score is 80 instead of 40, the maximum possible raw score for Level of Comprehension), the raw scores that correspond to a scaled score of 68 are 42, 39, 40, and 41 for Forms 2A, 2B, 2C, and 2D, respectively. The scaled scores in both Speed of Comprehension and Level of Comprehension on all four forms of the test are equivalent or comparable, thus making possible direct comparison of scores.

Derived scores differ in both their properties and the uses for which they are best adapted.   In the following sections, several of the most widely used types of derived scores are described.

Grade-equivalent scores.   Grade-equivalent scores are established by determining for a given test the average raw score obtained by pupils at each grade level for which the test is appropriate.   The grade level is usually expressed in tenths of a grade.   Table 2.5 shows the exact dates of the school year that correspond to each grade level, as these are ordinarily defined.*

TABLE 2.5

Grade Placement at Time of Testing

Date of Testing	Sept. 1– Sept. 15	Sept. 16– Oct. 15	Oct. 16– Nov. 15	Nov. 16– Dec. 15	Dec. 16– Jan. 15	Jan. 16– Feb. 15	Feb. 16– Mar. 15	Mar. 16– Apr. 15	Apr. 16– May 15	May 16– June 15
Grade Placement	.0	.1	.2	.3	.4	.5	.6	.7	.8	.9

Sometimes, the raw score corresponding to a given grade-equivalent score is the average raw score in a representative sample of all pupils at that grade level in American schools.   When this is the case, the grade-equivalent scores are called *total-group* grade-equivalent scores.   At other times, the raw score corresponding to a given grade-equivalent score is the average raw score of those pupils in a representative sample of all pupils at that grade

* See *Stanford Achievement Tests*, Intermediate and Advanced Complete Batteries, Forms J, K, L, M, and N (New York: Harcourt, Brace and World, Inc., 1953), table 2, p. 13.   Copyright 1953 by Harcourt, Brace and World, Inc. Copyright in Great Britain.   All rights reserved.   Reproduced by permission.

level who are approximately at the typical age.   In this case, the grade-equivalent scores are called *modal-group* grade-equivalent scores.   For Forms J, K, L, M, and N of the *Stanford Achievement Test*, modal-group grade-equivalent scores are provided that are based on the median raw score of pupils within six months of the most common age level for pupils at each grade level.   The norms samples for Forms S, W, X, Y, and Z of the *Stanford Achievement Test* include all pupils at a given grade level except for a few (1 to 2 per cent) who are extremely atypical with respect to age at grade level.   For the *Metropolitan Achievement Test*, modal-group grade-equivalent scores are provided that are based on the median raw score of pupils in the eighteen-month age range that includes the largest proportion of all pupils at each grade level.

The test performances of pupils who are either markedly over age or under age for their grade levels do not influence the establishment of modal-group grade-equivalent scores.   Since there are usually more pupils who are "held back" than "double-promoted," modal-group grade-equivalent scores ordinarily set a higher standard of comparison than total-group grade-equivalent scores.   It is more realistic to compare a pupil's test performance with that of others at his grade level than to compare it with the median of a group that includes retarded pupils who are greatly over age for their grade and accelerated pupils who are very young for their grade.   On the other hand, if the *average* grade-equivalent score in one class is to be compared with that in another class, it is better to use the total-group grade-equivalent scores than the modal-group grade-equivalent scores.

Grade-equivalent scores have both merits and defects.   One of their principal merits is that their units of measurement (tenths of a grade) are familiar to laymen as well as to educators.   In the lower grades especially, a record of each pupil's grade-equivalent scores over several years can be plotted on a cumulative record card to provide a quick assessment of his progress.   Grade-equivalent scores show in a readily comprehensible way the tremendous overlapping in achievement of pupils at different grade levels. For example, the Manual for the *Metropolitan Achievement Tests** shows that about 39 per cent of the pupils in the sixth month of grade 8 obtain Paragraph Meaning grade-equivalent scores of 7.6 or less, and are thus one grade or more retarded in reading.   About 27 per cent of them obtain grade-equivalent scores of 6.6 or less and are thus two or more grades retarded in reading.   About 17 per cent of them get grade-equivalent scores of 5.6 or less, and are thus three grades or more retarded in reading.   Approximately 7 per cent are four grades or more retarded in reading.   Grade-equivalent scores draw forcefully to the teacher's attention the range of achievement in

* *Metropolitan Achievement Tests*, Advanced Complete Battery, Forms A, B, C, D (New York: Harcourt, Brace and World, Inc., 1959), table 3, p. 14.

his class and thus tend to stimulate the use of grouping and other techniques for coping with the range of ability.

Among the defects of grade-equivalent scores is the fact that their units of measurement (tenths of a grade) do not represent reasonably equivalent amounts of the subject matter being measured.   This is clearly shown if one compares grade-equivalent scores on Forms J, K, L, M, and N of the *Stanford Achievement Test* with K scores for the same test.   K-score units may come reasonably close to representing equal amounts of the subject matter measured.   The comparison of grade-equivalent scores and K scores from the Arithmetic Computation section of the *Stanford Achievement Test* shown in Table 2.6 reveals that between grade-equivalent scores of 1.9 and

TABLE 2.6

K-Score Units Corresponding to Grade-Equivalent-Score Units in Arithmetic Computation*

Grade-Equivalent Score	K Score	K-Score Units per Tenth of a Grade
9.9	102.0	
8.9	90.2	1.18
7.9	76.8	1.34
6.9	62.2	1.46
5.9	49.1	1.31
4.9	41.2	.79
3.9	36.7	.45
2.9	33.0	.37
1.9	31.9	.11

* *Stanford Achievement Tests*, Intermediate and Advanced Complete Batteries, Forms J, K, L, M, and N (New York: Harcourt, Brace and World, Inc., 1953), table 6, p. 21.

2.9 a tenth of a grade represents .11 of a K-score point, whereas between grade-equivalent scores of 6.9 and 7.9 a tenth of a grade represents 1.46 K-score points.   In other words, a gain from a grade-equivalent score of 6.9 to 7.9 indicates that a pupil has improved about thirteen times as much as a gain from a grade-equivalent score of 1.9 to 2.9.   Grade-equivalent scores are not unique in this sort of distortion, but some other types of scores are less affected by it.

A second defect of grade-equivalent scores lies in the fact that they give an impression of a steady increase in the average performance of school children throughout the grades when this may not, in fact, be happening. Suppose that the average number of items marked correctly on a spelling test actually dropped during the summer vacation from eighteen in grade 6.8 to fourteen in grade 7.0.   Any pupil who marked eighteen items correctly should receive a grade-equivalent score of 6.8 and any pupil who marked fourteen items correctly should receive a grade-equivalent score of 7.0. Obviously, this sort of thing cannot be allowed to happen in establishing tables for converting raw scores into grade-equivalent scores.   It is avoided simply by testing a sample of pupils in each grade at the same time of year and assuming a steady progression in learning between testings.   This technique, however, is hardly applicable except in basic school subjects and cannot reasonably be used for establishing grade-equivalent scores in most secondary school subjects.   Therefore, grade-equivalent scores are not commonly employed for tests above grade 9.

A third defect of widely used grade-equivalent scores is that they were established by testing pupils in only a few of the grade levels that they cover. For example, the grade-equivalent scores for the *Stanford Achievement Test* were based on testing pupils only in grades 1 through 9.   Hence, grade-equivalent scores from 10.0 to 12.9 do not have the fundamental meaning of those from 1.0 to 9.9.   Nevertheless, they have been established in such a way that they are acceptably comparable from one subject-matter field to another.   Thus, they may be directly compared.

At this point, it may be appropriate to warn against a misconception about grade-equivalent scores.   Teachers and laymen have occasionally assumed that all pupils at a given grade level should attain or exceed the corresponding grade-equivalent score.   The nature of the scores is such that only about half of the members of a typical class can be expected to exceed the grade-equivalent score corresponding to their grade level.   However, in many schools where the pupils are above average in ability and in background of experiences, a majority of the pupils will attain grade-equivalent scores above their grade level.   This is also true in classes for intellectually gifted pupils in many communities.   It must be remembered that grade-equivalent scores are ordinarily established on the basis of representative samples of pupils throughout the country.   This is their frame of reference.

Finally, the frame of reference underlying grade-equivalent scores may not be the one regarded as most desirable in many schools or communities. Variations in curricula, equipment, and teaching methods may cause pupils in a given school or community to score generally higher or lower than the pupils in the representative samples of American school children used as a basis for establishing the grade-equivalent scores.   These considerations should be taken into account when the test scores are interpreted.

Age-equivalent scores.   The median obtained score of individuals at a single chronological age is defined as the age equivalent for that obtained score.   In practice, large representative samples of individuals at each chronological age are tested and the median (in years and months) of each age group is paired with the median obtained score. These pairs of scores (one for each age level) are then plotted, a smoothed curve is drawn through them, and a table of age-equivalent scores is read from the curve. In general, the defects of grade-equivalent scores are also present in age-equivalent scores.

The best-known type of age-equivalent score is the mental-age score. Since their introduction by Alfred Binet, mental-age scores have been widely used. Terman defined mental age in 1919 as "that degree of general mental ability which is possessed by the average child of corresponding chronological age."[*] In later years it became clear that the average scores of representative samples of Americans above the age of 16 to 18 increase very little on tests of general mental ability. The average obtained scores on a test of this sort remain about the same for representative samples at ages from 18 to about 25, beyond which they tend to decrease with advancing years. Between ages 3 and 12, the average obtained scores on tests of general mental ability of representative samples increase markedly, after which the rate of increase slows down. Figure 2.7 shows evidence of these trends. The solid line represents level of general mental ability; the vertical lines show the variability around points on this line. Each vertical line extends one standard deviation above and below the mean at a given age level.[†]

It is apparent that one month of mental age represents a different amount of the property being measured at different ages, and there is no way to express the mental ages of above-average individuals as they approach and pass the age of 18 except to create an artificial set of mental ages above, say, 18 years and 0 months. This was done to permit the computation of intelligence quotients (IQ's) for superior individuals from the usual equation, which follows:

$$\text{(Intelligence Quotient)} = 100 \, \frac{\text{(Mental Age)}}{\text{(Chronological Age)}}. \qquad (2.13)$$

In recent years, other methods have been used to obtain IQ's and age-equivalent scores, and mental-age scores are gradually falling into disuse. The method used to obtain IQ's for modern tests is described later in this chapter.

Percentile ranks. Percentile ranks (or percentile scores, as they are sometimes called) constitute a very useful way of reporting test scores. The

---

[*] L. M. Terman, *The Intelligence of School Children* (Boston: Houghton Mifflin Co., 1919), p. 7.

[†] N. Bayley, "On the Growth of Intelligence," *American Psychologist*, X (1955), 805–818.

FIGURE 2.7

The Growth of General Mental Ability.*

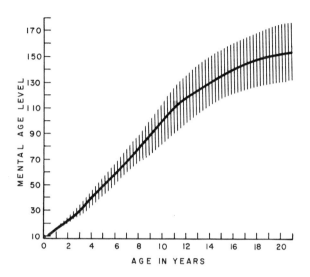

* After N. Bayley, *loc. cit.*, p. 811.

percentage of cases in a distribution that lie below any given score is called the percentile rank of that score. The computation of percentile ranks is discussed and illustrated in appendix B. Their relationship to other types of scores in the normal distribution is shown in Figure 2.8. It must be emphasized that percentiles may be obtained in distributions of any shape and are particularly useful in distributions that are *not* normal.

Both educators and laymen find percentile ranks easy to understand. Their use is illustrated in chapter 8. Once the group on which percentile ranks are based has been clearly defined, most teachers find it meaningful to be able to make statements like, "Suzanne's percentile rank on the reading test was 30. In other words, 30 per cent of the group she is being compared with did not perform as well as she did; 70 per cent performed better than she did."

Although percentile ranks are easy to understand, caution must be exercised in using them; when entered on a profile chart, they should usually be spaced to take account of the fact that differences between successive percentile ranks from 1 to 99 do not represent equal amounts of the property measured. A profile chart with the percentile ranks arranged in an appropriate way is shown in Figure 8.9 (p. 208). The arrangement of percentile

FIGURE 2.8

The Normal Distribution and Various Types of
Scores*.

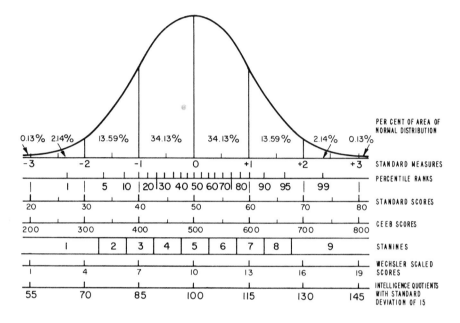

* Adapted from H. G. Seashore *et al.*, *Test Service Bulletin No. 47* (New York: Psychological Corporation, September 1954).

ranks on the profile chart in Figure 8.11 (p. 211) is *not* in accord with this principle.

It is often desirable to be able to compare a pupil's percentile ranks in several different groups. For example, the percentile rank in reading of a seventh grade pupil in a sample representative of all American seventh grade pupils may be compared with his percentile ranks in his own school and in his own community. In some subject-matter fields, it is important to have separate percentile norms for boys and girls. Table 2.7 gives selected percentile ranks for boys and girls in grade 12 on the Mechanical Reasoning Test of the *Differential Aptitude Tests*. The median for boys is 49 and for girls is 29. Obviously, separate tables of percentile norms are essential for meaningful interpretation of scores derived from this test.

To aid teachers, counselors, school psychologists, and administrators who may wish to establish local percentile norms, a recommended procedure is outlined and illustrated in appendix B.

TABLE 2.7

Percentile Norms for the *Differential Aptitude Tests*
Mechanical Reasoning Test, Form B

Boys		Girls	
Percentile Rank	Raw Score	Percentile Rank	Raw Score
99	67+	99	55+
97	65–66	97	51–54
95	62–64	95	47–50
90	60–61	90	43–46
85	59	85	40–42
80	57–58	80	38–39
75	56	75	36–37
70	54–55	70	35
65	53	65	33–34
60	52	60	32
55	50–51	55	30–31
50	49	50	29
45	47–48	45	28
40	45–46	40	26–27
35	43–44	35	24–25
30	41–42	30	22–23
25	39–40	25	20–21
20	37–38	20	17–19
15	34–36	15	15–16
10	29–33	10	12–14
5	23–28	5	8–11
3	17–22	3	5–7
1	0–16	1	0–4

Standard measures. As defined in this book, a standard measure is the deviation of an obtained score from the arithmetic mean of a distribution expressed in terms of the standard deviation of that distribution. To compute a standard measure, merely subtract the mean of a distribution from an obtained score and divide the resulting difference by the standard deviation of the distribution. The computation of standard measures is illustrated in appendix D. Their relationship to other types of scores in the normal distribution is shown in Figure 2.8. Standard measures may be computed for scores in distributions of any shape and themselves form a distribution shaped exactly like that of the original obtained scores.

Standard scores. In this book, the term *standard score* is reserved to designate a standard measure that has been converted to a different scale of measurement simply by multiplying it by one constant (to get rid of the decimal point) and adding the product to another constant (to get rid of the negative sign, if it had one). The computation of standard scores is discussed and illustrated in appendix D. The third line below the curve in Figure 2.8 shows standard scores with a mean of 50 and a standard deviation of 10. These were computed by multiplying each standard measure (shown on the first line below the curve) by 10 and adding the product to 50. Naturally, standard scores do not necessarily form normal distributions; they simply take the shape of the original distribution of obtained scores, whatever that may be.

Obtained scores on several different tests are sometimes converted to standard scores so that an examinee's performance on the various tests may be readily compared. Such comparisons rest on the assumption that scores equally deviant from the mean of a defined group that took all of the tests represent comparable levels of performance. This assumption is often reasonably well satisfied, but it must be remembered that the pattern of abilities in the defined group is the foundation on which all such comparisons are based.

Normalized standard scores. It has long been known that the score distributions of well-constructed tests in random samples of examinees at any given age or grade level tend to be normal. This observation led psychologists to conjecture that the true shape of the distribution of many human abilities is normal. This conjecture is supported by the fact that physical characteristics, such as height, weight, and waist measure, distribute themselves normally. The units of measurement for these characteristics (usually feet and inches, pounds, and inches, respectively) are clearly uniform throughout the scale so we know that their distributions are not made to look normal because of some peculiarities of the scale.

It is possible to obtain standard measures and standard scores that will form normal distributions regardless of the shape of the original distribution. The method for accomplishing this and illustrations of its use are given in appendix D. The resulting scores are called normalized standard measures or normalized standard scores. Since standard measures are useful mainly for research purposes, they will not be discussed further. Several types of normalized standard scores are in wide use and will be described briefly in the following sections.

Deviation IQ's. For various practical reasons it is difficult, if not impossible, to make IQ's computed from the ratio of mental age to chronological age have exactly the same meaning at every age level. For example, on Form L of the *Revised Stanford-Binet Tests of Intelligence*, the 84th percentile of the American population is represented at age 6 by an IQ of about 113 and at age 12 by an IQ of about 120. To eliminate this type of variation, deviation IQ's are now provided for many tests, including the 1960 revision of the *Stanford-Binet Tests of Intelligence*, Form L–M. Deviation IQ's are simply normalized standard scores expressed in units that have a mean of 100 and a preselected standard deviation. For most tests, the standard deviation of their deviation IQ's has been established as either 15 or 16.

Stanines. During World War II, psychologists in the Aviation Psychology Program of the U.S. Army Air Forces decided to express predictor scores for various air crew positions as normalized standard scores in only nine categories. From the words *standard* and *nine*, Laurance F. Shaffer coined the term "stanine" to denote scores of this type. They possess all the merits of normalized standard scores but divide examinees into only nine groups. Thus, they permit only rough measurement. With test scores having reliability coefficients of less than, say, .75, this coarseness of measurement may be desirable, since a false impression of precision is avoided. The standard error of measurement of a stanine of 5 when the reliability of the scores is .75 is one stanine. Thus, an examinee whose true stanine is exactly at the center of the range 4.5 to 5.5 may be expected to obtain a stanine of 5 on about 38 out of every 100 equivalent forms of the test that are administered to him.

Methods for establishing stanines are given in appendix D. A few words of caution may be in order for those who contemplate using these procedures: (1), the sample of examinees employed in establishing a set of stanines should be large, at least 100 and preferably 500 or larger; and (2), it is safest for several reasons to regard stanines as comparable only when they are based on the same sample.

T scores. Many years ago, William A. McCall defined T scores as normalized standard scores having a mean of 50 and a standard deviation of 10 in the population of twelve-year-olds in the United States. They constitute, therefore, a special type of normalized standard scores. They were named T scores in honor of Thorndike and Terman, two pioneers in the development of educational measurement.

Converted scores. Converted scores are three-digit scores used by the Educational Testing Service as derived scores for many of the tests they publish. For the *School and College Ability Tests*, for example, verbal converted scores were obtained by locating the raw scores on one form of the college-level test that represent, respectively, 60 per cent and 20 per cent of the maximum possible raw score. These raw scores were arbitrarily assigned converted-score values of 300 and 260, respectively. One-fortieth of the distance between these two raw scores, expressed in terms of normalized standard scores, was taken as one converted-score point. Tables were then developed to express verbal raw scores on all levels and forms of the test in these units. Analogous procedures were used to obtain quantitative and total converted scores.

The converted-score scale runs from about 150 to 400. This range was deliberately chosen so that the converted scores would not be confused with College Board scores (which run from 200 to 800), percentile ranks (which commonly run from 1 to 99), or other types of two- or three-digit scores that are in common use. It must be noted, however, that converted scores are not generally comparable from one test to another. That is, a verbal converted score of 200 on the *School and College Ability Tests* must not be regarded as indicating the same relative standing in the norms group as a quantitative converted score of 200.

Flanagan scaled scores. Flanagan scaled scores were developed for the *Cooperative Achievement Tests* and have been fully described by their originator.* They are essentially normalized standard scores with a mean of 50 and a standard deviation of 10. However, the fact that distributions of raw scores centering at several ability levels are used in establishing these scores makes them far more stable than normalized standard scores based on only one distribution of raw scores. This overcomes one weakness of the latter, since extremely high and low normalized standard scores are often poorly established. Another merit of Flanagan scaled scores is that they exhibit a stronger tendency than other types of normalized standard scores to form distributions of the same shape in different samples drawn from the same population. As used for reporting performance on the *Cooperative Achievement Tests*, a scaled score of 50 has special meaning. It represents the score the average American white child would make at the end of a given period of study if he had typical instruction for an average length of time at the usual grade levels. In this sense, a particular scaled score is comparable from test to test.

K scores. To overcome the need for forcing standard scores into normal distributions, Eric F. Gardner developed K scores based on overlapping distributions that need not be normal in shape. This procedure provides sets of scores in which the units represent more nearly equal amounts of the property being measured than do other types of scores. Up to the present time, K scores have been made available only for the parts of the *Stanford Achievement Test*.† For measuring the growth of an individual

* J. C. Flanagan, *The Cooperative Achievement Tests, A Bulletin Reporting the Basic Principles and Procedures Used in the Development of Their System of Scaled Scores* (New York: Cooperative Test Service, 1939).

† See, for example, *Stanford Achievement Tests*, Intermediate and Advanced Complete Batteries, Forms J, K, L, M, and N (New York: Harcourt, Brace and World, Inc., 1953), section 7. For a technical discussion of K scores, see E. F. Gardner, "The Determination of Units of Measurement Which Are Consistent with Inter- and Intra-Grade Differences in Ability," Ed. D. dissertation, Harvard University, Cambridge, Mass., 1947. K scores were so named in honor of Truman L. Kelley, one of the pioneers in educational measurement and guidance.

pupil over a period of time, K scores have great merit. Anyone who administers the *Stanford Achievement Test* for this purpose should consider using them.

Percentile bands. Since 1955, the Educational Testing Service has made provision for reporting the performance of an examinee on any one of several of their tests as a percentile band. A percentile band consists of a range of percentile scores that may, in effect, be regarded as having a designated probability of including the examinee's true score. This probability is expressed by the Educational Testing Service as follows, "The chances are 2 to 1 that the student's true score lies within this interval."*

Percentile bands emphasize the degree of inaccuracy in test scores. Whether it is better to report a band of scores or a single score plus an indication of the approximate range that has about two out of three chances of including the examinee's true score is a moot question. The answer probably depends on how the scores are to be used. To many test interpreters, percentile bands are confusing.

Quotients. Scores have sometimes been expressed as quotients, the intelligence quotient being the outstanding example. As stated earlier in this chapter, IQ's are now rarely expressed as actual quotients; instead, they are expressed as normalized standard scores with a mean of 100 and a standard deviation of about 15.

Educational quotients, such as reading quotients and arithmetic quotients, are now little used. The best way to compare an individual's obtained score on a test with the average score of a large sample representative of individuals at his age or grade level is presented and illustrated in chapter 8. A third type of quotient score, the accomplishment quotient, is no longer recommended for practical use. It was computed by dividing an individual's age-equivalent score in a subject-matter field (like arithmetic) by his mental-age score and multiplying the quotient by 100 to eliminate the decimal point. Recommended methods for comparing achievement- and aptitude-test scores of individuals and groups are given in chapter 11.

Estimated True Scores

As pointed out earlier in this chapter, an individual's true score is impossible to obtain. His obtained score is ordinarily used as an estimate

---

* *Cooperative School and College Ability Tests, Directions for Administering, Scoring, and First Interpretation of Forms 1A, 1B, 1C, 1D, 2A, 2B* (Princeton: Educational Testing Service, 1955), p. 12. Statisticians find this statement technically incorrect for reasons that lie beyond the scope of this discussion, but it has practical meaning and in my judgment should not be unduly criticized.

of his true score, but a better estimate can be obtained with the mean obtained score of the group in which he properly belongs and the reliability coefficient of the scores in this group. With his obtained score represented by X, his estimated true score by $\hat{X}$, the mean of the group by $\overline{X}$, and the reliability coefficient by $r_{XX'}$, equation 2.14 can be used to estimate his true score:

$$\hat{X} = \overline{X} + r_{XX'}(X - \overline{X}). \tag{2.14}$$

The standard error of measurement for estimated true scores is smaller than for obtained scores. It is given by equation 2.15:

$$s_{\text{meas }\hat{x}} = r_{XX'}s_X \sqrt{1 - r_{XX'}}. \tag{2.15}$$

When $s_{\text{meas }x}$ is substituted for $s_X \sqrt{1 - r_{XX'}}$, equation 2.15 becomes:

$$s_{\text{meas }\hat{x}} = r_{XX'} s_{\text{meas }x}. \tag{2.16}$$

Although estimated true scores are used mainly for research purposes, they are extremely helpful for measuring individual gains and for comparing individual scores on two different tests. They are, therefore, dealt with in practical terms in chapters 10 and 11.

Summary

The basic objective of measurement is the true score of an individual or of a group in the property that it is desired to measure. Since a true score can never be ascertained in practice, an estimate of it must be used. Ordinarily, this estimate is an obtained score. It may differ from the true score because it is subject to errors of measurement.

The extent to which an obtained score is subject to errors of measurement is indicated by the standard error of measurement. Important sources of error include:

1. Variation in the sets of items that make up equivalent test forms.
2. Variation in conditions of test administration.
3. Variation in the examinee's intent and motivation and in his physical and emotional states.
4. Guessing on the part of the examinee.

The relative precision of measurement of a set of test scores is indicated by their reliability coefficient. Among tests of equal validity those of highest reliability are preferred.

Validity is indicated by the extent to which examinees are ranked in the same order on a test as on the criterion, the latter being the property that it is desired to measure. A test may have a different degree of validity for each of many criteria. Different methods of determining test validity lead to a variety of estimates, as follows:

1. Empirical validity
   a. Predictor validity
   b. Concurrent validity
   c. Congruent validity
   d. Self-defining validity
2. Judgmental validity
   a. Constructor validity
   b. User validity
   c. Face validity
3. Empirical-Judgmental validity
   a. Inferential validity
   b. Factorial validity

Test scores are expressed in many ways.   Among these are:

1. Raw scores
2. Derived scores
   a. Grade-equivalent scores
   b. Age-equivalent scores
   c. Percentile ranks
   d. Standard measures
   e. Standard scores
   f. Normalized standard scores
   g. Deviation IQ's
   h. Stanines
   i. T scores
   j. Converted scores
   k. Flanagan scaled scores
   l. K scores
   m. Percentile bands
   n. Quotients
3. Estimated true scores

An understanding of the nature and properties of these scores is essential for anyone who uses tests.

Selected References

Cureton, Edward E., "The Definition and Estimation of Test Reliability," *Educational and Psychological Measurement*, XVII (1958), 715–738.

Cureton, Edward E., "Validity," in Lindquist, E. F., ed., *Educational Measurement*, Chapter 16. Washington: American Council on Education, 1951.

Ghiselli, Edward E., *Theory of Psychological Measurement* (New York: McGraw-Hill Book Co., 1964), Chapters 8 and 11.

Kelley, Truman L., "The Reliability Coefficient," *Psychometrika*, VII (1942), 75–83.

Thorndike, Robert L., "Reliability," in Lindquist, E. F., ed., *Educational Measurement*, Chapter 15. Washington: American Council on Education, 1951.

Chapter Three

SELECTION AND ADMINISTRATION OF STANDARDIZED TESTS

FACTORS TO CONSIDER IN SELECTING TESTS

Purpose of Testing

The first step in selecting tests is to define carefully and in detail the purpose for which they are to be used. A number of purposes for which tests have been found useful in education are listed in chapter 1. A supervisor of language arts in the elementary schools of a city may want information about the reading readiness of pupils entering grade 1 in order to help first grade teachers group pupils for preparatory exercises in reading. The guidance department in a junior high school may want to find out about the aptitudes and interests of ninth grade pupils during the first semester so that this information will be available to counselors when they confer with pupils during the second semester regarding their course of study in senior high school. Whatever the purpose, it should be clearly expressed in writing before measuring instruments are selected. Tests should not be used in schools without a clear understanding of their purpose and without detailed plans for their interpretation and use by competent personnel.

Test Validity

With a clear statement of the purpose of testing at hand, a teacher, counselor, or administrator may consult publishers' catalogues of tests, sources like the *Mental Measurements Yearbooks*, and experts in the field to find the tests that seem likely to be most useful. Copies of these tests can be secured for examination. If they are to be used to assess achievement or aptitude, their content can be analyzed and compared with the particular combination of skills, abilities, and knowledge that it is desired to measure. By this process, the user validity of each test under consideration is judged. If the tests are to predict performance in some criterion variable (such as marks in the freshman year of college), evidence regarding the predictive validity of each one may be found in the test manual or elsewhere.

TABLE 3.1

Average Product-Moment Correlation Coefficients between First-Term Course Grades and Scores on Six Aptitude Tests in Samples of Navy V-12 Students*

Test	First-Term Course Grades				
	English	History	Physics	Mathe-matics	Engineering Drawing
	N = 763	N = 761	N = 793	N = 751	N = 763
Verbal section, College Entrance Examination Board Scholastic Aptitude Test	.52	.49	.33	.14	.05
Verbal Reasoning	.46	.46	.42	.20	.20
Quantitative Reasoning	.26	.36	.46	.39	.39
Mathematics section, College Entrance Examination Board Scholastic Aptitude Test	.28	.39	.52	.36	.36
Spatial Visualization	.05	.07	.25	.59	.60
	N = 410	N = 408	N = 439	N = 422	N = 409
Mechanical Ingenuity	.12	.14	.33	.50	.50

* Weighted averages were computed by means of Fisher's *z* transformation. Three groups of beginning freshmen at Yale were tested at the time of admission in July 1943, November 1943, and March 1944. The Mechanical-Ingenuity Test was administered to only a few of the July 1943 entrants, and the data for this group have not been used.

The interval between administration of the aptitude tests and the assignment of course grades was one term, or about four months.

Reproduced by permission from F. B. Davis, *Utilizing Human Talent* (Washington, D.C., American Council on Education, 1947), table 2, p. 44.

FIGURE 3.1 Validity Coefficients of Scores Derived from the *Differential Aptitude Tests* for Predicting Course Marks.

For each test, the bars and accompanying numbers indicate how many coefficients fall within each range given in the left-hand column.

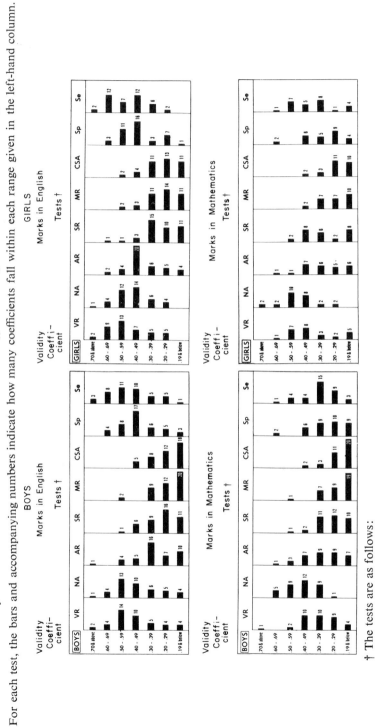

† The tests are as follows:

VR = Verbal Reasoning
CSA = Clerical Speed and Accuracy
SR = Space Relations

MR = Mechanical Reasoning
AR = Abstract Reasoning
Se = Sentence Structure

NA = Numerical Ability
Sp = Spelling

The types of data that may be available are illustrated by those provided in *A Manual for the Differential Aptitude Tests.** A graphic summary of validity coefficients for scores derived from these tests is reproduced as Figure 3.1.† Note how much better verbal-reasoning (VR) scores predict course marks in English than in mathematics and, conversely, how much better numerical-ability (NA) scores predict course marks in mathematics than in English.

Table 3.1 shows validity coefficients of several tests for predicting first-term marks in samples of Navy V-12 students at Yale University. The verbal and mathematical sections of the College Entrance Examination Board *Scholastic Aptitude Test* show very different patterns of correlation with marks in different subjects. As would be expected, the verbal scores are most effective for predicting marks in English and history; on the other hand, the mathematical scores correlate highest with marks in physics and lowest with those in English. Note especially the marked differences in the validity of the spatial-visualization scores for predicting marks in different courses. These data illustrate the principle stated in chapter 2 that the predictive validity of a set of scores may differ markedly from one criterion to another.

Characteristics of Scores

Having learned something about the many kinds of scores used to express test results, the student may wonder, "What are some of the general characteristics of scores that I should consider in selecting tests?" This section presents some information to answer this question.

Coarseness of units of measurement. The units in which scores are expressed differ greatly in size or coarseness. A glance at Figure 2.8 (p. 44) reveals that the number of score points between standard measures of $+3$ and -3 varies approximately from 9 for stanine scores to 600 for CEEB (College Entrance Examination Board) scores. The question that comes to mind is, "How many score points *should* there be in this range?" Unfortunately, there is no single answer. However, it is widely agreed that the number should depend on the purpose for which the scores are to be used and on their reliability coefficient. If we adopt, as a rule of thumb, the principle that the interval covered by one score point should be one-half of

* G. K. Bennett, H. G. Seashore, and A. G. Wesman, *A Manual for the Differential Aptitude Tests* (New York: Psychological Corporation, 1959), section 4.

† Reproduced by permission. Copyright © 1959, The Psychological Corporation, New York, N.Y. All rights reserved.

the over-all standard error of measurement of the scores, the resulting number of score points between standard measures of $+3$ and -3 can easily be determined for any degree of reliability.*   The results for eleven values of test reliability are shown in Table 3.2.

TABLE 3.2

Approximate Number of Score Points One-Half
a Standard Error of Measurement in Width
Between Standard Measures of -3 and $+3$ for
Eleven Values of Test Reliability

Test Reliability Coefficient	Approximate Number of Score Points
.99	120
.95	55
.90	38
.80	27
.70	22
.60	19
.50	17
.40	16
.30	15
.20	13
.10	13

Many standardized tests that are commercially available have single-grade reliability coefficients between .80 and .95.   For these, our rule of thumb indicates that there should be 27 to 55 score points in any one age or grade group.   Of the types of scores shown in Figure 2.8 (p. 44), CEEB scores with 600 points, percentile ranks with 99 points, and Wechsler intelligence quotients with 90 points greatly exceed these limits.   If CEEB scores were reported as two-digit normalized standard scores with a mean of 50 and a standard deviation of 10, they would not fall far outside the limits suggested by our rule of thumb, but this change would probably not be wise since the main purpose of CEEB scores is to rank applicants in order for college admission.   In the long run, the higher the CEEB score, the better qualified the applicant.   For reporting test results to the applicants and their parents, a 60-category scale would probably be more suitable than the 600-point scale.

The coarseness of stanines for reporting the results of even rather unreliable tests is clearly implied by the data in Table 3.2.   This is no reason

*If score intervals are one-half a standard error of measurement in width and if an examinee's true score is exactly in the center of one of these intervals, his raw score will in the long run fall in the same interval only about once out of every five testings.

for not using stanines if finer distinctions than are provided by nine score categories are unnecessary. Certainly, stanines avoid any unwarranted impression of great precision of measurement.

Equality of units of measurement. As noted earlier, raw scores on a test rarely represent equal amounts of the property measured throughout their range. Percentile ranks are notably deficient in this respect. For measuring growth in aptitude and in school achievement, it is desirable to use scores that do represent equal amounts of growth; for computing the growth made by two or more individuals or the growth made by an individual during one period with that made during another period, such scores are essential. Derived scores, like normalized standard scores, Flanagan scaled scores, and Gardner's K scores, come closer to meeting the need for equality of units than do other types of scores.

Equivalence and comparability of scores. If the growth of individuals and groups in aptitude or school achievement is to be measured, several forms of the test must be available. These forms of the same test should yield equivalent scores. (See p. 10.) If comparisons are to be made of achievement in two or more subject-matter fields or of achievement and aptitude, the tests used should yield comparable scores. (See p. 10.) In selecting tests, therefore, it is desirable to make sure that four or more equivalent forms are available and that their scores are inherently comparable or can be made so by conversion to percentile ranks, grade-equivalent scores, some type of normalized standard scores, or K scores.

Meaningfulness of scores. For many purposes, percentile ranks in carefully defined groups constitute the most satisfactory way of making test scores meaningful. It is often desirable to obtain an examinee's percentile rank in several different groups. Local percentile norms are often a valuable adjunct to national norms, for example. For indicating the achievement and mental levels of elementary school pupils, grade-equivalent and age-equivalent scores (such as mental age) are often intrinsically more meaningful to teachers and laymen than are other types of scores.

Scores that convey the examinee's ability to perform practical tasks are extremely meaningful but are currently available only in fields like typing and shorthand. That an applicant for a secretarial position can type 45 words per minute or 60 words per minute is highly informative to a pro-spective employer. Unfortunately, we do not have analogous scores in other fields. Regarding French, for example, it would be meaningful to report that a given examinee can read a typical issue of the popular French magazine *Match* and comprehend 90 per cent of its contents, that he can read the daily newspaper *Paris Soir* and understand 50 per cent, or that he can understand about 30 per cent of a novel by Françoise Sagan. A beginning has been made in providing this type of score for comprehension in English on one of the tests used in Project TALENT, a national survey of the abilities of American high school students. The number of questions answered correctly by the average pupil about passages of typical difficulty taken from several sources are shown in Table 3.3.

TABLE 3.3

Average Number of Items Answered Correctly by the Median American Pupil During the Second Semester of Grade 12 on Similarly Constructed Ten-Item Tests Based on Typical Passages from Ten Well-Known Authors and Magazines*

Author	Average Score	Magazine	Average Score
Alcott	6.3	*Silver Screen*	7.7
Stevenson	5.7	*Saturday Evening Post*	5.3
Cather	4.9	*Look*	4.6
Verne	4.6	*Reader's Digest*	4.3
Lewis	4.5	*Pageant*	3.9
Kipling	4.4	*McCall's*	3.7
Dostoevski	4.2	*Time*	3.4
Conrad	3.9	*Fortune*	3.2
Austen	3.3	*Saturday Review*	2.8
Mann	2.7	*Atlantic*	2.7

* These data are merely illustrative because the representativeness of the passages and of the ten items in each of the twenty tests has not been adequately established. They are derived from data gathered by Project TALENT of the University of Pittsburgh and are presented with the permission of Professor J. C. Flanagan, responsible investigator.

Norms

Meaning. Norms represent standards of performance in defined groups. As such, they are invaluable for interpreting test scores. They must not, however, be regarded as ideals or goals to be reached. There seems little doubt that well-motivated pupils taught in small groups with self-teaching devices available and properly used can learn a great deal more efficiently than typical pupils taught in conventional school classes. Norms based on the achievement of the latter should not be allowed to make educators or laymen complacent about the performance of gifted pupils taught in well-equipped schools staffed with superior personnel. Neither should they be used to disparage or discount the performance of underprivileged children taught in large classes by inexperienced teachers without modern equipment.

Tables of norms should always be accompanied by a description of the population or populations on which they are based and the methods by which the samples were drawn. Norms are likely to be more representative of the population defined as their base if small numbers of pupils from many schools are combined to form the sample than if large numbers of pupils from a few schools are so used.

Bases for norms. It is far better to have norms based on the testing of moderately large but properly representative samples of several well-defined populations than to have norms based on the testing of a very large sample drawn from the American population at a specified age or grade level. In the first case, test users can choose among several bases of comparison. How different the performance of pupils may look when the basis of comparison is changed is illustrated by comparing grade-equivalent scores on the *Advanced Stanford Achievement Test*, Form L, that correspond to the same percentile ranks in the national public school norms provided by the publisher and in independent school norms.* These data are shown in Table 3.4. Note that in Word Meaning and Arithmetic Reasoning the 25th

TABLE 3.4

Grade-Equivalent Scores Corresponding to the 25th, 50th, and 75th Percentile Ranks on the Stanford Achievement Test, Advanced Battery, Form L, March 2–8, 1962, Among Eighth Grade Pupils in 69 Member Schools of the Educational Records Bureau

Test	Grade-Equivalent Scores					
	25th Percentile		50th Percentile		75th Percentile	
	Public Schools	ERB Schools	Public Schools	ERB Schools	Public Schools	ERB Schools
1. Paragraph Meaning	6.9	9.8	8.6	11.0	10.4	12.1
2. Word Meaning	7.3	10.1	8.6	11.4	10.0	12.1
3. Spelling	7.4	8.6	8.5	10.2	10.0	11.7
4. Language Usage	7.1	10.8	8.6	11.6	10.9	12.2
5. Arithmetic Reasoning	7.4	10.5	8.6	11.3	10.2	12.1
6. Arithmetic Computation	7.6	9.8	8.6	11.1	10.1	11.9
7. Social Studies	7.1	10.1	8.7	11.2	10.4	12.2
8. Science	7.1	9.9	8.6	11.0	10.0	12.0
9. Study Skills	6.7	10.0	8.6	11.3	10.3	12.2

* "1962 Achievement Testing Program in Independent Schools, and Supplementary Studies," *Educational Records Bulletin*, No. 82 (New York: Educational Records Bureau, 1962).

percentile in the independent school norms represents a higher level of attainment than does the 75th percentile in the public school norms. These data illustrate the importance of defining norms groups in detail and of choosing them with great care for interpreting test results.

Test Reliability

Other things being equal, the test yielding the most reliable scores is of greatest usefulness. In judging the reliability data for various tests, it is necessary to make sure that the data are directly comparable. As noted in chapter 2, the reliability coefficient of a test can be raised by increasing the range of talent in the group used to compute the coefficient. For example, if the group includes examinees from two, three, or more grades, the reliability coefficient will be considerably higher than if all the examinees are at one grade level or one age level.

The method of obtaining the data used to compute a reliability coefficient also affects its magnitude. If equivalent forms of a test are administered seven to ten days apart, as recommended for getting the reliability coefficients of most tests, errors of measurement associated with variations of the examinees over the period of time affect the coefficient and tend to keep it lower than if the tests had been administered one right after the other. If a reliability coefficient is based on the scores on two halves of the same test (the split-half procedure), it is likely to be higher than if scores from two equivalent forms are used, because variations in the examinees' performance affect scores on both halves in a similar way.

Using split-half procedures to obtain reliability coefficients for speeded tests (in which very few examinees have a chance to try all the items) may result in spuriously high coefficients that give a misleading impression of the relative precision of measurement. This point is illustrated by the data in Table 3.5 on the reliability of scores on the Clerical Speed and Accuracy Test in the *Differential Aptitude Tests*. In grade 8, for example, the reliability coefficient of these scores in a sample of forty-eight boys was increased from .77 when scores from both Forms A and B were used to compute it to .990 when only the two halves of Form A were used and to .996 when only the two halves of Form B were used. In other samples, for which data are shown in the table, similar increases in the size of the reliability coefficient are apparent.

Sometimes, a reliability coefficient is estimated from data pertaining to the internal consistency of a test by means of Kuder-Richardson formulas 20 or 21, or their equivalents.* If used with speeded tests, these pro-

---

* G. F. Kuder and M. W. Richardson, "The Theory of Estimation of Test Reliability," *Psychometrika*, II (1937), 151–160.

cedures, like the split-half procedures, yield spuriously high coefficients. When properly used with unspeeded tests, these procedures ordinarily yield estimates similar to those obtained by split-half procedures.

TABLE 3.5

Reliability Coefficients for the Clerical Speed and Accuracy Test in the Differential Aptitude Tests Obtained by Equivalent-Forms and Split-Half Methods*

	Boys					Girls			
	Equivalent-Forms Method	Split-half Method				Equivalent-Forms Method	Split-half Method		
Grade	Form A vs. Form B	Form A	Form B	N	Grade	Form A vs. Form B	Form A	Form B	N
8	.77	.990	.996	48	8	.87	.992	.998	62
9	.83	.991	.989	50	9	.84	.994	.991	62
10	.93	.996	.985	45	10	.91	.997	.993	54
11	.86	.992	.993	50	11	.86	.994	.993	44
12	.92	.996	.969	43	12	.88	.986	.989	53

* G. K. Bennett, H. G. Seashore, and A. G. Wesman, *A Manual for the Differential Aptitude Tests* (New York: Psychological Corporation, 1959), p. 67. Reproduced by permission. Copyright © 1959, The Psychological Corporation, New York, N.Y. All rights reserved.

Ease of Administration

Several factors affect the ease and convenience with which a test is administered.

1. The *number* and *length* of the *parts*. The larger the number of parts to be timed separately and the shorter these time limits, the more likely it is that mistakes in timing will be made.
2. The *format* of the *booklets* and the *answer sheets*. Some tests have been printed with part of the material upside down so that examinees cannot look ahead and study what they are supposed to do in a later time period. Turning booklets around at the appropriate time requires close supervision by the examiner and proctors and may lead to difficulties. Occasionally, an answer sheet is to be used during more than one testing session, and keeping examinees who have looked up answers to questions they did not know during the first session from going back and filling in answers to those questions during the second session is

always difficult and often impossible.   Careful attention to arrangement and format by the test publisher can minimize sources of trouble like these.

3. The *directions*.   They should always state just how the test papers or answer sheets are to be scored.

If the directions are not clear, examinees often ask, "Is there a penalty for wrong answers?   Should I guess when I don't know the answer?"   It is only natural that examinees should want to know how their answers are to be scored.   Therefore, the directions should always deal explicitly with this point in a way that is appropriate to the age of the examinees.   If the scores on a test given to junior high school pupils are to be corrected for chance success (a procedure explained in chapter 4), the directions should include a statement something like this:

"It pays to answer items even when you are not sure that your answers are correct.   If you think that one (or more) of the choices in an item is definitely wrong, it will pay you to guess among the remaining choices.   On the other hand, if you have no idea of the answer to an item or do not have time to read it, you had better not mark an answer to it."

If the scores are *not* to be corrected for chance success, the directions should include a statement like this:

"Your score will be the number of items you mark correctly.   It will pay you to mark answers to all the items even if you have no idea of the correct answers to some of them or do not have time to read them."

These statements provide honest advice and tend to reduce the advantage held by pupils who have been coached on how to take objective tests, especially those for which scores are not corrected for chance success.

Another point that should be fully covered in the directions is the number of items and the time available to answer them.   It is *not* enough to say, "If you work at average speed, you will have plenty of time to try all the questions."   Pupils do not know what is meant by "average speed"; it may mean something different to each pupil.   The information about the time available may be stated in this form: "There are 30 questions in Part I, and you will have 15 minutes in which to answer them.   Work as rapidly as you can without making careless mistakes.   Do not spend too much time on any one item; if you cannot answer an item, go on to the others and come back to it later if you have time."

Ease of Scoring

Instructions for scoring tests should be straightforward and clear.   If answers are to be recorded in the test booklet (a convenience for examinees that has become too expensive), scoring stencils should fit accurately over

FIGURE 3.2. Rights Scoring Stencil for *ABC Comprehension Test.*

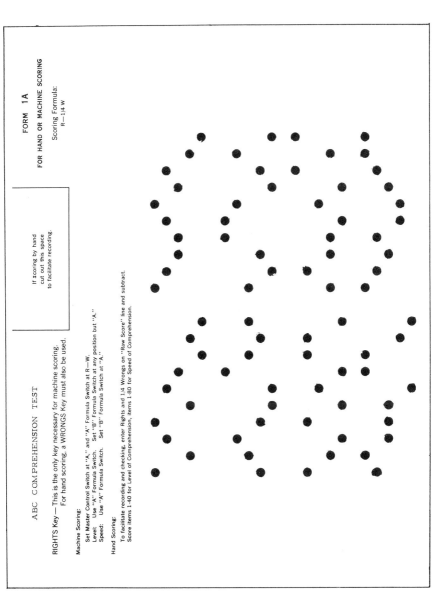

ABC COMPREHENSION TEST

If scoring by hand
cut out this space
to facilitate recording.

FORM 1A

FOR HAND OR MACHINE SCORING

Scoring Formula:
R—1/4 W

RIGHTS Key — This is the only key necessary for machine scoring.
For hand scoring, a WRONGS Key must also be used.

Machine Scoring:

Set Master Control Switch at "A," and "A" Formula Switch at R—W.
Level: Use "A" Formula Switch. Set "B" Formula Switch at any position but "A."
Speed: Use "A" Formula Switch. Set "B" Formula Switch at "A."

Hand Scoring:

To facilitate recording and checking, enter Rights and 1/4 Wrongs on "Raw Score" line and subtract.
Score items 1-40 for Level of Comprehension, items 1-80 for Speed of Comprehension.

FIGURE 3.3. Wrongs Scoring Stencil for *ABC Comprehension Test*.

ABC COMPREHENSION TEST

FORM 1A

FOR HAND SCORING ONLY

WRONGS Key (A Rights Key is also needed.)

Scoring formula: R—1/4 W. To facilitate recording and checking, enter Rights and 1/4 Wrongs on "Raw Score" line and subtract.
Score items 1-40 for Level of Comprehension, items 1-80 for Speed of Comprehension.

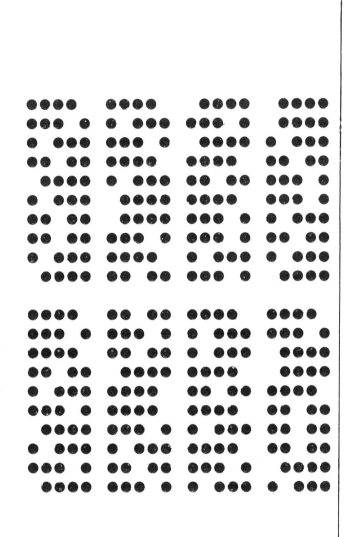

the pages with the correct answers printed next to the spaces where the examinee's responses appear. If answers are to be recorded on separate answer sheets, scoring stencils should be available for both hand scoring and machine scoring. Examples of these are shown in Figures 3.2 and 3.3. The first is intended for counting the correct answers and the second for counting the incorrect answers. Both numbers are required in obtaining scores corrected for chance success.

The amount of labor in preparing answer sheets for accurate machine or hand scoring depends partly on the scoring procedure. For reasons that are discussed fully in chapter 4, the preparation of answer sheets for scoring is less time-consuming if the scores are corrected for chance success.* This gain is partly offset in hand scoring by the fact that counts of wrong answers as well as of correct answers have to be made if the correction is used. In machine scoring, there is no difference in the time or labor involved in running the machine. The net result favors selecting tests that are scored with correction for chance success.

Aids to Interpretation

Test users should evaluate the aids to interpreting scores that are provided for the tests they are considering. In addition to norms and scores that are equivalent from form to form and comparable from part to part of multiscore tests, information of value to test interpreters includes standard errors of measurement, confidence intervals, and the smallest differences between scores that are worth interpreting. These are provided in various ways by test publishers. The standard errors of measurement of grade-equivalent scores on the *Stanford Achievement Tests* are shown as lines on the Individual Profile Charts. The chart for Form J of the Intermediate Battery is reproduced as Figure 8.5 on page 199. The percentile bands for the *School and College Ability Tests* are portrayed for each examinee on his Student Profile Chart. This is reproduced as Figure 8.11 on page 211. As mentioned in chapter 2, these percentile bands are 68-per-cent confidence intervals. The use of confidence intervals is discussed in chapter 8.

Differences between scores that are large enough to be worth interpreting are identified in several different ways. On the Student Profile Chart for the *School and College Ability Tests*, they are those between scores whose percentile bands do not overlap vertically. Appendix M gives tables for identifying such differences for many tests in common use. Various other ways of identifying differences of this kind have been provided by test publishers. It is important in selecting tests to make sure that information of this kind is available in some usable form.

---

* Except when the most modern photoelectric scoring devices are used.

SOURCES OF INFORMATION
ABOUT TESTS

A comprehensive bibliography entitled *Tests in Print** is the most up-to-date and most complete listing of tests available. Critical evaluations of hundreds of tests have been published in the *Mental Measurements Yearbooks*.† In addition, the yearbooks provide for each test the following information:

1. The title.
2. The grades or ages for which it is intended.
3. The date or dates of publication.
4. The number and types of scores yielded.
5. The auxiliary publications (manuals, etc.) and their prices.
6. The type of answer sheets used.
7. The price of the answer sheets.
8. The time limits.
9. The author or authors.
10. The publisher.

Selected References on Test Construction, Mental Test Theory, and Statistics, 1929-1949,‡ a compilation by Goheen and Kavruck published in 1950 by the U.S. Government Printing Office, stresses technical data. Other sources of information about tests are various professional journals. The *Review of Educational Research* publishes an issue on educational and psychological testing every three years; the most recent appeared in February 1962. The *Journal of Consulting Psychology,* the *Personnel and Guidance Journal,* the *Journal of Counseling Psychology,* and others have from time to time carried reviews of new tests as they appear on the market. Brief annotated notices of new tests appear regularly in *Psychological Abstracts* and announcements of their publication appear regularly in the *Education Index.*

Most test publishers prepare annual catalogues of their current offerings. In general, the tests are sold only to purchasers professionally qualified to use them. Students who wish to examine tests may do so in files kept for the purpose in many college and university libraries. If they wish to purchase tests for inspection or experimental use, this can usually best be

---

* O. K. Buros, ed. *Tests in Print* (New Brunswick, N.J.: Gryphon Press, 1961).

† See the list of references at the end of the chapter for bibliographical data.

‡ See references at the end of the chapter.

done with the cooperation of their instructor in educational or psychological measurement.

A list of the larger test publishers and their addresses follows:

> Bureau of Publications, Teachers College, Columbia University, New York 27, N.Y.
> California Test Bureau, Del Monte Research Park, Monterey, Calif.
> College Entrance Examination Board, 375 Riverside Drive, New York 27, N.Y.
> Committee on Diagnostic Reading Tests, Inc., Hendersonville, N.C.
> Consulting Psychologists Press, 270 Town and Country Village, Palo Alto, Calif.
> Cooperative Test Division, Educational Testing Service, Princeton, N.J.
> Harcourt, Brace and World, Inc., 750 Third Avenue, New York 17, N.Y.
> Houghton Mifflin Co., 2 Park Street, Boston 7, Mass.
> Psychological Corporation, 304 East 45th Street, New York, N.Y.
> Science Research Associates, 259 East Erie Street, Chicago 11, Ill.
> Sheridan Supply Co., Box 837, Beverly Hills, Calif.
> Stanford University Press, Stanford, Calif.

ADMINISTRATION OF TESTS

Preparing for Testing

The most important part of preparation for testing is telling the pupils the nature and purpose of the examinations they are to take and giving them reasons for trying to do as well as they can.   At least a week before standardized tests are to be given, the pupils should be told that the testing has been scheduled.   The content of the examinations should be described in general and the format of the items should be illustrated with samples so that everyone will know how to record his responses.   Care should be taken to avoid stirring up undue excitement, but the purpose and the importance of the tests should be made clear.

The date for testing should be chosen so that it will not be too close to that of any important or absorbing event in the school, such as a crucial football game or a prom.   The morning hours are usually best for testing since the pupils are likely to be most alert then.   The length of the testing sessions depends on the age of the pupils.   In the primary grades, the children cannot be expected to work for more than 20 to 30 minutes at a stretch.   In the senior high school, on the other hand, testing sessions up to 120 minutes in length may be scheduled, preferably with a 10 to 15 minute recess at the end of approximately the first hour.   In the case of competitive examinations, recess periods should be planned so that a different answer sheet is used after each recess.   This prevents examinees from changing responses or filling in blank spaces on the basis of information obtained during the recess.

All materials to be used in a testing session should be assembled at least a week ahead of time to make possible obtaining any items that may be found missing.   Test booklets, answer sheets, special pencils (as needed), scratch paper, labels for doors (such as "Quiet—Testing in Progress"), and timing devices should all be inspected to make sure they are ready for use.

Testing rooms should be selected that can be well ventilated, well lighted, and kept free from distractions.   Seating arrangements demand special attention.   If separate answer sheets are to be used, desks with tops large enough to spread out test booklets along with the answer sheets should be provided.   Tablet armchairs are not really satisfactory for the purpose although they are often used; they are particularly unsuited for left-handed examinees.   Experiments have shown that when all examinees place their answer sheets to the right of their test booklets on small tables, right-handed examinees have a slight advantage over left-handed examinees on highly speeded tests.*   These data suggest that, even if tablet armchairs or their equivalent must be used for right-handed examinees, desks or tables be provided for those who are left-handed.

Pupils should be seated at alternate desks unless the latter can be moved far enough apart to make copying very difficult.   This should be prevented by planning the seating in advance.   The use of answer sheets with objective tests makes it almost impossible for examinees who are seated close together to avoid seeing their neighbors' responses.   It is far more distracting and troublesome to the examinees than the possible noises and interruptions that are usually guarded against with so much care.   If it is physically impossible to provide adequate space between examinees, two or more equivalent forms of a test should be used and the pupils so informed.   Although they will still be subject to distraction, they cannot profit by copying their neighbors' responses or by checking their own against them.

Administering the Test

It goes without saying that directions for standardized tests must be carried out precisely as they are given in the manual and that time limits must be rigorously observed.   However, these requirements should be

* L. V. Gordon, "Right-Handed Answer Sheet and Left-Handed Testees," *Educational and Psychological Measurement*, XVIII (1958), 783–795.

carried out in the context of a pleasant, good-humored, but businesslike atmosphere. Before the directions have been read, questions that do not ask for specific information about test items should be answered frankly. In general, it does not pay to encourage questions at this point, but any that arise should be answered in a friendly and informative way.

When essay tests are given, examinees should be told how long their answers should be, how much detail they should include, whether relevant information not directly required to answer the question will be credited, how many points are allotted to each question, and on what bases the answers are to be graded. As in the case of objective tests, the time limits should be clearly stated.

Ordinarily, the directions for a standardized test end with "Are there any questions about what you are to do?" Sometimes, queries from the examinees can be answered merely by rereading a sentence or a phrase or two from the directions. At other times, they call for information not included in the directions. One that often comes up is, "How much is taken off for a wrong answer?" As stated previously, the examiner should respond frankly by saying, "One-quarter of a point," or "Nothing," or whatever is actually the case.

It is unwise to evade questions by saying, "I am not allowed to answer that question." If the examinee asks for information about the subject matter to be tested, the examiner should simply say, "We can't discuss the subject matter now." Various unexpected questions and occurrences may come up during a testing session, and the examiner must improvise suitable ways of handling them. He should be guided by two basic principles: First, the atmosphere of the testing session should be kept friendly, businesslike, and conducive to good work; second, any assistance that can be given to an examinee without providing help in answering the items themselves should be supplied quietly and individually. After the examinees have begun work on the items, the examiner and the proctors should move quietly and unobtrusively around to make sure that individual examinees are working on the proper pages, etc. This is more important with young children than with high school students.

When the testing is well under way, the examiner may systematically rate each examinee on the degree of effort he displays. The rating scale in Figure 3.4 may be used for this purpose. The letter ratings defined on the scale may be entered on the attendance list or on a seating plan for the testing session if one is available. Ideally, these ratings should be transferred to the lists of scores before these lists are sent to teachers, counselors, or administrators. It makes a great difference in how these individuals interpret a score on a test if they know that a pupil's lack of effort was so marked that the examiner judged that his score would be seriously affected. Whenever it is feasible to do so, a pupil in this category should be asked to come in for a conference, preferably with a school counselor or psychologist, within a few days. At this conference, the pupil should be given a chance to discuss his feelings about the test and his performance on it. Sometimes, he will offer to do his best on an equivalent form of the test. If possible, arrangements should be made for him to take one.

FIGURE 3.4

Scale for Rating Pupil Cooperation During Examinations

Rating	*Degree of Effort Displayed*
A	Examinee is unusually absorbed by the task.
B	Examinee is normally absorbed by the task and looks around only momentarily and occasionally.
C	Examinee works well but is distracted by any little sight or sound.
D	Examinee does not appear to work conscientiously even on the easier items. His score may be adversely affected by lack of effort.
E	Examinee does not appear to take the test seriously. His cooperation is so poor that his score should not be used.

If the clerical labor involved in making effort ratings and transferring them to score lists seems prohibitive, the examiner should keep a record of the names of examinees whom he rates as D or E on the scale in Figure 3.4. These names with the ratings may be turned over to the person in charge of testing together with the completed answer sheets for use when the test scores are interpreted.

Summary

Tests should not be used in schools without a clear understanding of their purpose and, if they are standardized tests, without detailed plans for reporting and interpreting the resulting scores.

In selecting standardized tests, evidence should be obtained about the

1. Validity of their scores.
2. Characteristics of their scores.
3. Norms provided for interpreting their scores.
4. Ease with which they can be administered.
5. Ease with which they can be scored.
6. Aids provided for interpreting their scores.

Information about published tests may be obtained from a variety of sources, chiefly the *Mental Measurements Yearbooks*.

Careful preparations should be made for administering standardized tests and they should be given with scrupulous attention to the directions that accompany them. Whenever possible, a record of the degree of cooperation of each examinee should be kept. A scale for rating cooperation has been suggested.

Selected References

Buros, Oscar K., ed., *The Nineteen Thirty-Eight Mental Measurements Yearbook.* New Brunswick, N.J.: Rutgers University Press, 1938.

Buros, Oscar K., ed., *The Nineteen Forty Mental Measurements Yearbook.* Highland Park, N.J., 1941.

Buros, Oscar K., ed., *The Third Mental Measurements Yearbook.* New Brunswick, N.J.: Rutgers University Press, 1949.

Buros, Oscar K., ed., *The Fourth Mental Measurements Yearbook.* Highland Park, N.J.: Gryphon Press, 1953.

Buros, Oscar K., ed., *The Fifth Mental Measurements Yearbook.* Highland Park, N.J.: Gryphon Press, 1959.

Buros, Oscar K., ed., *The Sixth Mental Measurements Yearbook*, Highland Park, N.J.: Gryphon Press, 1965.

Buros, Oscar K., ed., *Tests in Print: a Comprehensive Bibliography of Tests for Use in Education, Psychology, and Industry.* New Brunswick, N.J.: Gryphon Press, 1961.

Goheen, Howard W., and Samuel Kavruck, *Selected References on Test Construction, Mental Test Theory, and Statistics, 1929-1949.* Washington, D.C.: U.S. Government Printing Office, 1950.

Traxler, Arthur E., "Administering and Scoring the Objective Test," in Lindquist, E. F., ed., *Educational Measurement.* Washington: American Council on Education, 1951. Pp. 329–365.

Traxler, Arthur E., and Robert D. North, "The Selection and Use of Tests in a School Testing Program," in Findley, Warren G., ed., *The Impact and Improvement of School Testing Programs*, the Sixty-Second Yearbook of the National Society for the Study of Education, Part II, Chapter 10. Chicago, 1963.

Chapter Four

TEST SCORING

ESSAY TESTS

The scoring of essay tests poses many problems. First is the well-known fact that the same essay scored by several readers is likely to be assigned widely different marks. For example, in a study of the marking of written compositions of college freshmen made at the Educational Testing Service,* 300 essays were scored independently by each of fifty-three readers on a nine-point scale. The variation in grades was remarkable: 34 per cent of the essays received all nine possible grades; 37 per cent received eight grades; 23 per cent received seven; 5 per cent received six; and 1 per cent received five, which was the smallest number of different grades received by any essay.

These data illustrate the difficulty of getting reasonable agreement among judges on the quality of written compositions. Fortunately, essay examinations in subject-matter fields can be scored with greater consistency, expecially if appropriate scoring guides are provided. Nonetheless, it should be kept in mind that the greatest value of essay tests lies in encouraging pupils to organize material as they study and in providing practice in written expression. In short, they serve better as learning exercises than as measuring instruments.

To reduce differences among readers to a minimum, a detailed guide for scoring an essay examination should always be prepared. A teacher should make such a guide even for scoring an essay examination that she has written for use only in her own class. This guide should list the elements to be scored and the maximum number of points to be allotted each element. Table 4.1 shows a sample guide for use with a literature test in grade 12. If an essay test is to serve its purpose in measuring reasoning and organization, not many questions should be set. The examination for which the sample guide is given comprised five questions, the second of which was a list of ten terms to be defined briefly. Answers to this question were marked only on

* *Educational Testing Service Developments*, IX (Feb., 1961), 2.

factual content.   In the other questions, how well the answers were thought through, how well they were organized, and how smoothly they were written were marked along with originality of content and correctness of written expression.   In many subject-matter examinations, a teacher may not wish to assign any credit for smoothness or accuracy of written expression. However, in a twelfth grade English class, allotting test credit to how well and how correctly the students have expressed their ideas seems appropriate.

TABLE 4.1

Sample Guide for Scoring an Essay Test

Element to Be Scored	Maximum Number of Points for Question				
	1	2	3	4	5
Factual Content	10	10	5	5	5
Reasoning from Facts	10	0	5	10	5
Organization	5	0	5	5	5
Style: Smoothness	2	0	2	0	2
Mechanics of Expression	3	0	3	0	3
TOTAL	30	10	20	20	20

The use of a guide is intended to make the scoring more consistent from pupil to pupil but will not insure that proper weight is given to each question in determining the total score on the test.   The weight of a question in determining the total score depends on the variability of the marks on each question and on the intercorrelations of these marks.   Techniques are available for making the weight of each question correspond to a desired amount, but these lie beyond the scope of this book and are too cumbersome for use by teachers.*

When essay tests are scored, it is best to grade the first question for all examinees, then the second question for all examinees, and so on.   This procedure usually makes the marks on each question more consistent from examinee to examinee.   If some choice among the questions is permitted (e.g., answering any seven out of ten), the procedure should still be used.   In general, it is wise to make the sampling of subject matter as nearly alike as possible for the examinees by requiring them to answer all the questions on an examination.   Sometimes scorers of essay tests fail to make use of the entire range of scores permitted.   Say, for example, that in marking the test for which the scoring guide is given in Table 4.1, no one received fewer than 5 points on reasoning for his answer to question 1.   This often arises because

* See K. W. Vaughn, "Planning the Objective Test," in E. F. Lindquist, ed., *Educational Measurement* (Washington: American Council on Education, 1951), pp. 167–170.

the scorer supposes that the passing mark has been set in advance at 70 out of the 100 possible points on the test; therefore, he feels that he should use only the upper half of the range of possible scores. Since measurement is usually more precise when the full range, or nearly the full range, is used, scorers should be told that letter grades or marks will be determined in a separate step and that they should use the full range of scores if the performance of the examinees justifies that. A method by which letter marks or percentage marks can be obtained from raw scores is presented and discussed in chapter 13.

OBJECTIVE TESTS

Scoring of Standardized Tests

Standardized tests must be scored exactly as directed by the author and publisher if the latter's norms are to be used. If they are not, the user may score a test any way he likes and develop his own norms. In any event, great care must be exercised to insure accuracy in obtaining and recording the scores. In practice, this means that both of these processes must be checked by having each operation performed at least twice, preferably by different persons working independently.

Scoring Methods

Number-right scoring. Three methods of scoring objective tests are in fairly common use. As stated in chapter 1, we often assume that every item is equally relevant to the property that a test is measuring and assign a credit of one point to the correct response to each item and zero points to any incorrect response.

Let: X_R = raw score on a test scored by giving one point for each correct response, and

R_M = number of correct responses marked.

Then, if we score a test by giving one point for each correct response,

$$X_R = R_M. \tag{4.1}$$

A large percentage of tests are scored in this way. We shall call it number-right scoring.

Correction for chance success. A second method of scoring is correcting for chance success in marking responses. Since an objective test item includes a certain number of choices, one or more of which are keyed as correct, the possibility exists that an examinee who has no idea of the correct answer to an item, or who has not even read it, may mark the keyed choice or choices by chance. In the usual multiple-choice item where only one choice is keyed as correct, the probability of his doing so is one out of the number of choices in the item. In a five-choice item, this probability is 1 out of 5; in a two-choice item (such as a true-false statement), it is 1 out of 2. This means that an examinee who knows nothing about the subject matter being tested or who does not even bother to read the items but who marks a response to every one of 100 items in a true-false test is more likely to mark 50 items correctly than any other number. His number-right score will, therefore, be 50.

Fortunately, most examinees do not mark many responses on the basis of guessing, especially on tests where they have time to try every item. Nonetheless, under certain circumstances, guessing does occur. For example, an examinee who is taking a highly speeded test may use the last couple of minutes to mark responses at random to all the items that he has not been able to reach. The answer sheet reproduced in Figure 4.1 shows how this is often done. In this case, a student applying for admission to a program of graduate studies did not have time to read items 59 through 80 in the time limit, so he hurriedly marked answer space C for each of these items in the last couple of minutes of the time limit. Of these, he marked three correctly. It was most likely that he would have marked four of them correctly. Note that he marked two answer spaces for each of items 10, 21, 28, 33, and 45. In the case of two of these items, one of his two marks was correct.

Figure 4.2 shows the answer sheet of a student who marked answers at random to items 61 to 80 in the last minute of the time limit. This student marked answers in a diagonal pattern to make the basis of her marking less obvious. Needless to say, the majority of those who mark answers at random just before they hand in their papers avoid any pattern in their marking to make detection of their behavior more difficult.

Let us now consider an illustration of the practical effects of marking answer spaces at random. Suppose that Johnny Jones and Jimmy Brown are taking a speeded 100-item true-false test in arithmetic. Two minutes before the end of the time limit, each boy has marked sixty items and each has made fifty correct responses. Johnny uses the last two minutes to mark a response to each of the remaining forty items, which he has not had time to consider. Of these, he is most likely to mark twenty correctly, so his number-right score is 70. Jimmy uses the last two minutes to try two additional items, both of which he marks correctly. His number-right score is 52. The evidence we have, aside from their test scores, leads us to believe that the two boys are about equally accurate and work at about the same speed in arithmetic. Yet, by marking a lot of responses at random, Johnny obtained

FIGURE 4.1

Answer Sheet for the *Davis Reading Test* Showing Items 59 to 80 Marked "C" during the Last Two Minutes of the Time Limit.

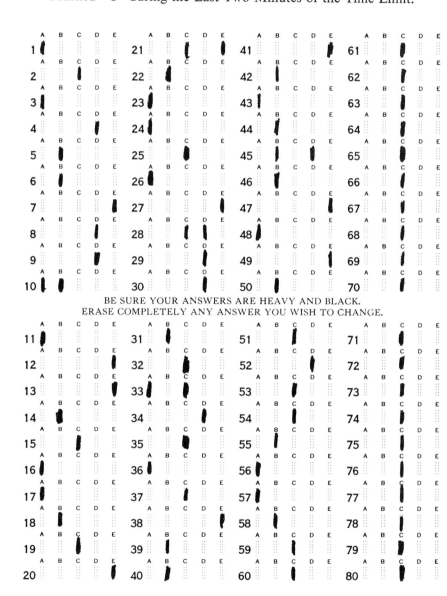

BE SURE YOUR ANSWERS ARE HEAVY AND BLACK.
ERASE COMPLETELY ANY ANSWER YOU WISH TO CHANGE.

FIGURE 4.2

Answer Sheet for the *Davis Reading Test* Showing Items 61 to 80 Marked in Side-to-Side Pattern during the Last Minute of the Time Limit.

BE SURE YOUR ANSWERS ARE HEAVY AND BLACK.
ERASE COMPLETELY ANY ANSWER YOU WISH TO CHANGE.

a much higher score. Translated into school marks, Johnny got an A and Jimmy a C in terms of number-right scores. Johnny's technique destroyed the operational validity of the test for measuring his speed and accuracy of arithmetic computation. In his own words, he "beat the test."

If this kind of result were unavoidable, it would be a severe indictment of objective testing. However, it can be prevented by scoring with a correction for chance success. The purpose of this correction is to provide an estimate for each examinee of the number of items to which he can respond correctly because he has enough information or skill to identify the correct choice, or at least to recognize the incorrectness of all other choices. This can easily be done if we assume that the examinee marks his responses only on the basis of (1) enough information or skill to identify the correct choice, or (2) guessing among all of the choices in each item. Thus all incorrect responses must result from guessing. This assumption over-simplifies the bases on which examinees actually mark responses; the manner and extent to which it is violated and the practical effects of these violations are discussed later in this chapter.

On the basis of the assumption, the number of items that an examinee marks correctly (R_M) may be expressed by equation 4.2:

$$R_M = R_K + R_G, \tag{4.2}$$

where: R_K = the number of items marked correctly on the basis of enough information to identify the correct choice; and
R_G = the number of items marked correctly on the basis of guessing.
Since we want to find R_K, we may rewrite equation 4.2 as follows:

$$R_K = R_M - R_G. \tag{4.3}$$

On any examinee's answer sheet we can count the number of items he has marked correctly and thus get a numerical value for R_M. We can also count the number of items he has marked incorrectly (W_M). The number of items to which the examinee has marked responses on the basis of guessing must equal the sum $(R_M + W_M)$ minus the number of items to which he marked answers on the basis of adequate information or skill (R_K). The most likely result of his guessing will be to mark $(R_M + W_M - R_K)/c$ items correctly, where c represents the number of choices in each item. Hence,

$$R_G = \frac{1}{c}(R_M + W_M - R_K). \tag{4.4}$$

Substituting $\frac{1}{c}(R_M + W_M - R_K)$ for R_G in equation 4.3, we get:

$$R_K = R_M - \frac{1}{c}(R_M + W_M - R_K). \tag{4.5}$$

This becomes:

$$R_K = R_M - \frac{R_M}{c} - \frac{W_M}{c} + \frac{R_K}{c},$$

or

$$R_K - \frac{R_K}{c} = R_M - \frac{R_M}{c} - \frac{W_M}{c}.$$

Then:

$$\left(\frac{c-1}{c}\right)R_K = \left(\frac{c-1}{c}\right)R_M - \frac{W_M}{c}. \tag{4.6}$$

If both sides of equation 4.6 are multiplied by $c/(c-1)$, we get:

$$R_K = R_M - \frac{W_M}{c-1}. \tag{4.7}$$

Under the conditions imposed, R_K represents an estimate of the number of items that an examinee actually knows (as distinct from the number that he marks correctly). It is also his score corrected for chance success. We usually represent the latter with the symbol X_C; the number of items marked correctly is represented by R, and the number of items marked incorrectly by W. Then the conventional formula for obtaining scores corrected for chance success is written as follows:

$$X_C = R - \frac{W}{c-1}. \tag{4.8}$$

In the special case where $c = 2$ (as in true-false items), this formula reads:

$$X_C = R - W. \tag{4.9}$$

Applying equation 4.9 to the test papers of Johnny and Jimmy, we obtain corrected scores as follows:

For Johnny: $X_C = 70 - 30 = 40$;
For Jimmy: $X_C = 52 - 10 = 42$.

Instead of showing Johnny with a considerably higher score (as did the number-right method), the corrected-for-chance method shows Jimmy to have a slightly higher score. This result is in accord with our evidence that both boys marked the same number of items correctly up to the last two minutes and that Johnny did no more real work in those minutes while Jimmy continued to work consistently until time was called. The corrected scores make sense even to the extent of penalizing Johnny for failing to work during the last two minutes. This illustration involves a highly speeded test of a basic subject like arithmetic; for unspeeded tests of more complex mental functions, the bases for responding to items are more varied. These bases will be discussed later in this chapter.

The procedure for scoring matching exercises is straightforward. A matching exercise may be defined as a set of related multiple-choice items.

An example is shown in Figure 4.3. Note that a term in the longer series may be the correct match to *more than one* of the items in the shorter series. Under these circumstances, equation 4.10 is recommended for scoring matching exercises with correction for chance success:

$$X_C = R - \frac{W}{cl - 1},\tag{4.10}$$

where R and W have the same meanings as in equation 4.8 and cl represents the number of terms from which the matching answers are selected.

FIGURE 4.3

Matching Exercise.*

Directions: For each city, blacken the letter of the state in which it is located. More than one of the cities may be located in the same state.

1. Augusta   A. Connecticut
2. Hartford   B. Georgia
3. Savannah   C. New Hampshire
                    D. Rhode Island
                    E. Vermont

* The keyed responses are: Item 1, B; Item 2, A; Item 3, B.

Choice-weighted scoring. A third method of scoring differs from the first two in that it rejects the assumption that every item is equally relevant to the variable being assessed or predicted. Instead, each choice in each item is assigned a number of scoring points, called a weight, proportional to its value in assessing or predicting that variable. Because the labor and cost of establishing reliable choice weights and of using them in hand-scoring and in some machine-scoring procedures are great, they have been little used except in certain tests of interests and personality.† Weights for an arithmetic-reasoning item are shown in Figure 4.4. The correct choice has a scoring weight of $+2$. The incorrect choices have weights of 0, -1, -2, and -3. The choice having the largest negative weight is the one that tends to be marked by examinees having the least ability to solve arithmetic-reasoning items of this type. Note that the item measures ability to *reason* about a simple mathematical problem and *not* (like most so-called arithmetic-reasoning items) mainly ability to compute accurately.

† For applications, see E. K. Strong, *Vocational Interest Blank for Men*, revised (Palo Alto, Calif.: Consulting Psychologists Press, Inc., 1961), and R. G. Bernreuter, *The Personality Inventory* (Stanford, Calif.: Stanford University Press, 1938).

FIGURE 4.4

Scoring Weights for Each Choice in an Arithmetic-Reasoning Item*

42. Three inspectors have time to inspect only two jet engines apiece. If the engines to be inspected are chosen at random from the 72 engines in a warehouse, what are the chances that any particular engine will be inspected?

		Scoring Weight
A.	1 in 36	−1
B.	1 in 24	0
C.	1 in 12	2
D.	Some other ratio	−2
E.	This cannot be determined from the information given.	−3

* The keyed response is choice C.

It has been reported that choice-weighted scoring tends to increase test reliability but seems to have little effect on congruent validity.† The use of electronic scoring techniques may in the immediate future encourage experimentation with choice-weighted scoring methods for achievement and aptitude tests since these machines permit rapid and economical calculation of weighted scores for examinees.

Bases for Responding to Items

On what bases do examinees decide which choice to mark as correct in an objective test item? This is a very interesting field for investigation and one about which there is not yet adequate information. Studies of the behavior of examinees while they are taking multiple-choice tests, logical analyses of the situation that confronts examinees, and inspection of the responses to test items made by large numbers of examinees indicate that most responses are made on one or more of the following bases:

1. Sufficient knowledge to identify the correct choice.
2. Partial knowledge that permits elimination of one or more of the *incorrect* choices followed by guessing among all of the remaining choices or by resort to irrelevant considerations like those listed in basis 6 below.
3. Guessing among all the choices after considering the item as a whole.

† F. B. Davis and G. Fifer, "The Effect on Test Reliability and Validity of Scoring Aptitude and Achievement Tests with Weights for Every Choice," *Educational and Psychological Measurement*, XIX (1959), 159–170.

4. Partial misinformation that leads to elimination of one or more choices, including the *correct* choice, followed by guessing among all of the remaining choices or by resort to irrelevant considerations like those listed in basis 6 below.

5. Sufficient misinformation to identify as correct one of the incorrect choices.

6. Characteristics irrelevant to the content of the item, such as length of the choices, precision of wording of the choices, number of times each choice position (A, B, C, D, E, etc.) has been marked as a correct choice, pattern of choice positions that appears on the answer sheet, etc.

7. Random marking of choices in items that have not even been read.

The extent to which these bases are employed varies from examinee to examinee and from test to test, depending on the nature of the subject matter, the cleverness and level of difficulty of the items, the purposes for which the test is being taken, the directions and scoring procedures, and the sophistication of the examinees in taking tests. It seems likely that, in reasonably typical circumstances, examinees rely heavily on bases 1, 2, 4, 5, and 7. Basis 3 is probably not widely used; guessing among all the choices occurs most commonly on items in speeded tests that an examinee has not had time to consider. Usually, if an examinee has considered an item, his guessing, if any, is among fewer than all the choices. Faint hunches and bits of information and misinformation generally lead him to rule one or more choices out of further consideration. Faced with a decision between two remaining choices, he may simply mark one as correct by making a stab in the dark, but often he recognizes frankly that he is simply guessing and decides to rely on some irrelevant consideration like those listed in basis 6 above. Most examinees do not realize that in a well-constructed test these characteristics have been carefully arranged to have no relationship to the correctness or incorrectness of the choices.

The use of proper directions and scoring methods can influence to a considerable extent the reliance of many examinees on the seven bases for marking choices. If an examinee is told that his score will be "the number of correct answers minus a fraction of the number of wrong answers" and that "it does not pay to guess wildly among all the choices in an item," he tends to avoid bases 3 and 7. Naturally this instruction cannot truthfully be given unless the scores are corrected for chance success. If he is further told that "it pays to answer questions even when you are not sure that your answers are correct," he feels encouraged to use bases 2 and 4. Because some examinees are more venturesome than others, these instructions do not result in equal avoidance by all examinees of guessing among all choices (bases 3 and 7) or among fewer than all choices (bases 2 and 4). However, they tend to produce this effect and warn those who hope to "beat the test" that only uncommonly good luck can help them.

Instructions for a few tests have urged the examinees to "mark answers to all of the items." This has been done in an effort to put all examinees on the same basis. Ordinarily, however, some examinees cannot bring themselves to follow these directions because they violate habits of admitting ignorance that they have built up over many years. It is particularly troublesome to many examinees to fill in answer spaces for items that they have not even had time to read. Yet they must do so if they do not have time to read all the items in the time limit and are to follow the instructions.

If the examinees actually follow these instructions, the penalty for achieving (or even approaching) uniformity of response set in this way is a decrease in accuracy of measurement that depends on the increase in the amount of guessing. The most serious objection to these directions is the long-term deterioration of confidence in objective examinations that their use engenders among students, educators, and the general public.

Estimating the Number of Items That an Examinee Knows

Equations 4.8, 4.9, and 4.10 provide a method for estimating the number of items to which an examinee knows the correct response, as distinguished from the number he marks correctly, provided that he responds to each item on the basis of either: (1) sufficient knowledge to identify the correct choice; or (2) guessing among all the choices. These are bases 1, 3, and 7 in the list given in the preceding section. Since examinees also use bases 2, 4, 5, and 6 to varying extents, we must consider their effects on the estimates yielded by the equations. Use of basis 2 causes the estimates to be too high while use of bases 4 and 5 causes them to be too low. In a well-constructed test, use of basis 6 should have no effect because in the long run it is no greater help to the examinee than is guessing among all the choices.

Since the effect of basis 2 is opposite to that of bases 4 and 5, these influences on the operation of the equations tend to cancel each other. Which of them is stronger depends on the nature of the items and how difficult they are for the examinee. Experience indicates that with many tests of appropriate difficulty they are reasonably well in balance and their net effect is close to zero.

An interesting experiment carried out by Mead and Smith* supplies data that illustrate the result of using equation 4.9 under circumstances that probably cause bases 4 and 5 greatly to outweigh basis 2 in their effect on the

* A. R. Mead and R. M. Smith, "Does the True-False Scoring Formula Work?" *Journal of Educational Research*, LI (1957), 47–53. See also F. B. Davis, "Use of Correction for Chance Success in Test Scoring," *Journal of Educational Research*, LII (1959), 279–280.

corrected scores.   Mead and Smith administered 148 exceedingly difficult true-false items to 100 volunteers, who indicated as they responded to each item whether they did so with: (1) confidence that they knew the correct response; (2) some doubt that their answer was correct; or (3) no confidence in their answer and regarded their response merely as a guess.

Since 100 examinees responded to 148 items, 14,800 decisions regarding these items were made.   Table 4.2 shows a classification of these decisions in terms of the seven bases for responding to objective-test items that we have

TABLE 4.2

Classification of Decisions Made by 100 Examinees
to 148 True-False Items

Basis for Decision	Outcomes		
	Correct Responses	Incorrect Responses	No Response
1. Sufficient knowledge to mark item with confidence	2,323		
2. Sufficient knowledge to mark item with some confidence	2,067		
3. Guessing	3,218	3,003	
4. Sufficient misinformation to mark item with some confidence		1,849	
5. Sufficient misinformation to mark item with confidence		1,271	
6. Did not want to venture a guess			1,069
TOTALS	7,608	6,123	1,069

discussed previously.   Responses were assigned in the light of each examinee's own statements and the correctness or incorrectness of his responses.   The examinees were permitted to refrain from responding to an item on which they did not care even to venture a guess; and this occurred 1,069 times out of the 14,800 decisions made.   Thus, 13,731 responses resulted in marking items correctly or incorrectly.   Of these, 7,608 were correct.   The mean number of items marked correctly per examinee was, therefore, 76.08.   On the basis of chance, half of the 13,731 decisions that led to marking responses would have been correct.   So 6,865.5 correct responses were expected by chance whereas 7,608 were actually made.   Clearly, the test was very difficult for the examinees since they obtained a mean number-right score of 76.08 when 74 was most probable if they had all responded to every item only by guessing (basis 3).

Of the 6,221 responses stated by the examinees to have been made by guessing, 3,218 were correct. If all of the 6,221 decisions had actually been made only on the basis of chance, it is highly unlikely that as many as 3,218 would have been correct. This implies that even when the examinees *thought* they were guessing they were actually using some bits of information or hunches that led them to mark correct responses very slightly more often than would be expected by chance.

The examinees made 3,594 decisions with confidence that they were correct; of these, 2,323 were correct (basis 1) and 1,271 were incorrect. The latter were presumably the result of misinformation (basis 5). Also accounted for by misinformation (basis 4) were the 1,849 incorrect responses out of 3,916 made with *some* confidence. The remainder of these, or 2,067 responses, were marked correctly on the basis of partial information (basis 2). Thus, misinformation accounted for 3,120 responses while partial information accounted for only 2,067 responses.

If equation 4.9 is used to estimate the average number of items to which the 100 examinees *knew* the correct answers, the result is as follows:

$$X_C = R - W = 76.08 - 61.23 = 14.85.$$

According to the examinees' own reports and their responses, they actually knew the correct answers to 23.23 items. The corrected-score estimate of 14.85 items is, when judged by this standard, too low. However, it is much closer to 23.23 than is the number-right score of 76.08. The reason why the corrected-score estimate is too low is that misinformation (bases 4 and 5) accounted for more responses (3,120) than partial information (2,067). This happened because the test was very difficult for the examinees. With tests of appropriate difficulty, partial information usually exerts more influence than misinformation and the corrected scores tend to be higher than they should be, but closer to the number of items to which the examinees really know the answers than are the number-right scores.

Teachers sometimes express the performance of pupils on essay and objective tests as a percentage of the total possible score. These percentage scores are rarely meaningful except for placing the examinees in rank order. Since this outcome is identical with placing them in order by raw score, expressing scores as percentages is usually wasteful of time and creates the danger that they will be interpreted as indicating the percentage of subject matter known by each examinee. If, nonetheless, objective-test scores are expressed as percentages, it is best to use corrected scores computed by equations 4.8, 4.9, or 4.10. Suppose, for example, that a pupil responds to ninety five-choice items by marking fifty of them correctly and 32 of them incorrectly, leaving eight items unmarked. His correct score is $50 - 32/4 = 42$. The corresponding percentage score is $\frac{42}{90}$, or 47 per cent (rounded to the nearest integer). This figure may be interpreted that he knows the correct answers to about 47 per cent of the particular ninety items in the test. It should *not* be concluded that he knows about 47 per cent of the subject matter covered by the test. One reason why this conclusion must be avoided is that simply by changing the incorrect responses in the ninety items, the test author could make it easier or more difficult. Such changes would cause the pupil's score to change without affecting his actual knowledge of the subject matter tested.

Correlation of Number-Right Scores and Corrected Scores

The correlation coefficient between corrected scores and number-right scores is usually very high, especially for unspeeded tests. For example, Jackson* reports a correlation of .91 between number-right scores on one form and corrected scores on a parallel form of a five-choice sixty-item vocabulary test administered with appropriately different directions to 106 college students. This seems like rather a high relationship between number-right and corrected scores, but a little calculation will show that if the number-right scores have a predictive validity coefficient of .60 for English marks, the predictive validity coefficient of the corrected scores could be as high as .88 or as low as .21. Thus, even a correlation as high as .91 between number-right and corrected scores must not be taken as proof that the two scores will have the same, or almost the same, predictive validity coefficients for any specified criterion.

Various Effects of Correcting Scores for Chance Success

Effect on validity. To the extent that the rank order of examinees with respect to their scores on a test is determined by guessing or by marking responses to items that the examinees have not had time to read in the time limit, the validity of the scores is reduced. Since correcting scores for chance success is one means of minimizing this effect (as illustrated by the scores of Johnny and Jimmy, pages 75–79), it can be expected to increase test validity. Both theoretical considerations and experimental data suggest that it does so.

Frederic M. Lord has presented† the equations with which the predictive validity coefficients of number-right and corrected scores derived from the

* R. A. Jackson, "Guessing and Test Performance," *Educational and Psychological Measurement*, XV (1955), 74–79.

† F. M. Lord, "Formula Scoring and Validity," *Educational and Psychological Measurement*, XXIII (1963), 663–672.

same test may be computed under reasonably typical conditions. He has found that corrected scores are likely to be more valid than number-right scores. The difference in validity appears to *increase* as the number of choices per item *decreases*, as the difficulty of the test *increases*, and as the examinees *differ more widely* in their tendency to guess. In practice, then, correction for chance success is probably maximally useful for a highly speeded true-false test administered to examinees for which it is very difficult. Although a test's predictive validity coefficient may be only .02 to .03 higher if corrected scoring instead of number-right scoring is used, this increase may be equal to that produced by doubling the length of a test that yields number-right scores. As Lord has stated, "In this case, failure to use formula scoring produces a decrement in validity equivalent to throwing away one-half of the test items and one-half of the testing time, or equivalent to ignoring one-half of each examinee's responses."*

Experimental studies yield results in harmony with Lord's theoretical discussion. In some respects, the most persuasive of these is one reported by Bryan, Burke, and Stewart.† They obtained both number-right scores and corrected scores for groups of 370 examinees on several tests. Next, they tabulated separately the number of incorrect choices for the items in a given test that displayed positive, zero, or negative correlation with number-right scores and with corrected scores. In a well-constructed, well-edited test, it would be expected that the *incorrect* choices in the items would show negative correlations with a measure of the subject matter covered by the items. The better the measure of this subject matter, the greater should be the number of incorrect choices displaying negative correlation with it. The authors present data showing that, in general, more incorrect choices show negative correlation with the corrected scores than with the number-right scores. They conclude, therefore, that corrected scores are more valid measures of the subject matter tested than are number-right scores. This result becomes more marked as the difficulty of the items increases and as larger numbers of examinees do not have time to consider all the items within the time limit. These findings are in accord with Lord's conclusions based on mathematical formulations. Table 4.3 summarizes the data on which the authors base their conclusions.

* *Ibid.*, p. 665.
† M. M. Bryan, P. J. Burke, and N. Stewart, "Correction for Guessing in the Scoring of Pretests: Effect upon Item Difficulty and Item Validity Indices," *Educational and Psychological Measurement*, XII (1952), 45–56. See also G. M. Ruch and M. H. DeGraff, "Correction for Chance and 'Guess' Versus 'Do Not Guess' Instructions in Multiple-Response Tests," *Journal of Educational Psychology*, XVII (1926), 368–375; B. D. Wood, "Studies of Achievement Tests," *Journal of Educational Psychology*, XVII (1926), 1–27, 125–139, 263–269; and E. P. Wood, "Improving the Validity of Collegiate Achievement Tests," *Journal of Educational Psychology*, XVIII (1927), 18–25.

TABLE 4.3

Number of Incorrect Choices Displaying Negative Correlations
with Measures of Subject Matter Tested*

Type of Test	Title of Test	Number of Incorrect Choices Showing Negative Correlations with Total Score	
		Corrected Scores	Number-Right Scores
Highly speeded	Cooperative Chemistry Test, Form 48A	192	95
Moderately speeded	Cooperative Intermediate Algebra Test, Form 48A	164	121
Unspeeded	Cooperative General Achievement Test: Social Studies, Form 48A	180	174

* Bryan, Burke, and Stewart kindly made their basic data available to the writer; from these, this table has been prepared. The numbers of examinees who did not reach certain items in the time limits for the Chemistry and Algebra Tests have been taken into account in assembling these data.

Effect on accuracy of measurement. It is reasonable to suppose that the more examinees resort to guessing in responding to test items, the more chance will enter into determining their scores and the less accurate these will be. Medley has shown that the standard errors of measurement of corrected scores do indeed increase as the amount of guessing involved in them increases.* He has also shown, as demonstrated earlier by Lord,† that number-right scores do *not* vary in accuracy on this account. These principles may be illustrated by comparing standard errors of measurement estimated for the number-right and corrected scores of Johnny Jones and Jimmy Brown previously discussed. The essential data are given in Table 4.4. It will be recalled that Johnny used the last two minutes of the allotted time to mark answers to forty items at random while Jimmy used those two minutes to read items 61 and 62 and mark responses to them. The standard error of measurement estimated for Johnny's number-right score of 70 is 4.6 while that for Jimmy's number-right score of 52 is 5.0. The difference between these standard errors of measurement is entirely due to the fact that the scores of 70 and 52 are unequally removed from a score of 50, which is

* D. M. Medley, "The Effects of Item Heterogeneity and Guessing on the Accuracy of a Test Score," *American Psychologist*, XVII (1962), 368.
† F. M. Lord, "Estimating Test Reliability," *Educational and Psychological Measurement*, XV (1955), 325–336, and "Do Tests of the Same Length Have the Same Standard Error of Measurement?" *Educational and Psychological Measurement*, XVII (1957), 510–521.

TABLE 4.4

Standard Errors of Measurement Estimated for the Number-Right Scores* and Corrected Scores† of Two Individuals

		Johnny		Jimmy	
		Number-Right Score	Corrected Score	Number-Right Score	Corrected Score
Score		70	40	52	42
Standard Error of Measurement		4.6	9.2	5.0	6.7

* as: $$s_{\text{meas } R_M} = \sqrt{\frac{R_M(n - R_M)}{n - 1}}$$

† as: $$s_{\text{meas } X_C} = \sqrt{\frac{X_C(n - X_C)}{n - 1} + \frac{W_M nc}{(n - 1)(c - 1)^2}}$$

where n represents the number of items in the test and the other symbols have the same meanings as in equations 4.1 through 4.9 in this chapter. See, D. M. Medley, *loc. cit.*

half of the maximum possible score. Although Johnny's score was greatly affected by guessing while Jimmy's was not, Johnny's score is indicated as more accurate than Jimmy's. This result seems misleading.

The standard error of measurement estimated for Johnny's corrected score of 40 is 9.2 while that for Jimmy's corrected score of 42 is 6.7. The difference between these standard errors of measurement is almost wholly due to the greater amount of guessing done by Johnny, whose corrected score is shown by these data to be less accurate than Jimmy's. The fact that the standard errors of measurement of the corrected scores are larger than those of the number-right scores does not mean that the relative precision of measurement of the latter is greater than that of the former. It simply means that the corrected scores spread more widely and therefore have a larger standard deviation. This point was discussed on page 22 with respect to the distributions of obtained scores in Figures 2.2 and 2.3.

Effect on reliability. It is reasonable to expect that the greater the amount of guessing done by examinees as they take a test, the lower the reliability coefficient of the test would be. In the limiting case, if every examinee answered every item on the basis of guessing among all its choices, the test reliability would be zero, or deviate from zero only by chance.

The amount of guessing done by examinees, especially on speeded tests, depends more on their expectation of how the tests are to be scored than on any other single factor. If the examinees know the scoring procedure includes a penalty for incorrect responses, they will tend to abide by directions that ask them to avoid marking items on the basis of wild guessing.   Thus, correction for chance success in test scoring makes it possible for the test to be administered with directions that tend to reduce the proportion of chance variance in the scores and thus to maximize their reliability.   As pointed out on page 62, the wording of these directions may be varied somewhat depending on the age, maturity, and degree of sophistication of the examinees in taking tests.

Once these directions have been given, the reliability of the resulting scores is likely to be about the same whether they are expressed as number-right or as corrected scores.   However, in any practical long-term use of tests, scores must be obtained in the manner specified in the directions.   Any other procedure will be found self-defeating in the long run since examinees will discover the deception and ignore the directions to avoid wild guessing. Furthermore, it is contrary to professional ethics to deceive examinees and engenders lack of public confidence in objective examinations.   In practice, correcting test scores for chance success appears to have only a small effect on their reliability coefficients, perhaps because most examinees do not indulge in a great deal of wild guessing or of marking responses at random to items they have not had time to read.

Effect on public acceptance of objective tests.   If examinees know that they can increase their scores on a test by marking responses to items to which they have no idea of the correct response or which they have not had time to consider, their attitude toward objective tests becomes cynical and con-temptuous even if the practical effect of their guessing has actually been small. This attitude is shared by many educators and laymen who do not realize that the fault lies in the scoring procedure and not in the technique of objective testing.   It can be greatly reduced or eliminated by the simple expedient of correcting scores for chance success and including appropriate warnings against wild guessing in the test directions.

Effect on labor of scoring.   Scoring involves two fundamental steps. The first is preparation of the test papers or separate answer sheets for scoring, and the second consists of counting responses and calculating a raw score. Sometimes a third step, that of converting raw scores to some kind of derived scores (such as scaled scores) is required.

Preparing answer sheets for machine scoring demands that unintentional stray marks be erased.   This process is usually unnecessary when the answer sheets are hand scored.   Next, intentional multiple marking of items must be considered if number-right scoring is employed.   It is obvious that if an examinee marks all the choices for an item, he will be given one point credit if the scorer or scoring machine merely counts one point for each keyed response that is marked.   In practice, examinees rarely mark all choices as correct; but they often mark the two or three choices that they think are most likely to be correct. The more sophisticated examinees know that the IBM Model 805 scoring machine sometimes counts marks that consist of small but heavily penciled dots. If they think that their answer sheets are to be scored by this machine, they place such dots at the end of one of the lines making up the answer spaces that they believe *may* be keyed as correct, in addition to filling in completely the answer space for each item that they think is *most likely* to be keyed. Examples of multiple marking are shown in Figure 4.5. Note that six items have been multiple-marked, three of them with dots.

FIGURE 4.5

Answer Sheet Showing Multiple Marking of Items
by Two Methods.*

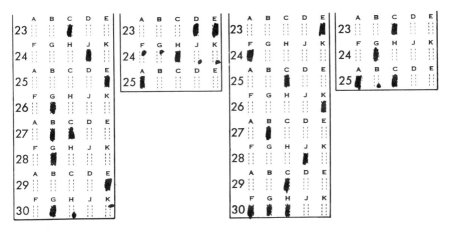

* Note especially that item 30 in column 1, item 24 in column 2, and item 25 in column 4 have dots placed on one or more of the answer spaces.

To prevent examinees from benefiting from multiple marking on answer sheets to be hand-scored number right, most test publishers suggest that the scorer inspect the papers, locating multiple-marked items and drawing a red pencil line through them so that no credit will be given. Before machine scoring, the marks for items that have been identified as multiple-marked must be either completely erased or covered with scotch tape. These procedures are time-consuming and tedious, especially if dots must be removed before use of the IBM Model 805 machine.

If scores are corrected for chance success, intentional multiple marks need not be identified or removed because the scoring process will automatically exact a penalty adjusted to the amount and kind of marking that has been done. A great deal of time and labor is saved.

If number-right scoring is used, raw scores are obtained simply by counting the number of correct responses (leaving out those in multiple-marked items). If correction for chance is employed, hand scorers must count correct and incorrect responses (including those in multiple-marked items) separately. They then subtract the required fraction of the incorrect responses (rounded to the nearest whole number) from the number of correct responses to obtain the raw score. Since a scoring machine does the counting and calculation of the raw score automatically, this step takes about the same amount of time on the machine whether the scores are number right or number right minus a fraction of the number wrong.* When scoring is done by hand, corrected scores require more time for counting and calculating than do number-right scores.

The net result of these factors is as follows: for machine scoring, correcting for chance success takes less time and labor than not correcting; for hand scoring the time and labor are approximately the same for the two methods.

Summary

It has long been recognized that if essay tests are to be scored with satisfactory consistency by several readers, detailed scoring guides must be used. The scorers should be urged to make use of the full range of score points allotted to each question and should mark responses of all examinees to question 1 before going on to question 2, and so on. The same questions should be answered by all examinees.

The unique merits of essay questions make them more suitable in learning exercises than in examinations.

Procedures for scoring objective test items should be carefully planned and followed; checks on the accuracy of scoring should always be provided. Three methods of scoring objective tests have been most commonly employed:

1. Number-right scoring.
2. Scoring with correction for chance success.
3. Choice-weighted scoring.

An analysis of the bases for responding to objective test items leads to the conclusion that the conventional formula for correcting for chance success should ordinarily be used in scoring objective tests especially if they are highly speeded or include many difficult items. In these circumstances

* Sometimes adjustment of the machine and reading the scores from the dial takes a bit longer for corrected scoring than for number-right scoring, but this difference is a negligible part of the time required for the whole scoring process.

some examinees are likely to leave items unmarked. For informal teacher-made tests, on which every examinee marks a response to every item, number-right scoring is satisfactory.

Studies by Lord, Medley, and others have shown that correction for chance success may be expected to yield scores that are more valid and more accurate than number-right scores. Evidence regarding the effect of correction for chance success on the relative precision of measurement (indicated by the test reliability coefficient) is not clear cut.

The most important reason for employing a correction for chance success in test scoring is to maintain public confidence in the integrity of objective testing techniques. If examinees know that they can increase their scores on a test by marking responses to items for which they have no idea of the correct answer or which they have not had time to consider, their attitudes toward objective tests become cynical and contemptuous even if the practical effect of their guessing has been small. These attitudes are naturally communicated to educators and to the general public who cannot be expected to recognize that the fault lies with certain test constructors and publishers and not with the technique of objective testing.

Selected References

Chen, L., "The Correction Formula for Matching Tests," *Journal of Educational Psychology*, XXXV (1944), 565–566.

Cronbach, Lee J., "Response Sets and Test Validity," *Educational and Psychological Measurement*, VI (1946), 475–494.

Davis, Frederick B., "Item Selection Techniques," in E. F. Lindquist, ed., *Educational Measurement*, Chapter 9. Washington: American Council on Education, 1951.

Graesser, Roy F., "Guessing on Multiple-Choice Tests," *Educational and Psychological Measurement*, XVIII (1958), 617–620.

Gulliksen, Harold O., *The Theory of Mental Tests*. New York: John Wiley & Sons, Inc., 1950. Chapter 18.

Horst, Paul, "The Chance Element in the Multiple-Choice Item," *Journal of General Psychology*, VI (1932), 209–211.

Michaels, William B., *et al.*, "An Experimental Determination of the Optimal Scoring Formula for a Highly Speeded Test Under Different Instructions Regarding Scoring Penalties," *Educational and Psychological Measurement*, XXIII (1963), 83–89.

Odell, Charles W., "The Scoring of Continuity or Rearrangement Tests," *Journal of Educational Psychology*, XXXV (1944), 352–366.

Phillips, Beeman N., and Garrett P. Weathers, "Analysis of Errors Made in Scoring Standardized Tests," *Educational and Psychological Measurement,* XVIII (1958), 563–567.

Stalnaker, John M., "The Essay Type of Examination," in E. F. Lindquist, ed., *Educational Measurement,* Chapter 13. Washington: American Council on Education, 1951.

Traxler, Arthur E., "Administering and Scoring the Objective Test," in E. F. Lindquist, ed., *Educational Measurement,* pp. 365–416. Washington: American Council on Education, 1951.

Chapter Five

MEASUREMENT OF ACHIEVEMENT

The primary purpose of achievement tests is to assess the knowledge, understandings, and skills of examinees at a specific point in time. A teacher-made test used once to measure the status of the pupils in a single class and a standardized test taken each year by hundreds of thousands of pupils share this purpose. However, as mentioned in chapter 2, tests constructed for assessment may be used for prediction. For example, the College Entrance Examination Board tests of achievement in English, mathematics, and other subjects are used to predict the relative performance of examinees in college courses in these fields. It is reasonable to assume that a college applicant who has learned a great deal of chemistry in high school will be able to learn a great deal of chemistry in college. The aptitudes and study habits that served him well in high school are likely to serve him well in college. Accumulated data indicate this to be true.

Achievement tests may be divided into two main groups: survey tests, intended to measure the full range of a defined subject-matter field; and diagnostic tests, intended to measure separately clusters of skills, understandings, or knowledge in a defined field in order to identify those clusters in which examinees are relatively strong or weak.

Two main emphases may be noted in the content of survey tests. The first of these displays itself in the *specific* learning demanded by most achievement tests. The test constructor consciously tries to formulate questions that can be answered only by examinees who have learned certain key facts or developed certain understandings or skills. He tries to make it impossible for a highly intelligent examinee who possesses a wide fund of general information but has not learned specific subject matter or skills to answer more questions correctly than would be most likely by chance. In practice, he is happy if he even approximates this goal, but it is essential that he have it in mind as he devises the test items.

The second emphasis calls for the use of questions that can be answered by an examinee who is able to learn new material and to understand basic concepts in the field. Tests of this kind often consist of passages taken from textbooks or other sources in the subject-matter field being tested, followed by questions requiring comprehension of the passages and application of the principles stated in them. Examinees of high general intelligence tend to obtain high scores on tests of this kind regardless of the subject-matter field they are intended to measure. It seems fair to describe them as specialized comprehension tests.

THE DESIGN OF
ACHIEVEMENT TESTS

To insure the intended validity of an achievement test, it is first necessary to define very closely the subject-matter field that it is supposed to measure. The definition must, however, be not only specific and unambiguous but also accepted as an adequate and accurate description of the field by people of good judgment in such matters—experts in the field. The test constructor must identify all subdivisions of the field to be tested and the relative importance, or weight, of each. To do so, he may analyze textbooks and courses of study used in representative school systems. He may ask authorities in the field to indicate the relative importance of the topics, understandings, and skills in a tentative list and to suggest other entries for the list. The resulting definition is likely to be an outline with each component topic weighted in proportion to its importance. More detailed information about the planning of achievement tests will be found in chapter 12.

THE MEASUREMENT OF
READING ABILITY

Importance of reading as a tool subject. Of all school subjects, reading is universally acknowledged as the most necessary. It is the tool that permits learning in virtually all subject-matter fields. Achievement tests in reading are, therefore, of paramount importance in education and are, in fact, more widely used than any other type of achievement test.

What is reading? To the layman, reading consists mainly of pronouncing written words or combinations of letters. Many years ago, reading instruction in schools was directed primarily toward developing the ability to do this. Horace Mann, the famous Massachusetts commissioner of education, once told of visiting an elementary school where the teacher boasted that her pupils had made such excellent progress that they could read newspapers at sight. Commissioner Mann handed a newspaper to a pupil and asked him to read from it. While the teacher beamed with pleasure, the pupil read word after word with fluency. Mann was puzzled, however, by the fact that, distinct though the individual words were, he could get no meaning from the whole. Taking the paper from the pupil, he was surprised to discover that the boy was reading directly across the page, completely ignoring the vertical lines dividing the page into columns!

To the educational psychologist, reading is a complicated agglomeration of habits, skills, and abilities that may be grouped loosely into three major categories: *mechanical skills, comprehension in reading*, and *rate of reading*. Let us consider these categories to discover the principal habits, skills, and abilities in each and how these may be measured.

Mechanics of reading. In ordinary reading, the eyes converge on a point on the line being read and remain fixed at that point for a tiny portion of time (about .33 to .24 of a second for readers of normal ability in grades 1 to 12).* During this pause, the normal reader perceives the characters on the line for a distance of about one-quarter to one-half inch either side of the point of fixation.† Then the eyes move along the line about one-half to one inch and the process is repeated. This occurs again and again. If perception is faulty in one or more pauses of the eyes, they go back and focus again on material previously covered. These backward movements are called regressions. On the average, first grade children make about fifty-two regressions per 100 words and high school seniors about seventeen regressions per 100 words.

If the visual form that the reader sees during a fixation is a word with which he is familiar, he associates that form with its meaning. If it is a part of a word or phrase with which he is familiar, he recognizes that fact, combines it with the remainder of the word or phrase, and associates the combination with its meaning. A series of these associations may be woven together to re-create the ideas expressed. This is a somewhat oversimplified description of the process by which highly skilled, mature readers get meaning from the printed page.

* S. E. Taylor, H. Frackenpohl, and J. L. Pettee, "Grade-Level Norms for the Components of the Fundamental Reading Skill," *EDL Research and Information Bulletin, No. 3* (Huntington, N.Y.: Educational Developmental Laboratories, 1960), p. 12.

† *Ibid.*

Less skillful readers may not be able to make associations between some of the visual forms that they perceive and the meanings of these forms. If a reader comes to a visual form with which he is not familiar, he may pronounce (vocally or subvocally) the sounds of each letter or diphthong in it, one after the other, blend these sounds together, and recognize the word or phrase he is pronouncing. Its meaning is then combined with others to re-create the ideas expressed.

Problems arise if the reader cannot associate a visual form with its meaning and does not know what sounds to associate with letters or diphthongs or does not know the real-life meaning of a word or phrase he pronounces correctly. We try to reduce these problems to a minimum when children are learning to read by teaching them the visual forms they are likely to encounter, by making sure that they do know the meanings of words used in the material they are to read, and by teaching them the sounds of the most common visual forms in the words and phrases they are likely to encounter often. As a matter of fact, we then include in pre-primers and primers only those visual forms whose sounds they have been taught. The catch is that in some languages, especially English, the same visual form may be pronounced in several different ways. Because of this fact, it seems best to teach children to associate the meanings of many whole words and phrases with their visual forms before introducing them to the problem of associating sounds with letters and diphthongs and of using these associations to pronounce unfamiliar words and phrases. No successful method of teaching beginning reading fails to provide practice in associating visual forms with meanings and in teaching the sounds of letters and diphthongs as part of the process of pronouncing words and phrases encountered in the reading. Differences among methods of teaching reading center largely around the emphasis given to certain aspects of the reading process and the order in which these aspects are introduced. Controlled experimentation has shown that normal children will learn to read about equally well despite fairly wide variations in the methods used to teach them.*

Measuring the mechanics of reading. To measure the mechanical elements in reading, many tests have been devised. Those intended to measure the number and duration of eye fixations and the number of regressions per 100 words require expensive eye-movement cameras and will not be discussed here. Among pencil-and-paper tests, the *Gates Reading Diagnostic Test, Revised Edition,*† has been found helpful. This test must

---

* F. B. Davis, "Phonic Method Versus Combination Method in Teaching Beginning Reading," *Newsletter No. 28* (Huntington, N.Y.: Educational Developmental Laboratories, 1963).

† A. I. Gates, *Gates Reading Diagnostic Tests, Revised ed.* (New York: Bureau of Publications, Teachers College, Columbia University, 1953), Forms I and II.

be administered individually and takes from sixty to ninety minutes. It yields twenty-one different scores, covering various aspects of:

Oral reading	Word analysis
Oral vocabulary	Oral spelling
Reversal tendencies	Visual perception
Phrase and word perception	Auditory perception.

Directions for administering it and norms for interpreting scores are included with suggestions for remedial procedures in the *Improvement of Reading*.* This test may be used to assess the status of elementary school pupils in various elements of the mechanics of reading, but it is most commonly used for diagnosing the sources of difficulty among pupils who are retarded in reading. Teachers will find it useful for both purposes. With a little practice, it is easy to administer.

Comprehension in reading. Educators and psychologists are widely agreed that reading is essentially a process of getting meaning. So far as the writer is aware, Edward L. Thorndike was the first to try to describe on the basis of experimental data the reasoning processes that evoke meaning. His general conclusion was that reading is a reasoning process "of the same selective and coordinating nature as the more obvious forms of reasoning in mathematics or science."† "It consists in selecting the right elements of the situation and putting them together in the right relations, and also with the right amount of weight or influence or force for each."‡

In 1929, Ivor A. Richards published the results of a study of the comprehension of poetry among university students.§ Most of his analyses and conclusions are also applicable to prose. Richards concluded that to comprehend accurately a reader must:

1. Determine correctly the literal sense meaning of what he reads.
2. Determine correctly a writer's feeling or mood.
3. Apprehend a writer's exact tone, or attitude toward the reader.
4. Recognize a writer's intention.

Many other authorities have suggested skills and abilities that appear to be called into play during the process of getting an author's meaning. In fact, a list of several hundred skills and abilities was compiled when the

* A. I. Gates, *The Improvement of Reading: A Program of Diagnostic and Remedial Methods*, Third ed. (New York: Macmillan Co., 1947).

† E. L. Thorndike, "The Understanding of Sentences," *Elementary School Journal*, XVIII (1917), 98–114.

‡ E. L. Thorndike, "Reading as Reasoning: A Study of Mistakes in Paragraph Reading," *Journal of Educational Psychology*, VIII (1917), 323–352.

§ I. A. Richards, *Practical Criticism* (New York: Harcourt, Brace and Company, 1929).

specifications for the *Cooperative Reading Comprehension Test* were prepared.* A few of the skills that did not lend themselves to measurement in
objective tests were dropped and the remainder were clustered into nine
categories:

1. Remembering word meanings.
2. Deducing the meaning of words from the context.
3. Following the organization of a passage, as in identifying ante-
   cedents and references.
4. Identifying the main thought of a passage.
5. Answering questions for which explicit or paraphrased answers are
   given in the material read.
6. Weaving together the ideas in a passage.
7. Drawing inferences about the content of a passage.
8. Recognizing literary devices and identifying the author's tone and
   mood.
9. Drawing inferences about the author's purpose and point of view.

Multiple-choice items were written to measure each of these nine
categories of skills and an experimental study was carried out among college
freshmen to determine the extent to which the categories would merge or
remain distinct from one another.† The results indicated that two general
mental abilities underlie comprehension in reading. These are:

A. Memory for word meanings.
B. Verbal reasoning.

In addition, the existence of three specific abilities was rather firmly
established. These are:

C. Following the organization of a passage, as in identifying ante-
   cedents and references.
D. Recognizing literary devices and identifying the author's tone and
   mood.
E. Drawing inferences from the content.

The data did not establish clearly the separate existence of skills in categories
2, 5, and 9. Consequently, it seems reasonable to merge the skills in
categories 2, 7, and 9 in specific ability E. The skills in category 5 do not
seem logically or experimentally to belong with those in any other category,
so they may be listed as a separate ability:

F. Answering questions for which explicit or paraphrased answers are
   given.

It seems reasonable to conclude that comprehension in reading is
adequately represented by a composite of abilities A through F and that

---

* F. B. Davis, *et al.*, *Cooperative Reading Comprehension Test, Form Q*
(New York: Cooperative Test Service, 1940).
† F. B. Davis, "Fundamental Factors of Comprehension in Reading,"
Psychometrika, IX (1944), 185–197.

tests of comprehension at the secondary-school and college levels should measure all of these abilities. In the elementary school grades, specific skill D is probably less important than the others and should, therefore, receive less emphasis in tests of comprehension.

Measuring comprehension in reading. For measuring reading comprehension in grades 1 through 12, a number of satisfactory tests are available. Listed alphabetically below are seven which yield scores that are not significantly affected by speed of reading for most pupils.

California Reading Test, 1957 Edition (Del Monte, Calif.: California Test Bureau, 1957). This test is available in five levels suitable for use in grades 1 through 14 (college sophomore). Time limits range from thirty minutes in grades 1–4 to fifty minutes in grades 9–14. Number-right scoring is used. Norms are provided in terms of total-group grade-equivalent scores. The test yields vocabulary, paragraph reading, and total scores.

Cooperative Reading Comprehension Test, 1960 Edition (Princeton: Educational Testing Service, 1960). This test is a revision of the first series of *Cooperative Reading Comprehension Tests* (Forms Q, R, S, T, Y, and Z). It is available in two levels, one for college freshmen and sophomores and one for grades 9 through 12. The Level-of-Comprehension score is essentially unaffected by speed of reading. Vocabulary, Speed-of-Comprehension, and Total scores are also obtained. The time limit is forty minutes. Number-right scoring is used. Percentile norms are provided.

Davis Reading Test (New York: Psychological Corporation, 1957–1962). This test is available in two levels for use in grades 8 through the college freshman year. The Level-of-Comprehension score is essentially unaffected by speed of reading. The test also yields a Speed-of-Comprehension score. The time limit is forty minutes. Scores are corrected for chance success. Percentile norms are provided. Superior pupils are more accurately measured than by other tests.

Metropolitan Reading Test (New York: Harcourt, Brace and World, Inc., 1959). This test is available at five levels for use in grades 1–9. The first three levels (grades 1–4) yield scores in word knowledge, word discrimination, and paragraph comprehension. The fourth and fifth levels (grades 5–9) yield only word-knowledge and paragraph-comprehension scores. The time limits range from sixty-nine minutes for the grade 1–3 test to thirty-nine minutes for the grade 7–9 test. Number-right scoring is used. Norms are provided in terms of age-controlled-group grade-equivalent scores, percentiles, and stanines.

Sequential Tests of Educational Progress: Reading (Princeton: Educational Testing Service, 1957). This test is available in four levels for grade 4 through the college sophomore year. The time limit is seventy minutes. Number-right scoring is used. Percentile norms are provided.

SRA Achievement Series: Reading (Chicago: Science Research Associates, 1957). This test is available in three levels for grades 2–9. It yields separate vocabulary and paragraph-reading scores. The time limits vary from sixty-five to ninety minutes for the three levels. Number-right scoring is used. Grade-equivalent and percentile norms are provided.

Stanford Reading Test (New York: Harcourt, Brace and World, Inc., 1964). This test is available in five levels for grades 1–9. Word meaning, paragraph-meaning, word-study skills, and total scores are provided. The time limits range from eighty-three minutes in grade 1 to thirty minutes in grades 7–9. Number-right scoring is used. Age-controlled-group grade-equivalent scores, stanines, and percentile norms are available.

Rate of reading. The measurement of rate of reading seems at first thought to be a simple undertaking: just ask a person to read for five minutes, count the number of words he reads, and divide this number by five to get his average rate in words per minute. However, a little consideration quickly reveals that the measurement of rate of reading is actually complicated and troublesome.

In the first place, a reader's rate is greatly affected by his purpose in reading. How greatly is illustrated by some data obtained by Frank Laycock.† These are shown in Table 5.1. When asked to read a passage so

TABLE 5.1

Rate of Reading of 391 Applicants for College
Admission*

Group	N	Rate in Words Per Minute		Gain in Rate (Words per Minute)
		Normal Rate	After Request to Read Rapidly	
All applicants	391	220.4	308.1	87.7

* After F. Laycock, *loc. cit.*, table I, p. 313.

they could answer simple questions afterwards, 391 applicants for admission to college read at an average speed of 220.4 words per minute. Asked to read a similar passage as fast as possible without missing important points on which test questions would be asked, they averaged 308.1 words per minute. A simple request to increase their speed without sacrificing comprehension resulted in an immediate average gain of 40 per cent in rate of reading.

† F. Laycock, "Significant Characteristics of College Students with Varying Flexibility in Reading Rate," *Journal of Experimental Education*, XXIII (1955), 311–330.

These data are merely illustrative, but they are typical of those obtained in experiments designed to discover the effect on rate of reading of changing a reader's purpose. Two important implications follow from them:

1. The measurement of rate of reading must be carried out when the purpose of the reader has been clearly defined and he fulfills that purpose. For example, if he is told to read as rapidly as possible without sacrificing comprehension, the rate at which he reads cannot be accepted unless a check on his comprehension of the material he has read shows that he did understand it acceptably well.

2. The results of training programs designed to increase speed of reading should be judged on the basis of procedures that exclude any increase in rate that a reader can make before the training is begun simply by stepping up his speed without appreciable loss of comprehension. Readers' purposes vary so widely that some of them hardly result in what is commonly accepted as reading. For example, a student's purpose may be to determine what topics are taken up in a book or an article and how they are organized. He, therefore, skims through the material without any effort to understand the content. This accomplishes his purpose but can scarcely be described as reading in any ordinary sense of the term. He has used techniques well suited to his purpose, but he has not *read* the material.

A second purpose, characteristic of reading novels for pleasure, is following the main thread of a story. A third purpose is discovering an author's ideas, understanding them, and weaving them together so as to draw conclusions from them or apply them in practical situations. A fourth purpose is learning certain facts or statements so that they can be reproduced from memory. Students read many assignments with this objective uppermost in their minds.

It is evident that if rate of reading is to be measured in words read per minute, at least four separate tests are needed to show an examinee's rate while he is skimming through material to find out how it is organized; following the main line of thought or action; understanding the principal ideas; and learning the principal ideas well enough to recall them. To determine whether he is accomplishing, or substantially accomplishing, his purpose, the examinee must pass a comprehension test along with each rate-of-reading measurement.

This brings us to the second factor that greatly affects rate of reading—the complexity or difficulty of the material. Data published by Flanagan illustrate the relationship between rate and difficulty.* He administered three equivalent twenty-item tests to 317 twelfth grade pupils in such a way

* J. C. Flanagan, "A Study of the Effect on Comprehension of Varying Speeds of Reading," in *Research on the Foundations of American Education,* Official Report of the American Educational Research Association (Washington: The Association, 1939), pp. 47–50.

that they worked on them at three different predetermined rates. The resulting data are shown in Table 5.2. The average score of the 317 pupils when they read at a speed enabling them to finish in eighteen minutes was 10.5; when they read at a speed enabling them to finish in twelve minutes was 9.7; and when they read at a speed enabling them to finish in six minutes was 7.0. These data indicate that with the purpose of the readers (to respond correctly to test items illustrated in advance by practice exercises) and the difficulty of the material held constant, they sustained an average loss of comprehension when their rate was increased 50 per cent and a further loss when it was again increased 100 per cent.

TABLE 5.2

Comprehension at Three Rates of Reading*

Group	N	Average Scores		
		Test 1 18 minutes	Test 2 12 minutes	Test 3 6 minutes
Grade 12 Pupils	317	10.5	9.7	7.0
Highest-scoring Third on Test 1			11.7	8.4
Middle-scoring Third on Test 1			9.6	7.0
Lowest-scoring Third on Test 1			7.6	5.3

* After J. C. Flanagan, *loc. cit.*, p. 3.

The fact that the highest-scoring pupils in the eighteen-minute period had about the same percentage loss in comprehension as the middle-scoring and lowest-scoring pupils when the time was reduced from twelve to six minutes suggests that there is a fairly consistent *inverse* relationship throughout the range of reading ability between rate of reading and amount of comprehension. Since the pupils could refer to the reading material while they answered the test questions, memory did not play an appreciable part in determining the results.

The finding that the faster a person reads the less he comprehends agrees so well with common sense that one wonders why anyone ever doubts it. We all know that we can read and understand a novel more rapidly than a textbook in statistics. Yet we often hear it said that faster readers tend to comprehend more of what they read. Actually, this statement is true but does *not* contradict the fact that, for any given individual, the faster he reads certain specified material the less he comprehends (motivation and purpose remaining constant). The explanation is that both rate of reading and extent of comprehension vary with ability to assimilate. The better an individual can weave ideas together, the faster and better he can comprehend. This ability to assimilate appears to be almost synonymous with verbal reasoning.

A classic study of the relationship between rate of reading (as measured by the number of words read per minute) and extent of comprehension showed a correlation coefficient of .30 in samples of 672 pupils in grades 11 and 12.* This may be interpreted to mean that, under carefully controlled experimental conditions, rate of covering words and comprehension of the content are positively, but only slightly, related to each other. It does *not* mean that an individual pupil who forces himself to skim over material more rapidly than is natural for him will thereby understand the material better.

Tests for measuring rate of reading in terms of words per minute are available but none of them is sufficiently meaningful to warrant listing here. Speed-of-Comprehension scores are yielded by two of the comprehension tests mentioned earlier: the *Cooperative Reading Comprehension Test* and the *Davis Reading Test*. Because these tests were deliberately constructed in such a way that few pupils finish the speed-of-comprehension items in the time limit, the number of items answered by an examinee depends on his rate of reading as well as his extent of comprehension.†

The tests and techniques commonly used to measure changes in reading rate brought about by "reading-improvement courses" and by various mechanical devices have often been seriously inadequate. *First*, tests needed to measure the rate at which reading takes place in fulfilling each of the four major purposes listed previously have not been available. *Second*, tests used to check comprehension of the material read while rate was being measured have often included items that could be answered by many examinees before they read the material. *Third*, tests used to check comprehension have often been administered with time limits so short that every examinee did not have time to consider every item and have then been scored without correction for chance success. When an examinee is tested at the beginning and at the end of a reading-improvement course, he may read so rapidly on the second testing that his comprehension is poorer than it was initially. Yet, under these circumstances, he may get a higher comprehension score on the second test simply by marking responses (at random,

* P. Blommers and E. F. Lindquist, "Rate of Comprehension: Its Measurement and Its Relation to Comprehension," *Journal of Educational Psychology*, XXXV (1944), 449–472.

† Since the number of items not considered in the time limit will vary considerably among the examinees, it is best to correct the scores for chance success. Scores on Forms Q, R, S, T, Y, and Z of the *Cooperative Reading Comprehension Test* and on all forms of the *Davis Reading Test* are so corrected. Scores on Forms A, B, and C of the revised *Cooperative Reading Comprehension Test* are not so corrected.

if necessary) to a greater number of items than on the first test. His scores will give the false impression that he has greatly increased his reading rate while maintaining or even improving upon his original extent of comprehension. *Fourth*, although estimates of individual and group gains in rate of reading and extent of comprehension are based on scores from equivalent forms of the same test properly administered and scored at the beginning and at the end of a reading-improvement course, the training given during the course may have so altered the examinees' purpose that the initial and final scores are actually not measures of the same reading skills. *Fifth*, estimates of individual and group gains in reading have often been affected by regression to population means, a problem that is discussed in chapter 10.

MEASURING ACHIEVEMENT IN THE ELEMENTARY SCHOOL AND JUNIOR HIGH SCHOOL

For a variety of reasons, the most generally satisfactory tests for measuring achievement in elementary and junior high schools are probably several of the well-known batteries, some of which include separately printed reading tests that have already been mentioned. Five of these batteries are listed alphabetically below. For the reader's convenience, the subject-matter areas covered, the publisher, and the date of publication are given. Time limits, forms available, and other details are not presented because they can be found in *Tests in Print*,* the *Mental Measurement Yearbooks*,† and publishers' catalogues, which will be sent free on request.‡

> *California Achievement Tests*, 1957 ed. (Del Monte, Calif.: California Test Bureau, 1957). Grades 1–9. Vocabulary, Paragraph Comprehension, Arithmetic Reasoning, Arithmetic Computation, Mechanics of English, Spelling, Handwriting.
> *Iowa Tests of Basic Skills* (Boston: Houghton Mifflin Co., 1956). Grades 3–9. Vocabulary, Paragraph Comprehension, Language Skills, Work-Study Skills, Arithmetic Concepts, Arithmetic Problems.
> *Metropolitan Achievement Tests* (New York: Harcourt, Brace and World, Inc., 1959). Grades 1–9. Vocabulary, Word Discrimination (Grades 1–4), Paragraph Comprehension, Arithmetic Problems, Arithmetic Computation, Language Skills, Language Study Skills, Social Studies, Social-Studies Study Skills, Science.

* O. K. Buros, *Tests in Print* (New Brunswick, N.J.: Gryphon Press, 1961).
† O. K. Buros, ed., *Mental Measurement Yearbooks*. See Selected References at the end of chapter 3.
‡ See page 67 for publishers' addresses.

Sequential Tests of Educational Progress (Princeton, N.J.: Educational Testing Service, 1957). Grades 4–9. Paragraph Comprehension, Listening Comprehension, Writing Skills, Social Studies Comprehension, Science Information and Comprehension, Arithmetic Problems, Essay Writing (not objectively scored).

Stanford Achievement Test (New York: Harcourt, Brace and World, Inc., 1964). Word Reading, Vocabulary, Arithmetic (Grade 1); Word Study Skills (Grades 1–4); Paragraph Meaning (Grades 1–9); Science and Social-Studies Concepts (Grades 2–3); Word Meaning (Grades 2–6); Language, Arithmetic Computation, Arithmetic Concepts (Grades 2–9); Science, Social Studies, Arithmetic Applications (Grades 4–9).

MEASURING ACHIEVEMENT IN THE SENIOR HIGH SCHOOL

Tests for senior high school pupils fall into two main types: *first*, those intended to measure the subject-matter content of specific courses; *second*, those intended to measure important knowledge, understanding, and skills in the major subject-matter fields. Most educators believe that both types of test are of value in appropriate circumstances. On the other hand, criticisms have been leveled at both types. Some educators have questioned the importance of the factual content in specific courses and, therefore, of efforts to measure this content by tests. Others have pointed out that if generalizations and applications are explicitly taught to pupils and not evolved out of a foundation of factual content, they become mere parroted learnings. Certainly it is true that tests requiring the comprehension of reading material and of tables, graphs, and charts measure predominantly verbal-reasoning ability. As a result, examinees who are highly intelligent (in the popular sense), who read a good deal, and who remember what they read tend to obtain high scores whether the content of the material is social studies, science, mathematics, or literature. At the same time, conscientious hardworking students who learn the specific content of their courses but who lack high verbal-reasoning ability may do poorly.

In selecting tests for the senior high school, these considerations should be kept in mind. Decisions are not easy to make, however, because the two types of tests are not clearly differentiated. In practice, a test properly designed to cover the specific content of a course measures understandings and applications of the factual material taught because they are important objectives of the course. Similarly, many items in tests like the *Iowa Tests of Educational Development* and the *Sequential Tests of Educational Progress* measure specific factual information.

For measuring specific content in many typical high school courses, the *Cooperative Achievement Tests* offer coverage and quality that cannot be matched in other series.*   The subject-matter fields covered by these tests are as follows:

Languages	*Science*
English expression	General science
French	Biology
Latin	Chemistry
Spanish	Physics
Mathematics	*Social studies*
Elementary algebra (through quadratics)	American government
Intermediate algebra (quadratics and beyond)	American history
Plane geometry	World history
Solid geometry	Ancient history
Plane trigonometry	Modern European history

Two series of tests intended to measure the outcomes of formal and informal learning acquired over a period of years in school and out of school have already been mentioned: the *Iowa Tests of Educational Development* (ITED) and the *Sequential Tests of Educational Progress* (STEP).   These tests are said to be less concerned with *what* factual information the pupils have learned than with how well they can *use* their information in solving practical problems and in acquiring new information and understandings. The tests in these series are listed below.   After each title (except the *STEP Essay Test*) appears either the word "information" or "comprehension" indicating whether more of the items in current forms of the test call for specific information (whether applied or not) or for general comprehension. These descriptions are, of course, based on subjective judgment.

Iowa Tests of Educational Development (Chicago: Science Research Associates, 1958).
1. Understanding of Basic Social Concepts (information).
2. Background in the Natural Sciences (information).
3. Correctness and Appropriateness of Expression (information).
4. Ability to Do Quantitative Thinking (comprehension).
5. Ability to Interpret Reading Materials in the Social Studies (comprehension).
6. Ability to Interpret Reading Materials in the Natural Sciences (comprehension).

* The *Cooperative Achievement Tests* are published by the Educational Testing Service, Princeton, N.J.

7. Ability to Interpret Literary Materials (comprehension).
8. General Vocabulary (information).
9. Use of Sources of Information (information).

Sequential Tests of Educational Progress (Princeton, N.J.: Educational Testing Service, 1957).
1. Reading (comprehension).
2. Listening (comprehension).
3. Writing (comprehension).
4. Social Studies (comprehension).
5. Science (information).
6. Mathematics (information).
7. Essay.

THE USES OF ACHIEVEMENT TESTS

Efficiency of Learning

The major purpose of measurement in education is to maximize the efficiency of the learning process for each individual.   Before considering the ways in which achievement tests can be used for this purpose, it may be helpful to state the conditions that lead to efficient learning.

1. The specific objectives to be reached must be clearly defined in advance for the learner.   He should know what kinds of knowledge, skills, or abilities he is expected to demonstrate at the end of the learning period and how he will be expected to demonstrate them.
2. The learner should see just how these specific objectives are related to his own goals.   These goals range all the way from wanting to please his teacher and get high marks to gaining admission to college and succeeding in the career that he visualizes for himself.
3. The material to be learned should be presented in a meaningful way and at a rate adjusted to the learner's ability to absorb and assimilate it.   He should have abundant practice in making correct responses.
4. The learner should have frequent opportunities to find out whether what he has learned is correct and is an adequate basis for progressing to the next stage.   Reteaching should take place at once when errors or gaps in learning are revealed.
5. The material should be reviewed systematically to make sure that what has been learned is not forgotten.
6. The end of the learning period should be marked by a well-planned opportunity for the learner to demonstrate the skills, abilities, and knowledge that he was expected to learn.   This opportunity may consist of an examination or the completion of some project.

In addition to increasing the efficiency of learning, measurements of achievement are used to assign marks, to predict achievement, to diagnose individual difficulties in learning, and to provide data for research studies.

Teacher-Made Tests

Determining initial status. Teachers at all levels of school and college often *act* as though all of the pupils in a class begin at the same level of knowledge, skill, or ability in the field to be studied, yet hardly any teachers really *believe* that this is true. Some of them *act* as though it were because they fail to measure the achievement levels of their pupils in the subject matter they are about to teach. Achievement tests given at the beginning of a learning period are usually called *pretests*. When they are given, great differences are usually revealed in the initial status of the learners. Steps should then be taken to individualize instruction and assignments. Material already known by most of the class members need not be retaught. It can be taken up in group work with those who have not already learned it. Time saved in this way can be used by most of the class members for additional learning exercises on material that is new to them.

A well-designed pretest provides an excellent means of illustrating the objectives of learning and of showing how these must be demonstrated. Ordinarily, it takes the form of an objective or essay test, but sometimes it consists of a practical demonstration. For example, a pretest before beginning piano lessons might involve turning on a tape recorder and asking the pupil to play at sight as much of a composition of appropriate difficulty as he can in 10 minutes.

Grouping. Classes are usually so large that complete individualization of instruction is not possible. The best that the teacher can often do is to form three or four groups of pupils for classroom teaching and then individualize the assignment of outside reading and other special projects. A pretest made by the teacher, perhaps by adapting a final examination used with a class at the end of the preceding year, often provides a set of scores that is better suited than any other to serve as a basis for grouping of this kind. The rate of learning in the groups should be adjusted to their differing capacities to absorb and assimilate the material.

Checking up on learning. Short tests or informal quizzes constructed by the classroom teacher to find out whether pupils have learned the material they have been studying are of great value to both the teacher and the pupils in showing them what has been learned and what has not been learned. This information alerts the teacher to material that should be retaught or reviewed and indicates to the pupils the extent to which they are learning the material that they are expected to learn.

Experimental data generally have shown that properly planned tests tend to motivate normal pupils to study, to review material that they have already studied, and to organize and knit together material that might otherwise remain fragmented. In short, teacher-made tests can be helpful in stimulating learning.

Assessing learning. At the end of a learning period, a comprehensive test of the material taught should be used to inform each pupil of the extent to which he has attained the objectives defined at the beginning of the period. Educators have properly been concerned with the effect of this information on pupils who find that they have learned very little. The causes of failure to learn should always be considered very carefully; measures to prevent its recurrence naturally vary as the causes vary. Sometimes lack of motivation or systematic habits or techniques of study account for failure to learn; sometimes, inappropriate techniques of teaching are responsible; in other cases, lack of the basic mental abilities required for learning of the material is responsible. Occasionally, emotional maladjustment or physical or emotional immaturity prevent effective learning from taking place. Whatever the causes of failure, they should be located and remedial measures begun whenever possible.

Scores on teacher-made tests ordinarily serve as a basis for marks. Methods for using them in this way are discussed in chapter 13.

Standardized Tests

Determining initial status. Some uses of teacher-made tests for determining the level of achievement of pupils at the beginning of a learning period have been discussed in the preceding section. When standardized tests are used at the beginning of a learning period, they make possible comparisons of the levels of achievement of individuals and groups with those of defined norms groups. Just as scores from teacher-made tests are of special value in forming small groups within a class, so scores from standardized tests of achievement are of value for sectioning grade groups into classes. Suppose that 300 sixth grade pupils are to be assigned to ten classes in English, mathematics, social studies, and science. If an appropriate standardized test in each of these four subjects is administered to them during the first week of school, they can then be assigned to classes at the appropriate level in each subject. For example, a boy might be assigned to the class that includes the thirty highest-scoring pupils in English, to the third-highest-scoring group in social studies, to the fifth-highest-scoring group in science, and to the next-to-the-lowest-scoring group in mathematics. Formation of homogeneous groups in each subject-matter field is likely to prove far more satisfactory than if mental-test scores are used to form them. In the first place, teachers will find the groups easier to work with because the pupils in them tend to be alike in regard to qualities that are relevant to the material being taught. Second, pupils do not get the impression that they have been branded as "bright" or "dumb" and are expected to behave accordingly.

The extent to which this type of grouping can be put into practice is limited by the programs of the teachers and pupils. Careful scheduling of classes and compromises in pupil placement are ordinarily required.

Scores from standardized tests are usually comparable from subject to subject. Profiles of scores for pupils who show unusual variations should be studied carefully. Those who vary greatly from subject to subject or who obtain exceptionally low scores should be referred for diagnostic studies to the school psychologist or to a child guidance center. Information provided by specialists in educational and psychological diagnosis may be of great value to a child's classroom teachers. If referrals are made in September, this information is likely to become available in time to be of practical use during the school year.

One of the most immediately useful results of pretest data is the identification of exceptionally capable pupils who already know a good deal of the material to be taught and who may waste most of their time even if they are placed in a homogeneous group of high-scoring pupils. These few outstanding pupils should be identified and given special assignments to supplement the classroom work, and even to replace it in some cases. It should be noted that differential assignments for gifted pupils can always be made and are almost always beneficial in an observable, if not striking, way. The benefits of differential assignments for exceptionally low-achieving pupils are not usually so obvious to parents and teachers.

Determining final status. Scores from a standardized achievement test given at the end of a period of learning may be used to compare the status of individuals or groups with that of defined norms groups. Thus, a teacher can determine how the average level of achievement in her class compares with that of her classes in previous years or with that of classes at various grade levels in specified types of schools throughout the country.

Predicting performance. Educators long ago discovered that scores on an achievement test constitute an excellent predictor of performance in a subsequent course in the same subject-matter field or in a closely related field. Achievement tests are, therefore, widely used for selecting students for admission to specialized schools and to colleges and universities.

Achievement tests are also useful in predicting performance in many occupations. They are, in fact, not only valid for this purpose, but they look as though they should be. Thus, they have high face validity as well as high predictive validity. This makes them especially useful as civil service examinations since they have wide public acceptance.

Guidance counselors have found that scores on achievement tests provide much of their most valuable information about the probable performance of pupils in the next grade or course. In this respect, they are more uniformly dependable than teachers' marks. The latter vary in reliability and validity from teacher to teacher.

In one high school, the guidance counselor was asked to select sixty pupils for an eleventh grade honors course in chemistry. He looked up the marks given at the end of the preceding year to fifty-nine eleventh grade pupils who were then completing this honors course. Next, he correlated these marks with the teachers' marks these pupils had been given in their tenth grade general-science course and with scores on the natural-sciences test in the *Iowa Tests of Educational Development*, which the pupils took at the end of grade 10. His computations showed the predictive validity coefficient of the natural-sciences test to be .46 and of the teachers' marks in general science to be $-.06$. Naturally, he selected for the next year's honors course in chemistry sixty pupils who had made high scores on the natural-sciences test.

These results showed a more striking difference between the predictive validity of achievement-test scores and a single set of teachers' marks than is usually found, but they do illustrate the predictive value of achievement-test scores.

Assessing change. The measurement of changes produced in each pupil's level of achievement with respect to the knowledge, skills, and understandings that constitute the objectives of a learning period is one of the most important problems in education. The essential data needed to carry out this type of measurement consist of scores on achievement tests given at the beginning and the end of the learning period. Methods of using these data are discussed in chapter 10.

Identifying underachievement and overachievement. Pupils who learn more than our estimates of their potential ability lead us to believe they will are called "overachievers"; those who learn less than we think they will are called "underachievers." Their identification requires that a pupil's level of achievement in a specified area be compared with his level of ability to learn material in that area. Methods of making this type of comparison are discussed in chapter 11.

Conducting research. School administrators and psychologists use achievement tests for a wide range of research purposes. Educators are coming to recognize that if educational problems and issues are to be solved wisely, research data rather than armchair philosophizing will provide the means.   Chapter 9 discusses the interpretation of group data, and appendixes A through L provide computational routines and interpretive aids for several of the statistics most commonly used in educational research.

Summary

Achievement tests are intended to assess the knowledge, understandings, and skills of examinees at a specific point in time.   They are, however, often used to predict performance in a certain subject-matter field as well as to assess competence in that field.

There are two main types of achievement tests: survey tests and diagnostic tests.   The former are sometimes constructed to measure specific learning; in these, the test builder tries to make it impossible for a highly intelligent person to answer items correctly unless he has learned the subject matter. At other times they are constructed to measure an examinee's ability to learn new material and to understand basic concepts in the field being tested. Examinees of high general intelligence are likely to get high scores on this kind of survey test.

Diagnostic tests are designed to find out in which particular elements of a field of knowledge or an ability an individual or a group is especially strong or weak.   For example, a diagnostic test in arithmetic may provide separate scores for the examinee's ability in (1) addition, (2) subtraction, (3) multiplication, and (4) division, so that a pupil's performance is broken down into four components and his teacher knows in which ones (if any) he needs instruction.

Reading is one of the most important fields measured by achievement tests.   Many instruments are available for measuring the mechanics of reading, speed of reading, and comprehension in reading.

Achievement tests for use in elementary and junior high schools include the following, which are listed alphabetically:

California Achievement Tests
Iowa Tests of Basic Skills
Metropolitan Achievement Tests
Sequential Tests of Educational Progress
Stanford Achievement Test

For testing achievement in senior high schools, the following tests have been suggested:

The Cooperative Achievement Tests (in many subject-matter fields)
The Iowa Tests of Educational Development
Sequential Tests of Educational Progress

One of the major purposes of measurement in education is to aid in increasing the efficiency with which pupils can learn. The conditions required for efficient learning include the following:

1. The objectives to be reached must be clearly defined in advance for the learner.
2. The relationship of these objectives to the learner's own goals should be clearly evident to him.
3. The material to be learned should be meaningful and should be presented at an appropriate rate for each learner.
4. The learner must have many opportunities to make correct responses, to identify his errors, and to correct them.
5. The material learned should be reviewed systematically to minimize forgetting.
6. The end of a learning period should be marked by an opportunity for the learner to demonstrate what he has learned.

Measuring instruments play an important part in conditions 1, 3, 4, 5, and 6. Teachers frequently use tests constructed by themselves to determine the initial status of their pupils in the material to be learned, to form groups within their classes, to check up frequently on the progress of their pupils, and to assess the extent of learning at the end of a unit of work or marking period.

Standardized tests are frequently used in schools at the beginning of a school year or term to compare the status of pupils who have come from various schools and teachers. The data are often used for sectioning all pupils and for identifying those who appear exceptionally advanced or retarded so that individual attention may be given to their special needs. Scores from standardized tests may also be used to compare individuals and classes with existing norms, to predict their later performance, to assess the changes produced by instruction, and to identify pupils who seem to be learning markedly more or less than would be expected.

Finally, achievement tests are commonly used in research studies designed to investigate the educational process.

Selected References

For the beginning student in educational measurement, one of the best and most accessible sources of information about achievement testing is the material in the manuals for well-known achievement tests. Among these are:

California Achievement Tests, 1957 ed. Del Monte, Calif.: California Test Bureau, 1957.
Iowa Tests of Basic Skills. Boston: Houghton Mifflin Co., 1956.

Iowa Tests of Educational Development.   Chicago: Science Research Associates, 1958.

Metropolitan Achievement Tests.   New York: Harcourt, Brace and World, Inc., 1959.

Sequential Tests of Educational Progress.   Princeton, N.J.: Educational Testing Service, 1957.

Stanford Achievement Test.   New York: Harcourt, Brace and World, Inc., 1964.

Chapter Six

MEASUREMENT
OF INTELLIGENCE
AND APTITUDE

GENERAL INTELLIGENCE

From time immemorial, men have observed that their fellows differ greatly in the ease and accuracy with which they perceive facts and ideas, remember them, draw logical conclusions and inferences from them, and benefit or learn from experiences. These qualities make up the core of what is commonly called *intelligence* or general mental ability. The extent to which this mental ability is possessed by adults or by children at any given age level varies tremendously; thus, we say that some individuals exhibit high intelligence and that others exhibit low intelligence.

In general, it is true that an individual who perceives facts and ideas accurately is able to remember them well and to reason with them. Likewise, the individual who is rather inaccurate in perceiving facts and ideas tends to forget them readily and has difficulty seeing their interrelationships and drawing conclusions from them. If perceiving, remembering, and reasoning (as we have used the terms) were all simply outward manifestations of a single general mental ability possessed in some degree by each individual, the true rank order of the members of any group in accuracy of perceiving, of remembering, or of reasoning would be exactly the same. As a matter of fact, most of the pioneer workers in measuring intelligence tacitly assumed that, barring errors of measurement, the rank order of individuals from the same environmental background was exactly, or almost exactly, the same in each one of the basic mental abilities like perceiving, remembering, and reasoning.

By the 1920s, psychologists had constructed and administered to large numbers of examinees separate tests of various basic mental abilities. The resulting data permitted experimental studies of the extent to which the rank orders of scores in the separate tests were alike.   For this purpose, Charles Spearman at the University of London developed a method of analyzing the interrelationships of scores derived from any set of tests.*   Applications of his method led him to the conclusion that the interrelationships could be accounted for if the examinees made use of *one general mental ability*, which he called *g*, plus as many specific skills as there were tests.   With regard to *g*, Spearman wrote,

> (It) enters into the measurement of ability of all kinds, and (it) is throughout constant for any individual, although varying greatly for different individuals.   It showed itself to be involved invariably and exclusively in all operations of eductive nature.   Whether there is any advantage of attaching to this *g* the old mishandled label of "intelligence" seems at least dubious.†

Spearman recognized, however, that certain sets of tests yielded scores that seemed to have some basic mental ability in common beside *g*.   For example, tests of logical reasoning seemed to involve a common element that may be called *l*, in addition to *g* and *s*.   Likewise, tests of arithmetic appeared to involve a common element that may be called *a*; among men, tests of mechanical comprehension involved a common element that may be called *m*; and tests of social judgment involved a common element that may be called *j*.   The first two diagrams in Figure 6.1 show how the elements that underlie test scores in reasoning, arithmetic, mechanical comprehension (among men), and social judgment might be organized in terms of Spearman's studies.   In the first diagram, *g* in varying proportions appears for all tests, with a different *s* for each test.   In the second diagram, *g* again appears for all tests, but the pair of tests in each of the four areas measured includes an element in common that is not shared by tests in the other three areas. Again, a different *s* appears for each test.

Spearman speculated that the appearance of *m* in mechanical-comprehension tests administered to men and its absence in the same tests administered to women indicates that it reflects the presence of experiences that men usually have with mechanical things that women often do not have. Elements common to the interrelationships of some tests but not to those of others may be attitudes, emotional reactions, or simply the ways item responses are to be recorded on an answer sheet; they need not represent mental abilities.   For example, element *a*, common to arithmetic tests, may indicate the existence of an emotional reaction to arithmetic that is shared by examinees at all levels of *g* and that has resulted from the fright and tension often aroused in children by their early teachers of this subject.

---

* C. Spearman, *The Abilities of Man* (New York: Macmillan Co., 1927).
† *Ibid.*, pp. 411–412.

FIGURE 6.1

Illustration of Mental Skills in Eight Hypothetical
Tests.*

Part A: Illustrating Spearman's Two-Factor Theory

Reasoning		Arithmetic		Mechanical Comprehension (Among Men)		Social Judgment	
Test 1	Test 2	Test 3	Test 4	Test 5	Test 6	Test 7	Test 8
g	g	g	g	g	g	g	g
$s\,1$	$s\,2$	$s\,3$	$s\,4$	$s\,5$	$s\,6$	$s\,7$	$s\,8$

Part B: Illustrating Spearman's Group Theory

Reasoning		Arithmetic		Mechanical Comprehension (Among Men)		Social Judgment	
Test 1	Test 2	Test 3	Test 4	Test 5	Test 6	Test 7	Test 8
g	g	g	g	g	g	g	g
		a	a	m	m	j	j
l	l						
$s\,1$	$s\,2$	$s\,3$	$s\,4$	$s\,5$	$s\,6$	$s\,7$	$s\,8$

Part C: Illustrating Multiple-Factor Theory

Reasoning		Arithmetic		Mechanical Comprehension (Among Men)		Social Judgment	
Test 1	Test 2	Test 3	Test 4	Test 5	Test 6	Test 7	Test 8
P	P	P	P	P	P	P	P
M	M	M	M	M	M	M	M
R	R	R	R	R	R	R	R
V	V	V	V	V	V	V	V
N	N	N	N	N	N	N	N
$u\,1$	$u\,2$	$u\,3$	$u\,4$	$u\,5$	$u\,6$	$u\,7$	$u\,8$
$e\,1$	$e\,2$	$e\,3$	$e\,4$	$e\,5$	$e\,6$	$e\,7$	$e\,8$

* The data used are fictitious and for illustration only.

The fact that the interrelationships of any set of test scores can be explained without the existence of a general mental ability like *g* was pointed out by Godfrey Thomson of the University of Edinburgh as early as 1920. In 1928, Truman L. Kelley published data accounting for the interrelationships of scores on several tests without the existence of a general mental ability.* Since that time, Kelley and many others, including notably Louis L. Thurstone, have used this general approach for determining the underlying abilities that make up human intelligence. The third diagram in Figure 6.1 shows how the mental abilities underlying the eight tests might be accounted for by abilities of perception (P), memory (M), reasoning (R) visualizing space relations (V), and numerical facility (N). No general mental ability is presumed to exist. The *u*'s represent elements unique to each test and the *e*'s represent errors of measurement in each set of test scores.

Extensive research studies over a period of many years suggest that a rather large number of separate mental abilities are required to account for human intelligence. Intellectual activities, however, can be largely explained in terms of five types of ability applied in three major fields. The five types of ability are *perception, memory, reasoning, ideational fluency,* and *visualization.* The three major fields, or kinds of materials, are *verbal, numerical,* and *spatial* in character. Each block in Figure 6.2 represents a distin-

FIGURE 6.2

Fifteen Important Abilities Underlying
Intellectual Activity.

	Speed and Accuracy of Perception	Memory	Reasoning	Ideational Fluency	Visualization
Verbal	(1) Pv	(4) Mv	(7) Rv	(10) Iv	(13) Vv
Numerical	(2) Pn	(5) Mn	(8) Rn	(11) In	(14) Vn
Spatial	(3) Ps	(6) Ms	(9) Rs	(12) Is	(15) Vs

guishable mental ability.   In general, the three abilities in any one column tend to be more closely related to each other than to abilities in other columns,

* T. L. Kelley, *Crossroads in the Mind of Man: A Study of Differentiable Mental Abilities* (Stanford, California: Stanford University Press, 1928).

and the five abilities in any one row also tend to be more closely related to each other than to abilities in other rows. However, research data indicate that there are substantial positive intercorrelations among all fifteen abilities, perhaps traceable to the presence of a general mental ability like *g* which, to varying degrees, underlies all of them.

The fifteen abilities included in Figure 6.2 by no means exhaust the list of human abilities. Even in the intellectual field, others could be added. There is evidence, for example, that speed of mental operation constitutes an ability or characteristic that is nearly independent of level of performance without regard for time in each of the five types of ability included in Figure 6.2.* Speed and accuracy of sensory-motor response also affect performance on intellectual tasks, especially at early age levels.† At the present time, many psychologists conceive of general intelligence as a weighted combination of abilities drawn mainly from those included in Figure 6.2. To understand the nature of intelligence, therefore, we need a description of each of these abilities and examples of how it may be measured in intelligence tests. The following brief descriptions are numbered to correspond with the blocks in Figure 6.2.

1. *Perceptual speed and accuracy in verbal materials* (Pv). Since speed of mental operation is of importance in practical tasks involving perception, this ability is measured in terms of both accuracy and speed. Owing to the low relationship between speed of mental operation and accuracy without regard for speed, this ability is not closely related to others included in Figure 6.2 that do not involve speed.

Sample items:

Directions: If the two words on a line are spelled in exactly the same way, blacken the space under S; if they are different, blacken the space under D. Work as quickly as you can without making careless mistakes.

			S	D
1.	Benghazi	Benghazi	S	D
			::::	::::
2.	Andaman	Andanan	S	D
			::::	::::

2. *Perceptual speed and accuracy in numerical materials* (Pn). (See description of ability 1.)

Sample items:

Directions: If the two numbers on a line are exactly the same,

---

* M. W. Tate, "Individual Differences in Speed of Response in Mental Test Materials of Varying Levels of Difficulty," *Educational and Psychological Measurement*, VIII (1948), 353–374.

† P. R. Hofstaetter, "The Changing Composition of Intelligence: A Study of *t*-Technique," *Journal of Genetic Psychology*, LXXXV (1954), 159–164.

blacken the space under S; if they are different, blacken the space under D.   Work as quickly as you can without making careless mistakes.

1.	54928364	54923864	S ::::	D ::::
2.	79364291	79364291	S ::::	D ::::

3. *Perceptual speed and accuracy in spatial materials* (Ps).   (See description of ability 1.)
Sample item:*

> *Directions:*   The first object on each line is the model.   Blacken the answer space below each of the remaining objects on the line that is *not* exactly like the first one.

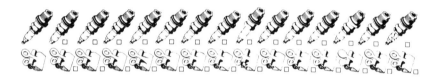

4. *Memory for verbal materials* (Mv).   By far the most important of the verbal-memory abilities is memory for meaningful materials over a long-term period.   Knowledge of word meanings is the key to this ability.
Sample item:

Odious most nearly means
A   hateful.
B   smelly.
C   apparent.
D   carefree
E   irreligious.

5. *Memory for numerical materials* (Mn).   As in the case of perceptual speed and accuracy, speed of mental operation is of importance in practical tasks involving numerical memory.   Therefore, scores on tests of the speed and accuracy with which basic numerical operations may be carried out tend to have little relationship to scores on tests that do not involve speed.
Sample item:

1. $97 - 2 + 3 + 8 - 5 =$	91 :::	98 :::	101 :::	105 :::	111 :::

* J. C. Flanagan, *Flanagan Aptitude Classification Tests* (Chicago: Science Research Associates, 1953), Test 1.   Reprinted by permission.

6. *Memory for spatial materials* (Ms).
Sample item:

Directions: I will show a card with a drawing on it. After 10 seconds, I shall take the card away. Then you should blacken the space on your answer sheet under the drawing that you saw.

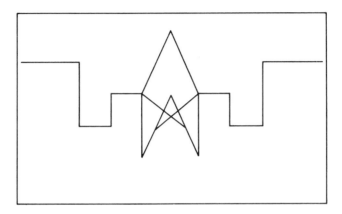

7. *Reasoning in verbal materials* (Rv).
Sample item:

Who is to *when* as *Mary* is to

A time.
B Jane.
C 8 P.M.
D person.
E girl.

8. *Reasoning in numerical materials* (Rn).
Sample item:

Directions: Read problem 1 to yourself as I read it aloud to you. Then find the correct answer to it.

1. A freight train made up of 60 cars is divided into 2 trains so that one of them will have 3 times as many cars in it as the other. How many cars will there be in the shorter train?

A 15
B 30
C 45
D Some other number
E We cannot find out from the information given.

9. *Reasoning in spatial materials* (Rs).
Sample item:

Directions: This is a test of your ability to recognize the relationships between figures. Look at the sample item below.

Notice the squares under the letters X and Y. Both are squares, but
the one under the letter Y is smaller than the one under the letter X.
The figure under the letter Z is a circle. The figure that goes with it in
the same way that figure Y goes with figure X is a small circle. This is
the figure under the letter B. Therefore, B is the correct answer to the
sample item. In each item in this part you are to locate the figure that
goes with Z in the same way that Y goes with X. Then blacken the
space on your separate answer sheet that has the same number and letter
as your choice.

10. *Ideational fluency in verbal materials* (Iv).
Sample item:

Directions: You will have 2 minutes to write on the lines below as
many words as you can that begin with the letter "s"—words like
"spook," "safe," or "shaft." Put one word on each line.

_____ _____ _____ _____ _____
_____ _____ _____ _____ _____

11. *Ideational fluency in numerical materials* (In).
Sample item:

Directions: Think of as many combinations of positive numbers
as you can that will make 32. For example, you might think of 16 + 16
or 2 × 16 or 15 + 15 + 2. You will have 2 minutes. Write each
combination on a separate line below.

16 + 16

2 × 16

15 + 15 + 2

12. *Ideational fluency in spatial materials* (Is).
Sample item:

Directions: You will have 2 minutes to write on the lines below as many objects as you can that have the same or almost the same shape as a baseball. The size does not matter. For example, you might begin with: basketball, soccer ball, ball bearing. Now you go on from there.

basketball _____ _____

soccer ball _____ _____

ball bearing _____ _____

13. *Visualization in verbal materials* (Vv).
Sample item:

Directions: On the line opposite each partially blotted word write what the word is.

1. _____ 1. _____
2. _____ 2. _____

14. *Visualization in numerical materials* (Vn)
Sample item:

Directions: On the line opposite each partially blotted number write what the number is.

A. _____ A. _____
B. _____ B. _____

15. *Visualization in spatial materials* (Vs). Sample item shown in Figure 6.3:

Directions: Imagine that you are the pilot of the delta-wing fighter aircraft headed away from the camera in the left-hand picture. How would the swept-wing aircraft look to you? Underline the space corresponding to the letter of the way it would look to you.

Although there is wide agreement among psychologists that general intelligence may be reasonably well defined as a weighted composite of the fifteen types of mental activities included in Figure 6.2, no common agreement on the amount of weight, or importance, to be given to each of them has been reached. This is primarily because no criterion measure of intelligence has been readily accepted to serve as a standard for comparison. In practice, most tests of general intelligence give greatest weight to reasoning abilities, to memory abilities (especially memory for word meanings and numerical computation), and to speed and accuracy of perception. Because

FIGURE 6.3

Sample Item for Visualization in Spatial Materials.

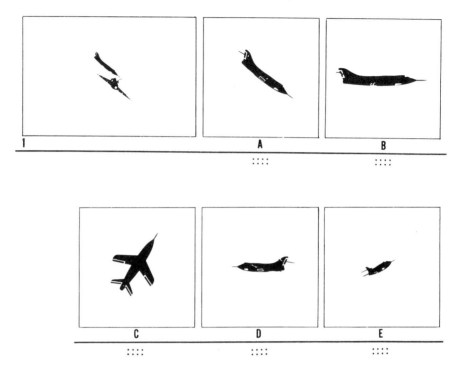

intelligence tests differ with respect to the abilities measured and the weights given to them, scores derived from these tests cannot usually be considered *equivalent*, as this term was defined on page 10. Their scores are, however, sometimes *comparable*, as the term was defined on page 10. It is this lack of equivalence of scores derived from different intelligence tests that accounts in part for the disparities sometimes noted in IQ scores of the same individual.

APTITUDE

Although there may be no objective way of determining how well scores in a given basic ability predict general intelligence, it is possible to determine objectively the relevance of any measurable basic ability or combination of basic abilities to a defined criterion variable. In this book, a basic ability or combination of basic abilities that is used to predict performance in a defined criterion variable is called an *aptitude*. Thus, a vocabulary test is a test of basic ability for remembering word meanings in a measure of general intelligence, but it is a test of scholastic aptitude if it is being used to predict performance in academic work. The difference between tests of basic ability and tests of aptitude is *not* one of content. It is one of function.

Suppose that a test is wanted to measure the scholastic aptitude of applicants for admission to the freshman class of a typical liberal-arts college. This test must be one that can be administered to these applicants during their senior year in high school to predict as accurately as possible their average marks in the freshman year at college. A test is given containing measures of ten of the fifteen basic activities included in Figure 6.2; a random selection of the applicants are admitted to the college without regard to their test scores; in June of their freshman year, the scores on each of the ten ability tests are correlated with the average marks of the students.

TABLE 6.1

Relationships of Scores on Certain Aptitude Tests Given at the Time of Admission to the Freshman Year at Yale University and Course Marks Obtained Four Months Later*

Predictive Validity Coefficients

Test	Basic Ability	English $N = 763$	History $N = 761$	Physics $N = 793$	Math. $N = 751$	Engin. Drawing $N = 763$
SAT Verbal Part	Mv	.52	.49	.33	.14	.05
Verbal Reasoning Test	Rv	.46	.46	.42	.20	.20
SAT Quantitative Part	Rn	.28	.39	.52	.36	.36
Quantitative Reasoning Test	Rn	.26	.36	.46	.39	.39
Spatial Visualization Test	Vs	.05	.07	.25	.59	.60
		$N = 410$	$N = 408$	$N = 439$	$N = 422$	$N = 409$
Mechanical Ingenuity	Rs, Vs	.12	.14	.33	.50	.50

* Based on data from A. B. Crawford and P. S. Burnham, "Educational Aptitude Testing in the Navy V-12 Program at Yale," *Psychological Bulletin*, XLII (1945), 301–309. These data also appear in Table 3.1.

In this way, an estimate can be made (by multiple-regression procedures that are beyond the scope of this book) of the weight to be given to the scores on each of the ten tests in order to obtain the combination of scores that will most accurately predict average grades in the freshman year. This result comes too late to be of any help in selecting members of the class already completing their freshman year, but in subsequent years the weighted composite scores can be used with every prospect of considerable success in selecting those applicants most likely to do well academically. In other words, the test is likely to have validity as a measure of scholastic aptitude.

In actual practice, it has been found that, if college marks in various subject-matter fields are used separately as criteria, the combinations of abilities of greatest value for predicting them are not the same. For example, the combination of ability scores of maximum utility for predicting course marks in languages (including English) and social studies is different from the combination of maximum utility for predicting marks in mathematics, science, and engineering. This point is illustrated by the data shown in Table 6.1. The predictive validity coefficients for the two verbal tests (the verbal part of the *Scholastic Aptitude Test* and a verbal reasoning test) are much higher for marks in English and history than for marks in physics, mathematics, or engineering drawing. The two numerical tests (the quantitative part of the *Scholastic Aptitude Test* and a quantitative reasoning test) have predictive validity coefficients that tend to be higher for course marks in physics, mathematics, and engineering drawing than for course marks in English. The two spatial tests (a spatial-visualization test and a mechanical-ingenuity test) display predictive validity coefficients that are considerably higher for marks in mathematics and engineering drawing than for marks in the other subjects.

NATIVE INTELLIGENCE OR NATIVE APTITUDE

An individual's *native intelligence* is sometimes defined as his innate or inborn capacity to adapt or to learn; this is conceived as being unaffected by his environment. Efforts to measure native intelligence have generally taken two forms: *First,* tests have been devised to measure an individual's learning ability or adaptive capacity in situations that are new to him, that he has never before experienced. To the extent that this can be done for all individuals tested, it is supposed that differences among these scores must be accounted for by differences in innate abilities rather than by differences in previous learning or environmental experiences.

Second, tests have been devised to measure the individual's learning ability or adaptive capacity in situations that are familiar to him. To the extent that this can be done for all individuals tested, it is supposed that their relative performances must be accounted for by innate abilities rather than by previous learning or environmental experiences. Since the latter would be the same or essentially the same for all individuals tested, they would not lead to differences in performance.

Unfortunately, neither method has been used very successfully for measuring intelligence unaffected by environmental influence. It is virtually impossible to devise test materials or problems that no examinee has dealt with. Even if this were possible and materials or problems were used that were completely novel at the time of publication of a test, it would not be long before some individuals who were scheduled to take the test would hear about them and practice with them. Likewise, it is difficult to find materials and problems that are about equally familiar to individuals with different cultural and ethnic backgrounds. For example, pictures and drawings have often been used as a basis for items in order to avoid the use of language, which obviously varies with cultural background. However, it has been found that the perception of pictures and drawings, especially those involving perspective in representing three dimensions, is also greatly influenced by cultural background and experiences. Thus, really satisfactory measures of innate intelligence are not available and will probably not become available. In practice, *all tests of intelligence measure a composite of functional abilities that represent a mixture of inborn capacities and acquired skills*. The student should note this point carefully. Intelligence-test scores (whether they are expressed as mental ages, intelligence quotients, percentiles, or in some other form) reflect the interaction of environmental influences and innate capacities. Even the most stimulating environmental circumstances cannot develop a high level of functional skills in an individual whose innate mental capacities are far below normal. Conversely, sparse environmental opportunities are often so completely exploited by individuals of outstanding innate mental capacities that they display functional abilities at exceptionally high levels. The exact relative contributions of innate capacities and environmental influences to the functional abilities of any one individual cannot be determined.

Efforts to measure native intelligence have been paralleled by efforts to measure *native*, or inborn, *aptitude*. These efforts have been equally unsuccessful, and for the same reasons. The fact that aptitude tests measure a mixture of inborn capacities and acquired skills rather than just the former does not seriously limit their value. In general, individuals with high native aptitude learn more than others from their environments and thus tend to obtain high scores on aptitude tests even though their environments vary considerably. Conversely, individuals with low native aptitude tend to learn less than others from their environments and thus tend to obtain low scores on aptitude tests despite fairly wide differences in their environments. Of course, the predictive accuracy of an aptitude test is poorest for individuals of high native ability who have had exceptionally barren or stultifying environments and for individuals of low native ability who have had exceptionally rich and stimulating environments.

THE MEANING AND USE OF INTELLIGENCE-TEST SCORES

In the early days of testing, scores derived from intelligence tests were expressed in terms of mental ages or intelligence quotients computed by dividing the examinee's mental age by his chronological age (up to about 16) and multiplying the resulting quotient by 100. To avoid a number of practical and theoretical problems involved in the use of such mental ages and IQ's, it now seems best to express intelligence-test and aptitude-test results as percentile ranks in carefully defined age or grade groups. To make it easy to transform IQ's derived from most tests into percentile ranks in the American population, Table 6.2 has been prepared. The table is entered in column 1 with IQ's derived from any test that yields IQ's having a standard deviation of approximately 16. Examples of such tests include Forms L and M (at most age levels) and Form L–M of the *Stanford-Binet Tests of Intelligence*, the *Lorge-Thorndike Intelligence Tests*, the *California Test of Mental Maturity*, and the *SRA Primary Mental Ability Tests*. Table 6.2 is entered in column 2 with IQ's derived from any test that yields IQ's having a standard deviation of approximately 15; the *Wechsler Adult Intelligence Scale* and the *Wechsler Intelligence Scale for Children* yield IQ's of this type. Percentile ranks are read from column 3 in Table 6.2. Naturally, an IQ of 100 corresponds to a percentile rank of 50 in the American population. IQ's higher than 135 and lower than 65 do not appear in the table because they represent performances in the highest and lowest one per cent, respectively, of the American population, and fractional parts of a percentile rank are not usually of practical consequence. In any case, most tests do not provide scores of sufficient accuracy to warrant such fine distinctions. It may be interesting to many students to note the percentages of the American population falling below various IQ scores. For example, in terms of Stanford-Binet IQ's, only about 3 per cent have IQ's below 70. About 90 per cent have IQ's below 120.

Table 6.3 provides descriptive terms for nine categories of IQ scores. These terms have been chosen because they convey to the nontechnical

TABLE 6.2

Percentile Ranks for IQ's in the American Population

COL. 1 Binet IQ ($s = 16$)	COL. 2 Wechsler IQ ($s = 15$)	COL. 3 Percentile Rank	COL. 1 Binet IQ ($s = 16$)	COL. 2 Wechsler IQ ($s = 15$)	COL. 3 Percentile Rank
135 and	133 and		99	99	47
above	above	99	98	98	45
134	132	98	97	97	42
133	131	98	95–96	96	39
132	130	98	94	95	37
131	129	97	93	94	34
130	128	97	92	93	32
129	127	96	91	92	30
128	126	96	90	91	27
127	125	95	89	90	25
126	124	95	88	89	23
124–125	123	94	87	88	21
123	122	93	86	87	19
122	121	92	85	86	18
121	120	91	84	85	16
120	119	90	83	84	14
119	118	88	82	83	13
118	117	87	81	82	12
117	116	86	80	81	10
116	115	84	79	80	9
115	114	82	78	79	8
114	113	81	77	78	7
113	112	79	75–76	77	6
112	111	77	74	76	5
111	110	75	73	75	5
110	109	73	72	74	4
109	108	70	71	73	4
108	107	68	70	72	3
107	106	66	69	71	3
106	105	63	68	70	2
104–105	104	61	67	69	2
103	103	58	66	68	2
102	102	55	65 and	67 and	1
101	101	53	below	below	
100	100	50			

person the degree of over-all brightness represented by scores in the nine categories. Teachers, counselors, and school psychologists will find these terms of value in communicating test results to parents and others. It is usually far more meaningful to a parent to hear that his child's scholastic-aptitude score is better than that of 73 per cent of children of his age and that he can be described as a bright boy than to hear that his child has an IQ of

TABLE 6.3

Classification of Intelligence Quotients

Descriptive Term	Binet IQ Range ($s = 16$)	Wechsler IQ Range ($s = 15$)	Approximate Percentage of American Population
Brilliant	139 and above	137 and above	.9
Very Superior	128–138	126–136	4.4
Superior	117–127	116–125	10.3
Bright	106–116	105–115	21.2
Normal	95–105	96–104	26.4
Dull	84–94	85–95	21.2
Inferior	73–83	75–84	10.3
Borderline Mentally Deficient	61–72	59–74	4.4
Mentally Deficient	60 and below	58 and below	.9

110.   Table 6.3 also indicates the approximate percentage of the American population that is found in each of the nine categories.

During World War II, the AGCT (*Army General Classification Test*) was used to measure the general mental ability of millions of Army draftees. The average AGCT scores of men in many occupational groups have been computed and provide interesting evidence of the way men tend to sort themselves into various jobs on the basis of their general mental ability. Table 6.4 shows the average AGCT scores of men in forty-eight occupational groups.   These groups were selected for Table 6.4 simply because each group included at least 100 men in a sample of 18,782 white enlisted men in the

TABLE 6.4

Average AGCT Scores and Estimated Average Binet IQ's of Draftees from Forty-Eight Occupations*

Occupation	No. of Men	Average AGCT	Estimated† Average IQ
Accountant	172	128	122
Chief Clerk	165	124	119
Teacher	256	123	118
Draftsman	153	122	118
Stenographer	147	121	117
Tabulating Machine Operator	140	120	116
Bookkeeper	272	120	116
General Clerk	496	118	114

TABLE 6.4 (*cont.*)

Occupation	No. of Men	Average AGCT	Estimated† Average IQ
Clerk-typist	468	117	114
Manager (Misc.)	235	116	113
Cashier	111	116	113
Radio Repairman	267	115	112
Printer; Pressman	132	115	112
Salesman	494	115	112
Manager (Retail Store)	420	114	111
Laboratory Assistant	128	113	110
Inspector	358	112	110
Stock Clerk	490	112	110
Receiving & Shipping Clerk	486	111	109
Musician	157	111	109
Machinist	456	110	108
Foreman	298	110	108
Airplane Mechanic	235	109	107
Sales Clerk	492	109	107
Electrician	289	109	107
Lathe Operator	172	108	106
Receiving & Shipping Checker	281	108	106
Sheet Metal Worker	498	108	106
Assembler	498	106	105
Mechanic	421	106	105
Machine Operator	486	105	104
Auto Serviceman	539	104	103
Riveter	239	104	103
Butcher	259	103	102
Plumber	128	103	102
Construction Carpenter	451	102	102
Welder	493	102	102
Auto Mechanic	466	101	101
Chauffeur	194	101	101
Tractor Driver	354	100	100
General Painter	440	98	98
Cook; Baker	436	97	98
Truck Driver	817	96	97
Laborer	856	96	97
Barber	103	95	96
Farmer	700	93	94
Farmhand	817	91	93
Miner	156	91	93

* T. W. Harrell and M. S. Harrell, "GCT Standard Scores of 18,782 AAF White Enlisted Men by Civilian Occupation," *Educational and Psychological Measurement*, V (1945), 229–239.

† IQ's having a standard deviation of 16 like those from Form L–M of the *Stanford-Binet Tests of Intelligence*.

Army Air Forces. For each group, the average Stanford-Binet IQ has been estimated. A glance at these estimates reveals marked differences in the average levels of general mental ability in the forty-eight occupational groups. The highest average IQ is 122 for accountants; the lowest is 93 for farmhands and miners. Although the averages do not reveal it, there is great variation among individuals in each occupational group, especially in the occupational groups having average IQ's below 100. The latter demand less formal education than the more specialized occupations in which the average IQ's are high. Consequently, individuals with wider ranges of mental ability are found in occupational groups characterized by low average IQ's.

It is a little risky to generalize from the samples of enlisted men in various civilian occupations to all American men in those occupations. For example, men whose AGCT scores were very low were not accepted in the Air Force. Therefore, it is likely that the average IQ's of all American men engaged in occupations near the end of the list in Table 6.4 are lower than the averages shown in the table for enlisted men who were in those occupations as civilians; conversely, some men in specialized occupations near the beginning of the list in Table 6.4 entered the armed forces as commissioned officers and did not take the AGCT. Consequently, it is likely that the average IQ's of all American men engaged in occupations near the beginning of the list are higher than those shown in the table.

Intelligence tests are often used for the following purposes:

1. Estimating the innate, or inborn, capacity of individuals.
2. Guiding the courts in deciding whether individuals should be judged feebleminded.
3. Grouping pupils in a given grade into somewhat homogeneous sections for instructional purposes.
4. Determining whether to admit students to a given course of study or to an educational institution.
5. As a more-or-less standardized interview during which an individual's mental and personality characteristics are subjectively evaluated by the examiner.

As noted earlier in this chapter, there is no conclusive evidence that intelligence tests provide satisfactory measures of innate abilities of practical significance without regard to environmental influences; therefore, it is best that they not be generally used for this purpose. They can, however, be properly included in an extensive case study of an individual. A study of this type includes data pertaining to the individual's medical and developmental history, his family background and relationships, his social and educational history, and his scores on several types of ability and achievement tests. With these kinds of data available, a skilled test interpreter can usually draw some valid inferences about the nature and level of his innate mental abilities. Usually, recommendations to a judge who is considering whether an individual is feebleminded or legally incompetent to manage his own affairs because of mental deficiency are based on intensive case studies. For the protection of individual rights they most certainly should be.

When pupils in a given grade are to be grouped for instructional purposes, intelligence-test scores are sometimes used. The justification for this practice is that these scores provide reasonably satisfactory predictions of pupil achievement; thus, pupils capable of learning with approximately the same degree of rapidity and effectiveness will be taught together. A glance at Table 6.1, however, indicates that the diverse mental abilities combined in most intelligence tests differ in the extent to which they predict performance in various kinds of subject matter. It is apparent that better prediction of pupil achievement in various subject-matter fields will ordinarily be obtained by using tests of different abilities to predict performance in different fields. In fact, it can be shown that the best predictor of performance in a given subject-matter field consists of scores on a properly constructed test of achievement in that field. For instance, the best predictor of achievement in seventh grade English is usually a test of achievement in sixth grade English; the best predictor of achievement in tenth grade geometry is likely to be a test of achievement in ninth grade algebra.

Given these facts, grouping should ordinarily be accomplished on the basis of achievement in the same subject or a closely related subject. When this is not possible, specialized aptitude-test scores should be employed. Only if none of these can be obtained are we justified in using intelligence-test scores for grouping. In such cases, the obtained scores or mental-age scores should be employed. Intelligence quotients should not ordinarily be used for grouping because they reflect the influence of chronological ages as well as of mental ages.

The factors affecting decisions about admitting a student to a given course of study are essentially the same as those affecting grouping for instructional purposes. In general, the same principles should be followed. Achievement tests or special-aptitude tests of appropriate types should be used to place the applicants for admission in rank order. The line of demarcation between those who are accepted and those who are rejected is usually determined by counting down from the top of the rank order to the number for which facilities are available. The more accurately the tests predict achievement in the course of study, the better the selection procedure will work.

When decisions about admitting students to an educational institution are made, the objective is usually to accept applicants most likely to obtain high average marks and to reject applicants least likely to do so. The marks entering into the averages are ordinarily those given in academic courses of widely divergent types, which means that they require the use of different kinds of basic mental abilities. An intelligence test that measures the usual assortment of verbal, memory, numerical, perceptual, and reasoning skills is likely to provide better prediction of average marks than of marks in any one subject-matter field. Thus, tests of general intelligence may often be used with success for selection of students by an educational institution. As in the case of grouping, the obtained scores or mental-age scores from intelligence tests should be used rather than IQ's expressed either as quotients or deviations.

A properly weighted combination of special-aptitude scores will usually predict average marks in a school or college better than intelligence-test scores. The data in Table 6.1 suggest, for example, that an engineering school would probably select students more effectively by arranging applicants in rank order on the basis of a combination of mechanical ingenuity, spatial visualization, and the SAT verbal and quantitative scores than on the basis of the two SAT scores alone. A liberal-arts college, on the other hand, might do better by using only the latter, which provide essentially a measure of general intelligence. In general, the more highly specialized a school's curriculum the less likely it is that intelligence-test scores will provide a close approximation to the best possible predictor of average academic performance.

The use of individually administered tests of intelligence such as the *Stanford-Binet Intelligence Tests*, the *Wechsler Adult Intelligence Scale* (WAIS), or the *Wechsler Intelligence Scale for Children* (WISC) as a sort of standardized interview is not new. Subjective observations of the examinee's thought processes, personality characteristics, and reactions to the examiner have always been valuable by-products of the examining process. The danger of making inaccurate inferences from these observations should, however, be kept clearly in mind. Efforts to determine the validity of inferences from diagnostic signs yielded by comparing part scores on the Wechsler tests of intelligence with the average of all part scores have, by and large, resulted in the conclusion that such signs have little value. Purely subjective impressions are probably of even less value. It is reasonable to suppose that standardized interviews especially designed to provide a basis for the observation of examinees' personality characteristics could be devised that would serve this purpose far better than individual tests of intelligence.

Consideration of several uses for tests of general intelligence leads to the conclusion that they are not well suited for grouping pupils for instruction, for selecting students for admission to designated courses of study, or for providing a basis for observation of personality characteristics. For selecting students likely to achieve high average grades in courses that require the use of a variety of mental abilities, intelligence tests are readily available and are serviceable measures, but a properly weighted combination of tests of achievement or basic skills is likely to prove more effective in the long run. For estimating innate ability or determining mental deficiency, intelligence tests have some value when they are skillfully used by clinical psychologists.

Our over-all conclusion is that tests of general intelligence are of very limited utility. Most of the uses to which they have been put can be better served by using properly constructed achievement tests or tests of more specialized basic abilities. With the advance of techniques of measurement in psychology and education, tests of general intelligence that yield single scores have become obsolete, but, like most things made obsolete by technological advance, they will disappear gradually.

Descriptions of Some Well-Known Intelligence Tests

Revised Stanford-Binet Intelligence Tests, Form L–M*

Ages: 2 to Adult.
Number of equivalent forms: 1.
Scores: Mental age and intelligence quotient.
Content: Items for Form L–M were chosen partly by the extent to which their scores are related to the total score on the test. Thus, mental ages and IQ's derived from the test are predominantly measures of general mental ability, as shown by McNemar for Forms L and M.† Inspection of the items and analyses of their interrelationships in these forms suggests that memory for word meanings and reasoning in verbal terms are the most important components of general mental ability. Memory for rote material, reasoning in numerical and in nonverbal but nonnumerical terms, and spatial visualization play smaller roles.

Interpretation of scores: Mental ages up to about 18 years and 0 months may be interpreted in the usual way as representative of the average performance of examinees at the corresponding chronological ages. Since mental growth appears to slow down markedly after about ages 12–13, the measurements of mental growth represented by a year's increase in mental age become smaller and smaller. After the age of approximately 18 the average American does not appreciably improve his performance on the kinds of skills tested by the *Stanford-Binet Intelligence Tests.* Hence, mental ages above 18 constitute artificial units that are needed to represent the performance of examinees who are above average in mental ability. The lack of uniformity of mental-age units and their artificiality above the level reached by average adults have been mentioned in chapter 2 as defects of all age scales.

* L. M. Terman and M. A. Merrill (Boston: Houghton Mifflin Co., 1960).
† Q. McNemar, *The Revision of the Stanford-Binet Scale* (Boston: Houghton Mifflin Co., 1942), chapter IX.

IQ's from Form L–M, like those from all other tests, are best interpreted in terms of percentile ranks in the American population; Table 6.2 makes this readily possible. An IQ of 120 on Form L–M corresponds to a percentile rank of 90. College students become accustomed to living and working with others whose IQ's are 110 or higher and sometimes forget that their companions are mostly drawn from the highest 25 per cent of the American population with respect to general mental ability. Table 6.3 shows that examinees with IQ's of 117 or higher fall in the top three categories of intelligence: superior, very superior, and brilliant. This table is convenient for translating numerical scores (like IQ's or percentile ranks) into descriptive terms understandable to parents and teachers.

Comments: The degree of accuracy of measurement represented by IQ's derived from Form L–M has not been specified by the authors except for their statement that it is at least as good as that for IQ's derived from Forms L and M of the 1937 Revision of the *Stanford-Binet Intelligence Scale.* These data are provided in Table 8.7. Their use is discussed in chapter 8.

The Pinneau Revised IQ Tables, provided in the manual for the third revision of the scale, constitute an important contribution in making readily available equivalent IQ's for examinees of all ages tested with Forms L, M, and L–M.* A somewhat similar table was prepared for the 1916 revision of the *Stanford-Binet Scale* in 1940.†

Wechsler Intelligence Scales‡

Ages: Adult Scale (WAIS): 16 and over.
 Children's Scale (WISC): 5–15.
Number of equivalent forms: Adult Scale: 1. Children's Scale: 1.
Scores: Verbal, Performance, and Full-Scale IQ's. Subtest Scaled Scores.
Content: Both the WAIS and the WISC include the following subtests.

Title of Subtest	Principal Mental Ability Measured
Verbal Score	
Information	Memory (for meaningful material)
Comprehension	Reasoning
Arithmetic	Reasoning

* L. M. Terman and M. A. Merrill, *Stanford-Binet Intelligence Scale,* Manual for the Third Revision, Form L–M (Boston: Houghton Mifflin Co., 1960), pp. 257 ff.

† F. B. Davis, "The Interpretation of IQ's Derived from the 1937 Revision of the Stanford-Binet Scales," *Journal of Applied Psychology,* XXIV (1940), table 3, 595–604.

‡ D. Wechsler, *Wechsler Adult Intelligence Scale* (New York: Psychological Corp., 1955). *Wechsler Intelligence Scale for Children* (New York: Psychological Corp., 1949). *Measurement and Appraisal of Adult Intelligence,* Fourth ed. (Baltimore: The Williams and Wilkins Co., 1958).

Similarities	Reasoning
Digit Span	Memory (for rote material)
Vocabulary	Memory (for word meanings)

Performance Score

Digit Symbol or Coding	Perceptual accuracy and speed
Picture Completion	Reasoning
Block Design	Perception and spatial visualization
Picture Arrangement	Reasoning
Object Assembly	Spatial visualization

In addition, the WISC includes an optional maze test that appears to measure principally spatial visualization.

Analysis of the interrelationships of the subtests suggests that they measure the following basic mental abilities: reasoning, memory, spatial visualization, and perceptual speed and accuracy. Cohen has shown that about half of the elements that determine Wechsler IQ's are attributable to a single general mental ability. He found that only about 14 per cent of what is measured by a typical subtest is unique to that subtest.* Differences among these subtest scores arise, therefore, as much from chance variation as from variations in mental skills and should be interpreted with great caution.

Interpretation of scores: The practical meaning of the IQ scores derived from the scales is probably best indicated by their percentile ranks, as shown in Table 6.2. The table should be entered in column 2. A functional classification of these IQ's is provided by Table 6.3.

Differences between verbal and performance IQ's that are smaller than 8 points for the WAIS or than 9 points for the WISC can occur fairly often by chance even though the true differences are zero. This is shown in Tables M.19 and M.20 in appendix M. Use of these is illustrated in chapter 8. When an examinee's verbal and performance IQ's differ by less than 8 points on the WAIS or less than 9 on the WISC, it is usually best to attach little importance to them and to use only his full-scale IQ. Differences among the scaled scores derived from the WAIS and the WISC should be interpreted only if there is considerable likelihood that they are not merely chance deviations from zero. The procedure for determining whether this is so is given in chapter 8 and is illustrated on page 205.

It has been suggested by Wechsler and others that an examinee's average scaled score on the subtests be computed and that each scaled score be compared with this average. He theorized that certain subtest scaled scores might be found consistently above average or below average for various types of mental disorders, such as brain injury and neurotic tendency. Thus far, no adequate evidence has been found to substantiate these theories. In any

* J. Cohen, "The Factorial Structure of the WAIS Between Early Adulthood and Old age," *Journal of Consulting Psychology*, XXI (1957), 283–290.

case, efforts to interpret patterns of deviations from the average scaled score of an examinee should take the possibility of chance deviations into account. The two right-hand columns of Tables M.19 and M.20 permit this to be done. The procedure is illustrated on pages 205 to 207.

Comments: The nature of the test items in the WAIS and the WISC and of the standardization group makes the full-scale IQ of value for estimating the relative general intelligence of examinees. Differences between verbal and performance IQ's may be interpreted cautiously if they are significant at the 15-per-cent level, or better. Interpretation of differences among subtest scaled scores should be made only by psychologists thoroughly familiar with the development and use of Tables M.19 and M.20, or other tables based on similar principles. Use of these differences to diagnose brain injury or personality disorders is not warranted on the basis of data accumulated up to this time.

*California Test of Mental Maturity (Long Form)**

Grades: Level 0: Kindergarten—Low 1.
Level 1: High 1–3.
Level 2: 4–6.
Level 3: 7–9.
Level 4: 9–12.
Level 5: 12 and above.

Number of equivalent forms: 1.

Scores: Percentile ranks, standard scores, and stanines for language, nonlanguage, and total-score IQ's and MA's. Percentile ranks, standard scores, and stanines for scores in:

1. Logical reasoning.
2. Spatial relationships.
3. Numerical reasoning.
4. Verbal concepts.
5. Memory.

Content: The language score is based on four subtests, as follows:

Title of subtest	*Principal mental ability measured*
Inference	Reasoning
Number Problems	Reasoning
Verbal Comprehension	Memory for word meanings
Delayed Recall	Memory for meaningful material

* E. T. Sullivan, W. W. Clark, and E. W. Tiegs, *California Test of Mental Maturity* (Monterey, Calif.: California Test Bureau, 1963).

The nonlanguage score is based on eight tests, as follows:

Title of test	Principal mental ability measured
Opposites	Reasoning
Similarities	Reasoning
Analogies	Reasoning
Rights and Lefts	Spatial visualization
Manipulation of Areas	Perceptual accuracy
Number Series	Reasoning
Numerical Values	Number facility (plus reasoning in following directions and layout)
Immediate Recall	Memory for rote material

With three exceptions, this categorization of the items agrees with that given by the test authors. The test titled "Manipulation of Areas" may measure accuracy of perception more than spatial visualization, and "Numerical Values" may measure number facility (accuracy of speed of computation) more than numerical reasoning, and "Verbal Comprehension" may measure memory for word meanings more than verbal comprehension, which implies the weaving together of word meanings to understand concepts.

Interpretation of scores: For most purposes, interpretations of IQ's and other scores from this test can best be made in terms of percentile ranks. These can be obtained conveniently by entering Table 6.2 in column 1.

Comparisons of the five ability scores can best be made in terms of standard scores by means of the technique described in chapter 8 on pages 201 to 204.

An Intellectual Status Index may be obtained corresponding to each IQ score. This is used to estimate the grade-equivalent scores that a given pupil should be expected to obtain on parts of the *California Achievement Test.* Comparison of this estimate with the grade-equivalent score actually obtained by the pupil on a part of the *California Achievement Test* provides a rough indication of whether he is underachieving, achieving up to expectancy, or overachieving. These comparisons must be interpreted with caution, as explained in chapter 11.

Comments: Although rate of work plays some part in determining scores on the *California Test of Mental Maturity,* it may be regarded essentially as a power test. The 1963 revision has corrected some of the faults of previous editions with respect to legibility of the drawings used in items and has increased the convenience of obtaining and interpreting the scores.

Kuhlmann-Anderson Intelligence Tests*

Grades: Kindergarten through 12.
Number of equivalent forms: 1.

* F. Kuhlmann and R. G. Anderson, *Kuhlmann-Anderson Intelligence Tests,* sixth ed. (Princeton, N.J.: Personnel Press, 1952).

Scores: Mental age and intelligence quotients.

Content: Thirty-nine subtests are used in covering the range from kindergarten through grade 12 in nine test booklets. A variety of types of items are employed. They appear to measure memory for word meanings, reasoning ability, numerical facility, perceptual speed and accuracy, and space conceptualization. The subtests are highly speeded.

Interpretation of scores: Mental-age scores are to be interpreted as indicating the levels of performance of examinees compared with the average of American children at each chronological age level included in the various groups. The variability of the IQ scores appears to change with age level; consequently, their meaning is not consistent from one age level to another.

Comments: The mixture of level of performance and speed of mental operation that determines scores derived from these tests and the variation in meaning of IQ scores from one age level to another make interpretation of scores difficult except for highly sophisticated users.

Kuhlmann-Anderson Test, Booklets G and H.*

Grades: Booklet G. 7–9. Booklet H. 10–12.

Number of equivalent forms: 1.

Scores: Beginning-of-the-grade percentile ranks for grades 7–12 for verbal, quantitative, and total scores.

Total-score IQ's and percentile ranks for these.

Content: The *Kuhlmann-Anderson Tests of Intelligence,* first published in 1927, have been revised several times. Booklets G and H, intended for use in grades 7 through 12, are the most recent revisions. The verbal score for Booklet G is based on four tests that may be described briefly as follows: (1) following verbal directions, (2) grouping words logically, (3) making sentences from words presented in scrambled order, and (4) arranging concepts in logical order. The verbal score for Booklet H is based on the first two of these four tests plus (3) verbal analogies and (4) word knowledge. It appears that the verbal scores measure principally general reasoning ability, word knowledge, and clerical accuracy.

The quantitative score in each of Booklets G and H is based on four tests that may be described briefly as follows: (1) number series, (2) arithmetic fundamentals, (3) simple equations, and (4) long division. Except for the number-series test, the quantitative tests are identical in Booklets G and H. It seems probable that the quantitative tests measure principally general-reasoning ability, clerical accuracy, and number facility.

Interpretation of scores: Verbal, quantitative, and total scores can best be interpreted in terms of their percentile ranks given in the *Norms Manual.*

---

* R. G. Anderson, *Kuhlmann-Anderson Tests,* Booklets G and H, seventh ed. (Princeton, N.J.: Personnel Press, 1960).

A pupil's percentile rank for any one of these three scores indicates how he compares, in the ability measured, with representative American school-children of the designated grade level, regardless of age.   On the other hand, a pupil's total-score IQ indicates how his level of general intelligence (as measured by the test) compares with that of representative American school-children of his own age, regardless of their grade level.   These total-score IQ's can be conveniently converted into percentile scores by means of Table 6.2.   This table should be entered in column 1.

Differences between verbal and quantitative obtained scores can be evaluated by using Table M.26 in appendix M.   Owing to the high correlation of these two sets of scores, only a small proportion of pupils will be found to have verbal and quantitative obtained scores that are sufficiently different to warrant the inference that there is a real difference between their verbal and quantitative abilities, as these are measured by Booklets G and H.

Comments: It is important to note that most pupils do not have a chance to try most of the items in the four parts of each booklet.   Thus, speed of performance greatly affects scores derived from these tests.   This was intended by the authors.   Teachers, counselors, or psychologists who wish to measure level of performance separately from speed of performance may find that this test does not meet their needs.   Since the test is highly speeded and scores are not corrected for chance, pupils who mark answers at random to all items they have not had time to read may thereby increase their scores considerably.

The Lorge-Thorndike Intelligence Tests*

Grades: Level 1: Kindergarten–1.
     Level 2: 2–3.
     Level 3: 4–6.
     Level 4: 7–9.
     Level 5: 10–12.
Number of equivalent forms: 2.
Scores: All levels: intelligence quotients.
     Levels 1–3: grade-equivalent and age-equivalent scores.
     Levels 4–5: percentile ranks by grade.
Content: Both verbal and nonverbal tests at all levels are intended to measure primarily the ability to work with ideas and to form relationships among ideas.   The nonverbal scores measure memory (for word meanings) by means of pictures at levels 1 and 2 plus reasoning ability by means of picture groupings.   They are, perhaps, more accurately described as non-reading, than as nonverbal, measures of mental ability.   At levels 3 to 5, the

* I. D. Lorge and R. L. Thorndike, *The Lorge-Thorndike Intelligence Tests* (Boston: Houghton Mifflin Co., 1954).

nonverbal scores measure reasoning ability through picture and figure groupings, figure analogies, and number-series items. The verbal scores at levels 3 to 5 appear to measure memory (for word meanings) and reasoning ability in both verbal and quantitative terms.

Interpretation of scores: Scores derived from the test are probably best interpreted as percentile ranks by grade for levels 4 and 5 and as IQ percentile ranks for all levels.   IQ percentiles may be obtained by entering Table 6.2 in column 1 and reading percentile ranks from column 3.   A difference between a pupil's percentile rank by grade and his IQ percentile rank is likely to occur if the pupil is either old or young for his grade placement.

Table M.25 (appendix M) has been prepared to facilitate the identification of differences between verbal and nonverbal IQ's that are worth interpreting.   It indicates that such differences must be at least 11, 13, or 12 points for IQ scores on levels 3, 4, and 5, respectively, to be significant at the 15 per-cent level.

Comments: The subtests in the *Lorge-Thorndike Test of Intelligence* are not markedly speeded.   The norms appear to be highly satisfactory. Finally, the content and the validity data provided in the manual offer assurance that the scores are useful for predicting academic performance in school and college.

THE MEANING AND USE OF APTITUDE-TEST SCORES

As stated earlier in this chapter, scores derived from any test of ability, achievement, interests, personality traits, or other properties of an individual become aptitude scores when they are used to predict performance in any defined criterion variable. Suppose, for example, that Harry Allen, a twelfth grade pupil, obtains a percentile rank of 93 in a representative sample of twelfth grade boys on a test of spatial visualization, indicating that he exhibits more of this ability than about 93 per cent of boys at his grade level. To predict Harry's performance in freshman courses in college, the correlation of the spatial-visualization scores with marks in certain courses must be known.   The test of ability in spatial visualization is likely to have different predictive validity coefficients for different courses.   As a matter of fact, this test of basic ability in spatial relations has been found to have a validity coefficient of .60 when it is used as an aptitude test to predict marks in typical college-freshman courses in engineering drawing and one of .05 when it is used to predict marks in typical college-freshman courses in English.   Since other ability and achievement tests have much higher predictive validity coefficients for marks in English, the spatial-relations test is never used as an aptitude test for English achievement.   If it were, scores derived from it would do very little better than chance in predicting Harry's performance in English.

For predicting the performance of an individual in any given criterion variable, an aptitude test with a predictive validity of zero is of no value. As the predictive validity coefficient is increased, the usefulness of the test also increases.   A reasonable question for the student to ask is "How high does a predictive validity coefficient have to be before any test should be used as an aptitude test?"   Unfortunately, there is no simple answer to this question.   In practice, the test or combination of tests that will yield the highest predictive validity coefficient is used as an aptitude measure until something better is available.   For most high-school and college courses, aptitude measures are available that have predictive validity coefficients between .50 and .70.   The middle of this range (.60) is reasonably representative of the validity coefficients of existing aptitude tests for predicting school and college marks.   A practical illustration of the accuracy attained in forecasting performance on a criterion variable from a predictor test having a correlation of .60 with that criterion is shown in Table 6.5.   If an examinee's score is in the top quarter on the test, we predict that he will be in the top quarter (of the same group or a similar group) with respect to performance on the criterion.   Out of every hundred examinees in the top quarter for whom we make this prediction, 54 will most likely be in the top quarter on the criterion.   This means that 46 of our predictions would be wrong.   Of these incorrect predictions, 28 would be in error by one quarter, 14 by two quarters, and 4 by three quarters.   The data in Table 6.5 also show the percentage of correct predictions that would be made for examinees in the second, third, and bottom quarters of the distribution of test scores that correlate .60 with the criterion.

Many teachers and counselors are dismayed to discover that aptitude tests of typical validity leave so much to be desired in accuracy of prediction. Certainly the data in Table 6.5 point to the need for continued research in the development of more effective aptitude tests, but it is better to make wise use of the imperfect measures now available than to rely on subjective judgments that ordinarily have far less predictive accuracy than the best tests.

In actual practice, the prediction of performance in freshman courses may be less clear-cut than it may at first seem to be.   For example, Harry's percentile rank in the spatial-visualization test was 93.   This put him in the top quarter of twelfth grade boys.   However, less than half of high school boys enter any kind of institution of higher learning the year following graduation.   The average spatial-visualization ability of those who do is somewhat higher than that of all twelfth grade boys.   Harry's classmates in engineering drawing are likely to be better in spatial visualization than college

TABLE 6.5

Accuracy of Prediction with Tests Having Predictive Validity Coefficients of .60 and of .40

Predictive Validity Coefficient	Quarter of Predictor Scores in Which Pupils Fall	Quarter of Criterion Scores in Which We Predict Pupils Will Fall	Percentage of Pupils in Each Quarter for Whom Prediction Is Most Likely to Be Correct	Percentage of Pupils in Each Quarter for Whom Prediction Is Most Likely to Be Incorrect by:		
				1 Qtr.	2 Qtrs.	3 Qtrs.
.60	Top	Top	54	28	14	4
	Second	Second	32	54	14	Not Possible
	Third	Third	32	54	14	Not Possible
	Bottom	Bottom	54	28	14	4
.40	Top	Top	43	28	19	10
	Second	Second	28	53	19	Not Possible
	Third	Third	28	53	19	Not Possible
	Bottom	Bottom	43	28	19	10

freshmen in general, especially if he enters a technical school or a college that is highly selective.   Under these circumstances, Harry's spatial-visualization score would correspond to a lower percentile rank among his classmates than among all twelfth grade boys.   If his rank among them is drastically lower than 93, he is likely to be in the second, third, or bottom quarter of the group in the work of the course.

It is clear from this example that prediction of a pupil's performance in academic work depends not only on the validity coefficient of the predictor test but also on differences between the distribution of the ability measured by the predictor test in the original group and in the group taking the course in which performance is to be predicted.

Prediction of vocational performance is even more complex and less accurate than prediction of educational performance, mainly because ratings of on-the-job performance are usually less meaningful and less accurate than instructors' ratings of course achievement.   Table 6.6 shows predictive validity coefficients for seven job-aptitude stanines derived from the *Flanagan Aptitude Classification Test.**

* J. C. Flanagan, *Technical Supplement, Flanagan Aptitude Classification Tests* (Chicago: Science Research Associates, 1953), table 5, p. 10.

TABLE 6.6

Predictive Validity Coefficients for Seven Job-Aptitude Stanines Derived from the *Flanagan Aptitude Classification Tests**

Job Stanine	Number of Examinees	Validity Coefficient†
Draftsman	15	.46
Electrician	33	.64
Mechanic	51	.54
Nurse	32	.29
Office Clerk	275	.30
Sales Person	170	.52
Structural Worker	45	.52

* L. Volkin, "A Validation Study of Selected Test Batteries Applied to Fields of Work," Ph.D. Dissertation, University of Pittsburgh, 1951.

† With predictor-test scores weighted equally in the computation of job-aptitude stanines and an interval of four years between the testing and the gathering of job-performance data.

The measure of job performance is reported to have been rate of salary increase adjusted according to whether increases resulted from seniority or special merit. The tests were given in the spring of 1947 while the individuals were twelfth grade pupils in Pittsburgh high schools and the measures of job success were obtained in 1951. For predictions of realistic criteria over the four-year period, the coefficients in Table 6.6 are surprisingly high. They must, of course, be interpreted cautiously because the number of workers for which ratings were obtained is small; for the two occupational groups (office clerk and sales person) for which large enough numbers of workers were available to provide reasonably stable data, the predictive validity coefficients were .30 (for office workers) and .52 (for sales persons). It is probable that with the addition of a few more predictor tests and the use of carefully determined weights in computing job-stanine scores, the *Flanagan Aptitude Tests* and others like them will be capable of providing predictions of on-the-job performance for many occupations that will be at least moderately useful to high school and college students and to the guidance workers and psychologists who counsel them.

What is now needed is an aptitude-test battery that has been administered to tens of thousands of high school pupils and that yields easily interpreted scores for which predictive validity coefficients for on-the-job performance in many common occupations are available. These data can be obtained only by actual follow-up studies of such scope that thousands of individuals

148   *Chapter Six*

tested several years previously in high school will have entered each occupation. Project TALENT, a research study conducted by the University of Pittsburgh under contract with the U.S. Office of Education, is now engaged in gathering this type of information.

Scores from most aptitude tests now available yield profiles of scores on their component parts. Figure 8.9 shows the scores of an eleventh grade girl plotted on the Individual Report Form for the *Differential Aptitude Tests.* Figure 8.11 shows the scores of a high school senior plotted on the Student Profile Chart used with the *School and College Ability Tests.* To interpret these profiles, the counselor must know the degree to which each test is predictive of performance in various courses of study and in many different occupations. He compares the pattern of scores of each individual with profiles of scores characteristic of others who have been successful in various courses of study or occupations. This can be a very time-consuming and tedious process. Consider, for example, the profile of a stanine score for Michael Breen, an eleventh grade pupil, on the parts of the *Flanagan Aptitude Classification Tests.* This is shown in Figure 6.4. His lowest

FIGURE 6.4

Aptitude-Test Profile for *Flanagan Aptitude Classification Tests.*

Name: Michael Breen   Age: 17–8   Grade: 11.8

Test No.	Test Name	Raw Score	Percentile for Grade 11.8	Stanine	Stanine 1 2 3 4 5 6 7 8 9
1	Inspection	59	85	7	
2	Mechanics	17	93	8	
3	Tables	42	45	5	
4	Reasoning	5	25	4	
5	Vocabulary	9	10	2	
6	Assembly	14	75	6	
7	Judgment and Comprehension	7	5	2	
8	Components	37	96	9	
9	Planning	18	23	4	
10	Arithmetic	47	53	5	
11	Ingenuity	9	20	3	
12	Scales	23	50	5	
13	Expression	23	5	2	
14	Precision	99	90	8	
15	Alertness	34	90	8	
16	Coordination	37	80	7	
17	Patterns	28	85	7	
18	Coding	93	24	4	
19	Memory	8	13	3	

stanines are in vocabulary, judgment and comprehension, and expression; his highest stanines are in components, mechanics, precision, and alertness. Since a score of 5 represents the average of eleventh grade pupils, it appears likely that Michael's aptitudes for academic work beyond the high school level are not good and that work requiring the sort of fine motor coordination measured by test 14 (precision), the spatial and mechanical abilities measured by tests 8 (components) and 2 (mechanics), and the practical judgment measured by test 15 (alertness) would be suitable for him.

Another type of profile, representing occupational stanines, is shown in Figure 6.5. In accordance with the instructions in the Student's Booklet for the *Flanagan Aptitude Classification Tests*, occupational aptitude

FIGURE 6.5

Occupational Aptitude Percentiles and Stanines with Suggested Minimum Levels.

Name: Michael Breen   Age: 17–8   Grade: 11.8

Occupational Group	Occupational Percentile	Stanine	Stanine* Those below Minimum for Each Occupation Are Shaded								
			1	2	3	4	5	6	7	8	9
College Student	8	2									
Mathematician	20	3									
Writer	12	3									
Bookkeeper	53	5									
Sales Clerk	53	5									
Airplane Pilot	80	7									
Construction Worker	65	6									
Draftsman	80	7									
Electrician	90	8									
Machinist	82	7									
Mechanic	82	7									
Plumber	86	7									
Policeman	51	5									
Printer	88	7									

* Stanines read from Table 3-4 in the Technical Report, *Flanagan Aptitude Classification Tests* (Chicago: Science Research Associates, 1959).

percentiles were computed for college performance and for several occupations that Michael's test scores suggest he might be suited for. In addition, his occupational aptitude percentiles were computed for several other occupations simply for illustrative purposes in this chapter.

Inspection of Figure 6.5 shows that Michael's aptitude for college work is low, considerably below the minimum suggested stanine level of 5 +. For the two groups listed next, Michael's aptitudes are also low. This would be expected since both of them actually presuppose college training or even graduate work.

The next two groups, bookkeepers and sales clerks, are in the business world. Michael's stanines, both of which are 5's, barely qualify him to consider bookkeeping but suggest that he might be reasonably successful as a sales clerk.

The remaining nine groups represent skilled trades or callings that Michael might well be interested in. His stanines, which range from 8 for electrician to 5 for policeman, are high enough to suggest that he has the requisite abilities to succeed in any one of them. The school counselor should discuss these occupations with him and his parents. Information about his previous school records, interests, and his ambitions should be combined with the data about his aptitudes to help him clarify his thinking about a choice of twelfth grade courses and of possible job openings after graduation from high school.

The interpretation of occupational percentiles and stanines of this type is obviously easier and more convenient for both the counselor and counselee than is the interpretation of profiles of aptitude scores believed related to academic success and on-the-job performance. The next major advance in vocational guidance almost certainly will consist of providing occupational stanines of well-established predictive validity and high reliability for all of the most common occupations. Similarly, the next major advance in educational guidance will be the provision of a coordinated series of scholastic-aptitude stanines capable of very accurate prediction of marks in all principal fields of specialization in secondary schools and colleges. At present, such scores are not available.

Descriptions of Some Well-Known Aptitude Tests

*Academic Promise Tests**

Grades: 6–9.

Number of equivalent forms: 2.

Scores: Percentile ranks in abstract reasoning, numerical ability, verbal ability, and language usage.

Percentile ranks in the following composites: abstract reasoning plus numerical ability, verbal ability plus language usage, total of all four scores.

Content: The abstract-reasoning test undoubtedly measures a basic reasoning ability, probably inductive reasoning. The numerical-ability test

* G. K. Bennett, *et al., Academic Promise Tests* (New York: Psychological Corp., 1962).

appears to measure a combination of speed and accuracy of numerical computation and reasoning ability. The sum of these two tests yields a composite score predominantly a measure of reasoning with nonverbal material and partly a measure of numerical facility.

The verbal-ability test appears to measure memory for word meanings and specific information as well as reasoning ability. The language-usage test measures specific learning of spelling, punctuation, and grammar. Learning of this type reflects principally memory ability, type and quality of teaching, and socio-economic status of the home. The combination of the verbal-ability and language-usage tests measures primarily memory for word meanings, reasoning ability, and specific information commonly taught in social studies and English classes.

The total of all four scores probably stresses reasoning ability (in verbal, quantitative, and spatial terms) and memory for word meanings. Numerical facility and specific information in social studies, English, and arithmetic appear to be measured to a smaller extent.

Interpretation of scores: A convenient profile chart has been provided on the Student Report Form for portraying each examinee's percentile ranks in graphic form. The chart has been designed in such a way that vertical distances between percentile ranks of a half inch or more identify differences regarded by the authors as large enough to warrant interpreting. (Technically, such differences are significant at about the 5-per-cent level, or better; this concept is explained in appendix I.) Vertical differences of three-eighths of an inch or more are significant at about the 15-per-cent level or better. The latter is the level of significance recommended in this book as appropriate for identifying differences among individual scores that are worth interpreting.

In general, the reliability of scores from the *Academic Promise Tests* is highly satisfactory. A great deal of data presented in the manual demonstrates that the scores possess useful predictive validity for marks in academic courses in grades 6–9.

Cooperative School and College Ability Tests

Grades: Level 1: 12, college freshmen and sophomores.
Level 2: 10, 11, 12.
Level 3: 8, 9, 10.
Level 4: 6, 7, 8.
Level 5: 4, 5, 6.
Number of equivalent forms:
Level 1: 2 for college freshmen and sophomores only.
2 for grade 12 and for college freshmen and sophomores.
Levels 2–5: 2.

Scores: Fall-semester percentile bands for grades 4 through the college sophomore level for verbal, quantitative, and total scores.

Content: The *School and College Ability Tests* were designed to estimate the capacity of students to benefit from additional schooling. The verbal score is based on two tests: (1) understanding single sentences; and (2) word knowledge. The quantitative score is also based on two tests: (1) performing numerical computations rapidly and accurately; and (2) solving arithmetic problems. The principal mental abilities represented by the verbal score seem to be memory for word meanings and reasoning ability and by the quantitative score to be numerical facility and reasoning ability.

Interpretation of scores: The verbal, quantitative, and total raw scores are immediately transformed into converted scores. These have no useful intrinsic meaning, but verbal converted scores from levels 1 through 5 are equivalent scores, as these are defined in chapter 2. Similarly, all quantitative scores and all total scores are equivalent. However, the verbal, quantitative, and total converted scores are not comparable, as such scores are defined in chapter 2. Comparisons of these three scores must be made in terms of percentile bands. The latter replace percentile ranks for reporting SCAT scores. The test user has merely to look up an examinee's converted score in the tables of grade norms to obtain the corresponding percentile band. Each band was obtained by laying off one standard error of measurement on both sides of a converted score and taking the two percentile ranks thus defined as the ends of the band. For every hundred percentile bands thus determined, about 68 will include the true percentile ranks of the examinees. When an examinee's verbal and quantitative percentile bands are plotted on the Student Profile Chart, as shown for one pupil in Figure 8.11, lack of overlapping of the bands provides reasonable assurance that the difference between his verbal and quantitative true scores is not zero.*

It is a moot question whether it is more helpful to report scores in terms of percentile bands than in terms of percentile ranks with some convenient indication of the size of the confidence interval. However, the use of percentile bands permits an easy graphic method to be employed for identifying differences among scores that are worthy of attention, and it also emphasizes the degree of inaccuracy of the scores.

The norms provided for SCAT scores seem to have been exceptionally well established by careful sampling procedures.

Comments: Scores from SCAT provide useful prediction of the performance of examinees in later schooling. In grades 9 and 11, the average correlations of SCAT verbal scores with English grades, of quantitative scores

---

* Differences that lead to nonoverlapping percentile bands are significant at about the 16-per-cent level, or better.

with mathematics grades, and SCAT total scores with grades in social studies and in science are about .50 to .55.   In grade 7, such correlations run as high as .65 to .70.

The four parts of SCAT are separately timed and vary somewhat in the extent to which they are speeded.   The tests on which the quantitative score is based are more closely timed than those on which the verbal score is based.   Scores from SCAT must be regarded as measuring a combination of speed and level of performance.

The Differential Aptitude Tests*

Grades: 8–12.

Number of equivalent forms: 2.

Scores: Percentile scores for boys and girls separately in grades 8 through 12.

Content: Eight subtests comprise the *Differential Aptitude Tests*.   Their titles and the basic mental abilities that they appear largely to measure are as follows:

Title	Probable mental ability measured
Verbal Reasoning	Memory (for word meanings)
	Reasoning ability
Numerical Ability	Number facility
	Reasoning (in numerical terms)
Abstract Reasoning	Reasoning ability
Space Relations	Space conceptualization
	Reasoning ability
Mechanical Reasoning	Space conceptualization
	Reasoning ability
Clerical Speed and Accuracy	Perceptual facility
Language Usage I and II	Memory (for specific learnings)

Interpretation of scores: Percentile ranks for examinees on each of the eight subtests and on a combination of the verbal-reasoning and numerical-ability subtests show the relative standing of the examinees among American schoolchildren in grades 8 through 12.   The manual includes a very large amount of information with respect to the predictive validity of these scores for school marks and for achievement-test scores in many subject-matter fields.

Differences among an examinee's percentile ranks on the eight subtests in the *Differential Aptitude Tests* can be evaluated by converting the percentile ranks into standard scores by means of Table D.5 (appendix D) and using Table M.22 (appendix M) to determine which differences are large enough to warrant interpretation.   Since there are eight subtests, we can obtain

* G. K. Bennett, H. G. Seashore, and A. G. Wesman, *The Differential Aptitude Tests* (New York: Psychological Corp., 1963).

twenty-eight differences among them.   To make the differences in an examinee's profile of scores worth interpreting, at least five should be significant at
the 15-per-cent level.   Whether this is true for any examinee is easily
established by comparing the differences among his standard scores with
corresponding entries in Table M.22.   An approximation to the same result
can be obtained by identifying points plotted on the Individual Report Form
shown in Figure 8.9 that are more than five-eighths of an inch apart in a
vertical direction.

Comments: Although the basic mental abilities that largely determine
general intelligence are mixed together to a considerable degree in most of the
eight subtests, useful insights into an individual's strengths and weaknesses,
if any exist, may be obtained from the *Differential Aptitude Tests.*   When
significant differences on an Individual Report Form have been identified,
the profile may be compared with examples in the casebook prepared to aid
in the interpretation of scores.*

Flanagan Aptitude Classification Tests† (FACT)

Grade or age groups: Grade 12 and above.   Age 17 and above.
Number of equivalent forms: 1.
Scores: Percentile ranks and stanines for grades 9–12 on nineteen tests.
Content: The purpose of the nineteen tests in this battery is to measure
in a context of practical tasks a number of basic mental abilities.   Table 6.7
shows how they may be grouped.   Of the basic mental abilities described
earlier in this chapter, only ideational fluency does not appear to be strongly
represented in the nineteen tests.

Interpretation of scores: Although stanines are provided for the nineteen tests based on the performance of pupils in grades 9 through 12,
occupational aptitude scores for thirty-seven types of careers are the most
important outcome of the FACT battery.   For example, the mental abilities
in tests 3, 5, 13, and 19 (identified by name in Table 6.7) are included in the
occupational aptitude score for the position of secretary.   The median
percentile rank of an examinee on these four tests is used as his occupational
aptitude score.   If this is lower than 45, the examinee is not advised to
consider the occupation as a serious possibility.   Some evidence that
occupational aptitude scores are positively correlated with rate of salary
increase in seven types of jobs has been provided by Volkin.‡   Additional

---

* G. K. Bennett, H. G. Seashore, and A. G. Wesman, *Counseling From
Profiles—A Casebook for the Differential Aptitude Tests* (New York: Psycho-
logical Corp., 1951).
† J. C. Flanagan, *Flanagan Aptitude Classification Tests* (Chicago: Science
Research Associates, 1957).
‡ L. Volkin, "A Validation Study of Selected Test Batteries Applied to
Fields of Work," Ph.D. dissertation, University of Pittsburgh, 1951.

TABLE 6.7

Basic Mental Abilities That Appear to Be Measured
by the *Flanagan Classification Tests*

Test	Principal Mental Abilities Measured*
1. Inspection	P
2. Mechanics	Sp, R
3. Tables	P, R
4. Reasoning	R
5. Vocabulary	M
6. Assembly	V, Sp
7. Judgment & Comprehension	R, M
8. Components	P
9. Planning	R
10. Arithmetic	N
11. Ingenuity	I
12. Scales	P, R
13. Expression	M, R
14. Precision	Se
15. Alertness	R, M
16. Coordination	Se
17. Patterns	Sp
18. Coding	M, P
19. Memory	M

* I = Ideational fluency   Se = Sensory-motor
  M = Memory   response
  N = Numerical facility   Sp = Spatial conceptualiza-
  P = Perception   tion
  R = Reasoning   V = Visualization

information about the validity of occupational aptitude scores for predicting on-the-job performance five years after testing is included in the *Technical Report* accompanying the *Flanagan Aptitude Classification Tests.** While the data are mildly encouraging, a great deal more data is needed to establish with even a reasonable degree of assurance the predictive validity of occupational aptitude scores. The author and publisher would be the first to insist on this.

The reliability coefficients of the scores on the nineteen parts of the FACT battery vary considerably. They range among twelfth grade pupils from .61 to .91. Their combinations that make up the occupational aptitude scores tend to be considerably more reliable. The reliability coefficients of a representative set of nine occupational aptitude scores among twelfth grade pupils vary from .84 (for plumber) to .93 (for chemist, engineer, and lawyer).

* (Chicago: Science Research Associates, 1959), chapter 6.

Comments: This battery of tests breaks away from the traditional presentation of comparable scores in several basic mental abilities and provides comparable stanines intended to be predictive of actual performance in many types of jobs. This is a development that has long been overdue. It is to be hoped that adequate norms and evidence of predictive validity for the occupational aptitude scores will be forthcoming in due course. Meantime, experimentally minded psychologists and guidance counselors may want to become familiar with these test materials.

*SRA Primary Mental Abilities Tests.**

Ages: 5–7; 7–11; 11–17.

Number of equivalent forms: 1.

Content: The test for ages 5 to 7 includes subtests that appear to measure memory (for word meanings), perceptual speed and accuracy, number facility, sensory-motor facility, and space conceptualization. The types of items used seem to measure simultaneously two or more of these basic mental abilities. Some numerical items measure memory for word meanings and many of the space items seem to require a good deal of perceptual accuracy. The intercorrelations of the scores support these subjective impressions.

The PMA test for ages 7 to 11 includes subtests that appear to measure memory (for word meanings), space conceptualization, reasoning ability, perceptual speed and accuracy, and number facility. In the test designed for ages 11 to 17, the perceptual subtest has been omitted and an optional word-fluency subtest has been included.

Interpretation of scores: In general, the PMA tests are given with time limits so short that many examinees do not have time to try every item. This fact must be remembered when the scores are interpreted.

The quotient scores for the subtests and for the total test can best be interpreted as percentile ranks obtained by entering Table 6.2 in column 1 with the quotients and reading the percentile ranks from column 3. Broadly speaking, the quotient scores yield percentile ranks that have about as satisfactory reliability and predictive validity for academic performance as those provided by other tests of mental ability. The fact that the subtests are rather highly speeded but are not all scored with correction for chance success means that examinees who are sophisticated enough to mark answers to items they have not had time to consider in the time limit may greatly increase their scores.

Differences among mental-age or quotient scores for subtests must be interpreted with great caution since large differences can occur by chance

* *SRA Primary Mental Abilities Tests* (Chicago: Science Research Associates, 1953–1958).

when the true difference is zero. Unfortunately, the data needed to prepare tables of differences significant at the 15-per-cent level (or some other level) are not available.

Comments: The chief value of a set of tests measuring several basic mental abilities lies in assessing separately an individual's level of performance in each of these abilities. Some psychologists and counselors have expressed doubt that subtest scores derived from PMA tests measure reasonably close approximations to the mental factors of the same names originally identified by Thurstone.* Even if they are close approximations, it is impossible with data now available to interpret with confidence differences among subtest scores derived from these tests. It seems likely, therefore, that the PMA tests are principally useful for providing a total mental age or quotient score measuring a mixture of rate of mental operation and level of general mental ability.

Summary

Human beings differ greatly in general intelligence, which is a combination of mental skills that display themselves in the ease and accuracy with which an individual perceives facts and ideas, recalls them, draws inferences and conclusions from them, and, finally, benefits through learning and understanding them.

These mental skills are positively correlated in varying degree. They form clusters in which the member skills are more closely related to one another than they are to the skills in any other cluster. Most of the skills involved in intellectual activity group themselves into five clusters, which may be called Perception, Memory, Reasoning, Ideational Fluency, and Visualization. Each cluster functions in three fields: the verbal, the numerical, and the spatial. For example, memory for word meanings plays a big part in determining an individual's recognition vocabulary; memory for number combinations underlies his numerical facility. The cluster that we have called Ideational Fluency includes most of the skills that are now designated by some investigators as components of Creativity.

The fifteen groups of skills formed by the functioning of each of the five clusters in each of the three fields do not include all mental traits. There is evidence, for instance, that speed of mental operation is to a large extent independent of most of these groups.

Psychologists generally agree that the level of mental skill displayed by an individual is a product of innate capacity and environmental stimulation. All existing intelligence tests measure a composite of functional abilities that are indissoluble mixtures of inborn potentialities and acquired skills and

* L. L. Thurstone, "Primary Mental Abilities," *Psychometric Monograph No. 1* (Chicago: University of Chicago Press, 1938).

attitudes. The relative contribution of "nature" and "nurture" to the abilities of any one individual cannot be exactly determined.

Scores from intelligence tests are best reported as percentile ranks in defined groups. Table 6.2 provides a means of estimating percentile ranks in the U.S. population corresponding to the IQ's derived from most intelligence tests. Consideration of the ways in which general-intelligence tests are commonly used leads to the conclusion that their value is limited. With the advances in techniques of measurement in psychology and education, tests of general intelligence that yield a single score have become obsolete.

Scores derived from any test of ability, achievement, interests, personality traits, or other property of an individual become measures of aptitude when they are used to predict performance in any criterion variable. In other words, to describe a test as an "aptitude test" defines its use—not its content. The utility of any aptitude test is, therefore, indicated by its predictive validity coefficients; and it can have as many of these coefficients as there are variables to serve as criteria.

No minimum figure for predictive validity coefficients can be set as that above which a test has value as an aptitude measure. Performance in high-school and college courses can ordinarily be predicted with the accuracy represented by coefficients of .60 to .70. Predicting performance in most occupations is more difficult; coefficients of .30 to .50 are considered good for time spans up to two years. Intensive research is needed to improve accuracy in the prediction of occupational success.

Selected References

Anastasi, Anne, "Heredity, Environment, and the Question 'How?'" *Psychological Review*, LXV (1958), 197–208.

Bayley, Nancy, "On the Growth of Intelligence," *American Psychologist*, X (1955), 805–818.

Bloom, Benjamin S., *The Use of Academic Prediction Scales for Counseling and Selecting College Entrants.* New York: The Free Press of Glencoe, Inc., 1961.

French, John W., and Robert E. Dear, "Effect of Coaching on an Aptitude Test," *Educational and Psychological Measurements*, XIX (1959), 319–330.

Guilford, Joy P., "The Structure of Intellect," *Psychological Bulletin*, LIII (1956), 267–293.

Guilford, Joy P., "Three Faces of Intellect," *American Psychologist*, XIV (1959), 468–479.

Kelley, H. Paul, "Memory Abilities: A Factor Analysis," *Psychometric Monograph No. 11.* Richmond, Va.: Psychometric Corporation, 1964. Chapter 5.

Littell, William M., "The Wechsler Intelligence Scale for Children: Review of a Decade of Research," *Psychological Bulletin*, LVII (1960), 132–156.

MacKinnon, Donald W., "The Nature and Nurture of Creative Talent," *American Psychologist*, XVII (1962), 484–495.

MacKinnon, Donald W., "What Makes a Person Creative?" *Saturday Review*, XLV (February 10, 1962), 15–17, 69.

Noll, Victor H., "Relation of Scores on Davis-Eells Games to Socio-Economic Status, Intelligence-Test Results, and School Achievement," *Educational and Psychological Measurement*, XX (1960), 119–129.

Thurstone, Louis L., "Primary Mental Abilities and Their Psychological Implications," in W. Leslie Barnette, Jr., ed., *Readings in Educational and Psychological Measurements*. Homewood, Ill.: Dorsey Press, 1963.

United States Department of Labor, *Guide to the Use of the General Aptitude Test Battery:* Section III, "Development." Washington: Government Printing Office, 1958.

Chapter Seven

MEASUREMENT
OF INTERESTS

An individual's performance both in and out of school is determined by many factors. Prominent among these are his achievement, his basic abilities, his interests, and his character and personality traits, such as industriousness and perseverance. The measurement of achievement was discussed in chapter 5 and that of basic abilities in chapter 6. In this chapter, the measurement of interests will be considered. The measurement of character and personality traits is not covered in this book; this material is omitted largely because practical tests of these traits that have satisfactory validity and reliability are not available. Hence, the use of character and personality tests should at present be confined to research studies conducted or supervised by psychologists thoroughly grounded in psychometric methods.

TECHNIQUES FOR MEASURING INTERESTS

In measuring an individual's interests, we are trying to determine the strength of his tendencies to take part in various kinds of activities. Three techniques for making this determination suggest themselves:

1. Obtain information about the activities to which he has devoted a good deal of time over the past few years. Since people tend to spend their time on things that interest them, information of this sort should delineate pretty well an individual's interests.
2. Find out how much knowledge he has in many fields of interest. Although the total amount of information in all fields that any individual possesses is closely related to his level of general mental ability, the pattern of his knowledge in various fields is likely to be indicative of his interests. This results from the fact that we tend to remember material that interests us and to forget material that doesn't.

3. Ask him to express his preferences and his likes and dislikes among many activities involved in a variety of fields of interest.

Information obtained by means of these three techniques can be combined and expressed in such a way as to reveal an individual's interests. More detailed descriptions of the techniques follow.

Biographical Data Blanks

Description. To find out about an individual's background and activities, biographical data blanks are often used. The individual answers questions about his date and place of birth, the type of community in which he grew up, participation in games, sports, activities at school, and so forth. Many other questions about his home, his parents, and his hobbies are also included in these blanks. Two guiding principles in choosing questions are: (1) that they deal with objectively verifiable events and facts rather than subjective preferences or expressions of interest; and (2) that they be relevant to some criterion variable or variables.

In answering questionnaires, examinees may not respond truthfully if they believe that it is to their advantage to lie and if there is no way of proving that they have done so. This is the Achilles heel of questionnaires. They may be highly useful when they are administered to examinees who have no reason to fake answers that they think will put them in a favorable light. Properly used in research studies or in counseling, questionnaires can be the most efficient method of gathering a great deal of data with minimum time and expense. Under these circumstances, the examinees realize that there is no purpose to be served by faking their responses. However, when questionnaires are used for practical purposes in selection of personnel for employment or for admission to schools and colleges, many examinees will deliberately fake responses in the way that they think will be most favorable to them.

If the questions in a biographical data blank call for factual answers, the accuracy of which can be verified by an investigator who has the necessary time and facilities, faking can be held to a minimum by warning the examinees that their responses can be verified and that some of them will be. In this situation, examinees who most want to make a good impression are the most reluctant to fake responses because they realize that if they are caught doing so they will have created the worst possible impression. Thus, biographical data blanks are usually subject to less faking of responses than are other kinds of questionnaires, especially those purporting to measure personality traits.

Scoring. The scoring of items in biographical data blanks, like that of items in most questionnaires, is usually accomplished by assigning a weight to each choice and adding the weights attached to the choices marked by an individual to get his total score. The weights may be assigned by any one of several methods. Suppose, for example, that a biographical data blank containing the sample item shown in Table 7.1 was administered to 1,000 ninth grade boys. Suppose that 500 of these boys entered a commercial course and 500 entered a mechanics-machinists course in junior college. The teachers' marks given to each of these boys during their junior college training can be used to compute an average mark for each of them. Now the 500 boys in the commercial course should be arranged in rank order by average mark. Next, count down from the top through the 135th boy. This group of 135 boys, consisting of the top-ranking 27 per cent of the entire 500, may be called the "high-commercial-marks" group, or the HCM group. The 135 boys who obtained the lowest marks may be called the "low-commercial-marks" group, or the LCM group. The same procedure should be followed to select the "high-mechanics-marks" (the HMM) group and the "low-mechanics-marks" (the LMM) group.

The next step is to examine the responses of each group to each bio-graphical-data-blank item. The percentage of pupils in each group who marked each choice of the sample item is shown in Table 7.1. The

TABLE 7.1

Choice Weights for a Sample Biographical Data Blank Item*

	Commercial Course			Mechanical Course		
	Per cent in HCM	Per cent in LCM	Scoring Weight	Per cent in HMM	Per cent in LMM	Scoring Weight
How many times have you taken the head off an engine of any kind to repair or clean it?						
A Never	25	35	−1	5	20	−4
B Once or twice	50	45	0	20	45	−3
C Three to ten times	20	15	1	50	30	2
D More than ten times	5	5	0	25	5	6
	100	100		100	100	

* The item and the data have been prepared for illustrative purposes only.

percentages for the HCM and LCM groups and for the HMM and LMM groups are then used to enter a specially prepared table in which the scoring weights shown in Table 7.1 are found.* Weights obtained in this way will

* F. B. Davis, "The Estimation and Use of Scoring Weights for Each Choice in Multiple-Choice Test Items," *Educational and Psychological Measurement*, XIX (1959), 291–298.

tend to maximize the predictive validity of scores for the criterion variable used to establish the weights.

The choice-by-choice scoring weights for the sample item show that no matter how an examinee responds, this item can have little influence on total scores used to predict teachers' marks in the commercial course. It contributes considerably more to the prediction of marks in the mechanics-machinists course. In general, the more often a boy reports he has taken the head off an engine to repair or clean it, the higher his score on this item. Notice that boys who obtained high marks in the mechanics-machinists course tended to have worked on engines more often than boys who obtained low marks in this course.

Uses. Biographical data blanks made up of 50 to 100 items covering a wide variety of activities of appropriate types are often highly effective in measuring interests associated with performance in courses of study and in occupations. For example, a Pilot Biographical Data Blank used by the U.S. Army Air Forces during World War II had a validity coefficient of .33 for predicting graduation or elimination from complete pilot training in a sample of 1,275 essentially self-selected applicants for this training.

The *Student Information Blank* used by Project TALENT includes 394 questions, most of which are of the biographical-data-blank type. This was administered to about 440,000 secondary school pupils in the spring of 1960. The questions deal with the pupils' personal experiences, their families and homes, and their plans for the future. Two sample questions about personal experiences follow:

> During the school year, about how many hours a week do you work for pay?
>
> A None
> B About 1–5 hours
> C About 6–10 hours
> D About 11–15 hours
> E About 16–20 hours
> F More than 20 hours
>
> How many times have you been president of a class, a club, or other organization during the last three years?
>
> A None
> B Once
> C Twice
> D Three times
> E Four times
> F Five times, or more

Two questions of the type used to obtain data about the family and home follow:

What was the last grade in school *completed* by your father?
A 1–3
B 4–6
C 7–9
D 10–12
E College years 1–4
F He took graduate work after completing college.

How many books are there in your home?
A None, or very few (0–10)
B A few (11–25)
C One bookcase full (26–100)
D Two bookcases full (101–250)
E Three or four bookcases full (250–500)
F A room full—a library (501, or more)

Biographical data blanks can be constructed in such a way as to yield scores bearing satisfactory predictive validity for many practical criteria, such as performance in courses of study and in occupations. They do this presumably because they measure combinations of interests, abilities, experiences, and personality traits that are relevant to performance in these criterion variables. For example, a blank of practical value to guidance counselors and school psychologists might be constructed by choosing the 100 most useful questions in the Project TALENT *Student Information Blank*.

Differential Interests Tests

Description. During the 1930s, the Cooperative Test Service began publication of annual contemporary-affairs tests that included sections measuring political events, social and economic events, science and medicine, literature, fine arts, and amusements. Norms were provided separately for students from grade 9 to the college-sophomore level. It soon became apparent that the variations in any individual's relative standings from one section to another reflected his interests. This is a reasonable expectation, as pointed out earlier, because people tend to remember what they find interesting and to forget what they find dull.

The measurement of interests in this way has an advantage over questionnaire techniques in that it is not easy to fake responses in such a way as to make a favorable impression. An individual can try to make his score lower in one field of interest than in another only by deliberately responding to items in one field incorrectly or omitting some or all of them. In doing so, he lowers his total score on all fields combined and cannot be sure how well he is doing in the field in which he wants his score to be high. Experience has shown that faking interests tests of this type is less common and less effective than faking questionnaires.

Scoring. Scoring of differential interests tests can best be done by expressing all part scores and the total score in terms of a set of normalized standard scores and reporting an individual's scores on each part as a deviation from his total score. Positive deviations indicate areas that are of greater-than-average interest to the individual, and negative deviations indicate areas that are of less-than-average interest to him. Whether these deviation scores are significantly different (at some designated level of confidence) from one another can be determined if the standard errors of measurement of the part scores are known.

Project TALENT Information Tests. In the spring of 1960, a *Student Information Test* that yields forty separate scores for each individual was included in the Project TALENT tests given to about 440,000 secondary school pupils. These forty sets of scores have been expressed in comparable standard scores, and separate norms have been established for each set. The following items illustrate the types that were used:

Literature.
Which of these was a knight of King Arthur's Round Table?
A Alfred
B Lancelot
C Merlin
D Ivanhoe
E Roland

Physical science.
Ozone is a form of
A electricity.
B air.
C oxygen.
D nitrogen.
E carbon dioxide.

Music.
Who wrote "Peter and the Wolf"?
A Prokofiev
B Bach
C Tchaikovsky
D Dukas
E Mozart

Table 7.2 shows the average standard scores in ten areas of information that were obtained by four groups of twelfth grade pupils who, a year after their graduation, had entered college and were majoring in English and literature or in engineering or who had gone to work as mechanics or secretaries.

TABLE 7.2

Information Scores and Ten Relative Interests Scores of Groups of High School Seniors Who Entered Courses of Study or Occupations Listed in Year after Their Graduation*

	Majoring in				Working as			
	English and Literature (N = 1,056)		Engineering (N = 1,729)		Mechanic (N = 263)		Secretary (N = 3,728)	
Area of Information	Information Score	Interest Deviation Score	Information Score	Interest Deviation Score	Information Score	Interest Deviation Score	Information Score	Interest Deviation Score
Vocabulary	58	2	59	1	51	0	48	0
Literature	61	5	59	−1	47	−4	50	2
Music	59	3	54	−4	47	−4	51	3
Social Science	57	1	59	1	51	0	48	0
Mathematics	58	2	64	6	49	−2	45	−3
Physical Science	56	0	63	5	52	1	45	−3
Biological Science	55	−1	58	0	51	0	46	−2
Electricity & Electronics	50	−6	64	6	59	8	44	−4
Mechanics	49	−7	60	2	60	9	43	−5
Home Economics	55	−1	47	−11	44	−7	55	7
Total Information	56	0	58	0	51	0	48	0

* While the data shown are real, for illustrative purposes only ten of the forty information scores have been used. The data are based on only one subsample of the twelfth grade pupils tested in 1960. The material was selected from data assembled by Dr. John T. Dailey for Project TALENT of the University of Pittsburgh and is presented by permission of Professor John C. Flanagan, Responsible Investigator.

As would be expected, the students who entered college had higher average total information scores (56 and 58) than those who became mechanics and secretaries (51 and 48). The differences are not, however, so great as might have been expected. The average interest deviation scores of these four groups show rather different patterns. The most striking differences between twelfth grade pupils who later majored in English and literature and those who later majored in engineering are in electricity and electronics, mechanics, and home economics. These differences no doubt reflect in part the fact that a larger proportion of men than women major in engineering and, conversely, a larger proportion of women than men major in English and literature. Norms based on men and women separately would probably provide more meaningful interest deviation scores.

The differences in the interest deviation scores of mechanics and secretaries agree with reasonable expectations and add weight to other evidence that patterns of information scores can be used to measure interests and help predict performance in various courses of study and occupations.

Air Forces General Information Test.   Elaborate studies of the predictive validity of groups of information items were made in the U.S. Army Air Forces during World War II. A combination of 100 of these items in a *General Information Test* especially designed to select aircraft pilots displayed a predictive validity coefficient of .51 for graduation or elimination from complete pilot flying training. This was the highest predictive validity of any single test used in the selection of pilots in an essentially self-selected sample of 1,275 men.

Summary.   Up to the end of 1963, no information test especially designed as a measure of differential interests was available for use by schools and colleges. Research data suggest that a well-constructed test of this sort would be of considerable value to guidance counselors, school psychologists, and college admission officers.

Interest Inventories and Questionnaires

A large number of questionnaires designed to measure interests have been published. Table 7.3 summarizes descriptive information about several of the best known. Additional information and critical reviews can be found in the *Fifth Mental Measurements Yearbook.**

As indicated earlier in this chapter, the chief merit of using questionnaires to measure interests is the fact that each individual can supply data

---

* O. K. Buros, ed., *Fifth Mental Measurements Yearbook* (Highland Park, N.J.: Gryphon Press, 1959). Earlier editions of the same yearbook may also be found helpful.

TABLE 7.3

Summary of Information about Well-Known Interest Questionnaires

Title	Publisher	Scores	Grade Level
Kuder Preference Record, Occupational, Form D	Science Research Associates 259 East Erie St. Chicago 11, Ill.	38 scores for specific occupations, e.g., forester, druggist	9–12 and college and adults
Kuder Preference Record, Vocational, Form C	Science Research Associates 259 East Erie St. Chicago 11, Ill.	10 scores for broad areas of interest, e.g., scientific, literary	9–12 and college and adults
Occupational Interest Inventory, 1956 Revision	California Test Bureau Del Monte Research Park Monterey, Calif.	10 scores in fields of interests, types of interests, and levels of interests	Intermediate: 7–12 and college and adults Advanced: 9–12 and college and adults
Vocational Interest Blank for Men, Revised; Vocational Interest Blank for Women, Revised	Consulting Psychologists Press 270 Town and Country Village Palo Alto, Calif.	Men's Blank: 56 occupational interest scores, plus 4 others. Women's Blank: 30 occupational interest scores, plus 1 other	12, college, and adults

about *himself*, his preferences, his activities, and his interests that are either difficult or impossible for anyone else to obtain. The chief defect of questionnaires is that the respondents need not, and often do not, give truthful answers if they have reason to believe that it is to their advantage to lie. Considerable evidence has been accumulated indicating that college students and others are able to make their patterns of interest scores resemble those of specified occupational groups. That is, many examinees have at least a rough idea of the kinds of interests that various occupational groups display and recognize how to mark specific items to influence their test scores. For example, suppose than an examinee wants to show an interest in literature and is confronted with an item like:

Mark which magazine you would choose to read if you had some spare time.
A *National Geographic*
B *Saturday Review*
C *New Republic*

He would be very likely to mark choice B even if he had never done more than glance at the *Saturday Review* on the library rack.

As a matter of fact, suggestions about how to fake scores on tests such as the Strong *Vocational Interest Blank for Men* have been provided by popular writers like Gross and Whyte.* As Gross has pointed out, revealing answers to specific test questions raises an ethical issue. He goes so far as to defend the practice on legal and moral grounds. It does create a difficult problem for anyone who wants to use well-known questionnaires under circumstances that make it worthwhile for examinees to fake responses. When answers to specific questions on achievement and aptitude tests become known to the public, it is necessary only to use a different set of equally valid and difficult questions about the same body of subject matter; but the nature of the content of questionnaires for measuring interests and personality traits is such that most examinees can tell what the questions are driving at and can deduce how new questions should be answered to produce a desired pattern of test scores. Therefore, coaching on such questionnaires cannot be effectively countered. Since there is no way to prevent some examinees from knowing how to respond, it follows that, to be fair, all examinees should be given the same information in advance about how to influence their scores or else these questionnaires should be used only under circumstances that make it reasonable to believe that all or nearly all of the examinees have nothing to gain from faking responses.

The three most widely used of the interest inventories listed in Table 7.3 will be described more fully. They are the Strong *Vocational Interest Blank for Men*, the Strong *Vocational Interest Blank for Women*, and the *Kuder Preference Record, Vocational*, Form C.† Since the two blanks prepared by Strong were developed in the same way, they will be discussed together.

The Strong *Vocational Interest Blanks*. Construction of these two blanks rested on the assumptions that people in a given occupation have many interests in common and that these patterns of interest remain fairly constant throughout youth and early adulthood. Each blank is made up of 400 items. The examinee expresses liking, indifference, or disliking for many occupations, school subjects, amusements, activities, and peculiarities of people. He also checks his preferences among various activities and rates his own abilities

* M. L. Gross, *The Brain Watchers* (New York: Random House, Inc., 1962); W. H. Whyte, *The Organization Man* (New York: Simon and Schuster, 1956).
† E. K. Strong, *Vocational Interest Blank for Men, Revised; Vocational Interest Blank for Women, Revised* (Palo Alto: Consulting Psychologists Press, 1959). G. F. Kuder, *Kuder Preference Record, Vocational* (Chicago: Science Research Associates, 1948).

FIGURE 7.1

Directions for the Strong *Vocational Interest Blank for Men.*

STRONG

VOCATIONAL INTEREST BLANK

FOR MEN

(Revised)

BY

EDWARD K. STRONG, JR.
STANFORD UNIVERSITY

T IS POSSIBLE with a fair degree of accuracy to determine by this test whether or not you would like certain occupations. The test is not one of intelligence or school work. It measures the extent to which **your** interests agree or disagree with those of successful men in a given occupation.

In addition to this question booklet, you should have a **special answer sheet or cards** on which to record your responses. MAKE NO MARKS AT ALL ON THIS BOOKLET. Please read the following directions carefully:

1. Do **not** use a ball point or any other kind of pen. If you have been given a special pencil, use it. If not, mark with any soft, black lead pencil.

2. If you make a mistake, erase carefully. If you accidentally make stray marks on the answer sheets, erase them also. Do not fold or crease your answer sheet in any way.

3. You must make one mark for each of the 400 questions. If you omit items, or make more than one mark, the machine cannot score your test. If you are not familiar with a particular item, guess how you might feel about it and mark accordingly.

4. Listen carefully to any instructions given orally. In some parts of the test, the directions change; read the instructions at the beginning of each part.

5. Be sure to fill in your name and other information requested on your answer sheet or card. In some cases, it is necessary to code your name by marking spots representing each letter.

and characteristics. Figure 7.1 shows the cover page of the *Vocational Interest Blank for Men.**
Scoring of these items is done with choice weights that were established by a procedure somewhat similar to that described earlier in the chapter for obtaining scoring weights for each choice in biographical-data-blank items. In determining scoring weights for the *Vocational Interest Blank for Men,* Strong obtained the percentage of a representative sample of American men who marked each choice for the 400 items. Then he obtained the percentage of a sample of successful men in each of many occupations who marked each item choice. The greater the difference between the percentages for a given choice in the two samples the larger the scoring weight for that choice. Table 7.4 shows these percentages together with other data pertaining to the three choices (Like, Indifferent, and Dislike) for the first item in the blank.

TABLE 7.4

Data Used to Obtain Scoring Weights for Interest in Engineering for Item 1 in Strong *Vocational Interest Blank for Men**

Item	Percentage of American Men			Percentage of Successful Engineers			Differences between Percentages			Choice Weights for Engineering Interest		
	Like	*Indif.*	*Dislike*	*Like*	*Indif.*	*Dislike*	*Like*	*Indif.*	*Dislike*	*Like*	*Indif.*	*Dislike*
1. Actor	21	32	47	9	31	60	−12	−1	13	−1	0	1

* Data taken from E. K. Strong, *Vocational Interests of Men and Women* (Stanford: Stanford University Press, 1943), p. 75.

The examinee is asked to indicate whether he would like to be an actor, is indifferent to that idea, or would dislike to be one. The data show that engineers tend to dislike the idea of being an actor; consequently anyone who marks "Dislike" for this item is credited with one point toward having interests that resemble those of engineers. Conversely, anyone who marks "Like" for this item has one point subtracted from his total score showing resemblance between his interests and those of successful engineers. The same technique is used to obtain choice weights for determining the resemblance between an examinee's interests and those of successful men in fifty-five other occupational groups. In addition, the blank yields scores for specialization level, occupational level, interest maturity, and masculinity-femininity.

Each score for an examinee is obtained by adding algebraically 400 choice weights. Since the men's blank yields fifty-six occupational scores plus the four others mentioned above, the clerical labor of scoring by hand is prohibitive. The women's blank yields thirty-one scores, so the situation is almost the same. For practical purposes, then, any plans to administer the *Vocational Interest Blanks* must include provisions for machine processing of special answer sheets. A number of scoring services are now equipped to do this.

Figure 7.2 shows the report used by National Computer Systems for reporting test scores.* The standard scores for a high school senior have been printed following the title of each interest score and plotted as black circles on the profile chart. The higher the occupational interest score, the more nearly the examinee's interests coincide with those of successful men in the occupation designated. Scores that fall in the shaded areas are inconclusive. A score plotted to the left of the shaded area may be interpreted as showing definite lack of correspondence of the examinee's interests with those of successful men in the occupation designated.

The young man whose scores have been plotted shows greatest correspondence of interests with physical therapists. He shows least correspondence of interests with bankers. In general, he tends to have interests like those of professional workers and unlike those of businessmen and salesmen. His scores in specialization level, occupational level, and masculinity-femininity are all normal for American men, but his interest maturity score is high, indicating that his interests are rather well developed for an 18-year-old.

The *Vocational Interest Blank for Women* was developed on the basis of the same principles as the blank for men. Its scoring system is similar. By 1964, it yielded interests scores for thirty occupations and for femininity-masculinity.

The most important point to keep in mind in the interpretation of scores on the Strong *Vocational Interest Blanks*, and others, is that they do not measure abilities; in fact, interest scores often have low correlations with ability scores. Yet both are important in predicting performance on the job and both should be considered when a guidance counselor discusses educational and vocational plans with pupils. There is considerable evidence to indicate that the occupational interest scores are highly reliable. Strong has also shown that the profiles of interest scores obtained by college seniors remain reasonably stable over a period as long as ten years. He has found that patterns of interests tend to become rather stable after the age of seven-

* National Computer Systems can score specially printed answer sheets for many tests. Address: 1015 South Sixth Street, Minneapolis 15, Minnesota.

Figure 7.2

Profile of Scores on the Strong *Vocational Interest Blank for Men.*

REPORT FORM—**STRONG VOCATIONAL INTEREST BLANK**—FOR MEN

		OCCUPATION	STD. SCORE
1	I	ARTIST	27
2		PSYCHOLOGIST	37
3		ARCHITECT	28
4		PHYSICIAN	55
5		PSYCHIATRIST	47
6		OSTEOPATH	55
7		DENTIST	35
8		VETERINARIAN	33
9	II	MATHEMATICIAN	23
10		PHYSICIST	23
11		CHEMIST	43
12		ENGINEER	32
13	III	PRODUCTION MANAGER	34
14	IV	FARMER	39
15		CARPENTER	32
16		FOREST SERVICE MAN	37
17		AVIATOR	41
18		PRINTER	47
19		MATH. SCI. TEACHER	52
20		INDUSTRIAL ARTS TEACHER	52
21		VOC. AGRICULT. TEACHER	55
22		POLICEMAN	41
23		ARMY OFFICER	44
24	V	Y.M.C.A. PHYSICAL DIRECTOR	43
25		PERSONNEL MANAGER	38
26		PUBLIC ADMINISTRATOR	48
27		VOCATIONAL COUNSELOR	42
28		PHYSICAL THERAPIST	60
29		SOCIAL WORKER	39
30		SOCIAL SCIENCE TEACHER	40
31		BUS. EDUC. TEACHER	37
32		SCHOOL SUPT.	25
33		MINISTER	37
34	VI	MUSICIAN	48
35		MUSIC TEACHER	39
36	VII	C.P.A. OWNER	27
37	VIII	SENIOR C.P.A.	45
38		ACCOUNTANT	29
39		OFFICE WORKER	33
40		CREDIT MANAGER	44
41		PURCHASING AGENT	19
42		BANKER	16
43		PHARMACIST	39
44		MORTICIAN	25
45	IX	SALES MANAGER	17
46		REAL ESTATE SALESMAN	27
47		LIFE INSURANCE SALESMAN	22
48	X	ADVERTISING MAN	26
49		LAWYER	26
50		AUTHOR-JOURNALIST	23
51	XI	PRES. MFG CONCERN	23
52		GROUP I	43
53		GROUP II	41
54		GROUP V	49
55		GROUP VIII	23
56		GROUP IX	26
57		SPECIALIZATION LEVEL	45
58		INTEREST MATURITY	61
59		OCCUPATIONAL LEVEL	46
60		MASCULINITY-FEMININITY	44

Scored by NATIONAL COMPUTER SYSTEMS—1015 South 8th, Minneapolis, Minn.   (SEE OTHER SIDE FOR EXPLANATION)   Form SVI-RM

teen. It would be very helpful if we had data showing the extent to which standard scores in a given occupational interest area obtained by high school seniors predicted later performance in that occupation. Such data are difficult and expensive to obtain and, to the best of my knowledge, are not available.

***Kuder Preference Record, Vocational,* Form C.** The objective of the *Kuder Preference Record, Vocational,* Form C is not to determine the extent to which an examinee's interests are like those of men or women who are successful in designated occupations, but to yield ten comparable scores that show the relative levels of interest of the examinee in broad vocational areas. Table 7.5 lists these ten areas and gives the author's descriptions of them. An eleventh score, the verification score, is provided to identify examinees who mark the blank carelessly or omit a large number of items.

TABLE 7.5

List of Broad Vocational Areas for Which Interest Scores Are Provided by the *Kuder Preference Record, Vocational,* and the Author's Brief Description of These Scores*

Code Number	Area	Brief Description
0	Outdoor	Indicates a preference for work that keeps one outside most of the time, usually dealing with animals and growing things.
1	Mechanical	Indicates a preference for work with machines and tools.
2	Computational	Indicates a preference for working with numbers.
3	Scientific	Indicates a preference for discovering new facts and solving problems.
4	Persuasive	Indicates a preference for meeting and dealing with people, and promoting projects or things to sell.
5	Artistic	Indicates a preference for doing creative work with one's hands. It is usually work that has "eye appeal," involving attractive design, color, and materials.
6	Literary	Indicates a preference for reading and writing.
7	Musical	Indicates a preference for going to concerts, playing instruments, singing, or reading about music and musicians.
8	Social Service	Indicates a preference for helping people.
9	Clerical	Indicates a preference for office work that requires precision and accuracy.

* G. F. Kuder, *Administrator's Manual, Kuder Preference Record, Vocational,* Form C (Chicago: Science Research Associates).

Each item is made up of a list of three activities. The examinee is asked to mark the one that he likes (or thinks he would like) the *most* and the one that he likes (or thinks he would like) the *least*. Thus, he is forced to make a

FIGURE 7.3

Directions for the *Kuder Preference Record, Vocational*, Form CH.

KUDER PREFERENCE RECORD
VOCATIONAL
FORM CH

Prepared by G. Frederic Kuder, Editor, *Educational and Psychological Measurement*

Professor of Psychology, Duke University

This blank is used for obtaining a record of your preferences. It is not a test. There are no right or wrong answers. An answer is right if it is true of you.

A number of activities are listed in groups of three. Read over the three activities in each group. Decide which of the three activities you like **most**. There are two circles on the same line as this activity. Punch a hole with the pin through the left-hand circle following this activity. Then decide which activity you like **least** and punch a hole through the right-hand circle of the two circles following this activity.

In the examples below, the person answering has indicated for the first group of three activities, that he would usually like to visit a museum **most**, and browse in a library **least**. In the second group of three activities he has indicated he would ordinarily like to collect autographs **most** and collect butterflies **least**.

EXAMPLES

Put your answers to these questions in column O.

P.	Visit an art gallery		● P ●
Q.	Browse in a library		● Q ○ ←—LEAST
R.	Visit a museum	MOST→	○ R ●
S.	Collect autographs	MOST→	○ S ●
T.	Collect coins		● T ●
U.	Collect butterflies		● U ○ ←—LEAST

Some of the activities involve preparation and training. In such cases, please suppose that you could first have the necessary training. Do not choose an activity merely because it is new or unusual. Choose what you would like to do if you were equally familiar with all of the activities.

In some cases you may like all three activities in a group. In other cases you may find all three activities unpleasant. Please show what your first and last choices would be, however, if you *had* to choose.

Some activities may seem trivial or foolish. Please indicate your choices, anyway, for all of the groups. Otherwise we cannot give you a complete report. Your answers will be kept strictly confidential.

Please do not spend a lot of time on one group. Put down your first reaction and go on. Do not discuss the activities with anyone. An answer is worthless unless it is your own judgment.

If you want to change an answer, punch two more holes close to the answer you wish to change; then punch the new answer in the usual way. Hold the pin straight up and down when you punch your answers.

Now go ahead with the activities on the next page.

Published by SCIENCE RESEARCH ASSOCIATES, 259 East Erie Street. Chicago 11, Illinois
Copyright under International Copyright Union. All rights reserved under Fourth International
American Convention (1910). Copyright 1948, by G. Frederic Kuder. Copyright 1948 in Canada.
Registered under Patent Nos. 1,500,777 and 2,052,369. Printed in the U.S.A.
To Reorder Use Code Number 7:291

choice among the three activities presented.   In the construction of the test, the combinations of activities for the items were carefully considered in an effort to have each item include activities of about equal attractiveness in the population that would also help to discriminate among the ten broad fields of interest to be measured.   The nature of the items and the method of marking them can best be understood by reading the directions for administering the questionnaire.   These are reproduced in Figure 7.3 for the hand-scored edition.   As stated in these directions, the examinee indicates his responses by punching holes with a special pin that is provided.

When an examinee's scores have been obtained (by a simple process that he may carry out for himself under supervision), they are plotted on a profile chart that is shown in Figure 7.4.   From this chart, the examinee's percentile ranks may be determined.   The scores of an eleventh grade boy, Wayne Atherton, have been plotted on this chart as large black circles.   Note that each score is entered in the column headed M (for male); the norms for men and women differ markedly in some areas.

Wayne's scores vary considerably; his computational, scientific, and mechanical interests are high (above the 75th percentile) and his artistic, literary, and musical interests are low (below the 25th percentile).   Whether there is significant variation in his profile of scores can be estimated at any desired level of significance by converting his percentile ranks into standard scores by means of Table D.1 (appendix D) and filling in a score-difference grid like that shown in Figure 8.8 for the *Wechsler Adult Intelligence Scale*.*   Figure 7.5 shows the grid filled in with differences among Wayne's standard scores in the ten interest areas.   The data indicate that the variations in his scores are significant at better than the 15-per-cent level.†   Directions are provided in the *Administrator's Manual*‡ for identifying various occupations that might be considered in discussing Wayne's educational and vocational plans with him.   Since these range from professional positions (like electrical engineer) to clerical positions, a counselor should have some idea of his level of mental abilities.   As it happens, Wayne took the *Wechsler Adult Intelligence Scale* two days before he took the *Kuder Preference Record* and obtained a verbal IQ of 96, a performance IQ of 126, and a full-scale IQ of 113.   The corresponding percentile ranks in the American population are 39, 96, and 81.   These data suggest that he might consider a semi-professional type of work (such as computer technician) or even some professional positions.   Additional information about his verbal aptitude would be helpful.

---

    * Strictly speaking, this procedure is not precisely correct because scores on the *Kuder Preference Blank, Vocational*, Form C are not completely free to vary independently of each other.

    † Table M.24 in appendix M shows minimum differences significant at the 15-per-cent level.

    ‡ *Loc. cit.*, table 1, pp. 6–18.

FIGURE 7.4

Scores of Wayne Atherton Plotted on Boys' Profile Chart* for the *Kuder Preference Record, Vocational*, Form C.

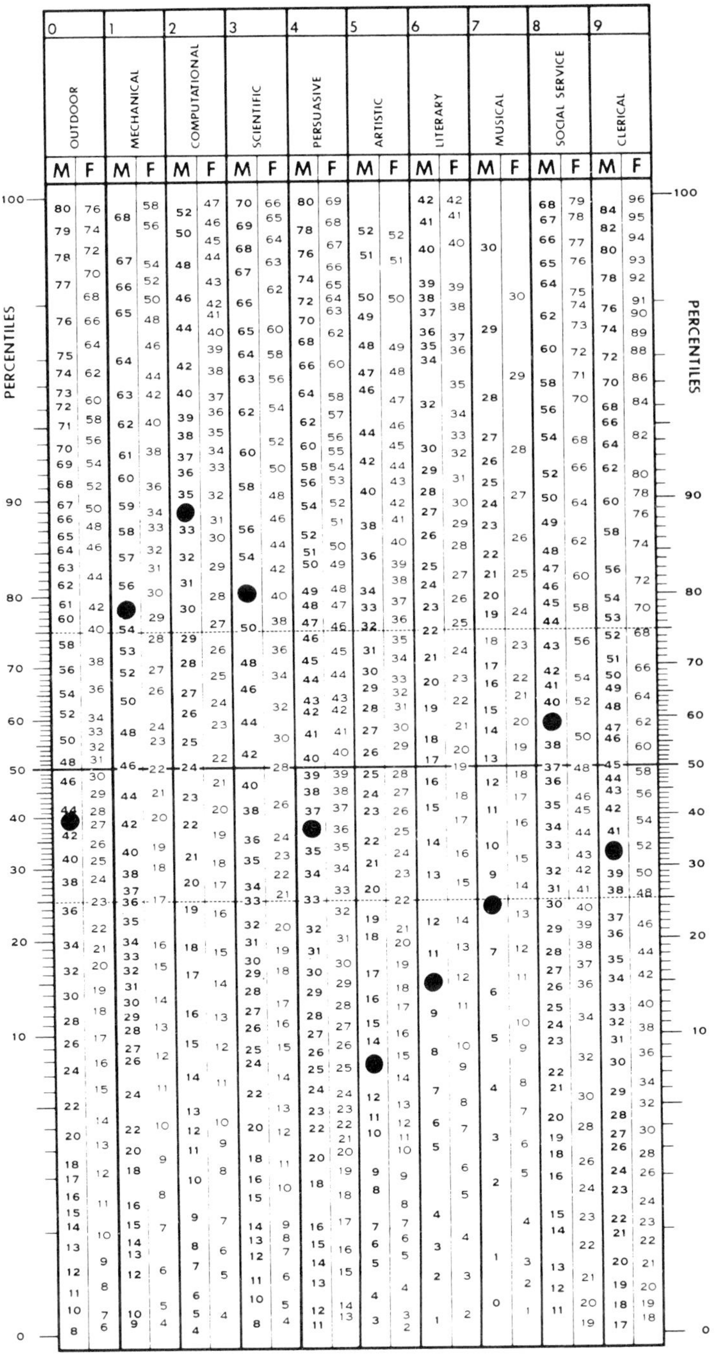

0	1	2	3	4	5	6	7	8	9
OUTDOOR	MECHANICAL	COMPUTATIONAL	SCIENTIFIC	PERSUASIVE	ARTISTIC	LITERARY	MUSICAL	SOCIAL SERVICE	CLERICAL

| M | F | M | F | M | F | M | F | M | F | M | F | M | F | M | F | M | F | M | F |

* Copyright 1958 by G. Frederic Kuder. Reproduced by permission of the author.

FIGURE 7.5

Differences among Wayne's Interest Scores on the *Kuder Preference Record, Vocational,* Form C.

Date: January 8, 1963 _____   School: _____

Name: Wayne Atherton _____   Test: Kuder, Vocational, C _____

Interest Area	Raw Score	Standard Score	0	1	2	3	4	5	6	7	8	9
0 Outdoor	43	47	−11	−15	−11	0	11	7	4	−5	2	
1 Mechanical	55	58			−4	0	11	22	18	15	6	13
2 Computational	34	62				4	15	26	22	19	10	17
3 Scientific	52	58					11	22	18	15	6	13
4 Persuasive	36	47						11	7	4	−5	2
5 Artistic	13	36							−4	−7	−16	−9
6 Literary	10	40								−3	−12	−5
7 Musical	8	43									−9	−2
8 Social Service	39	52										7
9 Clerical	40	45										

Number of Differences: 45
Number of Differences × .15: 6.75
Number of Circled Differences: 27

The reliability of interest scores derived from the *Kuder Preference Record, Vocational,* Form C is high. Like scores derived from the Strong *Vocational Interest Blank for Men* or *for Women,* they seem to be reasonably stable among high school and college students. Some evidence of the inferential validity of the scores has been provided; for example, the mean interest scores of men and women in various occupations agree rather well with expectations of what they ought to be. The *Kuder Preference Record, Vocational,* Form C is not expected to predict performance in occupations or in courses of study in school or college. Nonetheless, predictive validity coefficients with performance or degree of satisfaction in jobs and courses of study would be interesting and informative.

Counselors and school psychologists should recognize that the ten interest scores derived from the blank are not completely free to vary independently of each other.*   An examinee with several strong interests

* M. Katz, "Interpreting *Kuder Preference Record* Scores: Ipsative or Normative," *Vocational Guidance Quarterly,* X (1962), 96–100.

will necessarily score somewhat low in other interest areas—perhaps lower than another examinee with the same absolute level of interest but with no other strong interests. Thus, a certain amount of variation among the ten interest scores is a built-in feature of this test.

USES OF DATA ABOUT INTERESTS

Data regarding an individual's interests are useful to the counselor in several ways, whether they come from biographical-data blanks, information tests, or questionnaires. *First*, a thorough study of them before an interview gives the counselor a better understanding of the individual and raises questions in his mind that can be tactfully explored during the interview. *Second*, the scores from an interests test or questionnaire provide starting points for profitable discussions with the individual about his educational and vocational plans. *Third*, many examinees find that scores on interests tests draw their attention to scattered ideas and feelings that they have never organized and thought about in a systematic way; consideration of these ideas and feelings in the light of their interests scores and discussions about them with a skilled counselor often enable examinees to understand themselves better.

Summary

An individual's interests are revealed by how he spends his time, how he has spent it in the past, and how he would like to spend it. They are measured by determining, directly or indirectly, the extent to which he engages, has engaged, or would like to engage, in various activities. This can be accomplished by obtaining data as to how he actually has spent and is spending his time, by finding out how much information he has about each one of many different activities, or by asking him to express his opinions— that is, his preferences or likes and dislikes—about these activities.

Information about the activities in which an individual has taken part can be obtained economically by a biographical-data blank. The questions on this blank should deal with objectively verifiable facts and events and should be relevant to a criterion variable which it is desired to predict. When an examinee knows that his answers can be checked, he tends to be truthful even when he thinks that other answers would show him in a more favorable light.

Questionnaires that ask for opinions, feelings, or preferences should not be used to assess interests, attitudes, or personality traits in any competitive situation (such as admittance to college, employment, or promotion) where the examinee is tempted to answer untruthfully in order to "improve" his score by creating a certain impression on the examiner or the agency represented by the examiner. If they are so used, the boldest, least conscientious, and most sophisticated examinees are likely to get high scores. As this misuse of such questionnaires becomes known, public confidence in *all* educational and psychological measurement suffers.

When interests are measured by testing for specific information in many fields, the ability of an examinee to fake his responses so as to make a favorable impression is greatly limited. He cannot systematically inflate his scores; he can only lower some of them—and thereby perhaps make others stand out—by deliberately omitting or marking wrong answers to certain questions. Experience indicates that examinees rarely adopt this scheme because they know that to do so will automatically lower their *total* information scores.

Interests have been successfully measured by the differential subtests in the *Cooperative Contemporary Affairs Test*, the Air Force *General Information Test*, and the *General Information Test* used in Project TALENT.

A number of interest inventories have been published for use in educational and vocational guidance. Three of the best known are the *Kuder Preference Record, Vocational*, Form C, the Strong *Vocational Interest Blank for Men*, and the Strong *Vocational Interest Blank for Women*. The first of these has been widely used in secondary schools. The empirical basis used in deriving the scoring weights for the Strong blanks has been commended by authorities in measurement. All three instruments have been helpful to counselors as starting points for discussing educational and vocational plans with students, parents, jobseekers, and employees.

Selected References

McArthur, Charles, "Long-Term Validity of the Strong Interest Test in Two Subcultures," in W. Leslie Barnette, Jr., ed., *Readings in Psychological Tests and Measurements*. Homewood, Ill.: Dorsey Press, 1963.

Strong, Edward K., *Vocational Interests of Men and Women*. Stanford, Calif.: Stanford University Press, 1943.

Strong, Edward K., *Vocational Interests 18 Years After College*. Minneapolis: University of Minnesota Press, 1955.

Super, Donald E., "The Measurement of Interests," *Journal of Consulting Psychology*, I (1954), 168–172.

Super, Donald E., "The Use of Multifactor Test Batteries in Guidance," *Personnel and Guidance Journal*, XXXV (1956), 9–15.

Thorndike, Robert L., and Elizabeth P. Hagen, *Ten Thousand Careers*. New York: John Wiley & Sons, Inc., 1959.

Chapter Eight

INTERPRETATION
OF INDIVIDUAL
TEST SCORES

The raw score obtained by an examinee on a test is rarely meaningful in itself. Only when it is compared with those of other examinees or with the average scores of different groups does it become meaningful in a useful way. If more than one test is administered to an examinee, comparable scores from these tests may be compared to determine on which test or tests his performance is better than on others. To evaluate learning, equivalent forms of a test may be given to a pupil before and after the learning period. His equivalent scores may then be compared to estimate the change that has occurred in him.

Comparisons of scores are based on the differences among them; thus, almost all interpretations of scores involve the estimation and evaluation of differences, which are apt to be much less reliable than the scores themselves; they can also be highly misleading. Consequently, chapters 8 through 11 are devoted to the estimation of differences between individual scores, between individual scores and group means, and between means.

This chapter will consider the meaning and use of scores obtained by individuals. For illustration, scores obtained on several of the tests in most common use in American schools are used: the *Metropolitan Achievement Tests*, the *Stanford Achievement Test*, the *Davis Reading Test*, the *Wechsler Adult Intelligence Scale*, the *Differential Aptitude Tests*, the *Cooperative School and College Ability Tests*, and the *Revised Stanford-Binet Intelligence Scale*.

THE CONFIDENCE INTERVAL
FOR AN OBTAINED SCORE

The score that an individual obtains on any test (which is really a sampling of all the items that could be written about the field the test is intended to measure) is usually only an approximation of his true knowledge, skill, or ability. Therefore, it is important that his obtained score be interpreted in the light of the fact that it may be either too high or too low because of errors of measurement. To do this, a *confidence interval* is ordinarily used for each obtained score. The word *interval* in this term means a range of test scores. A confidence interval may be defined as a range of obtained scores that will, when it is applied to one obtained score after another, include the individual's true score a designated percentage of the times it is so applied. For example, a 95-per-cent confidence interval will include the individual's true score about 95 out of every 100 times that it is applied to obtained scores of successive individuals; an 85-per-cent confidence interval will do so about 85 times out of every 100; and a 68-per-cent confidence interval will do so about 68 times out of every 100.

In practice, the confidence interval is chosen which provides the desired degree of assurance that it includes the true score of each individual to whose obtained score it is applied. For most purposes in interpreting test scores, the 85-per-cent confidence interval provides an acceptable degree of assurance. The penalty for assuming that an individual's true score lies somewhere in the interval when it actually does *not* is usually not serious. Important decisions about pupils are rarely made without confirmatory evidence from teachers and parents, and opportunities to change decisions ordinarily present themselves as new data are obtained. Consequently, I recommend the 85-per-cent confidence interval for interpreting individual test scores. Some publishers have adopted an even less stringent level of assurance; the well-known *School and College Ability Tests* (commonly referred to as SCAT) and the *Sequential Tests of Educational Progress* (STEP), both published by the Educational Testing Service, use a 68-per-cent confidence interval expressed in terms of percentile ranks. The resulting percentile bands were described in chapter 2.

An extreme view is represented by some test interpreters who assume that an individual's true score is the same as his obtained score. The percentage of times that this assumption is correct varies from test to test but is always very low. For example, with grade-equivalent scores (such as 6.1, 6.2, 6.5) on the *Metropolitan Intermediate Reading Test*, the assumption would be correct only about 7 or 8 times out of every 100 times that it was made.

The underlying rationale for confidence intervals is given in appendix H; here, merely the practical procedure for setting them up and interpreting them is given. It is necessary only to multiply the standard error of measurement of an obtained score by a constant chosen to yield an interval that includes the true score the desired percentage of times. Table 8.1 gives the multipliers for establishing confidence intervals that include the true score with five different frequencies out of every 100 applications. A glance at the

TABLE 8.1

Multipliers Used to Set up Confidence Intervals at Selected Levels

Confidence Interval Desired	Multiplier (to two decimal places)
99 per cent	5.15
95 per cent	3.92
90 per cent	3.29
85 per cent	2.88
68 per cent	2.00

table indicates that the greater the percentage of times a confidence interval includes the true score, the wider it is.

Once the desired confidence interval has been computed, it can be used to interpret any obtained score for which it is appropriate simply by placing the obtained score at its center.   For example, the standard error of measurement of a verbal IQ derived from Level 5 of the *Thorndike-Lorge Intelligence Tests* is 6.1 IQ points.   The 85-per-cent confidence interval is, therefore, equal to 6.1 times 2.88 (as given in Table 8.1), or about 17.6 IQ points. Placing a pupil's verbal IQ of 105 at the center of this confidence interval, we see that the interval extends 8.8 points below 105 to 96.2 and 8.8 points above 105 to 113.8.   In practical work, it is best to round off the ends of the confidence interval to the nearest IQ point.   Then, we may infer that the pupil's true verbal IQ lies between 96 and 114, keeping in mind that out of every 100 inferences like this that we make it is most likely that 85 will be correct.

INTERPRETATION OF A SINGLE SCORE FOR AN INDIVIDUAL

The Confidence Interval

The first step in the interpretation of a single test score for an individual is to set up a confidence interval by finding the appropriate standard error of measurement in the test manual and using the procedure outlined in the preceding section.   The choice of probability level depends on the purposes of the interpreter.   As stated above, for most practical purposes in educational measurement the 85-per-cent confidence interval is satisfactory.   In the long run, the interpreter using 85-per-cent confidence intervals will be correct in 85 out of every 100 decisions he makes about the ranges of scores in which the true scores of individuals lie; this is a highly respectable degree of accuracy in drawing inferences about human behavior. At the same time, however, the 85-per-cent confidence intervals for most test scores are not so large as to make the use of these intervals seem futile. An example of the practical use of the 85-per-cent confidence interval for interpreting a pupil's score may be helpful:

Suzanne entered Miss Green's sixth grade class in September. On September 18 she took Form B of the *Metropolitan Intermediate Reading Test.* The directions and sample items for this test are reproduced in Figure 8.1.* Suzanne marked nineteen out of the forty-four items in this test

FIGURE 8.1

Directions and Sample Items for the *Metropolitan Intermediate Reading Test,* Form B.

DIRECTIONS

Read each story. Then read each question below the story. Find the best answer to the question and put a cross through the letter in front of the answer you have chosen. Certain questions refer to particular words in the story. These words can be found in the lines which have the stars (★) beside them. Study the sample below and notice how the questions have been marked.

SAMPLE

Frank has a good hobby. He collects stamps. He has stamps from many
★different places. Of course, he has many United States stamps. He saves them from the letters he gets from his Aunt Carrie in Texas and his Cousin Jack in Ohio. But Frank also has stamps from foreign countries.

A Frank's Aunt Carrie lives in —	B In this story, the word <u>saves</u> means —
[a] Ohio [b] New York	[e] rescues [f] protects
[c] Africa [X] Texas	[X] keeps [h] prevents

correctly. The first step in interpreting her score is to convert the raw score of 19 to a Metropolitan Standard Score. (This type of Standard Score is related to but is not the same as the standard measure referred to in chapter 2 and in appendix D.) To do so, a conversion table provided by the publisher is used; the pertinent part is reproduced in Figure 8.2.† Suzanne's Standard Score in reading turns out to be 45. This must be used to obtain her grade-equivalent score and her percentile rank for grade 6.1. Before getting these data we should obtain the 85-per-cent confidence interval for her Standard Score of 45. The booklet of directions for administering the test provides a standard error of measurement for the reading test, but the value given, which is 2.6, is in raw-score points.‡ Since the tables of grade

* Copyright 1959 by Harcourt, Brace and World, Inc. Copyright in Great Britain. All rights reserved. Reproduced by permission.

† Copyright 1959 by Harcourt, Brace and World, Inc. Copyright in Great Britain. All rights reserved. Reproduced by permission.

‡ *Directions for Administering, Metropolitan Achievement Tests,* Intermediate Battery—Complete (New York: Harcourt, Brace and World, Inc., 1959), table 8, p. 24.

FIGURE 8.2

Raw Score–Standard Score Conversion Table for the
Metropolitan Intermediate Reading Test,
Form B.

Reading

Raw Score	Standard Score
44	84
43	80
42	76
41	72
40	70
39	69
38	68
37	66
36	64
35	62
34	61
33	59
32	58
31	57
30	56
29	55
28	54
27	53
26	52
25	51
24	50
23	49
22	48
21	47
20	46
19	45
18	44
17	42
16	40
15	39
14	38
13	37
12	36
11	34
10	33
9	31
8	30
7	28
6	26

scores and percentile ranks for the test must be entered with Standard Scores, the confidence interval should be expressed in Standard Scores. A serviceable approximation to this can easily be obtained by computing the 85-per-cent confidence interval in terms of raw-score points and getting its equivalent in Standard-Score points. First, we multiply 2.6 by 2.88 (the appropriate multiplier, as shown in Table 8.1). The result is 7.5, rounded to the nearest tenth of a point. If the center of this confidence interval is placed at Suzanne's raw score of 19, it will extend $3\frac{3}{4}$ points above 19 to $22\frac{3}{4}$ and $3\frac{3}{4}$ points below 19 to $15\frac{1}{4}$. This range of raw scores has been bracketed in Figure 8.2. The range of Standard Scores corresponding to it extends from about 39 to about 49. This range can be used as the 85-per-cent confidence interval for Suzanne's Standard Score of 45 and, in practice, for any other Standard Score on this particular reading test.

The Grade-Equivalent Score

To find Suzanne's grade-equivalent score, a table provided by the test publishers is used; part of this table is reproduced as Figure 8.3.* A Standard Score of 45 on this reading test corresponds to a grade-equivalent score of about 5.1. This means that Suzanne's obtained score is about the same as the average score obtained by pupils in the first month of grade 5 who are within nine months of the modal (that is, most common) chronological age at that grade level. However, her true reading score is not likely to be the same as her obtained score; the chances are about 85 out of 100 that the range of Standard Scores from 39 to 49 includes her true score.† Converted into grade-equivalent scores, this range becomes 4.2 to 5.9. From these data, it is very unlikely that Suzanne's true reading score is up to her actual grade-placement level of 6.1, and it is likely that her reading ability is retarded by about one grade.

The Percentile Rank

To determine Suzanne's percentile rank with respect to American school-children entering grade 6, a table provided by the publishers is used.‡ Part of this table is reproduced as Figure 8.4. Entering the body of this table

---

* *Ibid.*, table 1, p. 20. Copyright 1959 by Harcourt, Brace and World, Inc. Copyright in Great Britain. All rights reserved. Reproduced by permission.

† This statement is of practical utility but it is cast in a form that makes it technically inexact. The confidence interval has already been defined, and appendix H presents its technical basis. Somewhat inexact statements that help beginning students to understand its practical implications occur occasionally in this book.

‡ *Ibid.*, table 3, p. 19.

FIGURE 8.3

Grade-Equivalent Scores Corresponding to Standard Scores for the Language Tests in the *Metropolitan Achievement Test*, Intermediate Battery, Form B.

Grade-Equivalent Scores

Standard Score	Word Knowledge	Reading	Spelling	Language Total (A-C)
71				10.0+
70				9.9
69				9.6
68			10.0+	9.4
67			10.0	9.2
66			9.8	8.9
65			9.4	8.7
64		10.0+	9.2	8.6
63	10.0+	10.0	9.0	8.5
62	9.8	9.7	8.7	8.3
61	9.2	9.2	8.4	8.1
60	8.9	8.9	8.1	7.9
59	8.7	8.7	7.8	7.7
58	8.3	8.4	7.6	7.5
57	7.9	8.0	7.3	7.3
56	7.6	7.7	7.1	7.1
55	7.4	7.3	7.0	7.0
54	7.1	7.1	6.8	6.8
53	6.9	6.8	6.7	6.6
52	6.6	6.6	6.5	6.5
51	6.4	6.3	6.3	6.3
50	6.2	6.1	6.1	6.1
49	6.0	5.9	6.0	5.9
48	5.8	5.7	5.7	5.8
47	5.6	5.5	5.6	5.7
46	5.5	5.3	5.5	5.5
45	5.3	5.1	5.3	5.4
44	5.1	4.9	5.1	5.3
43	4.9	4.8	5.0	5.1
42	4.7	4.7	4.8	5.0
41	4.5	4.5	4.7	4.9
40	4.3	4.4	4.4	4.8
39	4.2	4.2	4.3	4.7
38	4.0	4.0	4.2	4.6
37	3.8	3.8	4.1	4.4
36	3.7	3.7	3.9	4.3
35	3.6	3.6	3.7	4.1
34	3.4	3.5	3.6	4.0
33	3.3	3.3	3.4	3.9
32	3.1	3.2	3.3	3.7
31	3.0	3.1	3.1	3.5
30	3.0−	3.0	3.0−	3.4
29		3.0		3.2
28		3.0−		3.1
27				3.0−

FIGURE 8.4

Percentile Ranks Corresponding to Standard Scores on the *Metropolitan Achievement Test*, Intermediate Battery, Form B, for Grade 6.1.

Percentile Rank	Standard Scores										Percentile Rank
	Word Know.	Reading	Spelling	Lang. Total (A-C)	Lang. Stud. Sk.	Arith. Comp.	Arith. Prob. Solv. & Conc.	Soc. Stud. Info.	Soc. Stud. St. Sk.	Science	
98	71	70	70	71	70	71	71	71	70	71	98
95	66	66	66	67	67	67	67	67	67	66	95
90	63	62	63	63	63	63	63	63	63	63	90
85	61	61	61	60	60	60	61	60	61	61	85
80	59	58	59	58	58	58	59	58	59	59	80
75	57	57	57	57	57	57	56	57	57	57	75
70	55	55	56	55	56	55	55	55	55	55	70
65	54	54	54	54	54	54	54	54	54	53	65
60	53	53	53	52	52	52	53	53	53	52	60
55	51	52	52	51	51	51	51	51	51	51	55
50	50	50	50	50	50	50	50	50	50	50	50
45	49	49	49	49	49	48	49	49	48	49	45
40	48	48	48	48	47	47	48	47	47	48	40
35	46	46	46	46	46	46	46	46	46	46	35
30	45	45	45	45	45	45	44	45	44	45	30
25	43	43	43	44	43	43	43	43	43	43	25
20	41	41	41	42	42	41	41	42	42	41	20
15	39	39	40	40	39	39	39	40	40	39	15
10	37	37	37	37	36	37	37	37	37	37	10
5	33	33	34	33	32	34	33	34	33	34	5
2	30	30	30	29	30	29	29	29	30	29	2

with her Standard Score of 45 on the reading test, we find her percentile rank (shown in the left-hand column) to be 30. This means that her score is higher than the scores obtained by 30 per cent of American schoolchildren in the first month of grade 6 who are within nine months of the most common chronological age for pupils at that grade-placement level. It also means that about 70 per cent of these pupils obtained scores higher than Suzanne's. If the 85-per-cent confidence interval is applied to the percentile ranks, a range of Standard Scores from 39 to 49 is obtained; this corresponds to percentile ranks from 15 to 45. It is highly unlikely that Suzanne's true reading score is as high as the median (the 50th percentile) of pupils in grade 6.1. To some teachers, a percentile rank of 30 may seem to represent virtually a failing grade, but this is not a correct impression. In most cases, no more than the lowest one or two per cent of pupils in a grade are required to repeat it because of failure. As shown in Table 8.2, Suzanne's percentile rank of 30 places her slightly below the normal range of achievement. In many schools, the average reading ability of pupils entering grade 6 is no better than Suzanne's. Because of this wide variation among schools with respect to average pupil achievement, Suzanne's teacher should compare her

TABLE 8.2

Categories of Percentile Ranks That Minimize Errors of Grouping, with Suggested Description of Each Category

Range of Percentile Ranks	Achievement Level
90–99	Excellent
67–89	Good
34–66	Normal
11–33	Poor
1–10	Deficient

score with that of the average of her class and perhaps with that of the average of entering sixth grade pupils in her community. How to make a comparison of this kind is taken up in the next section of this chapter. Suzanne's teacher should also examine her answer sheet carefully to find what types of items Suzanne marked incorrectly and whether she had time to try all of the items. Analysis of a pupil's responses in this way often yields important clues about ways to help him improve.

Comparison of an Individual's Score with the Average of a Group of Which He Is a Member

Although comparison of an individual's obtained score with national norms is often informative and worthwhile, the wide differences that exist among school systems, among schools within the same system, and even among classes within a single school make it desirable to compare an individual's score with local norms or with the average of his own class. Naturally, if a teacher makes up a test and uses it in his own class, he has no norms for it and can compare a pupil's score only with the scores of other pupils in the class or with some measure of central tendency in the group, such as the class mean.

To compare an individual's score with the average of the class of which he is a member, it is necessary only to compute the arithmetic mean of the scores obtained by the members of the class and subtract it from the score of the individual. The computation of the arithmetic mean is explained and illustrated in appendix A. The difference between the individual's score and the mean will be a positive number if his score is higher than the mean, zero if they are the same, and negative if his score is lower. However, both the individual's score and the mean score include errors of measurement; therefore the difference between them may result entirely from these errors. That is, even if the individual's *true* score and the *true* class mean are the same, the difference between the individual's *obtained* score and the mean of the *obtained* scores in the class may turn out to be a positive or a negative number. For this reason, it is necessary to determine the smallest difference that can be accepted as *not* likely to have occurred as merely a chance deviation from a true difference of zero. This difference, and any larger difference, is called a *significant difference* at the level of probability specified.

In Figure 2.1 a distribution of errors of measurement around the true score of an individual was shown. This section concerns the distribution of errors of measurement around the difference between a true mean score of a class and the true score of one individual in the class. The "measuring rod" for these errors of measurement is, as would be expected, a standard error of measurement—this time the standard error of measurement of the difference between the average of obtained scores of the class members and the obtained score of one member of the class. The desired standard error of measurement is easily estimated simply by multiplying the standard error of measurement of an obtained score on the test by $\sqrt{(N-1)/N}$, where N represents the number of scores included in the average. This statement can be expressed in an equation of general usefulness, as follows:*

$$s_{\text{meas }(X-\bar{X})} = s_{\text{meas }X} \sqrt{\frac{N-1}{N}}, \tag{8.1}$$

where $s_{\text{meas }(X-\bar{X})}$ = the standard error of measurement of the difference between X and $\bar{X}$,

* F. B. Davis, "Interpretation of Differences among Averages and Individual Scores," *Journal of Educational Psychology*, L (1959), Case 2, 162–170.

$s_{\text{meas } X}$ = the standard error of measurement of an obtained
score on test X,

X = an obtained score on test X,

$\overline{X}$ = the arithmetic mean of scores on test X, and

N = the number of scores averaged.

To determine the smallest difference that may be considered significant at a designated level, the standard error of measurement of the difference is multiplied by an appropriate constant. Table 8.3 shows the multipliers to

TABLE 8.3

Multipliers Used to Determine Smallest Differences
Significantly Different from Zero at Selected Levels

Level of Significance Desired	Multiplier (to two decimal places)
1 per cent	2.58
5 per cent	1.96
10 per cent	1.64
15 per cent	1.44
32 per cent	1.00

use for this purpose. Students interested in the rationale of this procedure will find it in appendix I; here the estimation and use of a significant difference is simply illustrated by a practical example.

On September 16, near the beginning of the school year, Miss Black administered Form J of the *Stanford Intermediate Paragraph-Meaning Test* to the ten pupils in her class. As shown in Table 8.4, their grade scores were as follows: 97, 81, 60, 72, 58, 64, 47, 51, 43, and 35. Their average grade score was 60.80. Since the standard error of measurement of an obtained grade score on this test is six points, the standard error of measurement of the difference between the average score of 60.80 and the obtained score of an individual pupil in the class is obtained by multiplying 6 by $\sqrt{(N-1)/N}$. Inasmuch as N equals 10 (the ten pupils in the class), 6 times .95, or 5.7 (rounded to one decimal place), is the standard error of measurement of the difference. To estimate the smallest difference significant at the 15-per-cent level when a true difference of zero is postulated, the standard error of measurement of the difference (5.7) is multiplied by 1.44, the multiplier shown in Table 8.3 for estimating differences significant at the 15-per-cent level. The result is 8.2 (rounded to the nearest tenth of a point). Therefore, only scores of class members that are 8.2 points, or more, above or below the class average of 60.80 are significantly different from it at the 15-per-cent

TABLE 8.4

Grade Scores on *Stanford Intermediate Paragraph-Meaning Test* of Ten Pupils in Miss Black's Fifth Grade Class

Date of Testing	Form J September 16	Form K September 17	Form L June 16	Form M June 17
Pupil				
A	97	92	109	108
B	81	79	87	73
C	60	68	95	88
D	72	53	77	97
E	58	53	72	63
F	64	73	63	73
G	47	46	72	76
H	51	64	57	57
I	43	43	61	61
J	35	38	47	48

level. We infer with considerable confidence that the three pupils who obtained grade scores of 97, 81, and 72 are truly superior in paragraph-meaning skill to the class average and that the four pupils who obtained grade scores of 51, 47, 43, and 35 are truly inferior in this respect to the average of the class. However, we cannot be reasonably sure that the pupils who obtained grade scores of 64, 60, and 58 are either truly inferior or superior to the average of the class with respect to paragraph-meaning skill.

To determine which of the pupils in Miss Black's class obtained grade scores significantly different from the average of the class at the 1-per-cent level, 5.7 is multiplied by 2.58 (as indicated in Table 8.3). The product is 14.7 (rounded to the nearest tenth of a point). This is the smallest difference between the class average and the score of an individual that is significant at the 1-per-cent level. We may infer with great confidence that the two pupils with grade scores of 97 and 81 are truly superior to the class average and that the two with scores of 43 and 35 are truly inferior to the class average.

Different assignments in reading and in other subjects are often given to pupils identified as superior, normal, or retarded readers. Miss Black would have some real basis for giving assignments of different length and complexity to the group of three pupils whose paragraph-meaning scores were found at the 15-per-cent level to be significantly higher than the class average, to the group of three pupils whose scores were found to be insignificantly different from that average, and to the group of four pupils whose scores were found to be significantly lower than that average.

Comparison of an Individual's Score with the Average of a Group of Which He Is Not a Member

Sometimes it is desired to compare a pupil's score on a certain test with the average score of a group of which he is *not* a member. For example, after Miss Black's fifth grade class had been in school for about a month, a fifth grade pupil named Eva Andrews moved into the district and was placed in her class. Miss Black administered the same paragraph-meaning test to her as she had to the ten original members of the class on September 16. Eva obtained a grade score of 69. Since the class average was 60.80, Eva's score was 8.2 points above it. Miss Black wondered whether to place Eva in the superior reading group or the normal reading group. To help her decide, she wanted to know whether Eva's score of 69 was significantly higher than the class average at the 15-per-cent level.

The standard error of measurement of the difference between the average score of a group and the obtained score of an individual who is *not* a member of the group can be estimated by means of equation 8.2,* which follows:

$$s_{\text{meas } (X - \bar{X})} = s_{\text{meas } X} \sqrt{\frac{N + 1}{N}}. \tag{8.2}$$

The notation of equation 8.2 is the same as that used in equation 8.1, which it closely resembles.

The standard error of measurement of Eva's obtained score is 6 points, as given by the publisher of the test. The number of pupils whose scores were averaged was ten. Therefore, the standard error of measurement of the difference between Eva's score and the average of the class is 6.3 (rounded to the nearest tenth of a point). Multiplying 6.3 by 1.44 (as shown in Table 8.3), we obtain 9.1 as the smallest difference that we may consider significant at the 15-per-cent level. Since Eva's grade score is only 8.2 points higher than the average of the class, we conclude that her skill in paragraph meaning may not be truly higher than the class average. Unless other information alters her judgment, Miss Black would do well to group her with the normal readers rather than with the three pupils in the superior group.

Comparison of an Individual's Score with the Average of a Sample of Pupils Representative of National or Local Groups

The score of an individual is often compared with national or local norms, which are usually based on the testing of very large numbers representative of certain more or less homogeneous grade or age groups; almost

* F. B. Davis, "Interpretation of Differences among Averages and Individual Test Scores," *Journal of Educational Psychology*, L (1959), Case 4, 162–170.

never has the score of the individual under consideration been included in the norms group.   Under these circumstances, the smallest difference between the individual's obtained score and the arithmetic average of the scores in the norms group that may be regarded as significant at a specified level can be closely approximated by multiplying the standard error of measurement of an obtained score by an appropriate multiplier chosen from Table 8.3. Consider the score of Helen Meadows on the *Davis Reading Test*, Series 1. Helen, a twelfth grade pupil, took this test in November and obtained a score of 68 in Speed of Comprehension.   The average score in the norms group of 5,596 twelfth grade pupils tested in September and October of 1957 was 71.8 points.   Helen's obtained score is 3.8 points below this average. Is this difference significant at the 15-per-cent level?

To answer this question, the standard error of measurement of an obtained score on this test is used; this is given in the *Manual for the Davis Reading Test* as 2.9 points.*   Multiplying 2.9 by 1.44 (the appropriate multiplier for the 15-per-cent level, as shown in Table 8.3), we obtain a value of 4.2 for the smallest difference between an individual Speed-of-Comprehension score and the average of the twelfth grade norms group that is significant at the 15-per-cent level.   Helen's score is only 3.8 points below this average.   Hence, her true speed of comprehension in reading may not be lower than the average for pupils at her grade level.   There is no reason to be worried about her reading ability on the basis of these data.

As mentioned previously, the technique used to evaluate the difference between Helen's score and the average score in the twelfth grade norms group is an approximation procedure that is useful when the number of cases in the norms group is very large.†

INTERPRETATION OF TWO OR MORE SCORES FOR ONE INDIVIDUAL

When an individual takes one or more tests, each of the scores he obtains may be interpreted separately in terms of grade-equivalent scores, percentile ranks, and comparisons with the average scores of various national and local groups.   Methods for doing this with the aid of confidence

---

* F. B. Davis and C. C. Davis, *Manual for the Davis Reading Test*, Series 1 and 2 (New York: Psychological Corp., 1962), table 5, p. 14.

† For an exact procedure, see F. B. Davis, "Interpretation of Differences among Averages and Individual Test Scores," *Journal of Educational Psychology*, L (1959), Case 5, 162–170.

intervals and significant differences have been presented in preceding sections of this chapter.   The existence of two or more scores for an individual leads the test interpreter to compare these scores systematically with one another while maintaining due regard for errors of measurement.   Procedures for making such comparisons on a scientific basis are presented in this section of the chapter.

Comparison of an Individual's Scores on Two Forms of the Same Test

If an individual takes two equivalent forms of a test, one after the other, with no opportunity to learn any of the subject-matter content between testings, his true score remains the same.   If his obtained scores on the two forms differ, the variation must result from errors of measurement in one or both scores or from changes in his attention to the task or effort to do well on it.   We can readily estimate whether this variation is greater than can reasonably be ascribed to errors of measurement.   If it is, some explanation of the difference in scores should be sought even though one cannot always be found.

We are concerned here with a distribution of errors of measurement around a difference of zero between one individual's true scores on two equivalent forms of a test.   The "measuring rod" for these errors of measurement is again a standard error of measurement—this time the standard error of measurement of the difference between two obtained scores.   If we let X stand for an obtained score on one form and Y for an obtained score on another form, the desired standard error of measurement of the difference between two obtained scores is given by equation 8.3.*

$$s_{\text{meas}\,(X-Y)} = \sqrt{s^2_{\text{meas}\,X} + s^2_{\text{meas}\,Y}}. \qquad (8.3)$$

The next step is to estimate the size of the smallest difference between obtained scores that is acceptable, at a designated level of significance, as *not* likely to have occurred as a result of errors of measurement when the difference between the individual's true scores on the two forms is really zero.   As previously stated, this can be done simply by multiplying the

* For the original proof of this equation in terms of standard measures, see T. L. Kelley, "A New Method for Determining the Significance of Differences in Intelligence and Achievement Scores," *Journal of Educational Psychology*, XIV (1923), 321–333.   For its adaptation to comparable scores, made in 1953 by F. B. Davis, see A. E. Traxler, ed., *Education in a Free World* (Washington: American Council on Education, 1955), pp. 146–147.

standard error of measurement of the difference by a multiplier chosen from Table 8.3 to yield the desired level of significance.

Consider the scores on Forms J and K of the *Stanford Intermediate Paragraph-Meaning Test* (shown in Table 8.4). These forms were given on successive days to the ten pupils in Miss Black's class. The grade scores on the two forms are equivalent and the standard error of measurement of a grade score on either form is 6 grade-score points. The standard error of measurement of the difference between obtained scores is, therefore, $\sqrt{36 + 36}$, or 8.5. Multiplying 8.5 by 1.44 (the appropriate multiplier for estimating the 15-per-cent level of significance, as shown in Table 8.3), we obtain 12.2 (rounded to the nearest tenth of a point) for the size of the smallest difference between obtained scores on Forms J and K that is significant at the 15-per-cent level. Comparison of the Form-J and Form-K scores of each of the ten pupils in Miss Black's class, as shown in Table 8.4, indicates that the difference is significant at the 15-per-cent level only in the case of pupils D and H. Pupil D's grade score dropped 19 points from 72 on Form J to 53 on Form K and pupil H's score rose 13 points from 51 to 64.

Before it is concluded that the differences between the obtained scores of these two pupils are too large to be explained on the basis of variation due to errors of measurement alone, it is necessary to estimate the number of differences significant at the 15-per-cent level that would be the most likely number to appear by chance in this set of ten differences. This estimate is obtained by multiplying the number of differences (in this instance ten) by the level of significance employed. The estimate is equal to 10 times .15, or 1.5 differences. Naturally, we should not interpret as significant any differences in a set if the number of differences judged significant is no greater than might by chance alone have been identified as significant. A convenient rule of thumb is to consider all differences in a set as insignificant if the number identified as significant is no greater than our estimate of the number that would most likely be identified as significant by chance alone.

In Miss Black's class, two differences out of ten are identified as significant. Since this is a larger number than would be most likely to show significance by chance alone, it is proper to conclude that some adverse influence might have affected the performance of pupil H during the first testing and the performance of pupil D during the second testing. With this information, Miss Black, the counselor, or the school psychologist should check the report of the test administrator for each of these testing sessions to see if there are any clues to the variation in performance of pupils D and H. Both pupils should be interviewed privately in a friendly, informal way to discover what, if anything, affected their performances. Inferences about their true abilities in paragraph meaning should then be made in the light of the information obtained. Surprising facts sometimes come to light. On one occasion, a twelfth grade pupil who was interviewed privately about a highly significant difference between scores on two equivalent forms of a perception test given on successive days admitted confidentially that he had tried to answer as many items as possible *correctly* on the first day and as many as possible *incorrectly* on the second day. He was quite successful in reaching his objective on both days. Naturally, his score on the second form should be expunged from the records since it provides grossly misleading information about his true ability in perception.

The technique presented in this section for identifying pupils whose test performances are markedly inconsistent should be used more often than it is by teachers, counselors, and school psychologists. It can be employed most conveniently by using short tests that are available in several equivalent forms. It is often better to give two equivalent short forms of a test on successive days than to give one long form of the test in a single testing session; this is especially true in the testing of young children or of examinees who are emotionally upset. The two equivalent test scores for each child can be compared to identify any that are significantly different; then the two scores for each child can be averaged for comparing one child's performance with that of another or for making local norms.* The standard error of measurement of the average of two or more scores on equivalent forms of a test is simply the standard error of measurement of a score on one form divided by the square root of the number of forms for which scores were averaged. This can be put in the form of equation 8.4:

$$s_{\text{meas } \bar{X}} = \frac{s_{\text{meas } X}}{\sqrt{n}}, \tag{8.4}$$

where n = the number of equivalent forms for which scores are averaged,

$s_{\text{meas } \bar{x}}$ = the standard error of measurement of an individual's average score on n forms of test X, and

$s_{\text{meas } x}$ = the standard error of measurement of an obtained score on test X.

It should be emphasized that the comparison of scores discussed in this section has been confined to scores on equivalent forms of the same test administered on the same day or within a few days of each other. If a longer period of time elapses between testings, pupils' scores can be expected to change because the pupils will have learned some of the subject matter tested. The measurement of the amount of learning that takes place over a period of time is discussed in chapter 10.

* Note that it is not proper to compare such average scores for each pupil with norms based on the administration of a single form.

Comparison of an Individual's Scores on Two or More Different Tests

Tests that yield comparable scores. Grade scores derived from a co-ordinated battery of tests, such as the *Stanford Achievement Test*, are comparable in the sense that a given grade score on any one of the nine tests represents the same level of performance relative to the scores obtained by pupils in a large sample. That is, a grade score of 61 in any one of the nine tests in the *Stanford Achievement Test* represents the average level of perform-ance attained by a sample of pupils in the first month of grade 6, a grade score of 65 represents the average level of performance attained by a sample of pupils in the fifth month of grade 6, and so on. As pointed out in chapter 2, this comparability of test scores is valuable because, within certain limita-tions, it makes possible convenient and direct comparison of an individual's performance in one subject-matter field with his performances in other subject-matter fields. His strengths and weaknesses thus become apparent and form the basis for individualized instruction or as close an approximation to that ideal as a teacher's schedule will permit.

To help teachers identify these strengths and weaknesses, many test publishers make provision for plotting comparable scores on a pupil profile chart. Figure 8.5 shows the Individual Profile Chart for the *Stanford Achievement Test*, Intermediate Battery, with five scores of pupil J in Miss Black's class (see Table 8.4) plotted on it.* Pupil J is Jim Allen, who entered Miss Black's class in September. His age and his various test scores are given in Table 8.5. The first step in making an interpretation of his scores is

TABLE 8.5

Performance of Jim Allen on Five Tests in Form J of the *Stanford Achievement Test*, Intermediate Battery, on September 16

(Jim became 10 years of age on August 16, one month before the testing.)

Test	Subject Matter	No. Right	No. Wrong	No. Omitted	Grade Score	Grade-Equiv. Score	Grade 5.2 Per-centile	K Score
1.	Paragraph Meaning	15	2	31	35	3.5	10	73.2
2.	Word Meaning	18	1	29	41	4.1	20	69.3
3.	Spelling	10	30	32	24	2.4	below 2	69.4
5.	Arithmetic Reasoning	20	7	18	45	4.5	30	66.5
6.	Arithmetic Computation	26	1	18	59	5.9	80	49.1

FIGURE 8.5

Individual Profile Chart for the *Stanford Achievement Test*, Intermediate Battery, Form J.

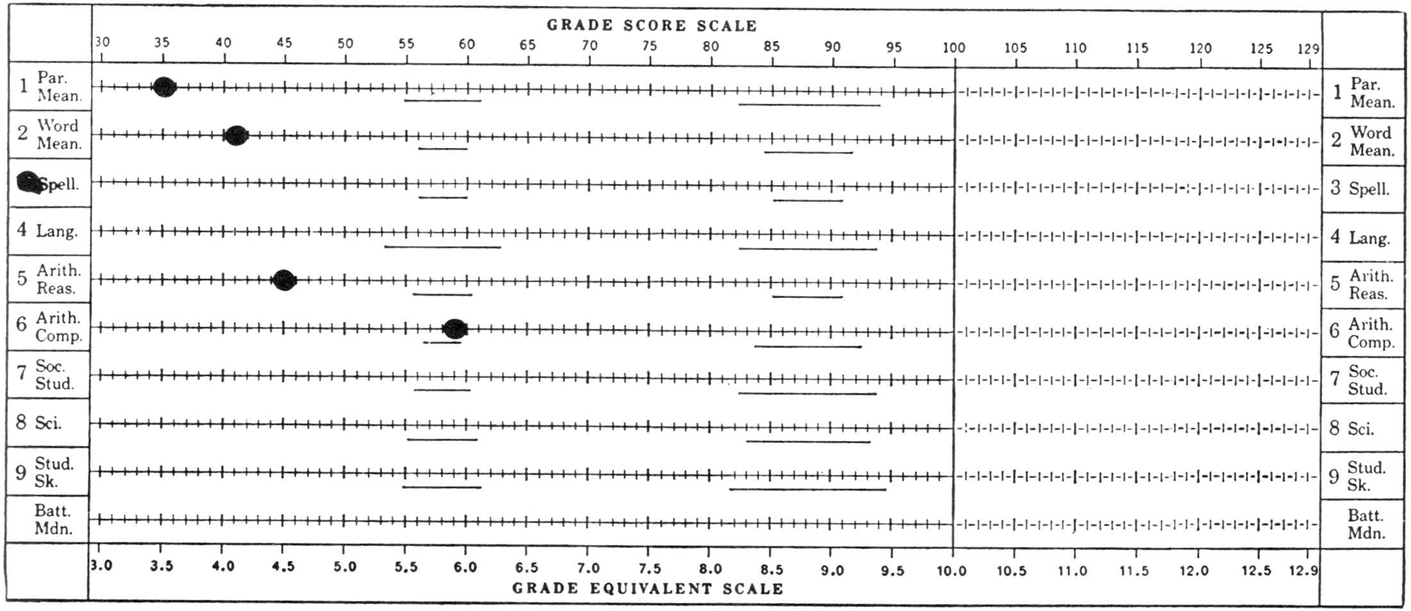

Grade equivalent values above 10.0 are extrapolated values and not to be interpreted as signifying the typical performance of pupils of the indicated grade placement. (See Directions for Administering.)

to note his age in relation to his grade placement. He was 10 years and 1 month old when he took the tests during his first month in grade 5. Data provided by the publishers indicate that the most common age for pupils at that grade level is 10 years and 1 month, so Jim is exactly at the expected age for his grade placement.* Of course, there is wide variation in age in any grade group. Within limits this is desirable to allow for differences among pupils in mental development and in social and physical maturity.

The second step in interpreting Jim's scores is to evaluate them relative to his grade placement. A glance at his grade-equivalent scores in Table 8.5 shows them below his grade-placement level of 5.1 in four of the five tests. Only in arithmetic computation does his obtained grade-equivalent score of 5.9 exceed his grade placement. The 85-per-cent confidence intervals for grade scores (not grade-equivalent scores) on all nine parts of Form J of the Intermediate Battery of the *Stanford Achievement Test* are given in Table M.3 in appendix M. For the five parts administered to Jim, they are: Part 1, 17.3; Part 2, 11.5; Part 3, 11.5; Part 5, 13.7; Part 6, 8.6. To convert these into grade-equivalent scores, move the decimal point one place to the left in each of them. When that has been done and the resulting confidence intervals have been centered around Jim's obtained scores, only for the two arithmetic tests (parts 5 and 6) do the confidence intervals include, or cover a range of scores above, his grade-placement level of 5.1. In the other subject-matter areas, therefore, it is likely that Jim is truly below his grade placement in achievement. His lowest score is in spelling, in which he is probably about two and one-half grades retarded. The data suggest the need for a careful diagnostic study of his spelling difficulty followed by systematic remedial work.

The third step in interpreting his scores is to compare his performance on each test with that of representative American school children at his grade level. For this comparison, percentile norms are satisfactory. These are provided by the publishers for the second, fifth, and eighth month at each grade level for which the tests are appropriate. For Jim, we use the norms for grade 5.2. The necessary table is reproduced as Figure 8.6.† Jim's percentile ranks are shown in Table 8.5. As would be expected from his

* *Stanford Achievement Test, Directions for Administering the Intermediate and Advanced Batteries,* Forms J, K, L, M, and N (New York: Harcourt, Brace and World, Inc., 1953), table 2, p. 13.

† To obtain percentile ranks from the table of norms, enter each column in the table with a grade score and read its percentile rank from the left-hand column of boldface numbers. If the grade score does not appear in the table, read as its percentile rank the boldface number corresponding to the grade score in the proper column that is closest in value to the grade score. If the grade score is exactly halfway in value between two grade scores in the column, take as its percentile rank the one of the two boldface numbers closest to it that is an even number. For example, a grade score of 31 on the paragraph-meaning part

grade scores, these percentile ranks are below 50 except in arithmetic computation.

It is interesting to note that, if the terms given in Table 8.2 are used to describe his achievement, Jim is "Deficient" in spelling and "Good" in arithmetic computation. This is not particularly unusual; differences of this magnitude will be found in the achievement levels in various subject-matter areas of many individuals. Such differences should be identified so that these individuals can be encouraged to develop their strengths to the maximum and to bring their weaker subjects up to at least an acceptable level.

The fourth step in the interpretation of Jim's scores is to find whether his five scores differ sufficiently from one another to warrant the belief that the strengths and weaknesses shown on his profile chart are not merely chance variations resulting from errors of measurement. To systematize this process, a score-difference grid, like the one shown in Figure 8.7, may be used. The rows and columns are numbered to correspond to the parts of the *Stanford Achievement Test* that were administered to Jim. His actual grade scores have been entered in the second column from the left. Next, the difference between each pair of scores is entered in the appropriate cell. For example, his grade score of 41 on part 2 is subtracted from his grade score of 35 on part 1 and the result (-6) is entered in row 1 at column 2. His score of 24 on part 3 is subtracted from his score of 35 on part 1 and the result (11) is entered in row 1 at column 3. The remainder of the cell entries are filled in as shown in Figure 8.7. In all, there are ten differences. Each of these must now be compared with the smallest value it could take and still be regarded as significant at the 15-per-cent level. To make this comparison readily possible, Table M.3 in appendix M has been prepared. Each of the differences in Table M.3 represents the smallest difference significant at the 15-per-cent level between a designated pair of scores on Forms J, K, L, M, or N of the *Stanford Achievement Test*, Intermediate Battery. It has been obtained by multiplying the standard error of measurement of the difference (as given by equation 8.3) by 1.44, as specified in Table 8.3.

A teacher, counselor, or school psychologist can easily make up a set of these minimum differences significant at the 15-per-cent (or any other) level for any test that he uses. Once this table has been made up, it can be used over and over to interpret the scores of any individual who takes the test. For the convenience of test users, sets of tables of this kind for many tests in common use have been included in appendix M.

---

is assigned a percentile rank for grade 5.2 of 5; a grade score of 32 is assigned one of 10, and so on. The slight errors introduced by failing to interpolate are not ordinarily of consequence for individual scores. Averages of two or more grade scores should not be used to enter the tables of percentile ranks for individual scores.

FIGURE 8.6

Percentile Ranks Corresponding to Grade Scores on the *Stanford Achievement Test*, Intermediate Battery, Form J.

Grade 5.2

Percentile Rank	Par. Meaning	Word Meaning	Spelling	Language	Arith. Reas.	Arith. Comp.	Social Studies	Science	Study Skills
98	93	90	73	91	76	66	93	92	97
95	81	80	69	84	71	63	83	86	86
90	74	70	65	77	66	61	75	77	77
85	69	65	63	74	63	60	69	73	71
80	65	62	61	70	61	58	65	69	66
75	63	59	59	67	58	57	63	65	64
70	60	57	57	64	56	56	61	62	61
65	58	55	55	61	55	55	58	59	59
60	56	54	54	58	54	54	57	56	56
55	54	52	53	55	53	53	54	54	54
50	52	51	51	52	52	52	52	52	52
45	49	49	49	50	50	51	51	50	50
40	47	47	47	47	48	50	50	47	48
35	46	45	46	44	47	49	48	44	46
30	44	44	44	42	46	48	47	42	45
25	42	42	42	38	44	46	46	40	42
20	40	41	40	36	43	45	45	38	40
15	38	39	38	31	40	43	44	36	38
10	34	35	35	27	38	40	43	32	35
5	30	31	31	19	33	36	41	29	32

FIGURE 8.7

Differences among Jim Allen's Grade Scores.

Date: September 16   School: Shadyside

Name: Jim Allen   Test: Stanford Intermediate, Form J

Test	Score	1	2	3	5	6
1	35		−6	⑪	−10	(−24)
2	41			⑰	−4	(−18)
3	24				(−21)	(−35)
5	45					(−14)
6	59					

Number of Differences: 10
Number of Differences × .15: 1.5
Number of Circled Differences: 7

To identify the differences in Figure 8.7 that are significantly different from zero, any one that is as large as, or larger than, the corresponding entry in Table M.3 has been circled: in row 1, the entries at columns 3 and 6; in row 2, the entries at columns 3 and 6; in row 3, the entries at columns 5 and 6; in row 5, the entry at column 6. Thus, out of ten differences, seven are found to be significant at the 15-per-cent level. As shown before, .15 times 10, or 1.5 differences would be most likely to show significance at this level as a result of errors of measurement alone. Therefore, the variations in Jim's obtained scores probably reflect true differences in his abilities and the differences found to be significant should be interpreted. It will be noted that they form a definite pattern, indicating that he is significantly lower in spelling (part 3) and higher in arithmetic computation (part 6) than in other subjects tested. His paragraph-reading, word-knowledge, and arithmetic-reasoning scores are not significantly different from one another. His special facility in computation should be recognized and encouraged and his interests in this type of skill should be stimulated; his spelling difficulty should be analyzed and appropriate remedial teaching should be initiated.

In Jim's case, seven of the ten differences are significant, indicating that his pattern of scores justifies interpretation. In many cases, however, it will be found that all of the differences among the scores could have been produced by errors of measurement alone even if the true scores were exactly alike. In such cases the data do not warrant interpretation, and a great deal of professional time and skill is wasted in an effort to derive meaning from differences in a set of scores that may reflect merely the operation of chance. The fifth and last step is to find what types of errors he has made by studying the items he failed. In spelling, for example, it would be useful to know whether he tries to spell phonetically, whether he uses the common rules (such as the "i before e" rule), and so on. Since this type of detailed analysis of test performance is time consuming, it can usually be employed only with the test papers of pupils whose total scores show that they need special attention.

Another illustration of the use of significant differences in the interpretation of test scores may be helpful. Roger, a twelfth grade pupil eighteen years of age, was tested by the school psychologist with the *Wechsler Adult Intelligence Scale.** Comparable scores derived from the eleven tests in this scale are called scaled scores (though they are not the same as the scaled scores developed by Flanagan for the *Cooperative Achievement Tests* and described in chapter 2). Roger's scaled scores and IQ scores are shown in Table 8.6 together with the difference between each of his scaled scores and his average scaled score on the remaining ten tests. The first step in interpreting Roger's scores is to determine whether his verbal IQ of 104 is

TABLE 8.6

Roger's Scores on the *Wechsler Adult Intelligence Scale* and Their Deviations from His Average Scores

Test	Scaled Score	Difference between Roger's Scaled Score on Each Test and the Average of His Scaled Scores on the Other Ten Tests
1. Information	10	.40
2. Comprehension	11	1.50
3. Arithmetic	9	−.70
4. Similarities	13	3.70
5. Digit Span	7	−2.90
6. Vocabulary	11	1.50
7. Digit Symbol	9	−.70
8. Picture Completion	9	−.70
9. Block Design	11	1.50
10. Picture Arrangement	9	.70
11. Object Assembly	7	−2.90

Verbal IQ: 104
Performance IQ: 94
Full-Scale IQ: 100

* New York: Psychological Corp., 1955.

significantly different from his performance IQ of 94. This is done by consulting Table M.19 in appendix M. The smallest difference between verbal and performance IQ's that is significant at the 15-per-cent level is eight points. Since Roger's verbal and performance IQ's differ by ten points, his verbal ability is probably truly superior to his nonverbal ability. If this difference between his verbal and performance IQ's were not significant, no further interpretation would be made of the verbal and performance IQ's separately; only the full-scale IQ would be considered.

The second step in interpreting Roger's scores is to convert his verbal and performance IQ's to percentile ranks in the American population. This can be done by reference to Table 6.2 (page 131), which shows that Roger's verbal percentile rank is 61 and that his performance percentile rank is 34. Table 6.3 indicates that his verbal ability may be described as " Normal " and his performance ability as " Dull."

The third step is to compute all the differences among Roger's scaled scores on a score-difference grid, as shown in Figure 8.8. Each difference on the grid is compared with the corresponding entry in Table M.19, and any one that is as large as, or larger than, its corresponding entry is circled to show that it is significant at at least the 15-per-cent level. Of the 55 differences, 17 are circled. Since the most likely number that would turn out by chance alone to be significant at this level is .15 times 55, or 8.25, all the variation in Roger's scaled scores cannot reasonably be ascribed to errors of measurement. Therefore, the pattern of significant differences among his scores is considered, and it is found that 15 of them pertain to test 4 (Similarities), test 5 (Digit Span), or test 11 (Object Assembly). Roger's reasoning ability (as demonstrated by his performance on the Similarities test) is significantly better than most of his other abilities, and his rote memory (as demonstrated on the Digit-Span test) and his spatial visualization (as demonstrated on the Object-Assembly test) are significantly lower than most of his other abilities. In general, Roger is of normal intelligence with no outstanding abilities among those sampled by this test.

The fourth step in the interpretation of Roger's scores is to explore the possibility that this pattern of scaled scores provides diagnostic indications, or "signs," of organic brain damage or of emotional maladjustment. This exploration falls outside the scope of an introductory course in educational measurement, but the presence or absence of one type of diagnostic sign suggested by Wechsler* can readily be ascertained by computing the difference between each of an individual's eleven scaled scores and the average of his scaled scores on the remaining ten tests. Whether such differences for any individual can reasonably be attributed to errors of measurement alone

* David Wechsler, *Measurement and Appraisal of Adult Intelligence*, fourth ed. (Baltimore: The Williams and Wilkins Co., 1958), chapter 11.

FIGURE 8.8

Differences among Roger's Scaled Scores.

Date: _____
Name: Roger

School: _____
Test: Wechsler Adult

Test	Score	1	2	3	4	5	6	7	8	9	10	11
1	10		-1	1	(-3)	(3)	-1	1	1	-1	1	(3)
2	11			2	-2	(4)	0	2	2	0	2	(4)
3	9				(-4)	2	-2	0	0	-2	0	2
4	13					(6)	2	(4)	(4)	2	(4)	(6)
5	7						(-4)	-2	-2	(-4)	-2	0
6	11							(2)	(2)	0	2	(4)
7	9								0	-2	0	2
8	9									-2	0	2
9	11										2	(4)
10	9											2
11	7											

Number of Differences: 55   Number of Differences × .15: 8.25   Number of Circled Differences: 17

can be determined by comparing each one with the smallest difference that is significant at the 5-per-cent (or any other) level. The smallest differences significant at the 5-per-cent level are given in Table M.19. When the difference between each of Roger's scaled scores and the average of his remaining ten scaled scores is compared with the appropriate entry in this table, only the one pertaining to his Similarities-test scaled score proves to be significant. Since the other differences may result from the presence of errors of measurement alone, they should not be considered seriously. The one difference that can be taken seriously is not, of itself, sufficient evidence on which to base any clinical inferences.*

The fifth and last step in the interpretation of Roger's scores is to analyze the quality and nature of his responses to individual items or to small groups of items. Inferences drawn from such analyses may be combined with subjective observations of the individual tested made by the psychologist during the examination. Valuable data may thus be obtained, but it must be handled carefully because individual item responses are highly unreliable and differences among them are even more so; furthermore, the psychologist's observations are subjective. The gathering and interpretation of these data clearly fall outside the scope of this book.

Tests that do not yield comparable scores. The interpretation of differences among test scores that are not comparable requires that some basis for making the scores comparable be found and used. Unless the test publisher has provided comparable scores, it is usually troublesome and sometimes impossible for the test user to do so. The process sometimes involves the establishment of local norms, which requires the testing of hundreds of examinees. If several tests have been given to the same group or to large groups drawn at random from the same population, percentile ranks for each test can be provided and may be regarded as reasonably comparable, especially if the tests are about equally reliable. The computation of percentile ranks is presented in appendix B.†

Some test publishers have prepared special profile charts on which percentile ranks for an individual may be plotted for each of several tests in a coordinated set. The Individual Report Form for the *Differential Aptitude*

* The testing of differences of this kind for significance and their use for interpreting scores derived from the *Wechsler Adult Intelligence Scale* and the *Wechsler Intelligence Scale for Children* are discussed in the following article: F. B. Davis, "Interpretation of Differences among Averages and Individual Test Scores," *Journal of Educational Psychology*, L (1959), Cases 1 and 2, 162–170. Table M.20 in appendix M includes the basic data required for interpreting scores derived from the *Wechsler Intelligence Scale for Children* (New York: Psychological Corp., 1949).

† The use of percentile ranks for making test scores comparable is described in J. C. Flanagan, "Units, Scores, and Norms," in E. F. Lindquist, ed., *Educational Measurement* (Washington: American Council on Education, 1951), pp. 747–760.

FIGURE 8.9

Individual Report Form for the *Differential Aptitude Tests.*

INDIVIDUAL
REPORT FORM

Forms L and M

DIFFERENTIAL APTITUDE TESTS [1963 EDITION]

G. K. Bennett, H. G. Seashore, and A. G. Wesman

Name *Mary Brown*   Year *63* Form *A* Grade *11* Sex *F*

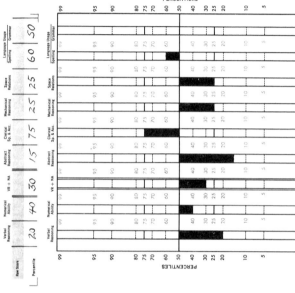

Profiling Your DAT Scores

The numbers that tell how you did on each test are in the row marked "Percentiles." Your percentile tells where you rank on a test in comparison with boys or girls in your grade. These percentiles are based on test scores earned by thousands of students in numerous schools across the country. If your percentile rank is 50, you are just in the middle — that is, one-half of the students in the national group did better than you and one-half did less well. (If your school uses local norms, your counselor will explain the difference.)

In the columns below each percentile you can draw your aptitude profile. For each test make a *heavy short line* across the column at the level which corresponds to your percentile rank on that test.

Your aptitude profile will be more visible if you black in each column *up to* or *down to* the 50-line from the short lines

How Big a Difference Is Important?

Of course we do not want to over-estimate small differences in ability on tests because a test cannot be perfectly accurate, and your score might not be exactly the same if you could take the same test twice.

To estimate the importance of a difference between your scores on any two tests on this profile, use a ruler to measure how much higher on the chart one mark is than the other. It is the *vertical* distance that counts, of course, *not* how far *across* the chart ╱ or ╲.

you have just made. The vertical bars just made. The vertical bars show the strength of your tested aptitudes, *up* or *down* from the rank of the *middle student* of your grade and sex.

Think of "percentile" as meaning "per cent of people." In your case, the people are boys or girls in your grade in many schools across the country. The percentile shows what per cent of this group scored no higher than you did. If your percentile rank on one test is 80, you are at the top of 80 per cent of the group — only 20 per cent made higher scores than yours. If you scored in the 25th percentile, this would mean about 75 per cent of the group did better than you on the test. Thus, a percentile rank always indicates your relative standing among a theoretical 100 persons representing a large "norm" group — in this case, students of your sex and grade. It does not tell how many questions (or what per cent of them) you answered correctly.

If the distance is *one inch or greater*, it is probable that you have a real difference in your abilities on the two tests.

If a difference between the two percentile ranks is *between a half inch and one inch*, consider whether other things you know about yourself agree with it; the difference may or may not be important.

If the vertical distance between two tests is *less than a half inch*, the difference between the two scores may be disregarded; so small a difference is probably not meaningful.

63-125S

Tests is one of these. This form is reproduced as Figure 8.9.* Note that the percentile ranks are spaced with unequal distances between them. The vertical distance between percentile ranks of 40 and 70 is about the same as that between percentile ranks of 95 and 99. To see why, suppose that the distribution of scores on a test of abstract reasoning is truly normal among a representative sample of tenth grade pupils in the United States. In such a distribution, the correspondence of standard measures and percentile ranks is shown in Figure 8.10. As the distance from the mean (the center line) of

FIGURE 8.10

The Normal Distribution and Various Types of Scores.†

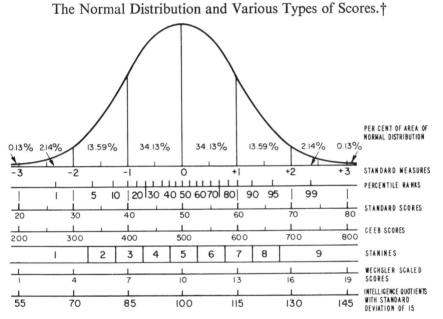

† Adapted from H. G. Seashore *et al., Test Service Bulletin No. 47* (New York: Psychological Corp., September 1954).

the distribution increases, the area under the curve for each half of a standard measure decreases. Since percentile ranks reflect areas under the curve, the distance between each two percentile ranks must be greater as the ranks are more distant from the mean. Thus, nineteen successive percentile ranks take up half of a standard measure from 0 to +.5 while only five percentile ranks take up half of a standard measure from +1.5 to +2.0. Obviously, each of the latter percentile ranks has to cover more distance along the base-line than each of the nineteen percentile ranks between 0 and +.5 standard measure. Equal distances along the baseline can be regarded as essentially equal increments of ability, and it is these distances that the Individual Report Form uses as the basis for the vertical placement of percentile ranks. Standard scores are employed as the units of measurement. On Figure 8.10 these standard scores are shown on the third line below the baseline of the curve. The method by which they are computed is given in appendix D. Their standard errors of measurement, their confidence intervals, and the minimum differences among them that are significant at the 15-per-cent level are provided in Table M.22 in appendix M. These data may be used to interpret standard scores derived from the *Differential Aptitude Tests* in the same way that such data were used to interpret grade scores derived from the *Stanford Achievement Test.*

For the *School and College Ability Tests* (SCAT),* the *Sequential Tests of Educational Progress* (STEP),† and other tests, the Educational Testing Service provides profile sheets on which a percentile band may be plotted for each test taken by an individual. This type of profile chart is illustrated in Figure 8.11, on which SCAT scores for a twelfth grade pupil named Betty Haven have been plotted.‡ Her percentile band for the verbal part extends from 83 to 94. In nontechnical terms, the chances are about 68 out of 100 that this range of percentile ranks includes her true verbal score. Similarly, the chances are 68 out of 100 that the range of percentile ranks from 53 to 72 includes her true quantitative score. When these percentile bands do not overlap, the difference between the abilities or skills that they represent can be regarded as significant at about the 15-per-cent level. Hence, Betty's true verbal ability is probably higher than her true quantitative ability. Since the total score on SCAT is the sum of the verbal and quantitative scores, lack of overlapping between the percentile band for the total score and that for either part score indicates a difference that is significant at a more stringent level than does a similar lack of overlapping between percentile bands for the two part scores. The explanation of this is outside the scope of this book.

Instead of using percentile ranks to make comparable scores from two or more different tests that have been administered to a large sample of pupils, a school psychologist or counselor can employ standard measures. In this case, scores on each test that correspond to the same standard measure

* *Cooperative School and College Ability Tests* (Princeton: Cooperative Test Division, Educational Testing Service, 1955).

† *Sequential Tests of Educational Progress* (Princeton: Cooperative Test Division, Educational Testing Service, 1956).

‡ *SCAT Student Profile* (Princeton: Cooperative Test Division, Educational Testing Service, 1957). Copyright 1957. All rights reserved. Reproduced by permission.

FIGURE 8.11 Student Profile Chart for the *School and College Ability Tests.*

Name *Haven* (Last) *Betty* (First) ______ (Middle)

School *Central High School* Grade or Class *12*

Age *16* (Years) *2* (Months) Date of Testing *Nov. 2* (Fall or Spring) *1963* (Year)

Norms Used

☒ Publisher's ☒ Fall Grade or Class ______

☐ Local ☐ Spring Other ______

Cooperative Test Division Educational Testing Service. Princeton, N.J. Los Angeles 27, Calif.

Here you can profile a student's percentile ranks corresponding to SCAT Verbal, Quantitative, and Total converted scores.

Recording. Directions for recording information and drawing percentile bands on the PROFILE form are included in the SCAT MANUAL FOR INTERPRETING SCORES.

Interpreting. To compare a student's Verbal, Quantitative, or Total SCAT performance with that of other students in the norms group used, note the unshaded parts of the column above and below the percentile band. For example, if the Verbal percentile band is 44-55, you know that 44 per cent of students in the norms group score lower than this student and 45 per cent score higher. In other words, this student's Verbal performance is about average with respect to the norms group.

To compare a student's Verbal and Quantitative standings, the following rules apply:

1. If the Verbal and Quantitative percentile bands overlap, there is no important difference between the student's Verbal and Quantitative standings.
2. If the Verbal and Quantitative percentile bands do *not* overlap, standing represented by the higher band is really better than standing represented by the lower band.

Examples: According to local norms, a student's percentile bands for SCAT Verbal and Quantitative are 39-50 and 45-57, respectively. The bands overlap; there is no important difference between the student's Verbal and Quantitative standings. Another student's percentile band for SCAT Verbal is 57-69 and for SCAT Quantitative is 35-46. The bands do not overlap; the student's Verbal standing is higher than his Quantitative standing.

A more detailed discussion of interpretations is contained in the SCAT MANUAL FOR INTERPRETING SCORES.

SCAT STUDENT PROFILE
SCHOOL AND COLLEGE ABILITY TESTS

Test	Verbal	Quantitative	Total
Form	1A	1A	1A
Converted Score	300	299	299

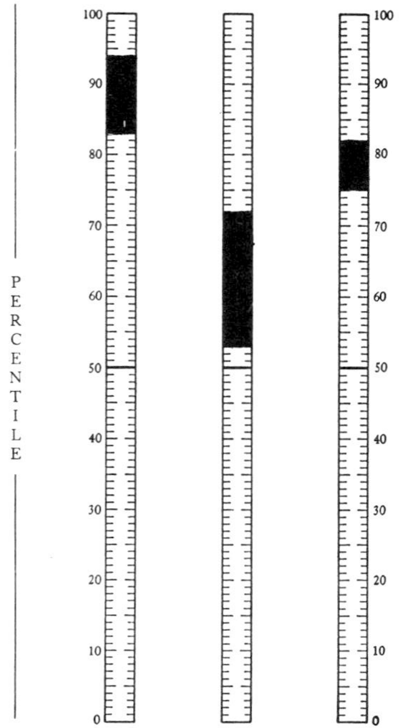

are regarded as comparable. The computation of standard measures is explained and illustrated in appendix D. If standard errors of measurement can be computed for scores on each of the tests, as shown in appendix E, confidence intervals for individual scores can be set up and the minimum differences significant at the 15-per-cent (or any other) level can be determined in terms of standard measures. The standard error of measurement of a set of standard measures (denoted $s_{\text{meas } z}$) is equal to the standard error of measurement of the raw scores (denoted $s_{\text{meas } x}$) divided by the standard deviation of the distribution of raw scores (denoted s_X). In the form of an equation, this reads:

$$s_{\text{meas } z} = \frac{s_{\text{meas } X}}{s_X}. \tag{8.5}$$

Comparison of Scores Obtained by Two or More Individuals

Table 8.4 shows the grade scores of ten fifth grade pupils on Form J of the *Stanford Intermediate Paragraph-Meaning Test*. Their scores, if placed in rank order, are as follows: 97, 81, 72, 64, 60, 58, 51, 47, 43, and 35. How large a difference between scores is required to give reasonable assurance that one score truly represents a higher level of paragraph-meaning skill than does another? This question is important because whenever the obtained scores of two individuals are compared, the possibility exists that the difference between the scores is attributable merely to a chance deviation from a zero difference between identical true scores. It is easily answered if the standard error of measurement of each obtained score is available.

The equation for the standard error of measurement of the difference between the scores obtained by two individuals (let us call them Frank and George) on test X is as follows:

$$s_{\text{meas } (XF - XG)} = \sqrt{s^2_{\text{meas } XF} + s^2_{\text{meas } XG}}, \tag{8.6}$$

where XF and XG = the scores of Frank and George, respectively, on test X; and

$s_{\text{meas } XF}$ and $s_{\text{meas } XG}$ = the standard errors of measurement of their scores.

If Frank and George took Form J of the *Stanford Intermediate Paragraph-Meaning Test*, the standard error of measurement of the grade score obtained by each of them would be 6 points; this value is given on the Individual Profile Chart for that test. According to equation 8.6, the standard error of measurement of the difference between any two individual scores on that test is $\sqrt{36 + 36}$, or 8.49. Multiplying 8.49 by 1.44 to estimate the smallest difference significant at the 15-per-cent level gives 12.22. Therefore, any difference of 13 points or more between obtained grade scores on this test is reasonable assurance that a true difference exists.

The rank order of scores on Form J in Miss Black's class shows that pupil A's score of 97 is significantly higher than pupil B's score of 81. However, pupil B's score is not significantly higher than pupil D's score of 72, and so on. The important point to keep in mind is that a definite conclusion that one pupil's achievement or ability is higher or lower than another's should be avoided unless the difference between their obtained scores is great enough to warrant the belief that a true difference exists. To permit convenient use of this technique, the tables in appendix M include the minimum number of score points that constitutes a significant difference between obtained scores on the same test. The minimum difference significant at the 15-per-cent level that we computed by means of equation 8.6 for Form J of the *Stanford Paragraph-Meaning Test*, which is test 1 in the Intermediate Battery of Forms J, K, L, M, and N of the *Stanford Achievement Test*, forms the basis for the entry of 13 at the left-hand end of row 1 in Table M.3. For test 2 in this battery (Word Knowledge), Table M.3 shows that the smallest difference between individual grade scores that is significant at the 15-per-cent level is nine points.

Tables for other tests will be found to yield minimum differences for comparing scores of individuals. For example, Roger's verbal IQ of 104 on the *Wechsler Adult Intelligence Scale* may be compared with the verbal IQ of 110 obtained by one of his classmates named Henry. The entry in Table M.19 at the junction of row 12 and column 12 shows that a difference of 7 IQ points is required for significance at the 15-per-cent level. Hence, we must conclude that we cannot be reasonably sure whether Roger or Henry has the higher true verbal IQ.

Some publishers offer standard errors of measurement that are appropriate for use with obtained scores in separate segments of the possible range of scores. For IQ's derived from Forms L–M, L, and M of the *Revised Stanford-Binet Intelligence Scale*, the standard errors of measurement shown in Table 8.7 have been provided. When equation 8.6 is used to obtain the smallest difference between IQ's of 130 or more that is significant at the 15-per-cent level, the result is 12 IQ points, as given in Table 8.7. Yet a difference of only 5 IQ points is significant at the 15-per-cent level for IQ's below 70. This is because low IQ's are more accurately determined by this test than are high IQ's. In actual practice this may be regarded as fortunate, since critical decisions with respect to children's placements in classes for the mentally retarded are made partly on the basis of IQ scores of about 70, where accuracy of measurement is nearly maximal on this test.

To determine the significance of differences between IQ's in ranges with different standard errors of measurement, the latter would be used appropriately in equation 8.6. Suppose, for example, that it is desired to determine

TABLE 8.7

Standard Errors of Measurement of IQ's and Smallest Differences Significant at the 15-Per-Cent Level between IQ's in Five IQ Ranges on the *Revised Stanford-Binet Intelligence Scale*, Forms L–M, L, and M

IQ Range*	Number of Cases†	Standard Error of Measurement*	Smallest Differences Significant at the 15-Per-Cent Level
130 and above	154	5.24	12
110–129	872	4.87	10
90–109	1,291	4.51	10
70–89	477	3.85	8
Below 70	57	2.21	5

* Data obtained from L. M. Terman and M. A. Merrill, *Measuring Intelligence* (Boston: Houghton Mifflin Co., 1937), table 11, p. 46.

† Data obtained from *ibid.*, table 10, p. 46. In the manual for the third revision, it is indicated (on pp. 257 ff.) that the accuracy of measurement of Form L–M is at least as good as that of Forms L and M, but no additional data are provided. See L. M. Terman and M. A. Merrill, *Stanford-Binet Intelligence Scale*, Manual for the Third Revision, Form L–M (Boston: Houghton Mifflin Co., 1960).

whether a difference of seven points between IQ's of 68 and 75 is significant at the 15-per-cent level. Equation 8.6 yields a value of $\sqrt{(2.21)^2 + (3.85)^2}$, or 4.44. Multiplying 4.44 by 1.44 gives 6.39. Thus, the difference of seven points between IQ's of 68 and 75 on the *Stanford-Binet Intelligence Scale* is significant at the 15-per-cent level. This kind of information is supplied without need for any calculation for the differences between most IQ's derived from these tests by the right-hand column in Table 8.7.

COMMUNICATING TEST RESULTS

The presentation of test results demands careful planning, accurate information, and a great deal of tact and patience. Because of the personal involvement of pupils and parents, the maximum need for tact and patience arises when test data are presented to them.

Before presenting test results to any individual or group, the interpreter should:

1. Consider the main objectives of the presentation.
2. Limit his objectives to those likely to be attainable within the amount of time available and with the amount and kind of explanation that can be understood.

3. Make sure that the data are accurate.
4. Make sure that he understands the meaning of the data and that they are in a form that minimizes the likelihood of their being misused.

During the presentation of test results, the interpreter should:

1. Maintain a friendly but matter-of-fact attitude and avoid dramatizing the findings.
2. Present favorable information first.
3. Provide opportunities for questions.
4. Avoid arguments about the data or their meaning.   Contradictory assertions should be met with statements like, "That's a point to consider.   Explain it more fully."

Two other basic rules for test interpreters are:

1. Treat all test data as confidential and make them available to school personnel only when there is reason to believe that the data will be used for the benefit of the pupils involved.   Under no circumstances should test data pertaining to one pupil be given to other pupils or to the parents of other pupils.
2. Treat as completely confidential any comments made or information volunteered by the pupil or parent unless the latter has willingly agreed that they should be discussed with some other person for the benefit of the pupil.

Inexperienced test interpreters tend to overestimate the extent to which pupils or parents accept their explanations or even understand them.   When most people are faced with information or explanations that they do not want to believe, they simply seal them off from their framework of beliefs. The inexperienced counselor or test interpreter is often surprised in later interviews to discover the pupil or parent expressing ideas that should logically have been modified by data or explanations already presented. This discovery should usually be a cue to him to encourage the pupil or parent to discuss the matter further.   With many people, this technique sooner or later results in their amalgamating new ideas into their framework of beliefs, thus causing them to make real changes in themselves.   It is sometimes surprising how long this process takes.

A great deal has been written about specific applications of the ten rules for test interpreters that have been given above.   It is only after practical experience in test interpretation, however, that this material becomes meaningful.   Test interpretation is based on technical competence and a thorough understanding of data, but it is, in practice, an art that can be developed through tact, experience, willingness to learn, and helpful guidance from someone versed in it.

Summary

An individual's obtained score on a test is usually not meaningful until it is compared with other examinees' scores or with mean scores or percentile scores in defined groups. These comparisons always involve differences, either explicitly or implicitly. Thus, interpretations of individual scores are based on differences between scores. It is well known that differences between scores are apt to be much less reliable than the scores themselves; they can be highly misleading, especially in estimating pupil growth or underachievement and overachievement. For these reasons, it is important that anyone who hopes to interpret psychological- or educational-test scores understand the nature and meaning of differences between scores.

To take account of the inaccuracy in a single test score produced by errors of measurement, the *confidence interval* of the scores should be used. The 85-per-cent confidence interval is recommended for this purpose. It represents a middle ground between the stringent levels of confidence used in research studies and the failure to recognize the existence of errors of measurement that is implicit in the naïve use of obtained scores as though they were true scores.

To take account of the inaccuracy in a difference between two individual test scores, the standard error of measurement of the difference should be used to establish the statistical significance of the difference. The 15-per-cent level is recommended for most purposes in the interpretation of such differences. It strikes a practical balance between the twin dangers of regarding a great many inferences as false when they are actually true and of regarding a great many other inferences as true when they are actually false.

The following types of test-score interpretation are explained and illustrated:

1. Use of the confidence interval for a single score;
2. Meaning of a grade-equivalent score;
3. Meaning of a percentile rank;
4. Comparison of an individual's score with the average of a group of which he is a member;
5. Comparison of an individual's score with the average of a group of which he is *not* a member;
6. Comparison of an individual's score with the average of a group representative of national or local groups (normative groups);
7. Comparison of an individual's scores on two forms of the same test;
8. Comparison of an individual's scores on two or more different tests that yield comparable scores;
9. Comparison of an individual's scores on two or more different tests that do *not* yield comparable scores;
10. Comparison of scores obtained by two or more individuals on the same test.

The information provided by these ten types of interpretive procedures must be organized and digested by the test interpreter before it can be communicated to pupils, parents, teachers, counselors, or administrators. The process of communication is an art that can be developed by those who have the technical knowledge to obtain accurate and meaningful data and the tact, the patience, and the personal warmth to put the data across effectively to others. The process does not lend itself to formulation by rule; it is at once scientific and artistic.

Selected References

Anastasi, Anne, "The Concept of Validity in the Interpretation of Test Scores," *Educational and Psychological Measurement*, X (1950), 67–78.

Bennett, George K., Harold G. Seashore, and Alexander G. Wesman, *Counseling from Profiles: A Casebook for the Differential Aptitude Tests.* New York: Psychological Corporation, 1951.

Berdie, Ralph F., *et al.*, *Testing in Guidance and Counseling.* New York: McGraw-Hill Book Co., Inc., 1963. Chapter 9.

Davis, Frederick B., "The Interpretation of Fall Test Results," in *1941 Fall Testing Program in Independent Schools, and Supplementary Studies.* Educational Records Bulletin, No. 35. New York: Educational Records Bureau, 1942, pp. 32–40.

Davis, Frederick B., "Interpretation of Differences among Averages and Individual Scores," *Journal of Educational Psychology*, L (1959), 162–170.

Durost, Walter N., "How to Tell Parents about Standardized Test Results," *Test Service Notebook, No. 26.* New York: Harcourt, Brace and World, Inc., 1961.

Kelley, Truman L., *Interpretation of Educational Measurements.* Yonkers: World Book Company, 1927.

Mosier, Charles I., "Batteries and Profiles," in E. F. Lindquist, ed., *Educational Measurement.* Washington: American Council on Education, 1951, pp. 794–808.

Thorndike, Robert L., and Elizabeth P. Hagen, *Measurement and Evaluation in Psychology and Education*, second ed. John Wiley & Sons, Inc., 1961. Chapter 18.

Traxler, Arthur E., *et al.*, *Introduction to Testing and the Use of Test Results in Public Schools.* New York: Harper and Row, Publishers, 1953. Chapters 7–10.

Chapter Nine

INTERPRETATION
OF GROUP SCORES

When the pupils in a class, a school, or a school system have been tested, we may want to compare the average performance of one class, school, or school system with that of another. Sometimes a principal or superintendent wants to compare the average performance of one class with the average of all pupils in the same grade or the average of all pupils in a single grade with the national average for that grade. This chapter provides the techniques for making these comparisons and others that may be of interest to teachers, counselors, psychologists, and administrators.

THE CHOICE OF AN AVERAGE

To represent the performance of a group of examinees by a single value, some sort of average can be employed. The phrase *some sort of average* is used because several different kinds of averages exist. For our purposes, the *median* and the *arithmetic average*, the latter often called the *arithmetic mean* or simply the *mean*, are the only two averages that need be considered. From the point of view of a mathematician, they are both averages but they differ with respect to the adequacy with which they represent the central tendency of a group of individuals and with respect to their standard errors. The median is usually the more representative in a distribution that is markedly skewed. A well-known example of a skewed distribution is that of family incomes in the United States. Most families have annual incomes between $1,000 and $10,000, but some have incomes running into the hundreds of thousands, and a very few have annual incomes running into millions of dollars.

Most of the distributions of test scores used in educational measurement are rather symmetrical, so the arithmetic mean is ordinarily more suitable than the median. Furthermore, these distributions tend to be either like the normal distribution in shape or a little flatter than the normal distribution. Under these circumstances, the arithmetic mean has a smaller standard error than the median; the standard error of the median of a normal distribution is about one and one-quarter times as large as that of the arithmetic mean of the same distribution.   Add to these considerations the fact that it is easier to work with the arithmetic mean mathematically than with the median, and it is easy to see why comparisons of groups and of individuals with groups should generally be made in terms of means.   The computation of the mean is very simple and is illustrated in appendix A.   The computation of the median is given in appendix B.

ERRORS IN ESTIMATING A TRUE MEAN

Chapter 8 showed how the obtained score of an individual can be used as an estimate of his true ability or of his knowledge in the subject matter tested.   In the same way, the average score of a group of individuals is used as an estimate of their true average.   A confidence interval can be set up for an arithmetic mean in much the same way as for an individual's obtained score.   Fortunately, the confidence interval for a mean is smaller than that for an individual's obtained score.   The larger the number of scores included in the average, the smaller the confidence interval becomes.

Errors of Measurement

The errors of measurement associated with an individual's obtained score arise, as shown in chapter 2, largely because of limitations of the test itself that cause it to be less than a perfectly accurate measure of the field it is intended to cover.   For example, the items in it ordinarily comprise only a small sample of all of the items that could be written on the subject matter tested.   Naturally, since an average is determined by the values of the scores that are used to compute it, the errors of measurement in individual scores also affect it.   But, since these errors are both positive and negative, they tend to cancel each other out when the scores containing them are averaged. The negative error in one individual's score tends to cancel the positive error in another individual's score.   The larger the number of scores that are averaged, the more opportunities there are for cancellation of errors and the smaller the error of measurement of the average becomes.

As would be expected, the distribution of successive arithmetic means obtained if the same group of examinees is tested with many equivalent forms of the same test approaches the shape of the normal distribution as the number of forms increases. The standard deviation of this distribution of means is used as the "measuring rod" for the error of measurement of the mean; it is called the *standard error of measurement of the mean*, and it is easy to estimate if the standard error of measurement of an obtained score is known. The latter is simply divided by $\sqrt{N}$, where N is the number of scores averaged, to estimate the standard error of measurement of the mean (denoted $s_{\text{meas }\bar{X}}$). This can be expressed compactly in equation 9.1.

$$s_{\text{meas }\bar{X}} = \frac{s_{\text{meas }X}}{\sqrt{N}} \tag{9.1}$$

A confidence interval can be set up for the mean by using an appropriate multiplier from Table 8.1. For the 85-per-cent confidence interval, this is 2.88. This can be illustrated by setting up a confidence interval for the mean grade score on Form J of the *Stanford Intermediate Paragraph-Meaning Test* for the ten pupils whose scores are shown in Table 8.4. Their mean grade score is 60.80. The standard error of measurement for a grade score on this test is given by the publisher as 6 points. Therefore, the standard error of measurement for the mean of 60.80 is estimated as $6/\sqrt{10}$, or 1.90. Multiplying 1.90 by 2.88 gives 5.5 (rounded to the nearest tenth of a point). Hence, we infer that the range of scores from 58.1 to 63.5 includes the true arithmetic mean of this class of ten pupils, recognizing that out of every 100 inferences like this that are made about 85 will be correct.

Errors of Sampling

Up to this point, only the errors of measurement resulting from the imperfections of a test in a particular sample have been considered. The illustration dealt with a class of ten pupils in grade 5. To estimate the true mean for an entire population, another kind of error must be taken into account—*sampling error* resulting from the fact that successive samples drawn from a population will not be perfectly representative of the population. It is easy to see that this is so: Write a different boy's name on each of fifty slips of paper and a different girl's name on each of fifty similar slips of paper, place the one hundred slips in a box, and mix them thoroughly; next, draw out ten slips of paper at random; five slips should have boys' names on them and five slips should have girls' names on them if our sample of ten children is to represent perfectly with respect to sex the population of one hundred children. But everyone knows that if this is done many times, each time putting the slips we have drawn back into the box and mixing them thoroughly before drawing another ten, groups will sometimes be drawn that are made up of six boys and four girls, four boys and six girls, seven boys and three girls, and so on. Once out of many drawings, a group made up of ten boys and no girls would be drawn. These variations in the number of boys and girls drawn constitute sampling errors. There would, of course, be no sampling error with respect to sex if five slips bearing boys' names and five slips bearing girls' names were always drawn, but this does not happen in real life so sampling variation must be taken into account in drawing conclusions about the means of populations.

For example, if a confidence interval is to be set up for the mean of the population of fifth grade pupils from which Miss Black's class of ten pupils was drawn, sampling variation as well as errors of measurement must be taken into account. To do this, the *standard error of the mean* is used. This may be denoted as $s_{\bar{X}}$ and estimated by equation 9.2.

$$s_{\bar{X}} = \frac{s_X}{\sqrt{N}} \tag{9.2}$$

In equation 9.2, s_X represents the standard deviation of the obtained scores of the ten pupils in Miss Black's class. As shown in Table F.1 in appendix F, it is 18.65 grade-score points. So the standard error of the arithmetic mean of 60.80 equals 18.65 divided by 3.16, or 5.90 points. Multiplying 5.90 by 2.88 (the appropriate multiplier given in Table 8.1 for estimating the 85-per-cent confidence interval) gives 17.0 (rounded to the nearest tenth of a point). Therefore, we conclude that the range of scores from 52.3 to 69.3 includes the mean paragraph-meaning score of the population of fifth grade pupils of which Miss Black's class is representative, recognizing that about 85 decisions out of every 100 of this sort that are made will be correct. This confidence interval of 17.0 points is much larger than the one of 5.5 points obtained for use in making inferences about the true mean paragraph-meaning score of Miss Black's class alone. The standard error of measurement of the mean is ordinarily smaller than the standard error of the mean—in fact, ordinarily much smaller. In educational measurement, the standard error of measurement of the mean is often appropriate for making comparisons of existing groups of pupils, but in research studies the standard error of the mean is ordinarily the more useful of the two values.

COMPARISON OF MEAN PERFORMANCES ON THE SAME TEST IN TWO SEPARATE GROUPS

On September 11, Form J of the *Stanford Advanced Paragraph-Meaning Test* was administered to all eighth grade pupils in the town of Dayville.

TABLE 9.1

Grade Scores in Four Eighth Grade Classes in Dayville Obtained on September 11 on Form J of the *Stanford Advanced Paragraph-Meaning Test* with Class, School, and Community Means

Pupil	Riveredge School		Mountain View School	
	Miss Brown's Class	Miss Green's Class	Miss White's Class	Miss Gray's Class
A	100	98	106	104
B	96	93	105	105
C	94	96	105	100
D	88	92	104	103
E	82	79	103	92
F	81	80	102	103
G	80	79	101	97
H	79	82	99	99
I	78	74	98	100
J	77	72	98	97
K	76	73	97	99
L	75	77	96	93
M	75	70	95	91
N	74	71	95	90
O	74	71	94	95
P	74	72	94	95
Q	74	74	93	87
R	73	66	93	88
S	73	70	92	79
T	73	71	91	91
U	72	68	91	92
V	72	70	90	90
W	71	71	90	86
X	70	60	89	90
Y	70	71	89	88
Z	69	70	88	84
AA	68	70	88	84
BB	68	65	87	89
CC	67	60	86	86
DD	67	63	85	75
EE	66	68	85	77
FF	63	67	84	83
GG	62	69	83	84
HH	60	62	82	80
II	58	62	81	76

Table 9.1—cont.

Pupil	Riveredge School Miss Brown's Class	Miss Green's Class	Mountain View School Miss White's Class	Miss Gray's Class
JJ	55	60	80	80
KK	54	55	78	77
LL	52	57	77	76
MM	51	53	74	77
NN	50	52	72	74
OO	44	47	48	49
$\bar{X}$	70.85	70.24	89.95	87.93
s	12.10	11.26	10.97	10.81

	Riveredge School	Mountain View School
$\bar{X}$	70.55	88.94
s	11.59	10.88

	Dayville
$\bar{X}$	79.74
s	14.51

There were 164 pupils tested, 82 in the Riveredge School and 82 in the Mountain View School. Their scores are shown in Table 9.1. The mean grade score in the Riveredge School is 70.55 and in the Mountain View School, 88.94. When these grade scores were converted to total-group grade-equivalent scores,* they became 7.55 for the Riveredge School and 9.39 for the Mountain View School. Since the pupils were all in the first month of grade 8, it is apparent that the mean of the Riveredge School is about a half grade below the level of paragraph-meaning skill expected of pupils at their grade placement. The mean of the pupils in the Mountain View School, on the other hand, is a little more than a grade higher than would be expected of them.

A difference between the means as great as 1.84 grade-equivalent points is almost surely large enough to warrant the belief that it is not the result of error alone; but to make fairly sure of this, we may estimate the smallest difference between means that is significant at any designated level. Since we are not interested in making inferences about the populations of which the

* See *Stanford Achievement Test, Directions for Administering the Intermediate and Advanced Complete Batteries*, Forms J, K, L, M, N (New York: Harcourt, Brace and World, Inc., 1953), table 1, p. 12.

pupils in the Riveredge and Mountain View Schools are representative but are concerned solely with the difference between the means of the 82 pupils in each of those schools, we make use of the *standard error of measurement of the difference between means.* *   This may be obtained by means of equation 9.3.

$$s_{\text{meas} (\bar{X}_A - \bar{X}_B)} = s_{\text{meas } X} \sqrt{\frac{1}{N_A} + \frac{1}{N_B}}, \qquad (9.3)$$

where $s_{\text{meas} (\bar{X}_A - \bar{X}_B)}$ = the standard error of measurement of the difference between the mean score of group A and the mean score of group B on test X,

$s_{\text{meas } X}$ = the standard error of measurement of an obtained score of any individual on test X, and

N_A and N_B = the numbers of individuals whose scores were averaged in group A and in group B.

The standard error of measurement of an obtained grade score on the *Stanford Advanced Paragraph-Meaning Test* is given by the publisher as 11.50 points.   This value can be used in equation 9.3 along with the numbers of pupils in the Riveredge and Mountain View Schools to obtain the standard error of measurement of the difference between the means of 70.55 and 88.94 grade-score points.   The computation becomes:

$$11.50 \sqrt{\frac{1}{82} + \frac{1}{82}} = 1.80.$$

Next, the standard error of measurement of the difference between means is multiplied by an appropriate entry from Table 8.3 in order to obtain the smallest difference significant at the desired level.   For the 1-per-cent level, this multiplier is 2.58.   Then 1.80 × 2.58 equals 4.64, which is the smallest difference between the grade-score means in the two schools that is significant at the 1-per-cent level.   Therefore, we conclude that the difference of 18.39 grade-score points between the means of the two schools is highly significant, and that the paragraph-reading ability of the pupils in the Mountain View School is, on the average, greater than that of the pupils in the Riveredge School.   Significant differences are often found between the mean achievement of pupils in different schools, even within the same school system. Pupils tend to go to schools in their own neighborhoods; neighborhoods tend to be somewhat homogeneous with respect to socio-economic and cultural levels.   Ordinarily, level of skill in school subjects, especially those dependent on verbal skills, is positively related to socio-economic and cultural level of the home.   However, some pupils of outstanding achievement and ability

* F. B. Davis, "Interpretation of Differences among Averages and Individual Test Scores," *Journal of Educational Psychology*, L (1959), Case 8, 162–170.

come from homes at low socio-economic and cultural levels and some pupils of limited achievement and ability come from homes at high socio-economic and cultural levels. One of the principal reasons why testing programs are needed in schools is to identify the skills and abilities of each individual pupil so that they can be used as a basis for guiding his learning experiences and his school career.

Equation 9.3 may also be used to determine whether differences between the mean grade scores of pupils in the two classes in the Riveredge School or in the Mountain View School are significant. Since there are forty-one pupils in each of the four classes, the smallest difference between the means of any two of them that can be considered significant at the 1-per-cent level is equal to $2.58 \times 11.50 \sqrt{(1/41) + (1/41)}$, or 6.55 grade-score points. The difference between the mean grade scores of 70.85 and 70.24 in the Riveredge School is .61 of a point; the difference between the mean grade scores of 89.95 and 87.93 in the Mountain View School is 2.02 points. Thus, neither of these two differences is significant at the 1-per-cent level. Apparently the two classes in each school are about the same with respect to paragraph-reading skill, although the means in the two schools are significantly different.

COMPARISON OF MEAN PERFORMANCES ON THE SAME TEST OF TWO OVERLAPPING GROUPS

It is sometimes desired to compare the mean performance of a group of pupils with that of another group that includes the first. For example, the school counselor may wish to compare the average ability of one class with the average ability on the same test of all classes at the same grade level in the school system, or a superintendent of schools may wish to know whether the mean IQ in one school is significantly different from the mean IQ of all pupils in the school system. To make comparisons of these types, the *standard error of measurement of the difference between the means of two partially overlapping groups* must be estimated with the aid of equation 9.4.*

$$s_{\text{meas } (\bar{X}_S - \bar{X}_T)} = s_{\text{meas } X} \sqrt{\frac{1}{N_S} - \frac{1}{N_T}}, \qquad (9.4)$$

* F. B. Davis, "Interpretation of Differences among Averages and Individual Test Scores," *Journal of Educational Psychology*, L (1959), Case 7, 162–170.

where $s_{\text{meas} (\bar{X}_S - \bar{X}_T)}$ = the standard error of measurement of the difference between the mean score of group S and the mean score of group T, when group S is wholly included in group T;

$s_{\text{meas} X}$ = the standard error of measurement of an obtained score on test X;

N_S and N_T = the numbers of individuals whose scores were averaged in groups S and T.

Notice that only the sign of the second term under the radical makes the form of equation 9.4 differ from that of equation 9.3.

Table 9.1 shows that the average grade score in Miss Brown's class of forty-one pupils is 70.85. The average grade score on the same test of all of the 164 eighth grade pupils in Dayville is 79.74. The standard error of measurement of the difference of 8.89 points between these two averages, as given by equation 9.4, is as follows:

$$11.50 \sqrt{\frac{1}{41} - \frac{1}{164}} = 1.55.$$

Multiplying 1.55 by 2.58 to obtain the smallest difference between the means that can be considered significant at the 1-per-cent level gives 4.00. Since the difference of 8.89 points between the means in Miss Brown's class and in all eighth grade classes in Dayville is larger than 4.00, we conclude that the mean paragraph-reading ability in Miss Brown's class is truly lower than that of all eighth grade classes in Dayville.

COMPARISON OF MEAN PERFORMANCES ON THE SAME TEST OF A PARTICULAR GROUP AND A NORMS GROUP

Teachers, school administrators, and others often wish to compare the mean score of a particular group, such as a class, with the published norm appropriate for the group. For example, Miss Steven's eleventh grade English class of thirty pupils took Form A of the *Davis Reading Test*, Series 1, in October. The average level-of-comprehension score in the group was 67.80 points. The norm for grade 11 is an average score of 66.00 for 5,857 eleventh grade pupils tested in September and October of 1957. The difference between these two averages is 1.80 points; to determine whether it is significantly different from a true difference of zero, it should be compared with an estimate of the smallest difference significant at the 1-per-cent level. This comparison requires the *standard error of measurement of the difference between the mean of a particular group and the mean of a representative sample of a defined population,* which is provided by equation 9.5.

$$s_{\text{meas } (\bar{X}_G - \bar{X}_S)} = \sqrt{\frac{s^2_{\text{meas } X}}{N_G} + \frac{s^2_{X_S}}{N_S}}, \tag{9.5}$$

where $s_{\text{meas } X}$ = the standard error of measurement of an individual obtained score on test X;

s_{X_S} = the standard deviation of obtained scores and N_S the number of cases in a large representative sample of a defined population; and

N_G = the number of cases in group G, none of whom are included in sample S.

The standard error of measurement for an obtained level-of-comprehension score on the *Davis Reading Test*, Series 1, is given by the publisher as 3.6 points. The standard deviation of obtained scores in the representative sample of 5,857 eleventh grade pupils is 7.06 points. Since Miss Steven's class comprises thirty pupils, the computation of the standard error of measurement of the difference we are concerned with becomes:

$$\sqrt{\frac{(3.6)^2}{30} + \frac{(7.06)^2}{5,857}} = .66.$$

Multiplying .66 by 2.58 to estimate the size of the smallest difference between the means that can be considered significant at the 1-per-cent level gives 1.70. Since the obtained difference between the mean of the class and the mean of the norms group was 1.80, we conclude that the average level of comprehension in Miss Steven's class is truly higher than the average level of comprehension in the norms group for grade 11.

Note that the second term under the radical in equation 9.5 becomes negligible if the number of cases in the norms group is very large, as is often the case in practice. Its value in the example above is only .008 (rounded to the nearest thousandth), so its omission does not change the result in the second decimal place.

COMPARISON OF MEAN PERFORMANCES OF THE SAME GROUP ON DIFFERENT TESTS THAT YIELD COMPARABLE SCORES

Level 5 of the *Lorge-Thorndike Intelligence Tests* was administered to all pupils in grade 12 of the Westbourne High School. The verbal and nonverbal IQ's yielded by this test measure somewhat different mental functions but are comparable in the sense that the percentile rank of a given IQ is essentially the same whether it is a verbal or a nonverbal IQ. In West-bourne, the average verbal IQ of the 169 pupils tested was 101.30 and the average nonverbal IQ was 102.61. The guidance counselor was surprised that the mean nonverbal IQ was higher than the mean verbal IQ and wished to find whether the difference of 1.31 IQ points between the means could be attributed only to errors of measurement. This problem can be solved by making use of the *standard error of measurement of the difference between means on two different tests*, which is given by equation 9.6.

$$s_{\text{meas }(\bar{X} - \bar{Y})} = \sqrt{\frac{s^2_{\text{meas } X}}{N_X} + \frac{s^2_{\text{meas } Y}}{N_Y}}, \qquad (9.6)$$

where $s_{\text{meas }(\bar{X} - \bar{Y})}$ = the standard error of measurement of the difference between means on two different tests, X and Y;

$s_{\text{meas } X}$ and $s_{\text{meas } Y}$ = the standard errors of measurement of obtained scores on tests X and Y, respectively; and

N_X and N_Y = the numbers of cases averaged to obtain $\bar{X}$ and $\bar{Y}$, respectively.

The standard errors of measurement of obtained verbal IQ's and non-verbal IQ's derived from Level 5 of the *Lorge-Thorndike Intelligence Tests* are 6.1 and 5.1, respectively.* Since the same pupils took the verbal and nonverbal parts of the test, both N_X and N_Y are 169. Computation of the desired standard error of measurement of the difference between the mean verbal IQ and the mean nonverbal IQ becomes:

$$\sqrt{\frac{(6.1)^2}{169} + \frac{(5.1)^2}{169}} = .61.$$

Multiplying .61 by 2.58 to estimate the smallest difference between the means that is significant at the 1-per-cent level gives 1.57. Because the difference of 1.31 points is smaller than 1.57, we conclude that in this partic-ular group of twelfth graders the true difference between the averages of their verbal and nonverbal IQ's may be zero or in the opposite direction from the obtained difference. In other words, the latter may be the result of errors of measurement alone.

---

* I. D. Lorge and R. L. Thorndike, *The Lorge-Thorndike Intelligence Tests, Technical Manual* (Boston: Houghton Mifflin Co., 1957), table 5, p. 9.

COMPARISON OF MEAN PERFORMANCES OF THE SAME GROUP ON TESTS THAT DO *NOT* YIELD COMPARABLE SCORES

If a group of examinees takes two or more tests that do *not* yield comparable scores, direct comparison of the mean scores of the group on the tests may not be meaningful. For example, the obtained scores on various tests in the *Differential Aptitude Tests* are not comparable.* However, norms based on the testing of large numbers of boys and girls in each one of several grades are available and can be used to permit expressing scores derived from various tests in comparable units. A practical illustration will make this clear.

In a tenth grade class in Eastboro High School, twenty boys obtained a mean score of 25.2 on the Verbal-Reasoning Test and a mean score of 26.5 on the Numerical-Ability Test.† Obtained scores on these two tests are not comparable because in the norms group of about 3,400 boys tested near the middle of grade 10 the mean and standard deviation of scores on the Verbal-Reasoning Test were 22.7 and 9.8 while on the Numerical-Ability Test they were 18.2 and 8.9, respectively. It is apparent that among tenth grade boys a score of 22.7 on the Verbal-Reasoning Test represents about the same relative level of ability as a score of 18.2 on the Numerical-Ability Test. Comparable scores for each of the twenty boys in the Eastboro class can be obtained simply by calculating a standard measure for him individually, in terms of the norms group, on the Verbal-Reasoning Test and on the Numerical-Ability Test. The computation of standard measures is explained and illustrated in appendix D. The mean standard measure of the twenty boys in verbal reasoning would then be comparable with their mean standard measure in numerical ability.

A short-cut method of computing these comparable mean standard measures is available that eliminates the labor of computing forty individual standard measures: Subtract the mean score of the tenth grade norms group from the mean score of the twenty Eastboro boys on the same test and divide

---

* G. K. Bennett, H. G. Seashore, and A. G. Wesman, *Differential Aptitude Tests* (New York: Psychological Corp., 1947).

† In Form A of the *Differential Aptitude Tests.*

the result by the standard deviation of the test. The computation of the comparable mean standard measures (denoted $\bar{z}_V$ and $\bar{z}_N$) is as follows:

$$\bar{z}_V = \frac{25.2 - 22.7}{9.8} = \frac{2.5}{9.8} = .3;$$

$$\bar{z}_N = \frac{26.5 - 18.2}{8.9} = \frac{8.3}{8.9} = .9.$$

Although the mean standard measure of the twenty Eastboro boys is above the mean of the tenth grade norms group on both tests, it is farther above the norms-group mean (which is zero) on the Numerical-Ability Test. To determine whether the difference of .6 between the average verbal-reasoning standard measure and the average numerical-ability standard measure is large enough to warrant the belief that it is the result of something other than errors of measurement, use equation 9.6 and multiply the result by an appropriate constant taken from Table 8.3.

First, the standard errors of measurement of obtained scores on the Verbal-Reasoning and Numerical-Ability Tests must be found. These are given by the publisher as 3.0 and 2.9, respectively, for boys in grade 10.* To express these standard errors of measurement in standard measures, each one must be divided by the standard deviation of obtained scores, as indicated by equation 8.5. The standard deviations of obtained scores estimated in the samples used by the publisher to establish the standard errors of measurement are given as 9.0 for the verbal-reasoning scores and 8.7 for the numerical-ability scores.† Using the data in equation 8.5, the standard errors of measurement for standard measures in verbal reasoning and numerical ability are as follows:

$$s_{\text{meas } z_V} = \frac{3.0}{9.0} = .3 \quad \text{and} \quad s_{\text{meas } z_N} = \frac{2.9}{8.7} = .3.$$

Next, the standard error of measurement of the difference between the means of the two tests is computed by equation 9.6. The computation becomes:

$$\sqrt{\frac{(.3)^2}{20} + \frac{(.3)^2}{20}} = \sqrt{.0090} = .09.$$

Multiplying .09 by 2.58 to estimate the size of the smallest difference significant at the 1-per-cent level gives .23 (rounded to the nearest hundredth). Since the difference of .6 between the average standard measures is larger

* G. K. Bennett, H. G. Seashore, and A. G. Wesman, *Manual for the Differential Aptitude Tests*, third ed. (New York: Psychological Corp., 1959), table 29, p. 67.
† *Ibid.*, table 27, p. 66. A sample of 960 boys was used.

than .23, we conclude that the mean numerical ability of the twenty boys in the class at Eastboro High School is truly greater than their mean verbal-reasoning ability.

CAUTIONS ABOUT THE INTERPRETATION OF GROUP SCORES

The Use of Group Data

When information about average achievement or aptitude levels of various groups in a school or a school system has been obtained, it can be helpful to teachers, counselors, supervisors, and administrators in many ways, such as: (1) evaluating differences within each age or grade group with respect to the average levels of pupils in various subject-matter fields and aptitudes, and (2) planning and revising curricula. The gathering and use of this valuable information should be carried out in such a way that its benefits will not be lost through abuses. Specifically, the testing programs in which the basic data are gathered should be planned and coordinated with the cooperation of committees of teachers, counselors, school administrators, and representatives of parent organizations. Pupils who take the tests should understand the purpose for which they are being given and should be made familiar with the general nature of the content to be measured.

When group means are compared, the purposes for which the tests were given should be kept in mind and invidious reflections on pupils and teachers should be avoided. For example, if the reading skill of elementary school pupils in a certain class or school is found to be lower, on the average, than that of pupils in other classes or schools, the reasons for the difference in achievement should be sought. Ordinarily, many factors will be found to be responsible and modifications in the teaching materials and procedures may be advisable. Children who lack a normal range of experiences can be taken on field trips and shown films to enrich their backgrounds, emphases in word analysis and phonetics can be changed, and teachers can alter the groupings of pupils in their classrooms. The main point to be kept in mind is that comparisons of group averages may be futile or even harmful if differences are ascribed to teacher incompetence or pupil stupidity. A major purpose of educational measurement is to identify the strengths and weaknesses of individuals and groups and to use this information for their benefit, and for the benefit of society as a whole. This purpose is defeated if hasty generalizations or improper inferences are made from the data obtained.

Limitations of Tests of Significance of Differences

As stated earlier in this chapter in the section on "Errors in Estimating a True Mean," there are two kinds of errors that may be taken into account when comparing means: (1) errors of measurement, and (2) sampling errors. In comparing the mean scores of two or more existing groups in order to make inferences about the differences among these particular groups, only errors of measurement need be considered. If errors of sampling are improperly taken into account, it may seem that certain differences are *not* significant at a designated level of probability when in fact they are. Equations 9.3, 9.4, and 9.6 are designed to take only errors of measurement into account; equation 9.5 allows for sampling errors as well as errors of measurement in the determination of a mean for the representative sample of a defined population but allows only for errors of measurement in the determination of the mean of the existing group. Like equations 9.3, 9.4, and 9.6, it serves a specific practical purpose in the interpretation of group scores. None of these equations should be used if inferences are to be made about the differences among means *in the population or populations* from which the samples used in computing the means were taken; this point is discussed in appendix I, and equation I.3 is provided as the basis for data that would permit such inferences as these to be drawn.

Summary

The mean scores of groups are usually most meaningful when they are compared with the mean scores of other groups. Inferences about the significance of differences between means are made in two quite different situations:

1. when the investigator is interested only in the particular groups for which he has means and is not interested in generalizing from these groups to other similar groups;
2. when the investigator is interested in generalizing from the particular groups for which he has means to the populations represented by these groups.

Teachers and school administrators are often interested only in the particular groups tested; when this is the case, they should use the *standard error of measurement* of the difference between means in judging whether a difference is significant. Research workers, however, are usually interested in the populations represented by the groups tested; when this is the case, they must use the *standard error* of the difference between means in judging whether a difference is significant.

Methods for computing and interpreting the standard error of measurement of the mean and the standard error of the mean are given. Also provided are techniques for interpreting the differences between the mean scores

1. of two particular groups on the same test;
2. of two particular overlapping groups on the same test;
3. of a particular group and a norms group on the same test;
4. of a particular group on different tests that yield comparable scores;
5. of a particular group on different tests that do *not* yield comparable scores.

The techniques listed above provide the data for meaningful interpretation of group performance. These data must be handled in such a way that invidious reflections on pupils or teachers are avoided. The major purpose of educational measurement is to obtain information about individuals and groups that will be used for their benefit and for the benefit of society. This purpose may be defeated if data of this kind are used to draw improper inferences or make hasty and unjustified generalizations.

Selected References

Diederich, Paul B., *Short-Cut Statistics for Teacher-Made Tests.* Evaluation and Advisory Service Series, No. 5. Princeton, N.J.: Educational Testing Service, 1960, pp. 20–27.

Kelley, Truman L., *Interpretation of Educational Measurements.* Yonkers: World Book Company, 1927. Chapter 3.

Traxler, Arthur E., *et al., Introduction to Testing and the Use of Test Results in Public Schools.* New York: Harper and Row, Publishers, 1953, pp. 56–67.

Chapter Ten

MEASUREMENT
OF CHANGE

In chapters 8 and 9, methods were presented and illustrated for assessing the status *at any given time* of an individual or of a group with respect to knowledge, skill, or ability.   In this chapter, methods of assessing the changes that occur *over a period of time* in an individual or a group are presented.   In some ways, this is the most important topic in educational measurement. The primary object of teaching is to produce learning (that is, change), and the amount and kind of learning that occur can be ascertained only by comparing an individual's or a group's status before the learning period with what it is after the learning period.   Yet this basic principle is often over-looked by teachers and school administrators.

Teachers sometimes assume that their pupils have started with zero knowledge or skill in the material being taught.   In a subject like history, for example, a teacher may give a test at the end of a marking period on the subject matter covered during that period and tacitly assume that any knowledge or understanding that the pupils display results from learning during the period.   Usually, this assumption is far from correct.   Before the period began, one pupil may have had virtually all of the information or understanding that he displayed on the test while another may have had little or none.   A third pupil may have been badly misinformed at the beginning of the marking period and may have had to unlearn the misinforma-tion in addition to learning accurate information on which to base new understanding.   Only by giving a test at the beginning of a learning period can a teacher ascertain the status of the pupils at that time.

Informal tests made up and administered by classroom teachers at frequent intervals during a school year are indispensable for determining whether pupils have learned the specific material taught or have acquired the understandings, skills, abilities, or attitudes that the teacher has tried to develop in them.   Informal tests are also useful for estimating the initial level of knowledge, understanding, skill, or ability of the pupils, for mo-tivating them to learn, for diagnosing the types of errors they make, and for

234

assigning grades to them. These tests are not, however, usually capable of serving as an adequate basis for making accurate estimates of pupil change. For this purpose, measuring instruments should be carefully selected from available standardized tests.

SELECTION OF TESTS TO MEASURE CHANGE

Test Validity

The first consideration in selecting an instrument for estimating the change in an individual or a group is to be sure that it measures the learnings that the teaching is intended to produce. This means that the teacher must have his objectives clearly in mind before teaching begins; the test that comes closest to measuring these objectives should be chosen. To determine which one this is, the outlines and descriptions provided by the publishers of relevant tests can be examined. Even more valuable information can be obtained by trying to answer the items in each test and deciding which one best measures the skills, knowledge, and understandings that constitute the objectives. Ordinarily, a teacher interested in measuring the improvement of a pupil during all or part of the school year wants to know how well the pupil has learned certain specific skills and facts and how much effect these specific learnings and his general maturation have had on his over-all proficiency. For example, in measuring reading ability in the lower grades, a teacher is interested in specific skills such as word recognition and pronunciation or the use of an index and in a general ability to understand what has been read. Only by studying carefully the available tests and their manuals and by taking the tests can a teacher decide which ones best measure the combinations of skills and abilities that are to be taught and that she expects the pupils to learn.

Directions for administering and scoring tests often play an important part in determining their validities: these should be taken into account in deciding which tests to use, as pointed out in chapters 3 and 4. The practice followed by some pupils of marking responses to all items in a test, even those they have not had time to consider seriously or even to read, is especially troublesome when tests that are not scored with correction for chance success are used to measure change. This is because changes in a pupil's method of taking a test or in the rate at which he works may lead to a gross overestimation or underestimation of his true growth in the skills, abilities, or understandings that the test is designed to measure.

This is a particularly important factor in measuring growth in comprehension in reading since many courses designed to improve reading stress techniques of reading rapidly by skimming or scanning as well as the acquisition of a fundamental understanding of the material read. If reading-test scores are not corrected for chance success, the mere marking of answers to a larger number of items on a test given at the end of such a course than on an equivalent form of the test given at the beginning may result in a rather spectacular increase in the score of a pupil who has made no true gain in reading ability. This possibility was illustrated by data obtained in 1949 by Murphy and Davis.* They tested 393 pupils in grades 11 and 12 in Nashville, Tennessee. The forty-seven pupils who obtained the lowest scores on the reading test were called in for retesting. They were encouraged to do better and to mark an answer to every item even if they did not know the answer. These instructions changed their mental set toward the task and their methods of work. Partly as a result of these changes, their average score rose from 25.53 items marked correctly on the first test to 46.32 items marked correctly on the second test. Since the scores on the tests were not corrected for chance success, the pupils were able to increase their scores simply by marking answers to more items on the second test. When a correction for chance success was applied to their scores, the average score on the first test was 13.62 and on the second test was 15.62, a difference small enough to be accounted for by regression to the mean of the group of 393 pupils from which the forty-seven were selected because of their poor performance on the first test. In other words, mere encouragement to read faster and to mark more items caused great increases in the scores of pupils when these scores were not corrected for chance success. Use of the correction, however, resulted in so small an increase in their average score that it can properly be ascribed to errors of measurement. This is a reasonable outcome, since the pupils had been given no real opportunity to improve their true comprehension in reading. These data illustrate how correction for chance success in scoring can lead to more valid measurement by avoiding the impression of false gains.

Another example may be used to illustrate how correction for chance success can help to maintain test validity by avoiding the impression of false losses. A ninth grade pupil who was markedly retarded in ability to recognize words was given the vocabulary section of a well-known reading test at the beginning of the school year in September. He found that he had great difficulty in reading the words so he moved rapidly along, marking an answer to each item even if he could not recognize the word and hoping to find others that he could recognize. Since he did recognize some words and

---

* H. D. Murphy and F. B. Davis, "A Note on the Measurement of Progress in Remedial Reading," *Peabody Journal of Education*, XXVII (1949), 108–111.

marked them correctly, his score was better than he would have obtained on the basis of chance alone. He got a score of twenty-three items marked correctly. According to the published norms, this corresponds to a grade-equivalent score of 11.0. Nine months later at the end of the school year in June, he was given an equivalent form of the same vocabulary test. During the course of the year, he had had systematic tutorial work in word recognition and other fundamental skills in reading, so he found that he could read the words more readily than on the test given in September. As a result, he tried each item seriously as he came to it and was able to attempt thirty-four of them in the time limit. Of these he marked fourteen correctly. The norms indicate that this corresponds to a grade-equivalent score below grade 9. A comparison of his grade-equivalent score at the end of the year with his grade-equivalent score at the beginning of the year might lead one to conclude that this boy had suffered a loss in ability to recognize words, but we can easily show that this conclusion is unjustified. After correction for chance success, his score at the beginning of the year was 4 points; at the end of the year, it was 9 points. Since norms for this test based on scores corrected for chance success are not available, we cannot express our estimate of this boy's gain in terms of grade-equivalent scores. But we have illustrated how correcting scores for chance can make an important difference in their interpretation. These examples point up the need for careful selection of tests used to measure change.

Test Reliability

Whenever scores of individuals are to be interpreted and used, high test reliability is desirable. When two scores are to be compared, as in the measurement of change, high test reliability becomes essential if small gains or losses are to be detected. This is because the difference between two scores is subject to the effect of the errors of measurement in both of them. Consequently, among tests of equal appropriateness in other respects, those with the highest reliability coefficients should be selected for measuring change. In fact, since virtually all published tests display reliability coefficients lower than are desirable for measuring change, the practice of administering two equivalent forms of a test initially and two more at the end of the training period should be followed whenever it is feasible. Change can then be expressed as the difference between the average of the individual's two initial scores and the average of his two final scores.

Range of Test Scores

Special attention must be given to selecting tests that cover a range of scores wide enough so that the lowest-ranking pupils at the time of initial testing will obtain scores above the minimum possible and that the highest-ranking pupils at the time of the final testing will obtain scores below the maximum possible. Otherwise, we cannot tell how much lower or higher these pupils might have scored, and the resulting gain or loss scores are underestimates of how much they have really changed.

Units of Measurement of Test Scores

It is commonly supposed that two pupils have displayed equal growth if the difference between initial and final scores on equivalent forms of the same test is the same for each of them. In practice, this is not strictly true. In many instances, it is not even approximately true unless the two pupils had the same initial score. The more widely the initial scores of two pupils differ, the more cautious we must be in comparing their gains and in drawing inferences from this comparison.

There are two main reasons why differences of the same size do not always represent the same amount of change: (1) each score point throughout the range of possible scores rarely represents the same increment of ability; and (2) the reliability of the scores is always less than perfect. To make all score points measure as nearly as possible equal increments of ability in the skill being measured, special types of scores have been developed. Gardner's K scores and Flanagan's scaled scores, described in chapter 2, are examples of these. The former are available only for the *Stanford Achievement Tests* and the latter for certain forms of the *Cooperative Achievement Tests*. Ordinarily, in the measurement of change, results must be expressed in terms of scores not especially designed for the purpose; this fact should be kept in mind, especially when comparisons are made of the growth made by pupils who have widely different initial scores.

ESTIMATION OF AMOUNT OF CHANGE FOR AN INDIVIDUAL PUPIL

The Difference between Obtained Scores

The simplest way to estimate the amount of change in an individual pupil is to administer two equivalent forms of the same test to him, one at the beginning of the training period and one at its end. The initial score is subtracted from the final score and the resulting difference is used as an estimate of the pupil's true growth. This simple procedure is by far the most common method used for estimating a pupil's growth, but it yields an acceptable estimate only if the equivalent forms of the test are highly reliable, if the pupil was *not* chosen from his age or grade group on the basis of his initial score, and if the estimate is *not* to be compared with similar estimates for other children. For example, a pupil named Alfred Baker is chosen at random from a fifth grade class. In September, his grade-equivalent score on the *Metropolitan Intermediate Word Knowledge Test* was 5.3; nine months later, his grade-equivalent score on another form was 6.6. A crude estimate of his true gain in word knowledge is 6.6–5.3, or 1.3 points. This gain is a little greater than the gain of .9 point made in a similar period by the typical American fifth grade pupil.

Is Alfred's gain of 1.3 points large enough to warrant the belief that it is not likely to have occurred merely as a result of errors of measurement in the two equivalent forms of the test given to him? To answer this question, compare his gain with the smallest gain that is significant at any desired level of probability. The standard error of measurement of the difference between two obtained scores is given by equation 8.3. With this equation, the standard error of measurement of an obtained score on the *Metropolitan Intermediate Word Knowledge Test* is used; this is given as .44 grade-equivalent score points in Table M.17. The standard error of measurement of the difference between Alfred's two scores is, therefore, computed as follows:

$$s_{\text{meas }(K-J)} = \sqrt{(.44)^2 + (.44)^2} = \sqrt{.39} = .62.$$

To obtain the smallest difference significant at the 15-per-cent level, choose the appropriate multiplier from Table 8.3. It is 1.44, so the smallest difference between scores on two forms of the *Metropolitan Intermediate Word Knowledge Test* that is significant at this level is .62 times 1.44, or .90. Hence, we conclude that Alfred's gain of 1.3 points is significant at the 15-per-cent level and that he really knows more word meanings at the end than at the beginning of the year.

Very often a pupil is chosen for measurement of change because he obtained a low score on an initial test and was put into a special class or given remedial tutoring during the school year. When this is the case, we must not use the test score that identified the pupil as in need of help as one of the scores for measuring his change unless we use a more elaborate technique than has thus far been presented. Instead, we should use the first testing only to identify him, give a second equivalent form of the test before he begins remedial work to serve as the initial test for measuring change, and administer a third equivalent form at the end of the remedial period to serve as the final test.

This procedure is illustrated by the measurement of Helen Johnson's progress in reading during grade 9. In September, Helen's class was given Form N of the *Stanford Advanced Paragraph-Meaning Test*. Her grade score was 56, which corresponds to a percentile rank of about 6 for pupils near the beginning of grade 9. Her score was so far below the average of pupils in her class that she was assigned to a special section of ninth grade English and was given individual remedial tutoring in reading for three hours each week during the school year. At the first tutoring session, she was given Form J of the *Stanford Advanced Paragraph-Meaning Test* and obtained a grade score of 60. In June at the end of the school year, she took Form L of the same test and obtained a grade score of 81. An estimate of her gain in reading during the school year should be made by subtracting her score on Form J from her score on Form L. Her score on Form N must not be used for this purpose because it constituted the basis for putting her in the special English class and giving her remedial work.

Her true gain from September to June is estimated as 81 − 60, or 21 grade-score points. This is over twice as large as the gain made on this test by typical ninth grade pupils during the same period of time. Is it also large enough to warrant the belief that it cannot readily be accounted for by errors of measurement in her scores on Forms J and L? To answer this question, equation 8.3 should again be used. The standard error of measurement of an obtained score on this *Stanford Advanced Paragraph-Meaning Test* is given by the publisher as about 11.5 grade-score points. Computation of the standard error of measurement of the difference between Helen's scores on Forms J and L is, therefore, as follows:

$$s_{\text{meas }(L-J)} = \sqrt{(11.5)^2 + (11.5)^2} = \sqrt{264.50} = 16.26.$$

Multiplying 16.26 by 1.44 to obtain the smallest difference significant at the 15-per-cent level gives 23.41. Only differences of 24 grade-score points or more between obtained scores on equivalent forms of the *Stanford Advanced Paragraph-Meaning Test* may be regarded as significant at this level. Since Helen's rather large gain of 21 grade-score points falls below this minimum, we must conclude that her reading ability in June may not be truly better than it was in September. This conclusion will surprise many students and teachers. It certainly illustrates the need for caution in the interpretation of differences between individual test scores—caution that can be exercised discriminatively only if a scientific technique for identifying significant differences is systematically employed. It may be noted that Alfred Baker's gain of 1.3 grade-equivalent-score points on the *Metropolitan Intermediate Word Knowledge Test* was shown to be significant at the 15-per-cent level by the same technique that revealed Helen's gain of 21 grade-score points, or 2.1 grade-equivalent-score points, to be insignificant at the same level. The explanation for this difference lies in the fact that the test used to measure Alfred's gain was more reliable than the test used to measure Helen's gain.

Fortunately, Helen was given Form K of the *Stanford Advanced Paragraph-Meaning Test* a day after she was given Form J and Form M the day after she was given Form L. Her September grade scores were 60 and 64, respectively, yielding an average of 62. Her June grade scores were 81 and 85, respectively, yielding an average of 83. The difference between her average scores in June and September is, therefore, 83 − 62, or 21 grade-score points. This happens to be the same gain obtained when only her scores on Forms J and L were considered.

The standard error of measurement of the difference between the averages on *n* equivalent forms of a test given at one time and on *m* equivalent forms given at another time is given by equation 10.1:

$$s_{\text{meas}} \left(\frac{\Sigma X1}{n} - \frac{\Sigma X2}{m} \right) = \sqrt{\frac{s^2_{\text{meas } X1}}{n} + \frac{s^2_{\text{meas } X2}}{m}}, \tag{10.1}$$

where n = the number of equivalent forms of test X given at the first testing session and

m = the number of equivalent forms of test X given at the second testing session.

For the difference of 21 grade-score points between Helen's average scores in June and in September, the standard error of measurement is found to be:

$$s_{\text{meas}} \left(\frac{J + K}{2} - \frac{L + M}{2} \right) = \sqrt{\frac{(11.5)^2}{2} + \frac{(11.5)^2}{2}} = \sqrt{(11.5)^2} = 11.5.$$

Multiplying 11.5 by 1.44 to estimate the smallest difference significant at the 15-per-cent level gives 16.56. Since Helen's gain of 21 points between her *average* scores in September and June is larger than 16.56, it is significant at the 15-per-cent level. By using the *averages* of two equivalent forms of the test before and after the remedial tutoring, the accuracy of measurement of the gain is sufficiently increased to indicate that Helen did gain in reading ability during the course of the year. The implication of this illustration for anyone who wishes to measure the growth made by individual pupils is that averages of two or more equivalent scores should be used as initial and final scores. Remedial teachers, school psychologists, and clinicians should find this technique especially helpful.

THE ESTIMATE OF TRUE CHANGE

The use of simple differences between obtained scores or between averages of obtained scores to estimate the true change in an individual pupil

TABLE 10.1

Speed-of-Comprehension Scores of 200 Twelfth Grade Pupils in Shadyside School

Test	Mean	Standard Deviation	Reliability Coefficient*	Correlation of Forms A and B
Form A (September)	70.30	7.30	.84	.65
Form B (June)	74.50	8.00	.87	

* Estimated by means of equations 10.2 and 10.3 from data in Table 5 in the *Manual for the Davis Reading Test*, Series 1 and 2 (New York: Psychological Corp., 1962), p. 14.

has been shown in the preceding section. However, comparisons of the amount of change displayed by different pupils must be made with a good deal of caution, particularly if the pupils have widely different initial scores. The best way to reduce the errors of measurement in estimates of change is to use highly reliable tests or averages of two or more equivalent forms of moderately reliable tests. Unfortunately, highly reliable tests are often not available in the three equivalent forms needed to provide one form for identifying pupils of exceptionally low or high ability, one form for initial testing, and one form for final testing; therefore, it may be necessary to use somewhat more complicated procedures for estimating the change in individual pupils. One of these procedures will be described in this section.*

In September, all the pupils in grade 12 of Shadyside School were given Form A of the *Davis Reading Test*, Series 1. The following June they were given Form B. As noted in chapter 5, this test yields both a speed-of-comprehension score and a level-of-comprehension score. For illustrative purposes, Table 10.1 shows only the speed-of-comprehension results of the testing in Shadyside School. These are based on the scores of 200 pupils who took both Forms A and B. The Form-A scores of those pupils who dropped out during the year are not included. All absentees on the testing dates were rescheduled for make-up tests. It will be noted that the average pupil at the beginning of the school year obtained a percentile rank of about 48 on the twelfth grade norms. The average of the group rose by 4.2 points during the school year so that in June the average pupil obtained a percentile rank of about 50 on entering-college-freshmen norms.

Separate reliability coefficients should be obtained for Forms A and B in the actual group of 200 pupils tested in September and June. If two

* Others are described in F. B. Davis, "The Assessment of Change," in *Tenth Yearbook of the National Reading Conference* (Milwaukee: Marquette University Reading Center, 1961), pp. 86–99.

equivalent forms have been given at each testing or if the items in an unspeeded test can be assigned to two separate groups, this can be done by one of the methods described in appendix F. In this case, however, only one form of a speeded test was given so the reliability coefficients must be estimated from data provided by the test publisher; this is frequently the procedure that must be followed. The estimation can be accomplished reasonably satisfactorily by assuming that the standard error of measurement of a given test remains constant in different but somewhat similar populations. Then, the reliability coefficient of Form A (the initial test), denoted $r_{AA'}$ and the reliability coefficient of Form B (the final test), denoted $r_{BB'}$, may be estimated by equations 10.2 and 10.3:

$$r_{AA'} = 1 - \frac{s^2_{\text{meas } A}}{s^2_A}, \tag{10.2}$$

$$r_{BB'} = 1 - \frac{s^2_{\text{meas } B}}{s^2_B}, \tag{10.3}$$

where s_A and s_B = the standard deviations of Forms A and B, respectively, estimated in the sample in which change is to be measured; and

$s_{\text{meas } A}$ and $s_{\text{meas } B}$ = the standard errors of measurement of Forms A and B, respectively, estimated in a large sample different from that used to obtain s_A and s_B.

One of the lowest-scoring pupils in the twelfth grade group at Shadyside School was Hazel Adams. Hazel obtained a score of 60 in September and of 65 in June. Her score of 60, in fact, was low enough to place her with the twenty pupils who were assigned to a special English class that met eight times a week during the school year for group work in remedial reading. To estimate Hazel's true gain in reading during the school year, it would not be proper merely to subtract her September score of 60 from her June score of 65 because she was selected as one of the lowest-scoring pupils on the basis of her score of 60. If we let A stand for her September score, B for her June score, and g for an estimate of her true change in the period between testings, equation 10.4 should be used to obtain a numerical value for g.

$$g = W_B B + W_A A + K. \tag{10.4}$$

Values for W_B, W_A, and K in equation 10.4 may be obtained from equations 10.5, 10.6, and 10.7, using the actual data shown in Table 10.1. These values need be computed only once for use in estimating the true gain (denoted g) of every one of the 200 pupils in grade 12 at Shadyside School. Equation 10.4 differs from pupil to pupil only with respect to each pupil's scores on Forms A and B. In fact, if two or more pupils have the same scores on Form A and the same scores on Form B, the numerical values yielded by equation 10.4 would be the same for these pupils. Their true gains would be estimated to be the same.

Equations 10.5 and 10.6 are as follows:

$$W_A = \frac{s_B r_{AB}(1 - r_{BB'}) - s_A(r_{AA'} - r^2_{AB})}{s_A(1 - r^2_{AB})}, \tag{10.5}$$

$$W_B = \frac{s_B(r_{BB'} - r^2_{AB}) - s_A r_{AB}(1 - r_{AA'})}{s_B(1 - r^2_{AB})}. \tag{10.6}$$

Equation 10.7 involves W_A and W_B as well as the average score on Form A (denoted $\bar{A}$) and on Form B (denoted $\bar{B}$).

$$K = \bar{B} - \bar{A} - W_B\bar{B} - W_A\bar{A} \tag{10.7}$$

For the group of 200 pupils in Shadyside School, the following numerical values are obtained for W_A, W_B, and K:

$$W_A = \frac{(8.00)(.65)(1 - .87) - (7.30)(.84 - .42)}{(7.30)(1 - .42)} = -.56,$$

$$W_B = \frac{(8.00)(.87 - .42) - (7.30)(.65)(1 - .84)}{(8.00)(1 - .42)} = .61,$$

$$K = 74.50 - 70.30 - (.61)(74.50) - (-.56)(70.30) = -1.88.$$

With these data we may estimate Hazel's true change as follows:

$$g = (.61)(65) + (-.56)(60) + (-1.88) = 4.17.$$

It may be noted that our estimate of her true change is .83 of a point smaller than the difference of five points between her obtained scores of 60 and 65. This does not mean, however, that the true change estimated for all other pupils in the group will be smaller than their change in terms of obtained-score points. To illustrate this fact and to show how easy it is to estimate the true change made by any pupil in the group when numerical values have been obtained for W_A, W_B, and K, let us estimate the true change made by George Crown who obtained an initial score of 70 and a final score of 75, and by Frank Sims who obtained an initial score of 87 and a final score of 92.

George's true change is estimated as:

$$g = (.61)(75) + (-.56)(70) - 1.88 = 4.67.$$

Frank's true change is estimated as:

$$g = (.61)(92) + (-.56)(87) - 1.88 = 5.52.$$

Although Hazel, George, and Frank each made a gain of five *obtained-score* points, different *true* gains are estimated for them; the higher their initial scores, the greater the estimate of their true gain. For Frank, a true gain larger than the difference between his obtained scores of 87 and 92 is estimated. Assuming that obtained scores ranging from 60 to 92 represent essentially equal increments in speed of comprehension, we may legitimately compare the true gains estimated for Hazel, George, and Frank because, in the process of estimating them, the reliabilities of the tests used and the pupils' initial and final score levels relative to the initial and final means in their twelfth grade class have been used. As pointed out earlier in this chapter, an assumption that all score points represent the same increment of ability is rarely justified, and evidence regarding its correctness is usually hard to find. In general, scores expressed as Gardner's K scores or Flanagan's scaled scores are more likely to satisfy the assumption than scores expressed in other ways. At any rate, it is estimated that Frank made a larger true gain than either George or Hazel and that George made a larger true gain than Hazel.

Is the amount of true change estimated for any individual pupil by means of equation 10.4 large enough to warrant the belief that it did *not* occur as a chance deviation from a true change of zero? If it is large enough to warrant this belief, it is a *significant* change at the level of probability specified as acceptable. To determine this in practice, multiply the standard error of measurement of the estimate of true change by an appropriate constant from Table 8.3 and compare the resulting product with the estimate of true change. The standard error of measurement of any estimate of true change found by equation 10.4 is defined by equation 10.8.

$$s_{\text{meas } g} = \sqrt{W^2_A s^2_{\text{meas } A} + W^2_B s^2_{\text{meas } B}} \tag{10.8}$$

For the group of 200 pupils in Shadyside School, the numerical values for W_A and W_B computed by equations 10.5 and 10.6 (and shown on page 244) may be used. The standard error of measurement of Forms A and B of the *Davis Reading Test*, Series 1, among twelfth grade pupils is given in the test manual as 2.9.* If these numerical values are used in equation 10.8, it becomes:

$$s_{\text{meas } g} = \sqrt{(-.56)^2(2.9)^2 + (.61)^2(2.9)^2} = 2.40.$$

If 2.40 is multiplied by 1.44 to obtain the smallest change significant at the 15-per-cent level (as shown in Table 8.3), the result is 3.46. Therefore, any estimate of true change for a pupil in grade 12 at Shadyside School that equals or exceeds 3.46 points may be regarded as significant at the 15-per-cent level. Thus, we conclude that Hazel, George, and Frank did make real gains in reading during grade 12.†

* *Ibid.*, Table 5.
† The standard deviation and reliability coefficient of estimates of true change may be obtained with equations 10.9 and 10.10:

$$s_g = \sqrt{W^2_A s^2_A + W^2_B s^2_B + 2W_A W_B s_A s_B r_{AB}}; \tag{10.9}$$

$$r_{gg'} = \frac{W^2_A s^2_A r_{AA'} + W^2_B s^2_B r_{BB'} + 2W_A W_B s_A s_B r_{AB}}{s^2_g}. \tag{10.10}$$

For the group of 200 pupils in Shadyside School, $s_g = 3.82$ and $r_{gg'} = .60$. These data are not required for most practical purposes.

ESTIMATION OF AMOUNT OF CHANGE FOR A GROUP OF PUPILS

The Difference between Average Obtained Scores

Teachers, school administrators, and psychologists sometimes need to estimate the change made over a period of time by a group of pupils. If every member of the group is given the initial and the final test, the best estimate of the true average change of the group is simply the difference between the average initial score and the average final score. If the average initial score is represented by symbol $\bar{A}$ and the average final score of the same pupils is represented by the symbol $\bar{B}$, the average change (which may be represented by the symbol $\bar{G}$) can be estimated from equation 10.11.

$$\bar{G} = \bar{B} - \bar{A} \tag{10.11}$$

For the group of 200 twelfth grade pupils in Shadyside School, equation 10.11 yields $74.50 - 70.30$, or an estimate of true change of 4.20 points during the school year. If the correlation of initial and final scores of the 200 pupils is not available, numerical values for W_A and W_B cannot be computed by means of equations 10.5 and 10.6; under these circumstances, the standard error of measurement of the average change may be obtained by means of equation 10.12.

$$s_{\text{meas } \bar{G}} = \sqrt{\frac{s^2_{\text{meas } A} + s^2_{\text{meas } B}}{N}}, \tag{10.12}$$

where $s_{\text{meas } A}$ and $s_{\text{meas } B}$ = the standard errors of measurement of obtained scores on tests A and B, and

N = the number of pupils whose scores were averaged on the initial (or on the final) test.

The standard error of measurement of an individual obtained score on either Form A or Form B of the *Davis Reading Test* is given as 2.9 for pupils in grade 12 by the publisher. Hence, for pupils in the twelfth grade at Shadyside School, the standard error of measurement of their average change is as follows:

$$s_{\text{meas } \bar{G}} = \sqrt{\frac{(2.9)^2 + (2.9)^2}{200}} = \sqrt{.0841} = .29.$$

Multiplying .29 by 1.44 to determine the smallest change significant at the 15-per-cent level gives .42 (rounded to the nearest hundredth). The average gain of 4.20 points is so much larger than .42 that it must be significant at far better than the 15-per-cent level.   Table 8.3 indicates that the multiplier appropriate for determining the smallest difference significant at the 1-per-cent level is 2.58.   (Remember that any change is actually a difference between initial and final scores.)   Multiplying .29 by 2.58 gives .75 (rounded to the nearest hundredth).   Clearly, the gain of 4.20 points is also significant at the 1-per-cent level.   There is no reasonable doubt that the average speed-of-comprehension score of this group of 200 pupils truly increased during the school year.

In June of the preceding school year, twenty-five of the 200 pupils were assigned on the basis of their achievement in the eleventh grade English class to an accelerated course in twelfth grade English.   The average change made during the course of their twelfth-grade year by these twenty-five pupils may legitimately be estimated simply by subtracting their average score on Form A (given in September) from their average score on Form B (given in June). Although this group of twenty-five pupils constituted a selected sample of the 200 pupils in grade 12, the selection was accomplished without regard to their scores on Form A.   (In fact, Form A was not given to any of the pupils until three months after the selection had been made.)

The average score of this selected group of twenty-five pupils was 77.50 on Form A in September and 84.00 on Form B in June.   To determine whether their average gain of 6.50 points is significant, we should first compute its standard error of measurement by equation 10.12.   The computation is as follows:

$$s_{\text{meas } \bar{G}} = \sqrt{\frac{(2.9)^2 + (2.9)^2}{25}} = \sqrt{.6728} = .82.$$

The smallest average change in this group that is significant at the 15-per-cent level is .82 times 1.44, or 1.18 points; the smallest average change that is significant at the 1-per-cent level is .82 times 2.58, or 2.12 points.   On the basis of these data, we conclude that a real average gain was made by the twenty-five pupils in the accelerated class during the school year.

Estimate of True Average Change

When the speed-of-comprehension scores on Form A for the 200 twelfth grade pupils in Shadyside School became available, the principal made arrangements to have the twenty lowest-scoring pupils placed in a special English class that met eight periods a week, three of which were devoted to group work in remedial reading.   Naturally, he was particularly interested in the change displayed by this group during the school year. Their average score was 60.1 on Form A (given in September) and 66.1 on

Form B (given in June). It would *not* be proper, however, to use the difference of 6 points between these averages as an estimate of their true change in speed of comprehension. The reason why this would not be legitimate is that the lowest-scoring twenty pupils on Form A were selected to make up the group. The errors of measurement in the obtained scores of the lowest-scoring pupils in a group are more likely to be negative errors of measurement than positive errors of measurement. This is because examinees whose scores happen by chance to include negative errors tend as a result to obtain lower scores than do examinees of the same true ability whose scores happen by chance to include positive errors. When these twenty lowest-scoring pupils on Form A are retested with Form B, their obtained scores on the latter test are as likely to include positive errors as negative errors; whether the error of measurement in an obtained score is positive or negative is assumed to be purely a matter of chance. This being so, the average score of the group on Form B is likely to be higher than their average score on Form A, even though their true average ability remains unchanged.

Note that this change in the average score of the group between the first and second testing is likely to be toward the average of the population of twelfth grade pupils in the Shadyside School. Thus, their second average score (on Form B) has *regressed* toward the mean of the 200 pupils in grade 12. This kind of effect is called *regression to the mean* and is quite widespread; it was first investigated by Sir Francis Galton between 1877 and 1888.

Scores that contain no errors of measurement are perfectly reliable. Unfortunately, perfectly reliable scores (for which the standard error of measurement would be zero and the reliability coefficient would be unity) are never obtained in practice. It is true that as test scores become more reliable, the increase in the average score of the lowest-scoring pupils in a group from the first to the second testing becomes smaller. One further point should be mentioned: not only do *average* scores regress toward the group mean; *individual* scores follow the same tendency and for the same reason.

Now suppose that we selected the pupil in grade 12 who obtained the *highest* score on Form A. His obtained score is more likely to include a positive error of measurement than a negative error of measurement; therefore, on Form B he is rather likely to obtain a *lower* score than he did on Form A. His score (like that of other high-scoring pupils in the group) tends to regress toward the mean of the 200 pupils in grade 12. Notice, then, that the effect of regression to the population mean is to *increase* the scores of the lowest-scoring pupils and to *decrease* the scores of the highest-scoring pupils.

If the principal of Shadyside School concludes that the twenty pupils in the special English class really gained 6 points between September and June on the basis of the difference between their average scores on Forms A and B, he is including any possible effects of regression in his estimate of change and may therefore be in error. To guard against this possibility, he should make allowance for these effects in estimating the change made by a group selected from an age or grade population on the basis of test scores that are also used as the initial scores in measuring growth.

The change score for an individual that does make this allowance for regression effects has been denoted by g. The average change of the twenty lowest-scoring pupils may be denoted by $\bar{g}_L$. If the average scores of this group on Forms A and B are denoted as $\bar{A}_L$ and $\bar{B}_L$ and the number of pupils by N_L, equation 10.13 may be used to compute $\bar{g}_L$.

$$\bar{g}_L = W_B\bar{B}_L + W_A\bar{A}_L + K \qquad (10.13)$$

In equation 10.13, W_A is given by equation 10.5, W_B by equation 10.6, and K by equation 10.7. These values have already been obtained for the group of 200 pupils, as follows: $W_A = -.56$; $W_B = .61$; and $K = -1.88$. $\bar{A}_L = 60.10$ and $\bar{B}_L = 66.10$, so equation 10.13 yields a value for $\bar{g}_L$ as follows:

$$\bar{g}_L = (.61)(66.10) + (-.56)(60.10) + (-1.88) = 4.78.$$

To determine whether this gain is significant at any desired level, compare it with the smallest change significant at the desired level. The standard error of measurement of an estimate of true average change is given by equation 10.14 as:

$$s_{\text{meas } \bar{g}} = \frac{s_{\text{meas } g}}{\sqrt{N}}. \qquad (10.14)$$

The numerical value of this standard error of measurement of the estimate of true average gain in the group of twenty pupils in the special English class is:

$$s_{\text{meas } \bar{g}_L} = 2.40/\sqrt{20} = .54.$$

Multiplying .54 by 2.58 gives 1.39, the smallest estimate of true change that is significant at the 1-per-cent level. Since the estimate of true gain of 4.78 is larger than 1.39, we conclude that average speed of comprehension in the special English class really increased during the school year.

Comparison of Estimates of True Average Change

Having found that the group of twenty pupils in the special English class really increased their average reading ability during the school year, the principal next wishes to compare his estimate of their true average gain with that of the entire twelfth grade group of 200 pupils. Equation 10.13 may be used to obtain the latter:

$$\bar{g}_T = (.61)(74.50) + (-.56)(70.30) + (-1.88) = 4.20.$$

This estimate of true average gain is identical to the difference between their average scores of 74.50 and 70.30 yielded by equation 10.11. The fact that these estimates of change are identical is not accidental. Average changes computed by these two methods will always be identical when the initial and final average scores of *all* of the pupils tested are compared. The estimate of true average gain in the special English class (4.78 points) is .58 point greater than that in the entire group (4.20 points). The standard error of measurement of the difference between estimates of true average change when one of the averages (in this case $\bar{g}_L$) is based on the scores of examinees who form part of the entire group tested is given by equation 10.15.*

$$s_{\text{meas }(\bar{g}_T - \bar{g}_P)} = s_{\text{meas }g} \sqrt{\frac{1}{N_P} - \frac{1}{N_T}}, \qquad (10.15)$$

where $\bar{g}_T$ = the estimate of true average change in the total group;

$\bar{g}_P$ = the estimate of true average change in part of the total group;

$s_{\text{meas }g}$ = the standard error of measurement of an estimate of the true change of one individual in the total group;

N_P = the number of examinees in the part of the total group tested;

N_T = the number of examinees in the total group tested.

Earlier in this chapter, equation 10.8 was used to estimate the value of $s_{\text{meas }g}$ as 2.40. For this comparison of averages, N_T is 200 and N_P is 20. Therefore, equation 10.15 yields:

$$s_{\text{meas }(\bar{g}_P - \bar{g}_T)} = 2.40 \sqrt{\frac{1}{20} - \frac{1}{200}} = .51.$$

Multiplying .51 by 1.44 to obtain the smallest difference between the estimates of true average change that is significant at the 15-per-cent level, gives .73. Since the change was only .58, it is not safe to conclude that the group in the special English class gained more than the entire twelfth grade group.

It may be of interest to compare the gain made by the group in the accelerated English class with that made by the group in the special remedial English class. To make the comparison, both gains must be expressed as estimates of true average change. For the special English class, this is 4.72. For the accelerated class, it may be found by equation 10.13. If $\bar{g}_H$, $\bar{A}_H$, and $\bar{B}_H$ refer to data pertaining to the accelerated class, we obtain:

$$\bar{g}_H = W_B \bar{B}_H + W_A \bar{A}_H + K,$$

$$\bar{g}_H = (.61)(84.00) + (-.56)(77.50) + (-1.88) = 5.96.$$

* For a detailed discussion of this, see F. B. Davis, "Interpretation of Differences among Averages and Individual Test Scores," *Journal of Educational Psychology*, L (1959), Case 7, 162–170.

Thus, the accelerated group gained 5.96 points, or 1.18 points more than the special English group.   To determine whether this difference between the estimates of true average gain is significant, first compute the standard error of the difference.   Equation 10.16 gives the standard error of measure‑ ment of any difference between estimates of true average change when the averages are based on scores in two different groups of examinees.

$$s_{\text{meas } (\bar{g}_L - \bar{g}_H)} = s_{\text{meas } g} \sqrt{\frac{1}{N_L} + \frac{1}{N_H}}. \tag{10.16}$$

If the appropriate numerical values are substituted in this equation, it becomes:

$$s_{\text{meas } (\bar{g}_L - \bar{g}_H)} = 2.40 \sqrt{\frac{1}{20} + \frac{1}{25}} = .72.$$

Multiplying .72 by 1.44 to obtain the smallest difference between estimates of true average change that is significant at the 15-per-cent level gives 1.04.   Assuming that the score points throughout the ranges of scores in the two groups represent essentially equal increments of ability in speed of comprehension in reading, we may conclude that the accelerated group made a larger average gain in speed of comprehension than did the group in the special English class.   This is not a surprising result; in fact, it is probably a tribute to good teaching that the group in the special English class gained on the average as much as they did.   By the time they have reached grade 12, poor readers are often so fixed in their faulty habits that, even when they have the verbal aptitude to permit improvement in comprehension to take place, it is difficult to cause marked improvement to occur.

Summary

The primary object of teaching is to produce learning—that is, change. Only by comparing an individual's or a group's status before and after a learning period can the kind and amount of learning that has taken place be determined.   Hence in one sense, measurement of change is the most important function of educational measurement.

The tests to be given at the beginning and at the end of the learning period must cover the material that the pupils are supposed to learn during the period.   It is especially important that they yield highly reliable scores corrected for chance success and that they measure over a range broad enough so that none, or only a small percentage, of the pupils get the lowest possible score at the beginning or the highest possible score at the end.

Change can be measured crudely by simply subtracting a pupil's initial score from his final score on an equivalent form of the same test.   Methods are described for determining whether this difference is large enough to warrant inferring that it was not the result of chance. This method of measuring change is appropriate only if the test forms are highly reliable, if the pupil or pupils were *not* selected for training on the basis of initial score, and if the estimate of change for the pupil or group of pupils is *not* to be compared with changes in the scores of pupils or groups of pupils whose initial scores were markedly different.

The best measure of change in an individual or a group is an estimate of the *true* change. Procedures for making these estimates are described and illustrated. Anyone who wishes to investigate the effects of teaching should study these procedures, plan to obtain the necessary data, and use the techniques described. It is especially important that these procedures be followed in assessing the gains made by pupils or groups of pupils selected for remedial training or for accelerated programs.

Selected References

Bereiter, Carl, "Using Tests to Measure Change," *Personnel and Guidance Journal*, XLI (1962), 6–11.

Davis, Frederick B., "The Assessment of Change," in Emery L. Bliesmer and Albert J. Kingston, eds., *Tenth Yearbook of the National Reading Conference for Colleges and Adults*. Milwaukee: Marquette University Reading Center, 1961, pp. 86–99.

Lord, Frederic M., "Measurement of Growth," *Educational and Psychological Measurement*, XVI (1956), 421–437.

Lord, Frederic M., "Further Problems in the Measurement of Growth," *Educational and Psychological Measurement*, XVIII (1958), 437–451.

McNemar, Quinn, "On Growth Measurement," *Educational and Psychological Measurement*, XVIII (1958), 47–55.

Chapter Eleven

MEASUREMENT OF UNDERACHIEVEMENT AND OVERACHIEVEMENT

DEFINITIONS

Underachievement is often defined as the situation existing when a pupil performs better, relative to the average of his age or grade group, on a test of aptitude or mental ability than on an achievement test in some subject-matter field. Overachievement is often defined as the situation existing when a pupil performs better, relative to the average of his age or grade group, on a test of achievement in a subject-matter field than on a test of aptitude or mental ability. These definitions *sound* better to the student unfamiliar with the problems of mental measurement than they really *are*. As soon as one examines existing tests of aptitude or mental ability, it is apparent that they measure a combination of native capacity to learn and knowledge of material already learned. As pointed out in chapter 6, these two elements are inextricably mixed in all the available tests of aptitude or mental ability. Consequently, it is impossible to make a clear-cut comparison of aptitude or mental ability on one hand with achievement in a defined subject-matter field on the other.

Suppose, for example, that all the eighth grade pupils in a small community take the nonlanguage section of the *California Test of Mental Maturity*, Junior High School Level, and the *Davis Reading Test*, Form 2A. If their scores on both tests are converted to stanines (as explained in appendix D), they may be regarded as essentially comparable. (Comparable scores are defined in chapter 2.) If an individual pupil obtains a nonlanguage stanine of 6 on the *California Test of Mental Maturity* and a speed-of-comprehension stanine of 3 on the *Davis Reading Test*, can we conclude that he is underachieving in reading?

253

Assume that the difference of three points between this pupil's nonlanguage stanine and his speed-of-comprehension stanine is significant at the 5-per-cent level; then it can properly be concluded that he is better (relative to the average of the eighth grade group) in the nonlanguage skills measured by the *California Test of Mental Maturity* than he is in the skills entering into speed of comprehension, as measured by the *Davis Reading Test*. But performance in reading is not primarily dependent on *nonlanguage* aptitude; it is mainly dependent on *language* aptitude.   It is entirely possible for an individual to be both significantly higher than the average of his age or grade group in nonlanguage aptitude and significantly lower than the average of the same group in language aptitude.   The most recent evidence regarding the nature and organization of human mental abilities indicates that general intellectual ability, or intelligence, is a weighted composite of at least five (and perhaps many more) loosely correlated clusters of skills.   It is, therefore, improper to conclude that a pupil is an underachiever or an overachiever simply because his achievement in a subject-matter field is significantly different from his general mental level, as measured by a test of general intelligence, or from his level of aptitude in some cluster of mental skills that may be comparatively unrelated to achievement in the subject-matter field.

Only if a pupil's level of achievement is significantly different from his level in an aptitude (or cluster of mental skills) that can be demonstrated to be crucial in learning the subject matter can the difference between these levels be used to draw conclusions about his underachievement or overachievement.   There is also the fact that a score on an aptitude test that purports to measure a cluster of mental skills employed in learning a certain body of knowledge may be simply another bit of information about his level of achievement in that body of knowledge.   For example, the *California Test of Mental Maturity* yields a language-aptitude score that depends in large measure on tests of ability to read and comprehend several kinds of material.   Hence, a comparison of stanines in this language-aptitude measure and in speed-of-comprehension on the *Davis Reading Test* can hardly be regarded as a means of determining the presence of underachievement or overachievement.   It is essentially a comparison of how well a pupil understands the material in the language-aptitude test and how well he understands the material in the reading test.

To find a measure of aptitude that is crucial in learning a certain subject-matter field but does not demand use of the skills and knowledge that make up the field is often difficult and sometimes impossible.   Yet only if such a measure is used can the difference between stanines on it and on an achievement test form the basis for meaningful inferences about a pupil's underachievement or overachievement.   Perhaps the closest we can come to a test of language aptitude that does not directly require reading but that measures the kind of aptitude for verbal learning that underlies comprehension in reading is a test of word knowledge like the vocabulary test in Form L of the *Revised Stanford-Binet Tests of Intelligence*. This test can be administered individually in 10 to 15 minutes to pupils in grade 8 by a trained examiner. The pupil being examined neither reads the questions nor writes his answers; he simply tells in his own words what each of the words in the test means. A good indication of level of verbal aptitude can be obtained by measuring in this way the extent of a pupil's word knowledge. Consequently, if this test and the *Davis Reading Test* are administered to all of the pupils in the eighth grade of a community and comparable stanines for each pupil in each of the two tests are obtained, comparison of a pupil's two scores may permit reasonably valid inferences to be drawn about the extent of his underachievement or overachievement in reading. That is, a much higher stanine in verbal aptitude than in reading comprehension is evidence that the pupil is not reading as well as his verbal aptitude would lead us to expect, or, conversely, if his stanine in reading is much higher than his stanine in verbal aptitude, we can conclude that his reading achievement is higher than his level of verbal aptitude would lead us to expect.

In summary, then, a meaningful measure of underachievement or over-achievement must consist of a difference score that is large enough to be significant at a designated level of probability and that is derived from comparable scores in subject-matter achievement in a carefully defined field and in aptitude for learning the subject matter of that field.

A CRUDE ESTIMATE OF UNDERACHIEVEMENT OR OVERACHIEVEMENT

A crude estimate of underachievement or overachievement may be obtained for any pupil selected at random from his age or grade group by taking the difference between comparable scores on an achievement test and on an appropriate aptitude test and comparing it with the smallest difference significant at a designated level of probability. The latter can be computed by using equation 8.3 in the manner described on page 195. It should be emphasized that, if a pupil is selected from his age or grade group because his achievement or aptitude seems to differ markedly from the average of the group, this method of estimating the extent of his underachievement or overachievement is not properly applicable. The more refined procedure described in the next section of this chapter should be employed.

Table 11.1 shows the data resulting from administering Form 2A of the *Davis Reading Test* and the vocabulary test in Form L of the *Revised Stanford-Binet Tests of Intelligence* to a large group consisting of all the eighth grade

TABLE 11.1

Stanines of Eighth Grade Pupils on the *Stanford-Binet Vocabulary Test* and on Speed of Comprehension as measured by the *Davis Reading Test*

Test	Mean	Standard Deviation	s_{meas}	Reliability Coefficient	Correlation Coefficient
Stanford-Binet Vocabulary Test, Form L	5	2.00	.78‡	.85*	
					.80
Davis Reading Test, Form 2A, Speed-of-Comprehension	5	2.00	.56‡	.92†	

* Estimated in the sample from the correlation of scores on odd and even words in the test. See appendix F for computational procedures for estimating the reliability coefficient.

† Estimated by means of equation 10.2 from data provided by the publisher indicating that the reliability coefficient of the speed-of-comprehension scores is .92 in grade 8.

‡ Estimated as $s_{meas\ X} = s_X \sqrt{1 - r_{XX'}}$.

pupils in a single community. A pupil drawn at random from the group is Hobart Price, whose stanine in reading is 3 and whose stanine in verbal aptitude is 5. When *D* represents a crude estimate of any pupil's extent of underachievement or overachievement, *A* represents the pupil's comparable score in achievement, and *B* represents his comparable score in aptitude,

$$D = A - B. \qquad (11.1)$$

For Hobart, the numerical result is $D = 3 - 5 = -2$. The negative sign of the difference indicates that Hobart appears to be underachieving in reading, but before any conclusions can properly be drawn, it must be determined whether the difference of -2 is significantly different from zero at a designated level of probability. To do so, use equation 8.3 to estimate the size of the standard error of measurement of the difference. With the standard errors of measurement of the stanines in Hobart's grade group (shown in Table 11.1), the following numerical result is obtained:

$$s_{meas\ (A-B)} = \sqrt{(.56)^2 + (.78)^2} = \sqrt{.92} = .96.$$

The smallest difference between two obtained stanines that is significant at the 15-per-cent level is equal to .96 times 1.44, or 1.38. At the 5-per-cent level, it is equal to .96 times 1.96, or 1.88. We conclude that a difference of one point between the two stanines is not significant at the 15-per-cent level and that a difference of two points (in the case of these particular tests in Hobart's grade group) is significant at the 5-per-cent level, or better.* Since Hobart's stanines differ by two points, he appears to be underachieving in reading and a more detailed study of his reading habits and performance would be worthwhile.

Therefore, it is proper to conclude that any individual drawn at random from the group tested or from a reasonably similar group whose speed-of-comprehension stanine differs by two points or more from his vocabulary stanine is an underachiever or an overachiever. If equation 11.1 is used, a positive difference signifies overachievement and a negative difference, underachievement.

ESTIMATE OF TRUE UNDERACHIEVEMENT OR OVERACHIEVEMENT

Whenever a pupil is chosen from his age or grade group because his achievement or aptitude is markedly different from the average of the group, it is important that the possibility of his being an underachiever or an over-achiever be investigated by a more refined technique than the one described in the preceding section. The more refined technique provides an estimate of the true difference between comparable scores obtained by a pupil in the group tested. Let us represent this estimate by lower-case letter d. Then, if an individual's comparable scores on an achievement test and on an appropriate aptitude test are represented by A and B, respectively, equation 10.4 can be rewritten as equation 11.2 to yield the desired refined estimate:

$$d = W_B B + W_A A + K, \qquad (11.2)$$

where W_A is given by equation 10.5,
W_B is given by equation 10.6, and
K is given by equation 10.7.

* An approximation to the exact significance level of a difference of two stanine points may be obtained by noting that a difference of this size is 2.08 times the standard error of the difference and then looking up the proportion of cases in the normal distribution (appendix K) more than 2.08 standard measures from the mean. The result is .04 (rounded to the nearest hundredth). So differences of two stanines are significant at approximately the 4-per-cent level.

For example, a pupil named Richard, who obtained a speed-of-comprehension stanine of 2 and a vocabulary stanine of 4, is selected for study because of his low relative standing in the eighth grade group for which the data are shown in Table 11.1. The values of W_A, W_B, and K are computed as follows:

$$W_A = \frac{(2)(.80)(.15) - (2)(.92 - .64)}{(2)(.36)} = -.44,$$

$$W_B = \frac{(2)(.85 - .64) - (2)(.80)(.08)}{(2)(.36)} = .41,$$

$$K = 5 - 5 - (.41)(5) - (-.44)(5) = .15.$$

With these values and Richard's stanines, the true difference between his achievement and aptitude stanines can be estimated by means of equation 11.2, as follows:

$$d = (.41)(4) + (-.44)(2) + (.15) = .91.$$

To determine whether this estimate of .91 stanine point is significant at any designated level, first estimate its standard error of measurement. To do so, revise equation 10.8 as shown in equation 11.3.

$$s_{\text{meas } d} = \sqrt{W^2_A\, s^2_{\text{meas } A} + W^2_B\, s^2_{\text{meas } B}} \qquad (11.3)$$

Numerical values for W_A and W_B are $-.44$ and $.41$, respectively, as shown above. Standard errors of measurement for stanines for Test A (the speed-of-comprehension score from the *Davis Reading Test*, Form 2A) and Test B (the Stanford-Binet vocabulary score) are given in Table 11.1 as .56 and .78, respectively. Hence,

$$s_{\text{meas } d} = \sqrt{(-.44)^2(.56)^2 + (.41)^2(.78)^2} = .40.$$

The smallest estimate of the true difference that is significant at the 5-per-cent level is .40 times 1.96 (as shown in Table 8.3). The result is .78. The smallest estimate significant at the 15-per-cent level is .40 times 1.44, or .58. Since our estimate of the true difference between Richard's speed-of-comprehension and vocabulary stanines is .91 point, it is significant at the 5-per-cent level, or better, and we may conclude that his verbal aptitude (as measured by the Stanford-Binet vocabulary score) is truly superior to his speed of comprehension in reading, as measured by the *Davis Reading Test*. This leads us to believe that he is underachieving in reading. The practical implications of this conclusion will be considered in the next section of this chapter.

At this point it should be noted that the values of W_A, W_B, K, and $s_{\text{meas } d}$, which were used to estimate the true difference between Richard's stanines and to establish the significance of this difference, can be employed for the same purposes with the stanines of other pupils. For example,

Arleen (one of Richard's classmates) obtained a speed-of-comprehension stanine of 7 and a vocabulary stanine of 9. The true difference between her stanines may be estimated as follows:

$$d = (.41)(9) + (-.44)(7) + (.15) = .76.$$

It is at once apparent that the estimate of the true difference between her stanines is not significant at the 5-per-cent level. The smallest difference significant at that level was given above as .78. It is desirable to maintain a fairly stringent level of significance in the identification of underachievers and overachievers; therefore, it is concluded that Arleen is not underachieving in reading.

Note that a difference of two obtained stanines does not lead to the same estimate of the true difference for pupils at various stanine levels in achievement or in aptitude. These estimates are, however, directly comparable if we assume that one stanine represents the same increment of ability in the function measured throughout the stanine scale from 1 to 9. This assumption is often reasonably well satisfied. A second assumption is that the stanines in the achievement and aptitude measures are comparable (as that term is defined in chapter 2). When they have been obtained on the basis of a large sample, this assumption is often satisfied well enough for practical purposes, especially if the tests are about equally reliable.*

REMARKS ON UNDERACHIEVEMENT AND OVERACHIEVEMENT

It is usually difficult to obtain suitable measures for estimating underachievement and overachievement; unless these can be found, it is best not to make the estimation since the result can be misleading. Unfortunately, this fact has not been recognized in some instances. For example, many teachers and school psychologists are still drawing conclusions about a child's aptitude or potential for learning to read on the basis of his scores on various types of nonverbal aptitude tests. It is true that these often require a minimum of reading of words because they make use of pictures and diagrams, but the possession of ability to perform nonverbal tasks is not necessarily indicative of equivalent ability to perform or to learn verbal

* If the tests differ widely in reliability, a more elaborate technique for obtaining comparable stanines should be employed. See J. C. Flanagan, "Units, Scores, and Norms," in E. F. Lindquist, ed., *Educational Measurement* (Washington: American Council on Education, 1951), pp. 747–760.

tasks.   In fact, there may be only mild exaggeration in the joking remark that scores on a nonverbal test of intelligence are chiefly useful in predicting scores on similar nonverbal tests of intelligence.

When suitable achievement and aptitude tests are found and administered to a large group of pupils in a single age or grade group, the conversion of scores to stanines and the estimation of a true difference score for each pupil will permit reasonably satisfactory identification of underachievers and overachievers.   Individual case studies can then be made of those pupils in need of special attention.   Overachievement is usually attributable to parental pressures to do well in school, to special talents, or to unusually intense interests and keenly pursued hobbies.   Occasionally, compulsive individuals exhibit their tendencies with regard to study habits and academic behavior, thereby becoming overachievers, as we have defined and measured overachievement.

Underachievement has many causes and is ordinarily of greater concern to teachers than overachievement.   Faulty learning in the past, poor study conditions or habits, special disabilities in learning, inadequate motivation, hostility to certain teachers or school personnel, and lack of reasonable cooperation in taking tests are common causes of underachievement.   In addition, the variations in mental alertness that sometimes accompany diseases such as diabetes, or personality disorders such as schizoid tendencies, may produce evidence of underachievement.   When the techniques for identifying underachievers and overachievers that are described in this chapter are used and the 5-per-cent level of significance is maintained, only a small number of pupils in any group are likely to be so identified.   Rather complete case studies should be made of each of these pupils if the benefits of the techniques of identifying them are to be realized in the form of help to the school, the home, and the pupil himself.

Summary

Underachievement is often described as the situation existing when a pupil performs better, relative to the average of his age or grade group, on a test of aptitude or innate capacity to learn than on an achievement test. Overachievement is often described as the situation existing when a pupil performs better, relative to the average of his age or grade group, on a test of achievement than on a test of aptitude or innate capacity to learn.   In practice, the mental functions actually measured by tests of achievement and of aptitude or innate capacity often overlap.   Consequently, it is impossible to make a clear-cut comparison of the two.   Furthermore, even if it were possible to make the comparison, we could not properly draw conclusions about under- or overachievement unless the aptitude or innate capacity measured actually served as the basis for performance in the specific type of achievement being measured.

Because a pupil is above average in spatial visualization and below average in reading comprehension we cannot conclude that he is under-achieving in reading. Ability in spatial visualization, which plays a large part in determining an individual's performance as a mechanic, has very little to do with his level of comprehension in reading. To estimate whether a pupil is under- or overachieving in reading, his level of comprehension should be compared with his level of capacity to understand verbal concepts. Perhaps the best available measure of this capacity is an individual test of word meanings, administered like the vocabulary test in the *Revised Stanford-Binet Tests of Intelligence.* Such a comparison is meaningful only if the two sets of scores are comparable.

In summary, a reasonably satisfactory measure of under- or over-achievement must take the form of a difference between comparable scores in achievement in a specified field and in innate capacity to learn the content and skills of that specified field. To interpret these differences properly, their statistical significance must be established at a designated level.

Procedures for making crude or refined estimates of under- or over-achievement are presented and techniques for establishing their significance are described and illustrated. They parallel the procedures used in chapter 10 for determining changes that take place as a result of teaching. The catch in estimating under- and overachievement lies in finding satisfactory approximations to measures of aptitude or innate capacity to learn the skills and content of any given subject-matter field. Since these are not often obtained, satisfactory estimation of under- and overachievement is rarely possible.

Selected References

Frankel, Edward, "Comparative Study of Achieving and Underachieving High-School Boys of High Intellectual Ability," *Journal of Educational Research*, LIII (1960), 172–180.

Thorndike, Robert L., *The Concepts of Over- and Underachievement.* New York: Teachers College, Columbia Univ., Bureau of Publications, 1963.

Chapter Twelve

CONSTRUCTING
TESTS FOR
CLASSROOM USE

By its very nature, test construction is creative; its essence is the conceiving of testable ideas and the expression of these ideas as items. If a test is to be standardized for widespread use, the construction process is lengthy, expensive, and highly technical. However, the expenditure of time, money, and statistical skill cannot make up for lack of scholarship or ingenuity in the test writer. This is true whether the intended responses are essays, sentences, words, or marks on a machine-scorable answer sheet. Building a test for a single class or school is a far less ambitious undertaking, but it, too, calls for planning, inventiveness, thorough knowledge of the material being tested, and painstaking care.

PURPOSE OF THE TEST

The first step is to state the purpose of the test, usually in the light of the objectives of a course, or of a particular part of a course. For example, a sixth grade teacher who wants to test his pupils at the end of a unit on the westward movement in American history might express the purpose as follows: "This test is to cover eight weeks' study of the westward movement. It is to measure understanding of the causes and results of the movement and their relationships to United States foreign policy and to the internal problems that led to the Civil War. Knowledge of frontier life and map reading should be included."

Sometimes, formulating a fairly precise statement of this sort will alert the teacher to the fact that some of the course objectives cannot be covered by a paper-and-pencil test and must be got at in some other way—by a class project, an oral report, or a term paper.

OUTLINING THE TEST

Unless the test content is adequately described in the statement of purpose (e.g., "To see whether the pupils can spell the words in Lists I through V"), an outline should be prepared with some indication of the importance, or weight, to be given each major topic. The outline may also suggest the types of items to be included and their approximate level of difficulty.

Specifying the optimum level of difficulty for items in a standardized test or in a test for admitting students to college or selecting employees is a rather complicated procedure. When a teacher wants to check on whether his pupils know certain essential concepts or basic skills that he has taught them, the question of difficulty hardly arises. An item testing one of these concepts or skills is likely to be easy in the sense that all the pupils have had ample opportunity to learn it. Tests made up of this kind of item are called *mastery* tests. They are often used on a school-wide or system-wide basis. The English department in a large urban high school prepares each year several forms of a short "Minimum Essentials" test in usage that every pupil has to take and continue taking (after reviewing the points he misses) until he achieves a perfect or near-perfect score.

For tests intended to rank pupils in terms of their scores, it is best to aim at items that about half the pupils will answer correctly. This tends to work out as a satisfactory rule of thumb because on classroom tests pupils usually have time to try all the items and do little random guessing.

An outline of a test on the westward movement is shown in Table 12.1. It calls for three types of items: 15 map-location matching items, 25 multiple-choice items, and 2 essay questions. A mixture of types of items is often desirable in informal classroom tests.

The weight given each topic is indicated roughly by the number of items and somewhat more exactly by the per cent of credit assigned to it. This outline, for example, calls for 42 items distributed as follows:

	NUMBER OF ITEMS	AMOUNT OF CREDIT	PER CENT OF CREDIT
1. American Frontier in 1800	5	5	10
2. Opportunities in the West	7	7	14
3. Transportation to the West	10	10	20
4. Life in the West	1	5	10
5. Expansion of Territory	19	23	46

In terms of facts, skills, and understandings, the item distribution is:

	NUMBER OF ITEMS	AMOUNT OF CREDIT	PER CENT OF CREDIT
Definitions and Facts	14	18	36
Map Locations	15	15	30
Understandings	13	17	34

These figures suggest that topic 3 will have somewhat more, and topic 5 considerably more, weight in the scores than will topics 1, 2, and 4. The teacher presumably gave more time and emphasis during the eight weeks of instruction to these two topics. Roughly equal weight has been assigned to facts, skills, and understandings.

TABLE 12.1

Outline for a Test on the Westward Movement

Time Limit	*Number and Type of Item*
50 minutes	15 map-location matching
	25 multiple-choice
	2 essay

Number of Items

Topic	Definitions and Facts	Map Loca-tions	Understandings Foreign Affairs	Understandings Domestic Problems	Total Credit
American Frontier in 1800	1	2	1	1	5
Opportunities in the West					
Farming	1	1		1	3
Trapping	1	1			2
Mining	1	1			2
Transportation to the West					
Trails	1	1			2
Roads	1	1			2
Canals	1	1		1	3
Railroads	1	1		1	3
Life in the West	1*				5
Expansion of Territory					
Louisiana Purchase	2	2	1	2	7
Annexation of Texas	1	1		2	4
Mexican Cession		1		1*	6
Oregon Territory	1	1	1		3
Purchase of Alaska	1	1	1		3
Totals	14	15	4	9	50

* These items are essay questions and are each given a credit of 5; that is, they are marked on a scale from 0 to 5.

The per cent of credit is only an *estimate* of weight based on the assumptions that all the items are equally difficult and are uncorrelated. In practice, neither of these assumptions is entirely justified. Nevertheless, the estimate should be made. Otherwise, tests with highly unjustifiable emphases are likely to result. The outline should be regarded as a *flexible* running guide during the construction process; the teacher should feel free to revise it on the basis of the testable points that occur to him and seem important.

TYPES OF ITEMS

Recall Items

Essay questions. Recall items require the examinee to bring to mind information or ideas, whereas recognition items offer him two or more choices among which he selects the one he thinks is correct or most nearly correct. The best-known type of recall item is a question (often in the form of a request) to which the examinee responds with an essay. The directions should usually indicate about how long the essay ought to be.

An essay question on the westward movement in the United States might read: "How did territory acquired from Mexico help bring on the Civil War?" or "Explain how territory acquired from Mexico helped bring on the Civil War."

In devising this question, the teacher first decided that he wanted to find out if his pupils understood how the westward movement created conditions that helped bring about the Civil War. His first version was, "Trace the causes of the Civil War created by the westward movement." It was apparent that to do this with reasonable completeness would take too much time. He first changed the question to the part territories acquired from other countries played in contributing to the causes of the Civil War and finally narrowed it to territory acquired from Mexico.

Teachers should think through the answer to be expected to an essay question rather systematically before using it. Compared with the difficulty of scoring a vague, ambiguous, or too-inclusive question, the effort of preparing one that can be scored more easily and fairly is small.

Short-answer, or completion, items. To require recall in a form that is easier to score than an essay, the short-answer question or incomplete statement is frequently used; e.g., "From what country did the U.S. purchase Louisiana? _____" or "The U.S. purchased Louisiana from _____." The expected answer in both versions is France, but "the French," "the French government," and "Napoleon" are also acceptable ways of completing the statement. In this example, the question form is superior since it pin-points the answer and is therefore easier to score.

One way to control the examinee's response to a short-answer question or incomplete statement is to supply either one or more letters or the number of letters in the expected response, or both. This technique works well in active-vocabulary items (where the object is to see whether the examinee can *think of* the *precise* word); e.g., "A verb meaning to play cards, etc., for money is _ _ M _ _ _." Supplying the number of letters and the letter M rules out such responses as "wager," which, though not so good as "gamble," might be defended.

Perhaps easier to write is the variation of this type in which a sentence using the wanted word is given as well as one or more letters and the number of letters; e.g., "How better could we fulfill the _ _ S _ _ _ Y (fate or fortune) for which we were created?"

This device of supplying letters and the number of letters must not be used when it will give the answer away. For example, if the blank in the incomplete statement, "The U.S. purchased Louisiana from _____," were changed to "F _ _ _ _ _" or to "_ _ _ _ _ E" or even to "_ _ _ _ _ _," the examinee would be able to rule out both England and Spain, the two most likely wrong answers, and get the item right on the basis of very little information. It would no longer be a good recall item.

An exercise that is really an extension of the completion item is often useful in helping less able pupils read and understand assigned material. Running text based on the material is prepared in which several blanks are to be filled in; e.g., "Most farm products from the West were shipped down the _____ River to the city of _____, where they were put on boats that could travel on the _____. This was possible because we had a treaty with _____, the country that then owned New Orleans ...." Pupils can do this kind of exercise while they are reading the material or just after they have read it. In either case, it is primarily a teaching, rather than a testing, technique.

Recognition Items

True-false items. A favorite form for many years, true-false items appear easy, but are actually tricky, to construct. Those that attempt to test complex ideas are likely to be ambiguous or to be given away by such words as "always" or "never," which more often than not indicate that a statement is false. Statements that begin, "The best way to...," "The chief factor in...," "The most effective method of...," "The main reason why...," and the like usually involve judgment and may confuse the examinee since he is not told the alternatives among which the test writer has made the judgment. It is better to put this type of question into multiple-choice form so that the examinee is able to consider the same alternatives.

The writer of true-false items should keep in mind that their principal advantage is their ability to test a single, clear-cut point in a natural, direct way. He should usually avoid testing, either purposely or inadvertently, more than one point per question; e.g., "John Adams and Thomas Jefferson died on the same day, July 4, 1826," covers two points: that the two men died on the same day and that that day was July 4, 1826. Statements that are basically true should not be made partly false (and therefore keyed as "False") by including an incorrect modifier; e.g., "John Quincy Adams, our fifth President, was the son of John Adams."*

Whenever possible, statements should be expressed positively. Examinees tend to think of "True" as "Yes" and "False" as "No."† When confronted with this item, "Mold from oak leaves should not be used for plants that require acid soil," those examinees who agree may mentally respond, "No, it should not be used," and mark the item "F." On the other hand, those who believe that oak leaf mold does produce acid soil (and therefore disagree with the statement) may think, "Oh yes, it should," and mark the item "T." Negatives tend to introduce irrelevant difficulty into true-false items.

Despite their many limitations, carefully worded true-false questions are a means of covering certain kinds of subject matter more economically and sensibly than multiple-choice items dealing with the same points—without the strained or absurd third, fourth, and fifth choices that appear when multiple-choice items are based on unsuitable topics. The true-false technique lends itself particularly to factual and quantitative material, as in, "A diameter of a circle divides the circle into two equal parts," or, "There were more people in the United States engaged in farming in 1860 than in 1960."

Multiple-choice items. Today the most widely used objective type, the multiple-choice item is highly flexible and can test many varieties of knowledge, ability, and skill. It consists of a stem and ordinarily two to five choices. The incorrect choices are often called "distracters."‡ The stem presents the idea or "problem" that the item deals with. It can be cast as either a question or a statement. Much of the time there is little to choose between the two forms, but occasionally one is superior. For example, "Which of the following events occurred earliest?" is shorter and less awkward than, "Of the following events, the one that occurred earliest

---

* John Quincy Adams was, in fact, our sixth President.
† The responses to true-false items are sometimes given as "Yes" and "No," or "Y" and "N."
‡ Other names for the incorrect choices are "foils," "decoys," and "misleads."

is ...." On the other hand, "The areas of two circles are to each other as ...," is hard to put into satisfactory question form. Sometimes a stem merely directs the examinee to perform an operation; e.g., "By interpolating in the table above, find sin 36°40′, correct to three decimal places." In this case, however, the teacher may prefer asking the examinee to supply the answer to having him choose among given responses.

The teacher is free to vary the number of choices to fit the point tested. He need not strain to concoct a fifth, a fourth, or even a third choice, if he is testing an either-or concept. Sometimes item writers actually weaken an item by splitting a natural, attractive choice into two inferior ones (which the test-wise examinee can sometimes rule out because they overlap, sound implausible, or are otherwise unlikely). The item below illustrates this.

> Thunder is heard
> A after you see the lightning.
> B before you see the lightning if it is far away.
> C at the same time you see the lightning.
> D before you see the lightning if it is nearby.

The pupil who does not know the answer may realize that it depends on which travels faster—sound or light. If the former, both B and D are correct; therefore neither is the answer and A is probably the one to mark. Another defect in the item is that, for all practical purposes, C is true if the flash is very close to you. Perhaps the most natural, efficient, and at the same time accurate way to test this point is:

> Underline the word or phrase in parentheses that correctly completes the statement.
>
> You see a distant flash of lightning (before, at the same time that, after) you hear the thunder that goes with it.

Many testable concepts in the physical world are two-choice or three-choice. Either something happens or it does not. A variable increases, remains the same, or decreases. An event occurs before, simultaneously with, or after another event.

Notice that in the revised thunder-lightning item, the choices come in the middle. Although they more frequently come at the end, they can occur anywhere when the item is expressed as a statement. This item can easily be put into tabular format as follows:

> In the blank space, write the letter of the choice that completes the statement correctly.
>
> You see a distant flash of lightning ... you hear the thunder that goes with it.
> A before
> B at the same time that
> C after

For the most common form of multiple-choice item—that in which just one response is keyed as correct, studies have shown that reliability *per item* increases as number of choices increases. On the other hand, reading time also increases. There is some evidence that maximum reliability *per unit of time* is obtained with about three choices per item.

Items with more than one keyed answer provide an efficient and space-saving method of testing certain kinds of material. Two examples follow:

1. Put an "X" before every choice that correctly answers the question.

Which of the following states are wholly or partly made up of land purchased by the U.S. from a foreign country?

——— Alaska   ——— Georgia
——— California   ——— Ohio
——— Florida   ——— Virginia

2. Write "Y" before each correct completion and "N" before each incorrect completion. Mark every choice.

Porpoises resemble people in that they

——— are born without teeth.
——— are unable to see at birth.
——— have "ranging" eyes.
——— sleep many hours each night.

The choices in both these examples are unequivocally right or wrong. In the first one, the scoring formula should include a penalty for putting an "X" before a wrong answer to guard against examinees who mark many choices to increase their chances of marking the correct ones. This danger does not arise in the second example.

Probably the multiple-choice technique is most valuable when, instead of being asked to select among responses that are unequivocally right or wrong, the examinee is asked to choose the one that is "best" or "most nearly correct" or when the item requires him to arrive at a new (that is, an unfamiliar) fact by putting two or more learned, or supplied, facts together. Such complex and important mental processes as making judgments, evaluating data, drawing inferences and conclusions, and exercising insight can be tested with these kinds of items. Some typical stems are:

The most far-reaching result of Alexander the Great's conquest was . . .
Which one of the following statements is completely justified by the data
     in the graph above?
The figures in the table indicate that . . .
Which of these headings for the paragraph quoted is most accurate?
The evidence in the paragraph suggests that . . .

The most important conclusion to be drawn from the experiment
described is that . . .
If this experiment were repeated, it is most likely that . . .
Which of the following terms includes the other four?
All the geometric figures listed below have perimeters of 5 inches.
Which one has the largest area?
Lady Macbeth is best described as . . .

Inspection of these stems reveals the most troublesome aspect of the
best-answer technique: the answer is sometimes a matter of opinion. This
is certainly true of the first and last ones and probably of some of the others.
This does not mean that objective items should not hinge on opinion, but
that if an opinion is involved, it should be perceptive and reasonably well-
informed, if not expert. It also means that responses that are very close to
being as good as the keyed answer should not ordinarily be used. Suppose,
for example, that the keyed completion to the stem about Lady Macbeth is
"ruthless"; "ambitious" and "determined" should not appear as distracters. On the other hand, the item writer should not automatically avoid
fine distinctions (if they are valid) and should usually not make an item less
difficult by eliminating an attractive distracter, unless, of course, it is a
defensible answer.

The teacher who reads or listens to criticisms of objective tests may
conclude that most items that involve opinion (and even some that do not)
have either more than one defensible answer or no good answer. We have
touched on the first point; the second is equally well taken. Far too many
items are written in which the examinee is actually choosing the *least incorrect*
answer. In the vocabulary item below, "empty" is closer to the meaning of
"pour" than are any of the other choices but is so far from being a synonym
that the item can almost be said to have no answer. To justify "empty" as
the best of those given abuses the technique.

Pour means most nearly

A read slowly.
B drive carefully.
C empty.
D pump.
E injure.

Matching exercises. A matching exercise may be regarded as a combination of two or more multiple-choice stems with choices in common.
Obviously the stems combined must be sufficiently homogeneous so that the
common choices are plausible matches for all of them. Usually the number
of choices should exceed the number of stems in order to reduce the likelihood of correct matching through elimination. If, as in the example on
page 80 in chapter 4, any of the choices (right-hand column) *may* be the

correct match for *more than one* of the stems (left-hand column), the examinee cannot depend on elimination to help him very much.

Matching exercises are suitable for associating definitions with terms, places with points on a map, authors with books, composers with operas, dates with events, and so forth.   Used with appropriate material, they save space and reading time and provide a change for the examinee, who often rather enjoys doing them.

PREPARING OBJECTIVE TESTS COOPERATIVELY

When several teachers are giving the same course, they may wish to work together in building the final examination.   If there is ample time in which to prepare the exam and very little time between the exam date and that on which course marks are due, short-answer or recognition items are preferable.   Because the multiple-choice type is familiar, versatile, and very easy to score, it is frequently used.   An optional essay question is sometimes offered at the end to occupy those pupils who finish early.

Once the teachers have agreed on an outline of the topics to be covered, each one usually becomes responsible for the items dealing with a particular section of the course and is expected to have a first draft ready by a specified date.   This first draft should normally include more items than the outline calls for so that some can be discarded.

The writer of multiple-choice items must somehow come by ideas that are sufficiently important to merit testing and that lend themselves to this testing technique.   Some good ideas will immediately occur to the average teacher; the inspiration for others can be found in textbooks, syllabi, old examinations, and indeed any likely source that is handy.   Expressing item ideas as clearly and smoothly as possible is ordinarily a trial-and-error process and takes time.   The next section of this chapter describes the difficulties a teacher had in phrasing a very simple graph-reading item.

Since indispensable steps in producing good objective items are having them criticized systematically by competent people and revising them accordingly, every teacher's items should be gone over by one or more of his colleagues.   This procedure is most effective when the critic does *not* have a key.   When the answer to an item is indicated, many critics tend to accept it and do not scrutinize the item nearly so carefully as when they themselves have to arrive at an answer.   Some of the faults commonly found in multiple-choice items for which a critic should be on the alert are illustrated later in this chapter.

EVOLUTION OF A MULTIPLE-CHOICE ITEM

This item is based on the chart in Figure 12.1. The point to be tested is whether the examinee can determine the amount of increase in gross national product between 1939 and 1942. The teacher first wrote the stem as follows:

> Gross national product in 1942 represented an increase over gross national product in 1939 of

This was awkward and wordy, so he tried the question form:

> How much did gross national product increase from 1939 to 1942?

This sounded satisfactory, so he supplied the correct answer as choice A: "$62 billion." He then realized that the chart hardly permits being sure of the *exact* amount and inserted a qualifier in the stem:

> Approximately how much did gross national product increase from 1939 to 1942?

This change overemphasized the inexactness so he went back to the incomplete-statement form and put the idea of increase at the beginning. For

FIGURE 12.1

Gross National Product, by Use of Product, United States, 1939–1943.

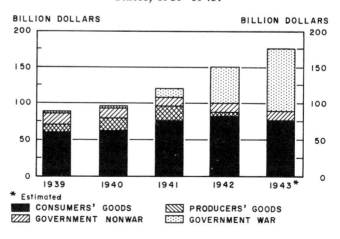

BILLION DOLLARS

* Estimated

CONSUMERS' GOODS   PRODUCERS' GOODS
GOVERNMENT NONWAR   GOVERNMENT WAR

three incorrect choices, he filled in the amounts resulting from what he regarded as likely mistakes. (The origin of each of these wrong answers is given below in brackets.) The item then read:

> The increase in gross national product between 1939 and 1942 was closest to
> A $62 billion.
> B $150 billion. [GNP in 1942]
> C $86 billion. [comparing 1943 with 1939]
> D $18 billion. [comparing consumers' goods instead of GNP]

To cover the many other possible mistakes, he decided to use "some other amount" as choice E. He then noticed that, as the stem was now stated, this choice might be a defensible answer, since the increase, if determined *exactly*, would almost certainly differ from $62 billion and would really be "closest to" some other amount. He again rewrote the stem and put the first four choices in order of size as follows:

> What was the approximate increase in gross national product between 1939 and 1942?
> A $18 billion
> B $62 billion
> C $86 billion
> D $150 billion
> E Some other amount

When "some other amount" or a similar phrase is used, it should come last, preferably follow a stem expressed as a question, and be called to the attention of the examinees in the test directions. Obviously, it must occasionally (and fairly early in the test) be the correct answer; otherwise, the examinees will come to disregard it. It should appear as the answer in rather easy items where the number of plausible wrong responses is limited, so that the likelihood of marking the keyed choice by reaching an unincluded wrong answer is minimized.

The open-end response, such as "some other amount" or "none of the above," is particularly useful in mathematics and other tests where the answers are quantitative. It tends to reduce, though it will not eliminate, getting the correct answer by working backwards; that is, by trying the various choices and marking the one that fits.

In objective spelling tests in which the examinee is to mark the mis-spelled word, if any, in each group, the use of "none wrong" as the fourth and last choice in every item and as the keyed response in about one-fourth of the items usually forces the examinee to scrutinize and come to a decision about all three words in those items and, since he can never be sure that an item in which he does not see a word he *knows* is misspelled actually does include a misspelled word, reduces his reliance on elimination to arrive at the keyed response in the other items.

"All of the above" used as the last choice in a best-answer item serves an entirely different purpose and is usually of dubious value. When it is the keyed response, all the choices preceding it have to be *correct* answers (though perhaps partial or incomplete), and the examinee must be emphatically warned to expect this situation and not hastily to mark the first correct choice he comes to. When "all of the above" is not the keyed response it is, of course, ruled out as a possibility as soon as the examinee spots one incorrect choice among those that precede it.

COMMON FAULTS IN MULTIPLE-CHOICE ITEMS

Unsuitable item idea. Many courses, particularly in the field of education, include material that is not sufficiently solid, specific, or unfamiliar to the student to be tested objectively. Multiple-choice items attempting to cover this material either belabor obvious points or have answers that are disputable—sometimes because expert opinions differ, but more frequently because the answer depends on circumstances that are not, and often cannot be, adequately described in the stem.

The items that follow were written for a comprehensive examination for prospective teachers; the first two exemplify points too obvious for multiple-choice testing.

1. An outstanding feature of the program in a good modern elementary school is its

   A formality.
   B predictability.
   C flexibility.
   D uniformity.

2. In developing a philosophy of education, the most important step consists of

   A choosing suitable and efficient methods.
   B planning the organization.
   C selecting the subject matter.
   D determining the objectives of education.

3. The best way to handle a "grouchy" child is to
A talk with him sympathetically.
B ignore him for a while.
C make good-natured fun of him.
D assign him impersonal tasks.

In the third item, any one of the choices might be the "best way"; to justify an answer, much more would have to be known about the child as well as something about the situation. The multiple-choice form does not fit this item idea.

Inadequate keyed response. Even items written by professional test constructors and presumably gone over by other experts are occasionally so worded that the intended answer is insufficient. The item below was paraphrased, but not essentially altered, from one in a social-studies test.

If each year in a certain state the number of wheat farms decreases, yet more wheat is raised, we *know* that the
A farms are becoming smaller.
B farmers are improving their methods.
C farmers are hiring more workers.
D farmers are working harder.

The keyed response, B, is the best of those listed, but it does not necessarily follow from the stem. If the average farm is becoming larger each year, there may easily be fewer farms and more wheat raised with no change in methods. The item could be made satisfactory by substituting "it is most likely" for "we know."

The author of the mathematics item below has fallen into a logical trap.

If all of *p* is part of *q*, and part of *q* is all of *r*, you *know* that
A all of *p* is *r*.
B *q* is all of *p* and all of *r*.
C some of *p* is *r*.
D none of *r* is part of *p*.

The bright pupil will mark B as the answer, but it is far from being right. To say that B is true is like saying that since Utah is part of the U.S. and part of the U.S. is Maine, the U.S. is Utah and Maine. Substituting "includes" for "is" rectifies B but makes it stand out from the other choices.

Defensible unkeyed response. This fault is often due to an ambiguous stem. The answer to "Which American city is the largest?" depends first on whether population or area is meant and, if the latter, on whether "American" refers just to the United States or to all of North and South America. Such words as "first," "second," and "last," which can refer to either time or position, are sometimes misinterpretable.* The danger of ambiguity is particularly great in tests composed of sentences taken out of context. The two examples below are from an exercise in which the pupil is to underline the correct grammatical form.

1. It is up to each of us to make the best use of what (we have, he has).
2. Laughing drunkenly, (she was shoved aside by one of the band, one of the band shoved her aside).

Whether the first sentence refers to what "we" as a group possess collectively or to what "each of us" has individually is impossible to tell. In the second example, it is more likely that one of the band was laughing drunkenly but not impossible that "she" may have been doing so. Either version is correct grammatically.

The following item, which appeared in a well-known English composition test some years ago, is a classic of its kind. It has three defensible answers. The examinee is to indicate which, if any, of the numbered words is incorrect.

Happiness is one of the intangibles which is wanted by almost everyone.
  1 2   3   4   5   C

Those who object to "which" in a restrictive clause will argue that 1 is the answer. Others will take the sentence to mean, "Happiness is one of those few intangibles which are wanted by almost everyone," and will mark 2. Still others will contend that the sentence means, "Happiness is that particular one of all the intangibles which is wanted by almost everyone," and will mark C, indicating that it is correct as it stands.

The need for avoiding distracters that are too close to the keyed response has been pointed out. In the Lady Macbeth item cited earlier, there is no dearth of suitable distracters; the item writer has only to select those that are clearly less applicable than "ruthless." In the item below, however, plausible *wrong* completions are hard to think of; choice D actually characterizes adolescent occupational interests about as well as does B, the keyed response.

As a rule, the occupational interests of adolescents are

A very clearly defined.
B not clearly defined.
C permanent.
D temporary.

---

* W. S. Miller, author of the analogies test that bears his name, and for a great many years professor of educational psychology at the University of Minnesota, often cited the graduate student who signed her registration card "Jane Smith" and maintained that she *had* written her last name first.

Since, in addition to having a defensible unkeyed response, this item contains an implausible distracter, "permanent," it would be better to avoid the problem of devising choices and express the idea in true-false form, as follows: "As a rule, the occupational interests of adolescents are clearly defined." Now the item tests a single point and does so briefly and directly; the statement is demonstrably false so there is no question about how to score it. Many weak multiple-choice items dealing with this type of subject matter can be recast into acceptable true-false sentences. This is true, of course, only when the point the item concerns is worth testing in the first place.

Nonparallel or nonhomogeneous choices. While distracters must not be defensible answers, they should be relevant and sufficiently plausible so that the pupil who gets an item right (without guessing) must really know or understand the point the item is designed to test, which should ordinarily be the point it appears to cover. In certain fields—spelling, arithmetic, algebra, physics—it sometimes pays to try items out in dictation or short-answer form to discover the errors that occur most frequently.

It is evident that the point actually tested by an item and therefore its difficulty depend on the distracters. Consider the following literary-acquaintance item:

> *The Vicar of Wakefield* was written by
> A _____   C _____
> B _____   D Goldsmith.

If choices A, B, and C are filled in as Galsworthy, Shaw, and Bennett, the item may test simply the fact that *The Vicar of Wakefield* and Goldsmith both belong to an earlier period than do the distracters. In other words, the four choices are not parallel chronologically. Isaac Newton, John Wesley, and William Pitt would be equally unsuitable distracters. Although they lived roughly during the same period as Goldsmith, the first is best known as a mathematician, the second as a religious leader, and the third as a politician; none was primarily an author. Good distracters for this item are Sheridan, Defoe, and Fielding.

The heterogeneity of the choices in this vocabulary item might prevent it from functioning effectively: "**repast**: meal, go by, beyond, rapid, over with." The examinee has merely to recognize that "meal" is the only one of the choices that is the same part of speech as "repast." The item cannot efficiently discriminate between those who know what "repast" means and those who do not. A better selection of distracters might be "rehearsal, witty remark, summary, jolly time."

That the choices in a vocabulary item should all be the same part of speech as the stem word is a special case of the principle that those in any item should be as parallel grammatically as is practical. In the item below, they are conspicuously and unnecessarily different in structure.

Thomas Edison is famous
A because he discovered several new chemical elements.
B because of his work in developing radio.
C for his practical applications of electricity.
D despite the fact that most of his work was theoretical.

The item can easily be rephrased to cover the same ideas much more smoothly:

Thomas Edison is famous for his
A discovery of new chemical elements.
B work in developing radio.
C practical applications of electricity.
D contributions to theoretical physics.

Choices should be reasonably similar in length and precision. In a praiseworthy effort to have the keyed response complete and accurate, the inexperienced item writer sometimes makes it considerably longer and more exact than the distracters, to which he devotes less time and thought. An example follows:

One of the strongest objections to compulsory voting is that it might
A be impossible to enforce.
B result in more people voting carelessly because some would vote only in order to fulfill the legal requirement.
C keep aliens from seeking citizenship.

There is no general rule for eliminating this fault. Sometimes part of the keyed response can be put into the stem and the distracters changed accordingly; at other times one or more of the distracters can be lengthened. Any abridgement of the keyed response must be done with care to keep its meaning clear and unchanged.

Overlapping choices. Sometimes it is predetermined that every item in a test, or section of a test, must have the same number of choices. The item writer is not permitted to select only as many plausible distracters as occur naturally with each item idea.* In a desperate effort to avoid unattractive

---

* One of my students wrote these stanzas after struggling through an assignment to produce a certain number of *five*-choice reading items.

To write the stem—that's like a breeze;   I rearrange the words just so
  I dash it off with carefree ease.   Till not one flaw there be.
Choice A's not hard; B's often faster.   But then the editors I know
  But oh, those C's and D's!   Will change what does comprise it.
And even when at last they please,   When next my item dear I see,
  I've still choice E to master.   I may not recognize it!

choices, he may come up with two choices that mean almost the same thing or two choices of which one includes or overlaps the other. If one of these is the keyed response, the informed examinee may be puzzled; he wants to mark both choices but knows that he must not. However, it is usually two distracters that overlap. This does not bother the examinee who knows the right answer but may provide unintended help to the uninformed but test-wise examinee. He reasons that if this particular choice is correct, this other one must also be and therefore neither is—and marks one of those remaining. Two examples follow:

1. Cotton comes from
   A an animal.
   B a plant.
   C a mineral.
   D a rock.
   E a sheep.

2. Where are quails most often found?
   A Near a marsh
   B Running across a road
   C Near a grain field
   D By a swamp

In item 1, choice A includes E, and C and D overlap, so the answer must be B. This item should have been limited to three choices—A, B, and C. In item 2, which was written as a sports question to be used in an interests test, choices A and D are almost synonymous. Also choice B is pretty weak. It may be that this item idea is unsuitable for multiple-choice testing and should be covered in some other way or discarded.

Overlapping of choices is not always caused by desperation or careless-ness in writing the choices. The stems of quantitative items (those in which the choices are amounts) can be so worded that if any one of certain of the choices is correct, one or more of the others are necessarily so. Consider this example: "Within the last decade, at least (75, 150, 250) skyscrapers have been built in London." If 250 is keyed, certainly 150 and 75 are defensible; if 150 is keyed, certainly 75 is defensible. An acceptable wording of this item idea is: "The number of skyscrapers built in London during the last decade is about (75, 150, 250)." Other phrases or words that invite this kind of overlapping are "as much as," "as many as," "less than," "fewer than," "more than," "over," "under," and "in excess of."

A subtler form of overlapping occurs in the logical-reasoning item on page 275. If choice A is correct, C must also be. This can be remedied by changing C to "some, but not necessarily all, of *p* is *r*."

Specific determiners. Anything in an item that can lead examinees who are completely ignorant of the subject it deals with to choose the right answer or to eliminate from consideration one or more distracters and thereby increase their chance of guessing the right answer is a *specific determiner*. Difference in choice length and overlapping of choices, both of which were discussed earlier, can operate in this way.   Two other types that should be mentioned are:

1. Distracters that do not follow the stem grammatically.   In the example below, "octagon" can be ruled out because it should have been preceded by "an."

> A closed plane figure with six sides is called a
> A cube.   C. hexagon.
> B pentagon.   D. octagon.

This defect is immediately corrected by omitting "a" from the stem and inserting "a" or "an" appropriately before each choice.   Obvious as this slip seems, it must be systematically watched for since it occurs with surprising frequency and can easily pass unnoticed (except by the examinees).

2. "Always," "never," and similar absolutes.   Just as a true-false item in history, economics, sociology, or allied fields that contains one of these words is likely to be false, so the presence of one of them in a choice suggests that that choice is not the keyed response.

Overlapping of items within a test or battery.   This term covers two quite different faults.   The first occurs when two or more items inadvertently hinge on the same, or almost the same, point.   It is apt to happen when several people write items for a test, when one person writes them over a long period, and when items are taken from a file according to statistical, rather than subject-matter, specifications.*

The second fault occurs when something in one item gives a clue to the answer to another item.   Words that are tested in the spelling section of an English composition test may appear, correctly spelled of course, in the grammar or punctuation section.   A term whose definition is required in the first part of a social studies test may be explained in a later reading passage.

The most successful way to catch these flaws—and many others—is to have at least one competent person who has not been involved in writing the test read over, or better still attempt to answer, all the items in a test or battery at one sitting.

---

* These "statistical specifications" are in the form of difficulty and discrimination indices, which are discussed in the next section of this chapter.   A striking example of how content can overlap when items are selected mechanically on the basis of item-analysis data occurs in the vocabulary part of a recently published English test: the fourth item requires the examinee to recognize that *ardent* means *fervent*, and the twentieth item that *fervor* means *ardor*.

ITEM ANALYSIS

What It Is

Items are analyzed in many ways. The test critic studies their content and wording. The teacher who looks over a test with a view to using it judges how suitable the items are for his pupils and how pertinent to what he has been trying to teach them. The pupils who eagerly discuss a test they have just taken expound their interpretations of, and reactions to, various items. The term "item analysis," however, has come to mean specifically "finding out how difficult an item is and how relevant it is to the variables measured by the test." Such data are routinely obtained for the items written for standardized tests before the final versions of these tests are published and often take elaborate forms that are beyond the scope of this book.

With only a modest investment of time and effort, a teacher can compute a simple item analysis by the method outlined in the next section. This method is appropriate when enough time has been allowed so that every pupil has had a chance to consider every item. Almost all tests made by teachers to use in their own classes satisfy this requirement. Exceptions include tests to measure how rapidly pupils can do arithmetic computation, how fast they can read, and how many words they can type per minute.

How to Do It

1. Draw up a worksheet like that in Table 12.2.
2. Write the item numbers and choice letters in columns 1 and 2.
3. Arrange the examinees' test papers in rank order of total score. Divide this pile of papers into three groups: those in the highest 27 per cent in rank order; those in the middle 46 per cent; and those in the lowest 27 per cent.
4. In column 3, make a tally mark on the line corresponding to the letter of the response made to each item by each examinee in the high group. If an examinee has made no response, make a mark opposite "Omit." In columns 4 and 5, follow this same procedure for the middle and low groups, respectively.
5. For each group, count up the number of responses in each item and enter the sum opposite "Total." Within each group, this figure should be the same for every item and should, of course, equal the number of examinees in the group.

TABLE 12.2

Item-Analysis Worksheet

COL. 1 Item Number	COL. 2 Choice Letter	COL. 3 Number in High-Scoring 27 per cent		COL. 4 Number in Middle-Scoring 46 per cent		COL. 5 Number in Low-Scoring 27 per cent		COL. 6 Total Number	COL. 7 Difference between Nos. in Cols. 3 and 5
		Tally	No.	Tally	No.	Tally	No.		
1	A	I I	2	I I I I	4	I I I	3	9	−1
	B	ⅡⅡⅠ	6	ⅡⅡⅡⅠ	7	I I	2	15	4
	C	I	1	I	1	I	1	3	0
	D	I	1	I I	2	I	1	4	0
	E		0	I I I	3	I I I	3	6	−3
	Omit	I	1	I I I	3	I	1	5	0
	Total		11		20		11	42	0
2	A								
	B								
	C								
	D								
	E								
	Omit								
	Total								
3	A								
	B								
	C								
	D								
	E								
	Omit								
	Total								

6. Add across on each line the number of marks recorded in columns 3, 4, and 5, and enter this sum in column 6. For each item, the "Total" figure in column 6 obtained horizontally should agree with that obtained vertically and should equal the total number of examinees.

7. For each line, subtract the number in column 5 from that in column 3 and enter this difference in column 7. If the number in column 5 is larger than that in column 3, this difference will have a minus sign. For each item, the "Total" of these differences should be zero.

How to Use the Data

The illustrative figures entered in Table 12.2 pertain to the following arithmetic-reasoning item, which was administered to 42 pupils in a ninth-grade class.

> 1. What is the selling price of a transistor radio on which a discount of 30 per cent equals $18?
>
>   A $58
> *B $60
>   C $78
>   D Some other amount
>   E This cannot be determined from the information given.
>
> * Keyed choice.

The teacher who devised this problem hoped that his pupils would solve it in this way: Let S be the selling price; then 30 per cent of S, or $.3S$, $= $18; and $S = $60. The data in Table 12.2 show that this problem was rather hard for these pupils; only 15 of them, or 36 per cent, answered it correctly. The rest got an incorrect result, or thought (wrongly) that more information was needed, or failed to mark an answer to it after considering it. It is clear that they need review of the procedure tested by the item and practice in following it.

A comparison of the responses of high-scoring and low-scoring pupils shows that more of the former than of the latter marked the keyed choice, B. This indicates that the item discriminates to some extent between pupils who have considerable arithmetic-reasoning ability and those who have little and is, therefore, relevant to the property measured by the test as a whole.

How well did the distracters (choices A, C, D, and E) function? The negative differences for A and E in column 7 of Table 12.2 show that these choices were marked by more low-scoring than high-scoring pupils. Choice E was an especially effective distracter. The zero differences for C and D show that they did not discriminate between these particular high and low groups, but the number of cases is so small that the teacher should probably wait for more data before trying to think of replacements for them.   The fact that they were marked, respectively, by about 7 and 10 per cent of the class shows that they are not deadwood.

When, by using an item with successive classes, a teacher accumulates enough cases so that the high and low groups each contain about thirty-five pupils, he is justified in paying more attention to the distracters.   He should try to figure out why a distracter that has a large positive difference in column 7 appeals to the high-scoring examinees.   Sometimes he will see an ambiguity in the stem that makes the distracter defensible as an answer and should reword the stem.   Sometimes he will decide that the distracter is too close to the keyed response and should be replaced.   At other times the stem will seem absolutely clear and the distracter indisputably wrong.   In this case, he should ordinarily not replace the distracter with one that he thinks will be less attractive to the able pupils.   To do so is usually to take the heart out of the item so that it no longer tests what it purports, and is intended, to test. It may be better not to re-use the item but to recognize that it may be suitable for pupils at a higher average level of ability or knowledge than that possessed by those to whom he has given it.

The teacher, then, can use informal item-analysis data in two general ways: as evidence of what his pupils have learned and what they need to have retaught and as a guide in producing a better test to be administered in the future.   In using the data for the latter purpose, he will ordinarily eliminate some items as too easy and others as too hard; he will revise some items by clarifying the stem and others by substituting what he hopes will be more effective distracters; and, unless he wants the items in logical or chronological order (as in a history test), he will arrange those that he selects for a second use in a more accurate order of difficulty (from easy to hard) than he was able to attain by subjective judgment.

As stated earlier, the method of item analysis described here is recommended only for classroom tests given with a generous time allowance to a relatively small number of pupils.   More elaborate procedures for tests administered to large numbers of examinees with time limits such that not all examinees can consider every item are available elsewhere.*

Summary

To produce a good test requires thorough knowledge of the subject matter or skill to be measured, a carefully considered plan, ingenuity, and

_____

* F. B. Davis.   *Item-Analysis Data: Their Computation, Interpretation, and Use in Test Construction.*   Harvard Education Papers, No. 2.   Cambridge: Harvard Graduate School of Education, 1946.   (Now available from Test Research Service, Inc., 10 Kent Road, Bronxville, N.Y.)

systematic attention to detail. Every test reflects the psychological insight, the taste, and the individuality of its author. It is this artistic, creative element in test construction that makes it at once a challenge and a source of satisfaction.

In building a test, a teacher should first have its purpose clearly in mind and then outline the material that must be covered to accomplish this purpose. The outline should usually indicate the importance, or weight, to be given each topic and the number and kinds of items.

Test items fall into two general categories: those that do not present answers but require them to be *recalled and produced* and those in which the examinee *recognizes and selects* the answer he thinks is correct or best from two or more choices that are supplied. In the first category are essay questions and short-answer, or completion, items. In the second are true-false statements, multiple-choice items, and matching exercises. Of these three objective types, the multiple-choice is the most flexible and widely used.

These faults commonly found in multiple-choice items are discussed and illustrated: unsuitable item idea, inadequate keyed response, defensible unkeyed response, nonparallel or nonhomogeneous choices, overlapping choices, specific determiners, and overlapping of items within a test or battery.

Despite great care in writing, criticizing, and rewriting items, some of them prove unsatisfactory in actual use. An item analysis will identify those that are too easy or too hard and those that do not discriminate between pupils who possess a large amount of the ability or knowledge being tested and those who possess little. This information guides test constructors in revising items for re-use and in discarding those that cannot be satisfactorily revised. A simple method of obtaining item-analysis data for the unspeeded tests commonly given by most teachers is described and the use of these data is explained.

Selected References

Davis, Frederick B., "Criteria for the Evaluation of Achievement Tests: From the Point of View of the Test Editor," in Educational Testing Service, *Proceedings of the 1950 Invitational Conference on Testing Problems.* Princeton, N.J., 1951.

Davis, Frederick B., "Estimation and Use of Scoring Weights for Each Choice in Multiple-Choice Test Items," *Educational and Psychological Measurement*, XIX (1959), 291–298.

Davis, Frederick B., *Item-Analysis Data: Their Computation, Interpretation, and Use.* Harvard Education Papers, No. 2. Cambridge: Harvard

Graduate School of Education, 1946. (Now distributed by Test Research Service, Inc., 10 Kent Road, Bronxville, N.Y.)

Davis, Frederick B., "Item-Analysis in Relation to Educational and Psychological Testing," *Psychological Bulletin*, XLI (1952), 97–121.

Davis, Frederick B., "Item Selection Techniques," in E. F. Lindquist, ed., *Educational Measurement*, Chapter 9. Washington: American Council on Education, 1951.

Ebel, Robert L., "Writing the Test Item," in E. F. Lindquist, ed., *Educational Measurement*, Chapter 7. Washington: American Council on Education, 1951.

Educational Testing Service, *Making the Classroom Test: A Guide for Teachers*, second ed. Educational and Advisory Service Series, No. 4. Princeton, N.J., 1961.

Educational Testing Service, *Multiple-Choice Questions: A Close Look*. Princeton, N.J., 1963.

Fan, Chung-Teh, *Item-Analysis Table*. Princeton, N.J.: Educational Testing Service, 1952.

Rimland, Bernard, and Edwin Zwerski, "Use of Open-End Data as an Aid in Writing Multiple-Choice Distracters; an Evaluation with Arithmetic Reasoning and Computation Items," *Journal of Applied Psychology*, XLVI (1962), 31–33.

Thorndike, Robert L., and Elizabeth Hagen, *Measurement and Evaluation in Psychology and Education*, second ed. New York: John Wiley & Sons, Inc., 1960. Chapters 3 and 4.

Travers, Robert M. W., *How to Make Achievement Tests*. New York: The Odyssey Press, 1950.

Vitola, Bart M., and G. K. Cantrell, *An Experimental Investigation of Multiple-Choice Item Structure*. Project 7717, Task 17131. Lackland Air Force Base, Texas: Personnel Laboratory, 1961.

Wood, Dorothy A., *Test Construction*. Columbus, O.: Charles E. Merrill Books, Inc., 1960.

Chapter Thirteen

SCHOOL MARKING
PROCEDURES

Probably the most disliked aspect of a teacher's job is marking. In the first place, the drudgery of marking reports and examinations occupies a good deal of the conscientious teacher's out-of-class time. Second, most classes include some pupils who show precious little evidence of having learned much, if any, of the material they have presumably been studying. In his marks, the teacher has the unpleasant task of conveying this information to the pupils and, often more unpleasant, to their parents. Third, most teachers know very little about the underlying rationale of marking procedures and what they do know has given them the impression that marks are rather unreliable and often not highly valid. Consequently, they have a vague feeling of dissatisfaction with the whole process of marking.

It is scarcely surprising that since marking often involves a good deal of drudgery and evokes feelings of dissatisfaction in teachers and feelings of frustration and disappointment in some pupils and their parents, a few educators have advocated abandoning marks altogether, or almost altogether. One can sympathize with this recommendation, but it is a bit like throwing the baby out with the bathwater. The purpose of this chapter is to explain marking procedures to teachers so that they can minimize the clerical labor involved and feel comfortable with the result.

HOW MARKS ARE EXPRESSED

Marks are commonly expressed in terms of:

1. Two categories, such as "satisfactory" and "unsatisfactory" or "passing" and "failing ."
2. Percentages running from 0 to 100.
3. Letter marks, such as A, B, C, D, and E.

287

4. Presence or absence of each element on a check list.
5. Oral or written reports that are descriptive, or both descriptive and analytical.

Each of these ways of expressing marks has some advantages and some disadvantages. These can best be discussed in connection with the purposes served by marks.

PURPOSES OF MARKING

Providing Information

The most fundamental and obvious purpose of marking is to tell each pupil and his parents how well he has attained the objectives of a course of study. Another purpose is to put this information on file for subsequent teachers, counselors, admissions officers of other institutions, and employers.

If the pupil and his parents are to be able to make immediate constructive use of information about his progress, marks must be given several times during a course, the first time not very long after it has begun. This practice should be followed throughout an individual's school career from grade 1 through undergraduate college years, but the method of expressing the marks must not remain the same. In the primary grades, and especially in grade 1, it is highly desirable that marks be expressed as descriptive reports. These should be prepared in written form but, whenever possible, they should be discussed before delivery with one or both parents. Not enough information is conveyed by a percentage or letter mark sent to a parent indicating that his child has failed to make satisfactory progress in beginning reading. The time to discuss the situation and agree on plans to diagnose the difficulty is when the symptoms first appear. The need for personal conferences with parents of primary-school children who are progressing normally, or better than normally, is less acute, but it still exists.

As children advance through the grades, the importance of expressing marks as written or oral reports decreases. After grade 3, reports can be used to supplement percentage or letter grades in the case of pupils for whom this seems desirable. When a teacher has a pupil in only one school subject, say mathematics or English, he often does not have detailed knowledge of the pupil's behavior and achievement except in his own subject. Unless these present some special problem, his comments are apt to be perfunctory.

As a matter of fact, one disadvantage of requiring that all marks take the form of reports is that the latter often become highly stereotyped. The writer has observed teachers writing out a dozen or two descriptive sentences about pupil behavior, such as: "_____ is doing work somewhat above average for his class but needs to study more if he is to realize his full potential," or "_____ needs special attention to his study habits and skills." Each sentence is then numbered and reports are prepared simply by asking the typist to use sentences 1, 3, 4, and 10 for John Jones, sentences 2, 3, 5, and 9 for Mary Smith, etc. Reports prepared in this way are not without value, but can be deceptive if parents are led to believe that each report represents a considered portrait of his child's school work.

Providing Motivation

Efficiency in learning requires that the learners be motivated. The most effective motivation is an intrinsic interest in the material being learned and a desire to learn it to reach intermediate and long-term goals. The implications of this principle for the classroom teacher are obvious. Among the natural and legitimate goals of most pupils is the desire for approval from their teachers and parents. One of the many ways of satisfying this desire on the part of pupils is to obtain satisfactory, or better than satisfactory, marks. This does not mean that excessive emphasis on marks or on competition among pupils for high marks need be encouraged or even condoned. It does mean that at regular intervals pupils should be informed of their progress so that, if desirable, they can modify their study habits with the teacher's guidance. It may be noted in passing that the results of the periodic examinations that often form the basis for marks are usually of considerable value to teachers in letting them know what points need re-teaching, which pupils need special attention, and how the class as a whole is progressing.

BASES FOR MARKS

Teachers and supervisors are often unsure about what should be the basis for marks. Some have argued that they should represent as accurately as possible *only* the relative levels of achievement of the pupils. Others have recommended that they should represent, at least in part, the amount of gain that the pupils have made during the marking period. These educators believe that a pupil who starts with a high level of achievement and makes little gain during the marking period should receive a lower mark than one who starts out at a low level of achievement and makes a large gain, even though the absolute level of achievement of the former at the end of the marking period is still higher than that of the latter.

Still other educators have suggested that marks should reflect the amount of effort that pupils display. They point out that two pupils with equal achievement levels at the beginning of a course who work equally hard may make widely different gains during a marking period because one has greater capacity for learning than the other. In this situation, if marks are based on amount of gain or on level of achievement at the end of the marking period, the pupil with the greater capacity for learning will get the higher mark. On the other hand, if effort is used as a basis for marking, both pupils will get the same mark.

It is apparent that any pupil's level of achievement at the end of a marking period is the joint product of at least three factors:

> 1. His level of achievement at the beginning of the period in the content (knowledge, skills, abilities, understandings, etc.) to be covered.
> 2. His capacity for learning the content.
> 3. The amount of effort he has devoted to learning it.

Theoretically, the gain that he makes would be accounted for mainly by the second and third of these factors. In actual practice, the first ordinarily plays a large part in determining the gain because, above a certain initial level, it becomes more and more difficult to make large gains and display them adequately. Thus, change in a pupil's level of achievement, the measurement of which is discussed in chapter 10, ordinarily involves all three factors and particularly the second and third, plus errors of measurement.

To determine the amount of effort that a pupil has exerted to influence his marks, his level of achievement at the end of a marking period, *relative to his* level of capacity for learning the subject matter, can be used. This would be the measure of underachievement or overachievement described in chapter 11. In theory, such a measure would be influenced mainly by the first and third factors. However, the practical difficulties in finding a measure of initial capacity to learn that is not strongly influenced by initial level of achievement are such that a measure of underachievement or overachievement usually involves mainly effort and errors of measurement.

As mentioned previously, the two major purposes of marking are to provide information about the levels of achievement reached by pupils and to motivate pupils to learn more effectively. By and large, marks given *at the end* of a marking period are intended to provide information about the pupils' achievement levels to them, to their parents, and to others; marks given *during* a marking period are intended primarily to motivate the pupils.

It is quite clear that to serve their first major purpose—that of providing information—marks should be based only on level of achievement. Since this information is an essential element in motivating the pupils, marks based on level of achievement also serve their second major purpose. Nevertheless, it is possible that pupils of limited capacity for learning in any given subject matter but who expend a great deal of effort can become discouraged if their marks based on level of achievement are consistently poor. To provide recognition of their effort and to encourage them, it is often desirable to supplement marks based on level of achievement with separate ratings of effort. These ratings can be obtained by several direct methods, one of which is described in a later section of this chapter.

ESTABLISHING CATEGORIES FOR MARKS

Even if a teacher accepts the idea that marks, whether they are given during or at the end of a marking period, should be based entirely on the levels of achievement of the pupils, he still has the problem of deciding how many pupils will be given marks that the school regards as "passing" or "failing." Usually, there is only one category or mark that represents failure, but the teacher must often assign pupils who "pass" to one of three or four categories and give marks accordingly. For instance, in one school system, marks in the secondary schools take the following form:

A. Work of the highest quality.
B. Good work.
C. Satisfactory work.
D. Passable but unsatisfactory work.
E. Failing work.

In this school, a teacher who is assigning marks must first decide which pupils in his class are to receive E's. Next, he must decide which ones deserve A's, B's, C's, and D's. The steps in making these decisions follow:

1. The pupils should be arranged in rank order on the basis of the best available evidence of their achievement in reaching the objective set for the marking period. Ordinarily, this evidence takes the form of composite scores involving examinations given during and at the end of the marking period and ratings made by the teacher of the classroom activities and individual projects of each pupil during the marking period. Methods of obtaining composite scores are given in a later section of this chapter.

2. The teacher must decide on the basis of his subjective judgment which point on the scale of composite scores represents the lower limit of the

minimum essentials covered in the marking period.   Any pupil at or above this score receives a passing mark; any pupil below this point receives a mark of E.

Choice of the passing point is entirely a subjective decision.   No statistic or "normal curve" of scores enters into the decision or can be expected to help the teacher in making the decision.   Any idea that marks should be assigned on the basis of the normal distribution should be discarded.   However, a consensus among a number of teachers giving sections of the same course regarding the essentials of achievement that a pupil must demonstrate to deserve a passing mark is very desirable.

The teacher's subjective decision about the minimum level of achievement that can be considered passable should be guided by the objectives of the course and the type of pupils in it.   For example, the level of achievement that can be regarded as representing the minimum essentials of a course in "practical arithmetic" for a group of ninth grade pupils with IQ's between 80 and 90 probably constitutes a smaller proportion of the material taught than the analogous level in a course in algebra given to college-preparatory pupils in grade 9.   It is this flexibility in the choice of a passing mark that prevents marks from being absurdly unrealistic, from discouraging most of the pupils with low capacity for learning, and from representing uniform achievement from teacher to teacher and from school to school.   If a counselor, school administrator, or college admissions officer wants data about pupil achievement that is uniform throughout a school, a school system, or the country as a whole, he needs scores from standardized tests that have been properly administered.

3. The teacher must decide, again on the basis of subjective judgment, which pupils in the "passing" group have done work of outstanding quality relative to the remainder of the class.   These pupils are given A's.   Similarly, the teacher sets his own standards for assigning B's, C's, and D's.   Since small classes of twenty to forty pupils can be expected to vary considerably from term to term, quotas calling for so many A's, so many B's, etc. are not dependable guides.   On the other hand, if a teacher finds himself giving A's to 90 per cent of his class, he ought at least to consider seriously whether the class really is exceptionally capable or whether his standards are too lenient.

Table 13.1 shows marks that were assigned by Miss Aylward to the thirty pupils in her class on an examination given at the end of the first marking period in an eleventh grade course in American history.   The examination consisted of 65 five-choice questions.   The scoring formula was (as recommended in chapter 4) $R-W/4$.   Corrected scores ranged from $62\frac{1}{2}$ down to $21\frac{1}{4}$.   The test was rather easy for the group, the median score being about 52.   Ordinarily, it is desirable to have rather easy examinations used for marking purposes because low scores on easy tests are usually spread more widely over the score range than on difficult tests.   Under these

TABLE 13.1

Corrected Scores of Thirty Pupils in an Eleventh Grade
History Class on a 65-Item Multiple-Choice Test,* and
Marks Assigned to Them

Examination Score	Number of Pupils	Mark Assigned
64–65	0	
62–63	1	A
60–61	0	
58–59	2	A
56–57	2	A
54–55	5	B
52–53	5	B
50–51	6	C
48–49	2	C
46–47	1	C
44–45	0	
42–43	3	D
40–41	1	D (Lowest Passing Score)
38–39	0	
36–37	0	
34–35	1	E
32–33	0	
30–31	0	
28–29	0	
26–27	0	
24–25	0	
22–23	0	
20–21	1	E
	30	

* Five-choice items.

circumstances, the low scores are more accurately determined than the high
scores. Since the percentage of pupils who will fail is usually small, the
lowest score judged passable is likely to fall in the more accurately determined
low scores. This passing mark is of critical importance, and errors of
measurement that cause a pupil's obtained score to fall below it when his
true score is above it must be minimized.

Miss Aylward first decided that scores below 42 represented too little
knowledge and understanding to warrant a passing mark. Then she noticed
that one pupil had obtained a score of 40 and that the next lowest score was
35. So she changed the passing mark from 42 to 40. This left only two
pupils with E's. Her next step was to determine the dividing lines between

the A's, B's, C's, and D's. The natural gap in the distribution (where no one got scores of 44 to 45) served nicely to separate the C's from the D's. It is always desirable to make use of natural gaps if they approach closely the dividing lines decided on after examination of the meaning of the scores themselves. The wider the gap, the less likely that pupils are misclassified as a result of errors of measurement.

EFFORT RATING

To supplement marks based on relative achievement levels, ratings of the amount of effort exerted by pupils are often effective for motivational purposes. Pupils who have somewhat limited capacities for learning often work very hard only to find that their marks in achievement are mediocre or even poor while their more intellectually gifted classmates may loaf along, expend very little effort, and obtain high marks in achievement. Some means of recognizing effort should be provided and separate ratings in this trait are probably best. If relative achievement and effort are combined in one set of marks, the latter become almost meaningless and a great deal of important and useful information is lost. For example, a pupil who has exhibited high relative achievement and low effort may receive the same mark as a classmate who has exhibited low relative achievement and high effort.

Effort ratings are usually as effective in motivating high-achieving pupils as low-achieving pupils. High achievers are in the habit of getting above-average marks. Low effort ratings are often sufficiently dissatisfying to cause them to increase their effort, and thus their achievement. Low-achieving pupils who obtain high effort ratings realize that their endeavors have not gone unnoticed and are encouraged to maintain them.

Figure 13.1 shows a form that may be used to obtain effort ratings from classroom teachers. Each pupil is rated in five characteristics:

1. Classroom participation.
2. Completion of assignments.
3. Readiness to learn.
4. Self reliance.
5. Teachableness.

A total score is obtained by summing the weights representing a pupil's ratings in the five characteristics. In successive revisions, the descriptive terms on each of the five rating scales were modified so that teachers would tend to spread their ratings of pupils in typical classes over the entire range, or nearly the entire range.* The weights for the five rating scales are

* The form was developed for use at Avon Old Farms School under the direction of Dean R. H. Sears by W. F. Gookin and F. B. Davis.

FIGURE 13.1

Avon Old Farms, Statement of Progress

Name .... Course .... Date ....

EFFORT

	(8)	(6)	(4)	(2)	(0)
Class Room Participation	Contributes intelligently	Eagerly acquisitive	Normally interested	Not sufficiently interested	Inattentive, or indifferent

	(12)	(9)	(6)	(3)	(0)
Effort Applied to Completing Assignments	Works to the limit of his ability in this subject	Works harder than most of his group	Does reasonably thorough work	Often works carelessly or superficially	Neglects work

	(4)	(3)	(2)	(1)	(0)
Readiness to Learn Subject Matter	Determined to master subject matter	Intent on doing superior work	Wants to do well	Displays "Get by" Attitude	Has little interest in learning subject matter

	(4)	(3)	(2)	(1)	(0)
Self Reliance	Intelligently self-directing	Shows initiative	Normally self-reliant	Follows directions mechanically	Requires prodding

	(4)	(3)	(2)	(1)	(0)
Teachableness	Exceptionally eager to receive instruction	Eager to receive instruction	Always cooperates	Usually cooperates	Rarely cooperates

Total Effort Rating   32   28   24   20   16   12   8   4   0

ACHIEVEMENT

(a) In Terms of College Preparation	Honors	Good	Passable	Weak	Failing
(b) In Terms of His Class Group	Excellent	Good	Satisfactory	Poor	Very Low
Work Habits	Highly Efficient	Fairly Efficient	Moderately Effective	Ineffective	Completely Unorganized
Quality of Composition Skills Shown in Written Work	High	Good	Average	Poor	Low

Specific Recommendations:

(Master) ....

proportional to their judged importance in a pupil's academic effort. The tendency of a pupil to complete assignments was regarded as most important and given a weight of 3; the nature of his participation in classroom work was judged next most important and given a weight of 2; his readiness to learn, degree of self reliance, and teachableness were each given a weight of 1.

These weights were used as multipliers for the five rating scales on the assumption that the intercorrelations of scores on the five scales would be very high. Total scores in effort, therefore, could range from 32 down to 0.

The correlation coefficients among the five rating scales are shown in Table 13.2 along with the corresponding means and standard deviations.

TABLE 13.2

Intercorrelations, Means, and Standard Deviations of Five Effort-Rating Scales
(N = 90)

Scale	1	2	3	4	5
1. Participation	—	.66	.81	.83	.77
2. Completion	.66	—	.83	.82	.76
3. Readiness	.81	.83	—	.89	.83
4. Self Reliance	.83	.82	.89	—	.82
5. Teachableness	.77	.76	.83	.82	—
Mean	6.04	8.42	2.81	2.86	3.08
Standard Deviation	1.21	2.24	.67	.82	.64
Maximum Possible Score	8	12	4	4	4

As expected, the five aspects of effort are closely related to one another. Nevertheless, a factor analysis reveals that the scales seem to measure five different basic components of the trait judged to be pupil effort. This conclusion is based on the data shown in Table 13.3. Note that the variance

TABLE 13.3

Percentage of Variance of Each of Five Rating Scales That Enter into Variances of Five Components of Pupil Effort

Scale	Component 1	Component 2	Component 3	Component 4	Component 5	Scale Variance
1. Participation	7	71	10	7	5	100
2. Completion	72	6	10	6	6	100
3. Readiness	20	17	14	10	39	100
4. Self-Reliance	18	19	13	42	8	100
5. Teachableness	12	13	63	6	6	100

of each rating scale is concentrated to at least a considerable degree on a different component.*

* A more technical description of the findings lies beyond the scope of an elementary textbook. Students who did well in high school or college mathematics can pursue the matter further by consulting K. J. Holzinger, "A Comparison of the Principal-Axis and Centroid Factors," *Journal of Educational Psychology*, XVII (1946), 449–472; and F. B. Davis, "The Interpretation of Principal-Axis Factors," *Journal of Educational Psychology*, XVIII (1947), 471–481.

THE RELIABILITY AND VALIDITY OF TEACHERS' MARKS

Reliability

There is no entirely satisfactory way of estimating the reliability coefficient of a set of marks given by a teacher unless the marks have been based entirely on scores from examinations, each of which was administered in two separately timed parallel forms. In practice, therefore, only rough estimates of the reliability coefficients of teachers' marks can be obtained. These estimates indicate that the coefficients vary greatly from one teacher to another and from one set of marks to another and that the marks are usually not highly reliable.

The best way to obtain marks of satisfactory reliability is to base them on a combination of scores or ratings. At the United States Military Academy, for example, where every cadet is given a mark for every class period, average marks for a semester are extremely reliable. Most teachers would not want to assign so many marks, but they can and should make sure that marks for a term or semester are based on scores from several examinations plus ratings on the quality of classroom participation, laboratory work, and reports on individual projects.

Many teachers would be surprised at the low reliability coefficients of most tests that they construct and administer in their classes. Table 13.4

TABLE 13.4

Reliability Coefficients, Means, Standard Deviations, and Ranges of Scores for Seven Tests in Science in Grade 3*

Test	N	Score Range	Mean	Standard Deviation	Reliability Coefficient
1	54	10–19	14.53	1.96	.34
2	56	10–20	16.27	2.02	.74
3	56	12–22	17.00	2.41	.53
4	57	11–18	14.18	1.57	.39
5	55	7–16	12.22	1.87	.51
6	55	10–19	14.45	2.29	.52
7	54	8–18	15.00	2.00	.41

* G. S. Lesser, F. B. Davis, and L. Nahemow, "The Identification of Gifted Elementary School Children with Exceptional Scientific Talent," *Educational and Psychological Measurement*, XXII (1962), Table 3, 349–364.

shows the reliability coefficients, means, standard deviations, and score ranges of short objective tests given at the end of each of seven units of work in a third grade science class. The items were administered in such a way that the pupils were able to understand them and respond to them without pressure of time. The test reliability coefficients vary from .34 to .74. None of these is, alone, high enough to use as a basis for marks. If the seven scores for each pupil are simply added to yield a total score, the latter has a reliability coefficient of .83, which is high enough to be reasonably satisfactory for marking purposes.

When several marks expressed as letters (such as A, B, C, D, E) are available for each pupil and are to be combined at the end of a marking period, it is usually satisfactory to transform the letters into numerical equivalents as follows: A = 4; B = 3; C = 2; D = 1; E = 0. The numerical equivalents can then be averaged for each pupil and transformed back into letters, if that is desired, as follows: A = 3.5–4.0; B = 2.5–3.4; C = 1.5–2.4; D = .5–1.4; and E = 0–.4.

It has already been pointed out that, to obtain greatest accuracy of measurement at the line of demarcation between passing marks (usually A, B, C, and D) and a failing mark (usually E), it is ordinarily best for a teacher to construct examinations that are rather easy for the class. This generally works out to be the rule because the percentage of pupils who get E's is likely to be small. The same rule of thumb leads to the conclusion that if a teacher wants to obtain greatest accuracy of measurement at the line of demarcation between marks of A and B, he ought to make his examinations rather difficult for the class—for example, if a few pupils are to be selected for special awards at the end of a course.

Validity

When a teacher builds a test for use as a basis for marks in his own class, the test's constructor validity and user validity are identical. As pointed out in chapter 2, constructor and user validities are determined by judging the extent to which a test measures the properties and characteristics that the test constructor and user want measured. The procedures by which a teacher can build a test to measure as nearly as possible what he wants it to measure are discussed in chapter 12.

The validity coefficients of marks for predicting performance in later courses in the same subject-matter field are usually moderately high. The averages of pupil's marks in grades 10, 11, and 12 have been found to have predictive validity coefficients of about .55 to .65 for performance in college-freshman courses. Few data are available to indicate the predictive validity of average high school or college marks for performance in jobs after graduation; so far as now known, these coefficients are ordinarily not high enough to be of practical utility in vocational counseling.

PROBLEMS IN MARKING

Expressing Marks in Prescribed Form

Schools and colleges often define letter marks of A, B, C, D, or E in terms of percentages. One college, for example, states in its catalog that A = 90–100 per cent; B = 80–89 per cent; C = 70–79 per cent; D = 60–69 per cent; E = 0–59 per cent. Taken literally, this statement means that a student who gets a score of 65 per cent on any examination should be given a mark of D; one who gets a score of 89 per cent should be given a mark of B, etc. Fortunately, no one takes the statement literally because it is self-evident that to get 65 per cent on a difficult examination might be the equivalent of getting 89 per cent on an easy examination. As noted earlier in this chapter, the lines of demarcation between marks must be determined by the teacher according to his best judgment.

To reconcile the proper procedure for choosing lines of demarcation with the requirement that marks must represent designated percentage ranges, a diagram like the one shown in Figure 13.2 can be used. On a sheet of graph paper, test scores (number right, corrected, etc.) may be placed on the horizontal dimension. If the test is of the essay type, the scores may be in terms of the possible number of points or in terms of percentages. Both scores and percentages are entered on the horizontal dimension in Figure 13.2. The maximum score is 50 points, which corresponds to 100 per cent.

Marks, expressed either as percentages or as letters, are entered on the vertical scale of the diagram. In this case, the teacher judged that the lowest test score to be assigned a mark of D should be 23, or a test percentage of 46. The official rule of the school requires that this be entered in the records as a mark of 60 per cent. A point, therefore, is plotted at the intersection of a dotted line rising vertically from a test score of 23 with another dotted line extending horizontally from a numerical mark of 60 per cent. The teacher also judged that the lowest test scores to be assigned marks of A, B, and C should be 42, 36, and 31, respectively. Points are plotted at the proper places to the right of numerical marks of 90, 80, 70, and 60 per cent, respectively.

Next, straight lines are drawn between the points plotted and the two

FIGURE 13.2

Transformation of Test Scores and Percentages to
Marks Expressed as Letters or Percentages.

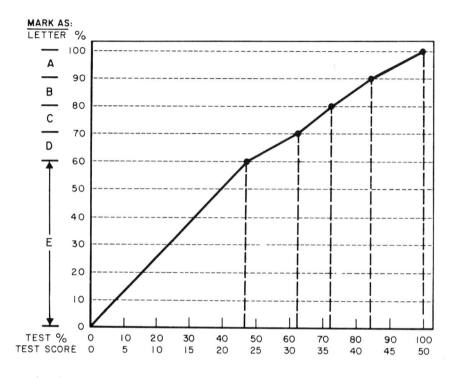

end points of 0 and 100.   From the resulting line, any test score or test percentage can be transformed into a corresponding numerical mark or letter mark.   A test percentage of 50, for example, would be reported as a numerical mark of 62 (rounded from 62½) or as a letter mark of D.

Combining Scores into a Composite

It has already been pointed out that the best way to obtain marks of satisfactory reliability is to base them on a combination of scores or ratings. In combining marks, the teacher may want their influences on the composite scores to vary.   For example, Mr. Abernethy, a twelfth grade English teacher, wishes to base the term marks for his pupils on a composite of the midterm test, his ratings of their contributions to class discussions, a term paper, and a final examination.   In the composite scores, he wants the

midterm test to count 10 per cent; his rating of their contributions to classroom discussions, 20 per cent; the term paper, 40 per cent; and the final
examination, 30 per cent. Table 13.5 shows the entries in his class record

TABLE 13.5

Marks Obtained by Twenty Pupils in a Twelfth Grade English Class

Name	Midterm Test	Classroom Contributions	Term Paper	Final Examination
Mona	C	B	C	B
Alfred	E	B	C	C
Nadine	D	E	C	C
Clarence	B	C	B	A
Danforth	D	B	B	D
Harold	A	C	B	C
Emma	C	D	C	D
Thomas	D	B	D	C
Mary	B	C	B	A
Alice	C	A	B	D
Fletcher	B	A	A	A
Deborah	D	C	C	C
Nancy	C	B	C	C
Douglas	D	C	D	E
Whitney	C	B	D	B
Nettie	D	C	B	C
Jan	C	B	C	B
Daphne	B	C	C	D
Kirby	A	B	C	B
Paul	C	C	B	B

book. The pupils' marks are recorded in the form of letters since that is the
system used in his school. Mr. Abernethy followed the procedure suggested
on pages 291–292 for assigning letter marks to the midterm test scores, to his
ratings on the term paper and on classroom contributions, and to the final
examination. Pluses and minuses are not allowed in the marking system of
his school.

As a first step in combining the five marks to form a composite, Mr.
Abernethy transformed the letter marks into numerical equivalents, as
follows: A = 4; B = 3; C = 2; D = 1; and E = 0. (If his school used
pluses and minuses, he would alter his numerical equivalents accordingly—
A+ = 15; A = 14; A− = 13; etc.) Next he computed the means,
sample standard deviations, and sample variances of each of the four sets of
marks, using equations A.1 (appendix A) and C.1 (appendix C). The
resulting data are shown in Table 13.6. The average mark on the midterm test was 2.00, which is exactly equivalent to a letter mark of C. In

TABLE 13.6

Means, Standard Deviations, and Variances of Four Sets of Marks

Variable	Mean	Sample Standard Deviation	Sample Variance
1. Midterm test	2.00	1.05	1.10
2. Classroom contributions	2.45	.92	.85
3. Term paper	2.30	.78	.61
4. Final examination	2.25	1.09	1.19

the other three sets of marks, the averages were a little higher. The variances differ considerably; for example, the variance of the final-examination marks is about twice as great as that of the term-paper marks.

The weight, or importance, of each variable that enters into a composite depends on its variability and its correlations with the other variables in the composite. If the intercorrelations of the variables are all zero (a phenomenon that rarely occurs), the weight of each variable is proportional to its variance. If the intercorrelations are all equal to 1 (a phenomenon that never occurs in practice), the weight of each variable is proportional to its standard deviation. Since the intercorrelations ordinarily vary among themselves and take values between 0 and 1, the variables that make up a composite cannot be precisely weighted unless their intercorrelations are known. If we are satisfied with a rough approximation to the desired weighting, we can avoid the labor of computing the intercorrelations by assuming that their values are all zero or all 1.

Mr. Abernethy knows that marks based on short tests or on ratings made by a single teacher are apt to be rather unreliable. This consideration and the fact that his four sets of marks are based on different types of data lead him to believe that their intercorrelations may be rather low. Hence, to obtain a rough estimate of the correct weights, he makes the assumption that the intercorrelations are zero.

The next step is to adjust the variances shown in Table 13.6 so that: (1) the variance of the classroom-contributions marks will be twice that of the midterm-test marks; (2) the variance of the term-paper marks will be four times that of the midterm-test marks; and (3) the variance of the final-examination marks will be three times that of the midterm-test marks. To make .85 (the classroom-contributions variance) equal 2.20 (twice the midterm-test variance), it should be multiplied by a weight of 2.20/.85, or 2.59 (rounded to the nearest hundredth). The weights for the term-paper variance and the final-examination variance are 7.21 and 2.77, respectively.

It can easily be shown algebraically that the square roots of these weights for the variances are the proper multipliers to use with the variables them-

selves.   For Mr. Abernethy's marks, these multipliers are shown in Table
13.7.   They have been computed to the nearest hundredth and rounded to

TABLE 13.7

Adjusting Weights for Variances, Multipliers for Marks, and Composite Numerical and Letter Marks for Pupils in a Twelfth Grade
English Class

Variable	Original Variance	Adjusting Weight	Adjusted Variance	Multiplier for Marks	
				2 decimals	1 decimal
1. Midterm test	1.10	1.00	1.10	1.00	1.0
2. Classroom contributions	.85	2.59	2.20	1.61	1.6
3. Term paper	.61	7.21	4.40	2.69	2.7
4. Final examination	1.19	2.77	3.30	1.66	1.7

Pupil's Name	Composite Numerical Mark	Composite Letter Mark
1. Mona	17.3	C
2. Alfred	13.6	C
3. Nadine	9.8	D
4. Clarence	21.1	B
5. Danforth	15.6	C
6. Harold	18.7	B
7. Emma	10.7	C
8. Thomas	11.9	C
9. Mary	21.1	B
10. Alice	18.2	B
11. Fletcher	27.0	A
12. Deborah	13.0	C
13. Nancy	15.6	C
14. Douglas	6.9	D
15. Whitney	14.6	C
16. Nettie	15.7	C
17. Jan	17.3	C
18. Daphne	13.3	C
19. Kirby	19.3	B
20. Paul	18.4	B

the nearest tenth.   In practice, a teacher would rarely need to use multipliers
correct to more than one decimal place; in fact, in many instances, the
multipliers may be rounded to the nearest whole number without appreciably
changing the rank order of the resulting composites.   Table 13.7 also shows

the numerical composites and the composite letter marks for the twenty pupils in Mr. Abernethy's class.

The numerical composites are obtained simply by multiplying the numerical equivalent of each mark for a given pupil by the appropriate multiplier and adding the products. For example, Mona obtained marks of C, B, C, and B. Thus, her numerical composite equals $(1.0 \times 2) + (1.6 \times 3) + (2.7 \times 2) + (1.7 \times 3)$, or 17.3.

Conversion of the numerical equivalents into letter marks can be accomplished by using the same standards originally set in getting the four sets of letter marks. A pupil who received four A's would get a numerical composite of $(1.0 \times 4) + (1.6 \times 4) + (2.7 \times 4) + (1.7 \times 4)$, or 28.0. One who received four B's would get a numerical composite of $(1.0 \times 3) + (1.6 \times 3) + (2.7 \times 3) + (1.7 \times 3)$, or 21.0. The numerical composite halfway between 21.0 and 28.0 is 24.5. A little computation will show that the numerical composites halfway between letter marks of B and C, C and D, and D and E are 17.5, 10.5, and 3.5, respectively. Table 13.8 presents these data in convenient form.

TABLE 13.8

Letter Marks Corresponding to Numerical Composites in a Twelfth Grade English Class

Composite Range	Letter Mark
24.5–28.0	A
17.5–24.4	B
10.5–17.4	C
3.5–10.4	D
0.0– 3.4	E

Although teachers are not likely to check up on the accuracy with which a set of composite marks reflects the desired weights of its parts, it is desirable to do so here for two reasons: (1) to illustrate the method; and (2) to show how well the approximation procedure serves its purpose. The data required are provided by Table 13.9.

Let V_c represent the sample variance of the composite marks;

V_I, V_{II}, V_{III}, and V_{IV} represent the contributions of variables 1–4 to the composite;

V_1, V_2, V_3, and V_4 represent the sample variances of variables 1–4;

S_1, S_2, S_3, and S_4 represent the sample standard deviations of variables 1–4;

m_1, m_2, m_3, and m_4 represent the multipliers used with variables 1–4; and r_{12}, r_{13}, r_{14}, r_{23}, r_{24}, and r_{34} represent the correlations among variables 1–4.

TABLE 13.9

Intercorrelations, Means, Standard Deviations, and Variances of Four Sets of Marks

Variable	Intercorrelations*			
	1	2	3	4
1. Midterm test	—	.10	.37	.44
2. Classroom contributions	.10	—	.16	.18
3. Term paper	.37	.16	—	.38
4. Final examination	.44	.18	.38	—
Mean	2.00	2.45	2.30	2.25
Sample Standard deviation	1.05	.92	.78	1.09
Sample Variance	1.10	.85	.61	1.19

* Computed by equation G.1 (appendix G), using sample standard deviations instead of population estimates. The substitution has no effect on the value of r.

Then:

$$V_c = V_I + V_{II} + V_{III} + V_{IV}; \tag{13.1}$$

and

$$V_I = m_1 S_1 (m_1 S_1 + m_2 S_2 r_{12} + m_3 S_3 r_{13} + m_4 S_4 r_{14}), \tag{13.2}$$

$$V_{II} = m_2 S_2 (m_1 S_1 r_{12} + m_2 S_2 + m_3 S_3 r_{23} + m_4 S_4 r_{24}), \tag{13.3}$$

$$V_{III} = m_3 S_3 (m_1 S_1 r_{13} + m_2 S_2 r_{23} + m_3 S_3 + m_4 S_4 r_{34}), \tag{13.4}$$

$$V_{IV} = m_4 S_4 (m_1 S_1 r_{14} + m_2 S_2 r_{24} + m_3 S_3 r_{34} + m_4 S_4). \tag{13.5}$$

If numerical values from Table 13.9 are substituted in equations 13.2 to 13.5, we obtain: $V_I = 2.93$; $V_{II} = 3.29$; $V_{III} = 7.89$; and $V_{IV} = 6.96$. These are the contributions of the four variables to the variance of the composite marks. This variance, given by equation 13.1, equals 21.07. Hence, the midterm test contributes 2.93/21.07, or 14 per cent, of the composite variance; the classroom-contributions rating contributes 16 per cent; the term-paper rating contributes 37 per cent, and the final examination contributes 33 per cent.

The multipliers provided by the rough-approximation procedure yield percentages that are rather close to those desired. As shown in Table 13.10, variables 1 and 4 yield percentages slightly higher than desired and variables 2 and 3 yield percentages somewhat lower than desired. If the intercorrelations of the four sets of marks had not been rather low and somewhat similar in value, the rough approximations that Mr. Abernethy obtained by assuming that the intercorrelations were all zero would have been less satisfactory than they turned out to be.

How much more satisfactory these rough approximations are than the weights yielded by simple addition of the numerical equivalents of the four marks for each pupil is shown in Table 13.10. If these equivalents are simply added, 30 per cent of the variance of the composite marks is contributed by

TABLE 13.10

Multipliers Used for Marks in Mr. Abernethy's Class and Percentages
of Composite Variance Yielded by Their Use

Variable	Desired Per-centage	Multipliers and Percentages of Composite Sample Variance Yielded by					
		Rough Approximation Method		Close Approximation Method		Simple Addition Method	
		Multi-plier	Per cent	Multi-plier	Per cent	Multi-plier	Per cent
1. Midterm test	10	1.0	14	.76	10	1.0	30
2. Class contribu-tions	20	1.6	16	1.85	20	1.0	18
3. Term paper	40	2.7	37	3.01	40	1.0	20
4. Final examina-tion	30	1.7	33	1.70	30	1.0	32

the midterm test instead of the desired 10 per cent; and 20 per cent is contributed by the term paper instead of the desired 40 per cent. This comparison
illustrates the fact that the user validity of composite marks can be regarded
as satisfactory only if the weighting of the variables in the composite is
considered and if proper multipliers are used to make the contributions of
these variables to the composite variance approximate those desired.

It is possible to obtain multipliers that will make the contribution of
each variable to a composite exactly what is desired. Essentially, this is done
by substituting modifications of the rough-approximation multipliers in
equations 13.2 to 13.5 until a combination of multipliers is found that yields
percentages satisfactorily close to those desired. For the marks in Mr.
Abernethy's class, this close-approximation method yields the multipliers
shown in Table 13.10. It will be observed that they provide exactly the weights
that Mr. Abernethy specified.*

MAKING MARKS COMPARABLE

One Teacher's Marks in the Same Class

Comparable scores were defined in chapter 2 as measuring different
characteristics or properties but as having identical means and distributions.

_____

* Computation routines that minimize the labor of the close-approximation
method have been developed but fall beyond the scope of an elementary textbook.

Procedures exist for transforming several sets of a teacher's marks for the same pupils into numerical equivalents that have essentially identical means and distributions, but their use when the number of pupils is small is probably inadvisable. Chance fluctuations begin to play a larger and larger part in determining the numerical equivalents as the number of cases decreases. All things considered, it is perhaps most satisfactory in these circumstances simply to regard a teacher's marks as comparable if they have been determined by the method described on pages 291–292. The four sets of marks in Mr. Abernethy's class may be used as an illustration. Their means and standard deviations are, in fact, somewhat similar, as shown in Table 13.6. It is possible that the differences among the means and among the standard deviations may reflect, at least in part, real variations in pupil performance from one type of activity to another.

Marks from Several Teachers or Schools

Everyone familiar with school or college marks recognizes that teachers vary greatly in their marking practices. Even in parallel sections of the same course, different teachers maintain different standards. Table 13.11 shows the average marks given in twenty-nine parallel sections of a college English-composition course. Letter marks were transformed into numerical equivalents, as indicated at the bottom of the table. The average scholastic aptitude of pupils in each section is also shown in numerical equivalents comparable to those used for the marks. The sections vary somewhat in average scholastic aptitude—from 2.4 to 3.2. Their average marks in English composition range from 1.5 to 3.0; that is, from the equivalent of a mark midway between a C and a D in sections 5 and 20 to a B in section 23. Note that the average scholastic-aptitude level of the thirty pupils in sections 5 and 20 is very close to that of the sixteen pupils in section 23. This suggests that the difference of 1.5 points between their average marks in English composition is attributable mainly to differences in the marking standards of their teachers.

To make the marks in all of the sections as nearly comparable as possible, the numerical equivalents of the letter marks in each section can be expressed as standard scores with a standard deviation equal to that of the distribution of numerical equivalents of letter marks in all sections. Then these standard scores are adjusted to take care of the fact that the marks are affected by differences in level of scholastic aptitude. The relationship between marks and scholastic-aptitude scores of the 436 pupils in the twenty-nine sections may be expressed as a correlation coefficient. This procedure for making marks approximately comparable is stated compactly in equation 13.6.

$$Z_M = S_{Mt}\left(\frac{Ms - \overline{Ms}}{S_{Ms}}\right) + \overline{Mt} + S_{Mt}r_{MA}\left(\frac{\overline{As} - \overline{At}}{S_{At}}\right), \qquad (13.6)$$

TABLE 13.11

Average Numerical Equivalents of Marks and of Scores in Scholastic
Aptitude Obtained by Pupils in Twenty-Nine Parallel Sections of an
English-Composition Course

Section	Number of Pupils	Average Numerical Equivalent of Mark*	Average Numerical Equivalent of Aptitude Score
1	15	2.6	2.6
2	18	2.3	2.7
3	18	1.8	2.8
4	17	2.2	2.5
5	15	1.5	2.6
6	17	2.8	3.1
7	13	2.2	3.0
8	19	1.9	2.7
9	15	2.5	2.9
10	14	2.1	3.0
11	17	2.4	2.6
12	13	2.1	2.5
13	13	2.3	2.8
14	17	2.2	2.5
15	15	1.7	2.7
16	17	1.9	2.9
17	18	2.3	3.2
18	18	2.2	2.9
19	17	2.4	2.7
20	15	1.5	2.8
21	15	2.3	2.5
22	16	1.8	2.4
23	16	3.0	2.6
24	9	2.3	3.1
25	10	2.8	2.9
26	8	2.2	2.8
27	16	2.6	2.5
28	12	1.8	2.9
29	13	2.1	3.2

* A = 4; B = 3; C = 2; D = 1; E = 0.

where Z_M = the adjusted standard score for any given mark (A, B, C, D, or E);

S_{Mt} = the sample standard deviation of the numerical equivalents of marks in all sections combined;

Ms = the numerical equivalent of any given mark in section s;

$\overline{M}s$ = the average numerical equivalent of all marks in section s;

S_{Ms} = the sample standard deviation of the numerical equivalents of all marks in section s;

$\overline{M}t$ = the average of the numerical equivalents of marks in all sections combined;

r_{MA} = the product-moment correlation coefficient between the numerical equivalents of marks and aptitude scores in all sections combined;

$\overline{A}s$ = the average of aptitude scores in section s;

$\overline{A}t$ = the average of aptitude scores in all sections combined; and

S_{At} = the sample standard deviation of aptitude scores in all sections combined.

The basic data needed to use equation 13.6 to obtain adjusted standard scores for pupils in sections 20 and 23 are presented in Tables 13.11 and 13.12. These two sections have been chosen simply for illustrative purposes; the procedure may be used to obtain adjusted standard scores for pupils in all sections. The correlation coefficient between marks and aptitude scores is +.07. That the coefficient is so low was unexpected. Ordinarily, scholastic-aptitude scores of the type used display coefficients of about .50 with marks in English-composition courses given a semester or two later. Some possible implications of the low relationship found between these two variables in the 436 pupils in these twenty-nine sections will be discussed in the next section of this chapter.

For a mark of C in section 20, equation 13.6 yields:

$$Z_{C20} = (.85)\left(\frac{2.00 - 1.53}{.62}\right) + 2.20 + (.85)(+.07)\left(\frac{2.80 - 2.77}{.76}\right) = 2.85.$$

For a mark of D in this section, it yields:

$$Z_{D20} = (.85)\left(\frac{1.00 - 1.53}{.62}\right) + 2.20 + (.85)(+.07)\left(\frac{2.80 - 2.77}{.76}\right) = 1.48.$$

For a mark of E in this section, it yields .10. There were no marks of A or B given in section 20.

For a mark of A in section 23, equation 13.6 yields:

$$Z_{A23} = (.85)\left(\frac{4.00 - 3.00}{.79}\right) + 2.20 + (.85)(+.07)\left(\frac{2.56 - 2.77}{.76}\right) = 3.26.$$

For marks of B and C in section 23, equation 13.6 yields: $Z_{B23} = 2.18$; and $Z_{C23} = 1.10$. No marks of D or E were given in section 23.

Since all of the letter marks in sections 20 and 23 have been made approximately comparable, they can be placed on a common scale; this has been done in Figure 13.3. Note that a letter mark of C in section 20 represents approximately the same level of achievement in English composition as a mark of A— in section 23 and that a mark of D in section 20 represents approximately the same level of achievement as a mark of C+ in section 23. This is evidence that, even with pupils having the same scholastic

TABLE 13.12

Distributions of Marks in Sections 20 and 23 and in All Sections of English-Composition Course

Letter Mark	Numerical Equivalent	Section 20		Section 23		All Sections	
		Number of English Marks	Number of Scholastic Aptitude Marks	Number of English Marks	Number of Scholastic Aptitude Marks	Number of English Marks	Number of Scholastic Aptitude Marks
A	4	0	3	5	2	19	74
B	3	0	6	6	6	137	198
C	2	9	6	5	7	204	156
D	1	5	0	0	1	63	5
E	0	1	0	0	0	13	3
Number of Pupils		15	15	16	16	436	436
Mean		1.53	2.80	3.00	2.56	2.20	2.77
Sample Standard Deviation		.62	.75	.79	.79	.85	.76

FIGURE 13.3

Letter Marks in Sections 20 and 23 Expressed in Terms
of Adjusted Standard Scores.

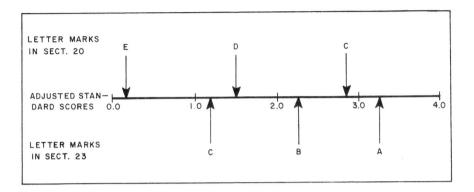

aptitude, the teacher of section 20 would tend to give lower marks than the teacher of section 23.

Equation 13.6 can be used to obtain adjusted standard scores for marks in all twenty-nine sections of the English-composition course. Since the distribution of all marks in the twenty-nine sections was used as a basis for establishing the adjusted standard scores, the letter marks in this distribution have adjusted-standard-score values as follows: A = 4; B = 3; C = 2; D = 1; and E = 0. The average adjusted standard score in the distribution is 2.20, or a little higher than a C.

If the pooled judgment of all the teachers of the twenty-nine sections with regard to marking standards is accepted, letter marks can be assigned to all pupils in the twenty-nine sections in accordance with the data in column 3 of Table 13.13. For example, any pupil in section 20 who was given a mark of C has an adjusted standard score of 2.85, so he has an adjusted mark of B. Any pupil in section 23 who was given a mark of A has an adjusted standard score of 3.26, so he is also given an adjusted mark of B. If the marking system of the school includes pluses and minuses, the adjusted standard scores of pupils like these would be B and B+. It is probable that the adjusted letter marks of these pupils are more nearly indicative of their actual relative achievement in English composition than the original letter marks assigned by their teachers. However, this is not certain because in adjusting the marks, several assumptions were made, such as that all of the teachers cause pupils of a given level of aptitude to reach about the same level of achievement.

To set standards in assigning adjusted marks different from those represented by the marks given in all sections combined is easily done—for

TABLE 13.13

Adjusted Letter Marks Corresponding to Adjusted Standard Scores in English Composition

Adjusted Letter Marks		Standards Represented by Marks Given in All Sections Combined	Standards Represented by Regarding Average Adjusted Standard Score (2.20) as Center of Range for Adjusted Mark of C
Column 1	Column 2	Column 3	Column 4
A	A	3.80 and above	4.00 and above
A	A −	3.50–3.79	3.70–3.99
B	B +	3.20–3.49	3.40–3.69
B	B	2.80–3.19	3.00–3.39
B	B −	2.50–2.79	2.70–2.99
C	C +	2.20–2.49	2.40–2.69
C	C	1.80–2.19	2.00–2.39
C	C −	1.50–1.79	1.70–1.99
D	D +	1.20–1.49	1.40–1.69
D	D	.80–1.19	1.00–1.39
D	D −	.50– .79	.70– .99
E	E +	.20– .49	.40– .69
E	E	.19 and below	.39 and below

example, the average adjusted standard score might be made to correspond to the center of the C range for adjusted marks. Column 4 in Table 13.13 shows the resulting ranges of adjusted standard scores for each letter mark. Given these standards, any pupil in section 20 who was given a mark of C would receive an adjusted mark of B −, and any pupil in section 23 who was given a mark of A would receive an adjusted mark of B.

Equation 13.6 is generally useful for rendering comparable the marks given by different teachers and in different courses; its use has been illustrated with marks given by different teachers in different sections of the same course in a single school. If these sections of the course were scattered among several different schools, the procedure would still be applicable. Marks in any given subject from different schools may thus be made approximately comparable; however, pupils in all the schools would have to have taken the same aptitude test.

IMPROVING MARKING PROCEDURES

Most teachers can improve their marking procedures by gaining a better understanding of the basic principles underlying the assignment of marks and putting these into practice. Studies of marks given in a school or college often serve as stimuli to reconsidering and improving marking procedures. An example of this is provided by the data gathered to permit obtaining comparable marks in the twenty-nine sections of the English-composition course. It was a little surprising to find that marking standards differed so greatly from teacher to teacher that one gave no A's or B's while another gave no D's or E's. It was startling to find that marks displayed so low a relationship with level of scholastic aptitude. It is reasonable to expect that most of the skills taught in English-composition courses will correlate markedly with customary measures of scholastic aptitude; and a great deal of data that have been gathered indicates that they usually do. The fact that this set of 436 marks correlated so low with scholastic-aptitude scores suggests that the marks were to a large extent based on elements other than skills and knowledge in English composition. If so, they are clearly invalid, since teachers, administrators, pupils, and parents expect them to represent achievement in this subject-matter field.

These data point to the need for a study of marking practices in this English-composition course by a committee of teachers in that field. To be effective, a committee of this sort usually needs the support and encouragement of school administrators and the technical assistance of someone versed in evaluation and research techniques. If school marking procedures are to be effective, they must be subject to periodic scrutiny and revision by faculty committees.

Summary

Teachers dislike marking partly because of the clerical drudgery involved, partly because it requires conveying unpleasant information to some pupils and their parents, and partly because they are unsure of the procedures to follow and of the validity of the results. Knowledge of how to construct adequate short-answer and objective tests can help to reduce the clerical labor of marking while at the same time often improving its validity. Constructive use of marks for motivation and guidance of pupils tends to make their reception less disagreeable. Understanding of the principles underlying the assignment and use of marks enables the teacher to improve their validity and to have greater confidence in them. With this confidence, the task of obtaining marks and of communicating them to pupils and parents is far less onerous than it otherwise would be.

The two major purposes of marking are to provide information about the levels of achievement reached by the pupils and to motivate them to learn more effectively. These two purposes are interdependent; knowledge of the level of achievement attained often serves as a spur to further effort, especially on the part of pupils who find that their levels of attainment are unsatisfactory. By and large, however, marks given during a learning period are intended primarily to inform them about their status.

Three principles that underlie marking may be stated as follows:

1. Marks should be clearly labeled to identify exactly what they are intended to measure. If necessary, separate marks should be given for subject-matter achievement, for effort expended, and for other factors judged important—such as conduct.
2. Marks should be based on reliable evidence strictly relevant to what is intended to be measured. Marks supposed to indicate achievement should ordinarily be based on composite scores representing examinations and ratings made by the teacher regarding the classroom activities and individual projects of the pupils.
3. The distribution of marks should reflect the teacher's best judgment of the extent to which the pupils have progressed toward the goals set for them. Any idea that marks should be distributed on the basis of a normal curve or of fixed percentages of A's, B's, etc. should be discarded.

The reliability of teachers' marks is often disappointingly low. To maximize their reliability, teachers should give several carefully constructed short tests during each marking period and keep accurate records of the pupils' class activities and out-of-class projects. The reliability of composite scores based on several tests and ratings is likely to be far greater than that of any one of the scores or ratings that enter into the composite. Methods of obtaining composite scores are discussed in the chapter. A graphic procedure for transforming scores into letter marks or percentages is also given.

There is considerable evidence to show that marks given by different teachers or even by the same teacher in different classes are not comparable. For example, an A from one teacher may represent the same level of performance as a C from another teacher. For most practical purposes, marks are regarded as comparable if the teachers who assigned them have been thoroughly briefed regarding the types of performances to be marked, the standards to be maintained, and the method for establishing marks. If these requirements have not been met or if refined techniques are to be employed, as in research studies in a school system, the methods described in the section on "Making Marks Comparable" may be followed.

Finally, it should be emphasized that evaluation procedures should always be planned to accompany any kind of learning exercises. Ordinarily, their outcomes can be usefully expressed as marks. In most schools, periodic reviews of marking procedures by faculty committees, aided by consultants in evaluation and measurement, are needed to keep the marking system functioning properly.

Selected References

Hamaleinen, Arthur E., *An Appraisal of Anecdotal Records.* Teachers College Contributions to Education, No. 891. New York: Teachers College, Columbia Univ., Bureau of Publications, 1943.

McCall, William A., *Measurement.* New York: Macmillan Co., 1939. Chapters 23, 24, and 28.

Smith, Eugene R., *et al., Appraising and Recording Student Progress.* New York: Harper and Row, Publishers, 1942.

Thorndike, Robert L., and Elizabeth P. Hagen, *Measurement and Evaluation in Psychology and Education,* second ed. New York: John Wiley & Sons, Inc., 1961. Chapter 17.

Traxler, Arthur E., *Techniques of Guidance.* Revised Edition. New York: Harper and Row, Publishers, 1957. Chapter 14.

Wrinkle, William L., *Improving Marking and Reporting Practices in the Elementary and Secondary Schools.* New York: Holt, Rinehart, and Winston, Inc., 1947.

APPENDIXES

THE ARITHMETIC MEAN

The arithmetic mean, often called the arithmetic average, is useful for representing with a single value the central tendency of a set of scores. In fact, it is ordinarily the most stable value that can be employed for the purpose. The major exceptions to this rule arise if a distribution is markedly skewed (that is, if the scores in it are piled up toward one end) or if almost all of the scores in a symmetrical distribution are concentrated on a few score values near the center. In these circumstances, the median may be the most stable value.

TABLE A.1

Computation of the Mean
Score of Ten Pupils on a Fifteen-Item
Vocabulary Test

Pupil	Score
A	6
B	1
C	4
D	9
E	0
F	5
G	3
H	6
I	7
J	5

$$\Sigma X = 46$$

$$\bar{X} = \frac{\Sigma X}{N}$$

$$\bar{X} = \frac{46}{10} = 4.60$$

The arithmetic mean of a set of scores is computed merely by adding the score values in the set and dividing by the number of scores. For convenience, the arithmetic mean of scores on test X is represented by $\bar{X}$. If we let the Greek $\sum$ (sigma) stand for "the sum of" and the number of scores by capital-letter N, we may write equation A.1 for computing the arithmetic mean.

$$\bar{X} = \frac{\sum X}{N} \qquad \text{(A.1)}$$

If the arithmetic mean of a very large number of scores is to be computed, a desk calculator or an adding machine is of great convenience. If no machine is available and the arithmetic mean of a very large number of scores must be obtained, computational short cuts can be employed.*

Computation of the mean score of ten pupils on a fifteen-item vocabulary test is illustrated in Table A.1.

---

* Any one of many texts in elementary statistics provides these short cuts. See, for example, N. M. Downie and R. W. Heath, *Basic Statistical Methods* (New York: Harper and Row, Publishers, 1959), pp. 29–32.

PERCENTILES, PERCENTILE RANKS, AND PERCENTILE NORMS

THE MEDIAN

The median is the numerical value of the score below which lie 50 per cent of the scores in a distribution.   Since it is regarded as a point (without dimension), 50 per cent of the scores in the distribution also lie above it.   It is identical with the 50th percentile.   It can usually be computed more quickly than the arithmetic mean, and in a distribution that is very tall and

TABLE B.1

Distribution of Scores Obtained by Ten Pupils on a Fifteen-Item Test

Score at Center of Interval	Interval	Pupil	Frequency of Scores	Cumulative Frequency through Each Successive Interval
10.00	9.50–10.49	D	1	10
9.00	8.50–9.49	None	0	9
8.00	7.50–8.49	I	1	9
7.00	6.50–7.49	A and H	2	8
6.00	5.50–6.49	F and J	2	6
5.00	4.50–5.49	C	1	4
4.00	3.50–4.49	G	1	3
3.00	2.50–3.49	None	0	2
2.00	1.50–2.49	B	1	2
1.00	0.50–1.49	E	1	1
0.00	−0.50–0.49	None	0	0

thin (with most of the scores concentrated close to the center) or that is highly skewed, it is more reliable than the arithmetic mean.   Furthermore, the median is easy to interpret to laymen because 50 per cent of the cases in a distribution lie below it and 50 per cent lie above it.

Computation of the median is very straightforward since it is simply the numerical value of the score at the center of a distribution.   The first step is to arrange the scores in rank order from highest to lowest.   In Table B.1 this has been done for ten scores.   It is obvious that half of the ten cases lie below the center of the score interval that runs from 5.50 to 6.49.   Its center is a score of exactly 6.00.   If half of the ten cases lie below the point represented by a score of 6.00 and half of the ten cases lie above this point, 6.00 must be the median of the distribution.   More systematically, we obtain the median by using equation B.1.

$$Mdn = LL + i\left(\frac{.5N - cfb}{f}\right), \tag{B.1}$$

where N = the number of cases in the distribution;

i = the range of scores covered by the interval that includes $.5N$;

LL = the lower limit of the interval that includes $.5N$;

cfb = the cumulative frequency of cases below LL;

f = the frequency of cases in the interval that includes $.5N$.

For the distribution of ten cases shown in Table B.1, equation B.1 yields the median as follows:

$$Mdn = 5.50 + 1\left(\frac{5 - 4}{2}\right) = 5.50 + .50 = 6.00.$$

ANY PERCENTILE

Any percentile in a distribution may be computed by using a generalized form of equation B.1 in which p, defined as the proportion corresponding to any desired percentile, is substituted for .5.   For example, the tenth percentile corresponds to a p of .10; the 25th percentile (sometimes referred to as the first quartile) to a p of .25; the 50th percentile (the median or second quartile) to a p of .50; and the 75th percentile (the third quartile) to a p of .75.   The general equation for computing any percentile is B.2.

$$X_p = LL + i\left(\frac{pN - cfb}{f}\right), \tag{B.2}$$

where X_p = the desired percentile;
$\quad\quad N$ = the number of cases in the distribution;
$\quad\quad i$ = the range of scores covered by the interval that includes pN;
$\quad\quad p$ = the proportion corresponding to the desired percentile;
$\quad\quad LL$ = the lower limit of the interval that includes pN;
$\quad\quad cfb$ = the cumulative frequency of cases below LL; and
$\quad\quad f$ = the frequency of cases in the interval that includes pN.

For the distribution of cases shown in Table B.1, the 25th and 75th percentiles are as follows:

$$X_{.25} = 3.50 + 1\left(\frac{2.50 - 2.00}{1}\right) = 3.50 + .50 = 4.00.$$

$$X_{.75} = 6.50 + 1\left(\frac{7.50 - 6.00}{2}\right) = 6.50 + .75 = 7.25.$$

It should be pointed out that we never obtain values for the 100th percentile or for the zero percentile. In fact, the smallest percentile to be computed in any distribution is equal to one hundred times the number of cases in the lowest interval that includes any cases divided by the number of cases in the distribution. For the distribution shown in Table B.1, the smallest percentile that should be computed is equal to 100/10, or 10. The largest percentile that should be computed in any distribution is equal to 100 minus one hundred times the number of cases in the highest interval that includes any cases divided by the number of cases in the distribution. For the distribution shown in Table B.1, the largest percentile that should be computed is equal to $100 - (100/10)$, or 90. Beyond these limits, percentiles in this particular distribution are too unreliable to be worth computing.

To compute a percentile of 90 in the distribution shown in Table B.1, we first obtain pN, which equals .90 times 10, or 9.00. Notice that 9 appears twice in the cumulative-frequency column in Table B.1 since the interval that runs from 8.50 to 9.49 has no cases in it. Half of the range of this interval should, therefore, be merged with the interval next below it. The other half should be merged with the interval next above it. Then the range of scores in the interval that includes the cumulative frequency pN becomes 1.50. Hence

$$X_{.90} = 7.50 + 1.50\left(\frac{9.00 - 8.00}{1}\right) = 7.50 + 1.50 = 9.00.$$

ANY PERCENTILE RANK

The percentage of cases in a distribution that lies below any given score value is called the *percentile rank* of that score. This can be computed by equation B.3.

$$P_X = 100\left[\frac{cfb}{N} + \frac{f(X - LL)}{iN}\right], \tag{B.3}$$

where X = the score for which the percentile rank is desired;

P_X = the percentile rank of score X;

N = the number of cases in the distribution;

i = the range of scores covered by the interval that contains score X;

LL = the lower limit of the interval that includes score X;

cfb = the cumulative frequency of cases below LL;

f = the frequency of cases in the interval that includes score X.

The percentile rank of a score of 6 in the distribution shown in Table B.1 may be computed as follows:

$$P_6 = 100\left[\frac{4}{10} + \frac{2(6.00 - 5.50)}{(1)(10)}\right] = 100(.40 + .10) = 50.$$

This result could also be stated as "Pupil F has a percentile rank of 50," or as "Pupil J's percentile rank is 50." Strictly speaking, then, we should never refer to a pupil's percentile or to his percentile score but always to his score or to his percentile rank.

To compute the percentile rank of a score of 10, we must take into account the fact that the interval of which the center is 9.00 includes no cases; therefore, half of the range of this interval should be merged with the interval of which 10.00 is the center. (The other half should be merged with the interval of which 8.00 is the center.) Then, LL becomes 9.00 and i becomes 1.50. The computation of the percentile rank of a score of 10 follows:

$$P_{10} = 100\left[\frac{9}{10} + \frac{1(10.00 - 9.00)}{(1.50)(10)}\right] = 100(.900 + .067) = 96.7.$$

The percentile rank of a score of 10 is 96.7; this will ordinarily be rounded off to the nearest whole number, making it 97.

PERCENTILE NORMS

In many schools or school systems, occasions arise when local percentile norms are desired. Sometimes, these are needed for a test that has been constructed locally and for which norms do not exist; sometimes, they are needed because existing norms were developed on the basis of pupils quite different with respect to mental or achievement level from those in the community. To establish a set of percentile norms, the best procedure is to compute a set of 15 to 20 percentiles by means of equation B.2 and to plot these values on graph paper. Although it is not necessary to use arithmetic probability paper in making such a plot, its use makes easier the drawing of a smooth curve through the points plotted.

Table B.2 shows in column 2 the frequency distribution of scores on a thirty-item language-aptitude test given to 1,497 children a week after they

TABLE B.2

Frequency Distributions and Estimated Population Percentile Ranks for Obtained Scores on a Language-Aptitude Test Given in the First Week of Grade I

Score	Frequency of Scores	Cumulative Frequency of Scores	Estimate of Population Percentile Rank from Figure B.1
		1497	
30	15		99
		1482	
29	62		98
		1420	
28	100		93
		1320	
27	142		86
		1178	
26	163		75
		1015	
25	183		63
		832	
24	162		52
		670	
23	124		42
		546	
22	118		33
		428	
21	112		25
		316	
20	91		19
		225	
19	62		14
		163	
18	46		10
		117	
17	37		7
		80	
16	18		5
		62	
15	20		3

Score	Frequency of Scores	Cumulative Frequency of Scores	Estimate of Population Per-centile Rank from Figure B.1
		42	
14	17		2
		25	
13	8		2
		17	
12	3		1
		14	
11	6		1
		8	
10	6		1
		2	
9	0		below 1
		2	
8	2		below 1
TOTAL	1,497		

enrolled in grade 1. The corresponding cumulative frequency distribution appears in column 3. Equation B.2 was used to compute 13 percentiles from 99 down to 1. These are shown in Table B.3 and have been plotted in Figure B.1. The vertical dimension in this figure is in terms of percentile ranks and the horizontal dimension is in terms of percentiles (which are obtained scores). A smoothed curve has been drawn as a solid line through

TABLE B.3

Selected Percentile Ranks and Corresponding Obtained Scores in Distribution Shown in Table B.2

Percentile Rank	Obtained Score
99	29.50
95	28.53
90	27.77
80	26.70
70	25.83
60	24.86
50	23.98
40	22.93
30	21.68
20	20.32
10	18.21
5	16.21
1	11.82

Figure B.1

Smoothed Curve Relating Percentile Ranks and Obtained Scores.

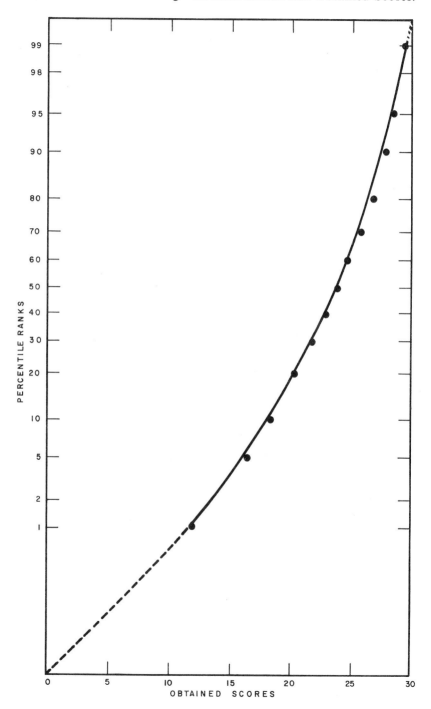

the points plotted.   Beyond the extreme values plotted, the smoothed curve has been extrapolated as a dotted line.

The percentile rank of the horizontal line that passes through the point on the curve corresponding to each obtained score from 8 through 30 has been read from Figure B.1 and entered in column 4 of Table B.2.   These ranks are estimates of the population percentile ranks of the obtained scores and are used as percentile norms.   The smoothing of the curve after the points have been plotted tends to reduce the influence of sampling variations and one or two other irrelevant factors on the percentile norms.

THE STANDARD DEVIATION

SAMPLE STANDARD DEVIATION

The standard deviation is used in elementary educational measurement principally as a sort of yardstick or measuring rod by which the spread of scores around the mean of a distribution is indicated. The standard deviation in greatest use is that of the distribution of errors of measurement around an individual's true score; as stated in chapter 2, this is called the *standard error of measurement*. Fortunately, it is ordinarily supplied by the test publisher for each age or grade level at which a test is to be used; therefore, in practical work, it is rarely necessary to compute standard deviations. However, a computational procedure is given here to make it possible for the student to do so when required and to provide a better understanding of the concepts underlying the standard deviation.

The scores of ten pupils on a fifteen-item vocabulary test, first given in appendix A, are shown in Table C.1. If we let S stand for the standard

TABLE C.1

Scores of Ten Pupils on a Fifteen-Item Vocabulary Test

Pupil	Score	Score Squared
A	6	36
B	1	1
C	4	16
D	9	81
E	0	0
F	5	25
G	3	9
H	6	36
I	7	49
J	5	25

$$\sum X = 46 \qquad \sum X^2 = 278$$

328

deviation in this tiny sample; X for any score; N for the number of scores; and the Greek $\sum$ (sigma) for "the sum of," the standard deviation of the distribution in the sample is defined by equation C.1.*

$$S_X = \sqrt{\frac{\sum X^2}{N} - \left(\frac{\sum X}{N}\right)^2} \qquad (\text{C.1})$$

To obtain $\sum X^2$, we must first square each score (as shown in the right-hand column in Table C.1) and then add these squares. The sum of the 10 squares is 278; the sum of the 10 scores is 46. N is, of course, 10. The computation of the sample standard deviation is as follows:

$$S_X = \sqrt{\frac{278}{10} - \left(\frac{46}{10}\right)^2} = \sqrt{27.80 - (4.60)^2} = \sqrt{27.80 - 21.16}$$

$$= \sqrt{6.64} = 2.58.$$

The standard deviation is the square root of the variance, which we may represent by the letter V. Hence, $S = \sqrt{V}$; or $S^2 = V$. For the scores of the ten pupils, the sample variance is simply the value under the square-root sign—6.64.

ESTIMATE OF THE POPULATION STANDARD DEVIATION

To estimate the standard deviation in the entire population of pupils from which our sample of ten pupils was drawn at random, a slight adjustment must be made in the variance computed in the sample (6.64). Let us represent the estimate of the population variance by v and the estimate of the population standard deviation by s. Then the estimate of the population variance is given by equation C.2.

$$v = V\left(\frac{N}{N - 1}\right) \qquad (\text{C.2})$$

For the population represented by the ten pupils whose scores are shown in Table C.1, our estimate of the variance is:

$$v_X = 6.64\left(\frac{10}{9}\right) = 7.38,$$

* As noted in chapter 2, the sample standard deviation is denoted in this book by S; an estimate of the standard deviation in the population of which the sample is representative, by s; and the population standard deviation, by σ. The variances corresponding to these three standard deviations are denoted by V, v, and σ^2 respectively.

and $$s_X = \sqrt{v_X} = \sqrt{7.38} = 2.72.*$$

The estimate of a population variance is always larger than the sample variance, but the increase is negligible if the number of cases is 100 or more.

A convenient way of computing an estimate of a population standard deviation is to make use of equation C.3, which is a slight modification of equation C.1.

$$s_X = \sqrt{\frac{\sum X^2}{N - 1} - \frac{(\sum X)^2}{N(N - 1)}}. \qquad (C.3)$$

For the scores in Table C.1, equation C.3 yields:

$$s_X = \sqrt{\frac{278}{9} - \frac{(46)^2}{90}} = \sqrt{30.89 - 23.51} = \sqrt{7.38} = 2.72.$$

* v is an unbiased estimate of the population variance, but s is not precisely an unbiased estimate of the population standard deviation. The reason for this seeming paradox lies beyond the scope of this book.

Appendix D

STANDARD MEASURES AND STANDARD SCORES

STANDARD MEASURES

The terms *standard measure* and *standard score* are often used interchangeably, but in this book a distinction is made between them. *Standard measures* are expressed as deviations from the mean of a distribution in terms of the standard deviation of that distribution. Their mean is always zero and their standard deviation is always unity. The symbol used to represent a standard measure is usually the small letter z. If X represents any one score in a distribution; $\bar{X}$, the arithmetic mean of the scores; and S, their standard deviation; equation D.1 defines a standard measure.

$$z = \frac{X - \bar{X}}{S_X} \qquad (D.1)$$

Each score in the distribution of ten scores for which the mean, standard deviation, and median have been computed in appendixes A, B, and C can be converted into a standard measure. Since $\bar{X}$ equals 4.60 and S_x equals 2.58, the standard measure corresponding to a score of 9 would be computed as follows:

$$z_{(X=9)} = \frac{9.00 - 4.60}{2.58} = \frac{4.40}{2.58} = 1.71.$$

The standard measure corresponding to each of the ten scores in the distribution is shown in the fourth column of Table D.1. These standard measures take negative and positive values; their sum is (within rounding errors) zero; their mean is also zero; and their standard deviation is unity. The shape of their distribution and of the distribution of deviation scores (shown in the third column of Table D.1) is the same as that of the original obtained scores. Standard measures do not necessarily form normal distributions.

331

TABLE D.1

Obtained Scores, Deviation Scores, Standard Measures, and Standard
Scores for Ten Pupils on a Fifteen-Item Vocabulary Test

Pupil	Obtained Score	Deviation Score $X - \bar{X}$	Standard Measure $\left(\dfrac{X - \bar{X}}{S_X}\right)$	Standard Score When $A = 50$ $C = 10$	Standard Score When $A = 500$ $C = 100$
A	6	1.4	.54	55.4	554
B	1	− 3.6	− 1.40	36.0	360
C	4	−.6	−.23	47.7	477
D	9	4.4	1.71	67.1	671
E	0	− 4.6	− 1.78	32.2	322
F	5	.4	.16	51.6	516
G	3	− 1.6	−.62	43.8	438
H	6	1.4	.54	55.4	554
I	7	2.4	.93	59.3	593
J	5	.4	.16	51.6	516
Sum	46	0.00	0.01	500.1	5,001
Mean	4.60	0.00	0.00	50.0	500
Sample Standard Deviation	2.58	2.58	1.00	10.0	100

STANDARD SCORES

Standard scores are defined in this book as standard measures that have
been converted to a different scale of measurement simply by multiplying
each standard measure by a constant and then adding another constant to
the product. Ordinarily, this is done to get rid of negative values and
decimal points, which are a nuisance both clerically and computationally.
If we represent a standard score by Z, the constant used as a multiplier by C,
and the constant to be added by A, equation D.2 defines a standard score.

$$Z = \frac{C(X - \bar{X})}{S_X} + A \qquad (D.2)$$

Standard scores obtained by using two of the sets of constants often
employed by test publishers are shown in the fifth and sixth columns of
Table D.1. In one set, the constant used as a multiplier is 10 and the
constant added to the product is 50; in the other set, the constant used as a

multiplier is 100 and the constant added to the product is 500. For each set of resulting standard scores, the shape of the distribution remains the same as that of the original obtained scores. It is not made normal by changing the scale of measurement.

NORMALIZED STANDARD
MEASURES AND SCORES

It is possible to obtain standard measures and standard scores that form normal distributions regardless of the shape of the distribution of the original raw scores. They are called *normalized standard measures* and *normalized standard scores*. Normalized standard scores expressed in a nine-point scale are called *stanines*. The use of normalized scores (of one type or another) is justified if it is reasonable to assume that the distribution of the variable measured by the test is normal in the underlying population that is represented by the sample of examinees who were actually tested and if the number of cases in the sample is large—200 or more. Perhaps the most satisfactory procedure for obtaining normalized standard scores is as follows:

1. Set up a table like that shown in Table D.2 in which the first column consists of the normalized standard measures in any distribution beginning at the median and progressing in half-standard-deviation steps to $+3.00$ and -3.00.
2. In the second column, express these normalized standard measures as normalized standard scores in the scale of measurement desired. Equation D.2 is used to convert standard measures into standard scores. In Table D.2, the normalized standard scores in the second column have a mean of 50 and a standard deviation of 10. (Each half-standard-deviation step is, therefore, represented by 5 normalized-standard-score points.)
3. In the third column, enter the percentile rank that corresponds in a normal distribution to each standard measure in the first column. Table K.1 provides these ranks: for standard measures at or above 0.00, add 50.00 to the corresponding percentage in column two; for those below 0.00, subtract the corresponding percentage from 50.00.
4. In the fourth column, enter the score (in the distribution of raw scores) that corresponds to each percentile rank in column three. Each one can be computed by means of equation B.2.
5. Set up on graph paper a diagram like Figure D.1 in which one dimension is raw score and the other is normalized standard score. Then plot the point represented by the percentile rank of each corresponding raw score and standard score. On this diagram for the data in Table D.2, a point has been plotted for a standard score of 80 and its corresponding raw score of 77.62, and for each of the other twelve pairs of standard scores and raw scores listed in Table D.2.

TABLE D.2

Computation of Basic Data for Normalized Standard Scores on an Eighty-Item Test in a Group of 1,353 Ninth Grade Pupils

Normalized Standard Measure	Normalized Standard Score*	Percentile Rank	Raw Score
3.00	80	99.87	77.62
2.50	75	99.38	74.60
2.00	70	97.72	71.95
1.50	65	93.32	65.06
1.00	60	84.13	57.93
.50	55	69.15	48.22
.00	50	50.00	37.11
−.50	45	30.85	26.99
−1.00	40	15.87	16.81
−1.50	35	6.68	7.59
−2.00	30	2.28	1.62
−2.50	25	.62	—
−3.00	20	.13	—

* The scale of measurement uses 50 as the mean and 10 as the standard deviation.

6. Draw a smooth curve that fits the points plotted, extending the ends of the curve smoothly to the highest and lowest levels of raw scores that can be obtained.

7. Read from the curve the normalized standard score corresponding to each raw score, rounding off the result to the nearest whole number.

Table D.3 presents the data read from Figure D.1.

TABLE D.3

Normalized Standard Scores Corresponding to Selected Raw Scores for Data Shown in Figure D.1

Raw Scores	Normalized Standard Scores (Mean 50; $S = 10$)
80	82
70	70
60	62
50	56
40	51
30	46
20	41
10	36
1	29

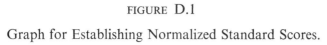

FIGURE D.1

Graph for Establishing Normalized Standard Scores.

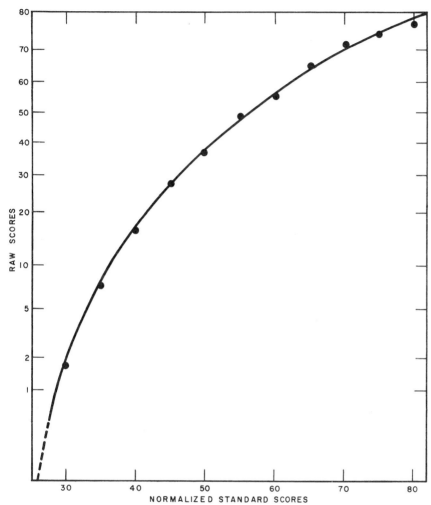

Stanines, or normalized standard scores expressed in nine categories, can readily be obtained by assigning to each stanine category a designated percentage of the raw scores in a distribution. Table D.4 shows these percentages and the percentile-rank limits of the nine stanine categories to be formed. It also shows the raw scores on the eighty-item test for which data are presented in Table D.2 that are assigned to each stanine category when these percentages were used to establish stanine scores in a sample of 1,353 ninth grade pupils. The right-hand column in Table D.4 gives the

336   *Appendix D*

TABLE D.4

Specifications for Establishing Stanines and Results for
Eighty-Item Comprehension Test

Stanine	Desired Percentage	Percentile- Rank Limits	Raw Score	Actual Percentage
9	4.580	95.421–99.999	69–80	4.287
8	6.830	88.591–95.420	61–68	7.095
7	12.074	76.517–88.590	53–60	13.082
6	16.994	59.523–76.516	43–52	15.817
5	19.044	40.479–59.522	33–42	19.142
4	16.994	23.485–40.478	23–32	17.443
3	12.074	11.411–23.484	13–22	11.826
2	6.830	4.581–11.410	6–12	6.504
1	4.580	.001– 4.580	0– 5	4.804

actual percentages of these pupils who fell in each stanine category. Note that these percentages differ somewhat from the desired percentages as specified in column 2 of the same table. Such differences will almost always occur and will usually be larger than those appearing in this case. They are small here because the number of cases in the sample was large and the distribution of obtained scores was regular in shape.

A distribution of stanines in which the percentages falling in each

TABLE D.5

Normalized Standard Scores, Including Stanines, Corresponding to
Obtained Scores with Percentile Ranks from 1 to 99

Percentile Rank	Stanine	Normalized Standard Score	Percentile Rank	Stanine	Normalized Standard Score
99	9	73	89	8	62
98	9	71	88	7	62
97	9	69	87	7	61
96	9	68	86	7	61
95	8	67	85	7	60
94	8	66	84	7	60
93	8	65	83	7	60
92	8	64	82	7	59
91	8	63	81	7	59
90	8	63	80	7	58

Per-centile Rank	Stanine	Normalized Standard Score	Per-centile Rank	Stanine	Normalized Standard Score
79	7	58	39	4	47
78	7	58	38	4	47
77	7	57	37	4	47
76	6	57	36	4	46
75	6	57	35	4	46
74	6	56	34	4	46
73	6	56	33	4	46
72	6	56	32	4	45
71	6	56	31	4	45
70	6	55	30	4	45
69	6	55	29	4	44
68	6	55	28	4	44
67	6	54	27	4	44
66	6	54	26	4	44
65	6	54	25	4	43
64	6	54	24	4	43
63	6	53	23	3	43
62	6	53	22	3	42
61	6	53	21	3	42
60	6	53	20	3	42
59	5	52	19	3	41
58	5	52	18	3	41
57	5	52	17	3	40
56	5	52	16	3	40
55	5	51	15	3	40
54	5	51	14	3	39
53	5	51	13	3	39
52	5	51	12	3	38
51	5	50	11	2	38
50	5	50	10	2	37
49	5	50	9	2	37
48	5	49	8	2	36
47	5	49	7	2	35
46	5	49	6	2	34
45	5	49	5	2	33
44	5	48	4	1	32
43	5	48	3	1	31
42	5	48	2	1	29
41	5	48	1	1	27
40	4	47			

category are exactly those specified as desired in Table D.4 will have a mean and standard deviation of 5.00 and 2.00, respectively.*

If percentile ranks have already been computed for scores in a distribution, the transformation to normalized standard scores, including stanines, can be done most economically by using Table D.5, which is entered with the percentile rank of any obtained score. The corresponding normalized standard score or stanine is simply read from the table.

* H. F. Kaiser, "A Modified Stanine Scale," *Journal of Experimental Education*, XVI (1958), 261.

Appendix E

THE STANDARD
ERROR OF
MEASUREMENT

The standard error of measurement was described and the general procedure for computing it outlined in chapter 2. Here its computation is illustrated by obtaining the standard error of measurement of Form J and of Form K of the *Stanford Intermediate Paragraph-Meaning Test* in a tiny sample of ten fifth grade pupils tested at the beginning of the school year. Form J was administered on September 16 and Form K on September 17. It should be made clear that a sample of ten pupils is far too small for determining the standard error of measurement. I recommend that at least 400 cases be used for this purpose. A sample of only ten cases is used here because this permits showing the computations in detail without taking up too much space.

Table E.1 shows the scores of each pupil on Form J and Form K, the algebraic difference between each pupil's pair of scores, and the calculation of an estimate of the population variance of the distribution of these algebraic differences. This variance equals 82.10. Since Forms J and K were constructed to measure the same mental skills in paragraph meaning and are composed of items drawn from a large pool of items, it is reasonable to assume that the variance of the differences is attributable only to errors of measurement. This point was discussed in chapter 2. Furthermore, it is reasonable to assume that the variance of the differences is attributable equally to errors of measurement on Form J and Form K. On the basis of these two assumptions, it is easy to show that the variance of the differences need only be divided by 2 to obtain the variance of errors of measurement of scores on either Form J or Form K. This division yields 41.05. The square root of this, 6.41, is the standard error of measurement for obtained grade scores on either Form J or Form K in the sample of ten pupils.

The method shown in Table E.1 illustrates what many authorities consider the most defensible way of obtaining an estimate of the standard error of measurement of a test.   When two parallel forms of the same test are administered with an interval of at least a day between testings, variations in the performance of pupils that are the result of day-to-day fluctuations in motivation, physical condition, and the circumstances of testing add their influence to that of pure chance in determining the standard errors of measurement.   Moreover, since the tests are administered with separate time limits, it does not matter if they are so highly speeded that many examinees do not have a chance to try every item.   Equation E.1 may be used to compute the standard error of measurement.

$$S_{\text{meas } A} = S_{\text{meas } B} = \sqrt{\frac{\sum(A - B)^2}{2N - 2} - \frac{[\sum(A - B)]^2}{2N(N - 1)}}, \tag{E.1}$$

TABLE E.1

Calculation of the Standard Error of Measurement of Form J and of Form K of the *Stanford Intermediate Paragraph-Meaning Test* in a Fifth Grade Class of Ten Pupils

Pupil	Grade Scores		Difference Scores	
	Form J	Form K	$(J - K)$	$(J - K)^2$
A	97	92	5	25
B	81	79	2	4
C	60	68	-8	64
D	72	53	19	361
E	58	53	5	25
F	64	73	-9	81
G	47	46	1	1
H	51	64	-13	169
I	43	43	0	0
J	35	38	-3	9
Sum			-1	739
Mean			-0.1	73.9

$$s^2_{(J-K)} = \frac{739}{9} - \frac{(-1)^2}{(10)(9)} = 82.11 - .01 = 82.10$$

$$s^2_{\text{meas } J} = s^2_{\text{meas } K} = \frac{s^2_{(J-K)}}{2} = \frac{82.10}{2} = 41.05$$

$$S_{\text{meas } J} = S_{\text{meas } K} = \sqrt{41.05} = 6.41$$

A convenient computing procedure is provided by equation E.1, as follows:

$$S_{\text{meas } J} = S_{\text{meas } K} = \sqrt{\frac{739}{18} - \frac{(-1)^2}{(20)(9)}} = \sqrt{41.06 - .01} = \sqrt{41.05} = 6.41$$

where A and B represent obtained scores on parallel forms that measure the same mental functions and have variances that differ (if at all) insignificantly.

If only one form of a test is available, there is no satisfactory way of obtaining its standard error of measurement if it is administered with a time limit so short that not all examinees have the opportunity to try every item. If a test is unspeeded, the standard error of measurement of a test for which there is only one form may be estimated by creating two half-length tests within it.   This is done by matching pairs of items for content and difficulty and assigning at random one item of each pair to Halftest A1 and the other to Halftest A2, as we may call them.   The standard error of measurement of Test A (denoted $s_{\text{meas }A}$) can then be obtained from the scores of the examinees on Halftest A1 and Halftest A2 by equation E.2.

$$s_{\text{meas }A} = \sqrt{\frac{\sum(A1 - A2)^2}{N - 1} - \frac{[\sum(A1 - A2)]^2}{N(N - 1)}}, \qquad \text{(E.2)}$$

where $A1$ and $A2$ represent obtained scores on Halftests A1 and A2, respectively, and these half tests measure the same mental functions.

There are other methods of obtaining the standard error of measurement for both speeded and unspeeded tests, but these lie outside the scope of this book.   The relationship of the standard error of measurement and the reliability coefficient is considered in appendix F.

Selected References

Davis, Frederick B., "Interpretation in Measurement," in Benjamin Wolman and Ernest Nagel, eds., *Scientific Psychology: Principles and Approaches.* Basic Books, 1964.

Lord, Frederic M., "Do Tests of the Same Length Have the Same Standard Error of Measurement?" *Educational and Psychological Measurement,* XVII (1957), 510–521.

Lord, Frederic M., "Estimating Test Reliability," *Educational and Psychological Measurement,* XV (1955), 325–336.

Medley, Donald M., "The Effects of Item Heterogeneity and Guessing on Accuracy of a Test Score," *American Psychologist,* XVII (1962), 368.

THE RELIABILITY COEFFICIENT

In chapter 2, the reliability coefficient was defined and its practical meaning discussed; here its computation, which may be accomplished in several ways, is illustrated. If we have the standard error of measurement for a set of scores, we can obtain a serviceable estimate of their reliability coefficient by equation F.1. Its use assumes that the two sets of scores employed in computing the standard error of measurement are equally reliable and have insignificantly different variances.

$$r_{AA'} = 1 - \frac{s^2_{\text{meas } A}}{s^2_A},\tag{F.1}$$

where $r_{AA'}$ = the reliability coefficient of test A in the sample used to compute s^2_A;

s^2_A = the variance of scores on test A; and

$s^2_{\text{meas } A}$ = the variance error of measurement of scores on test A.

Equation F.1 may be used for computing the reliability coefficient of scores on Form J and Form K of the *Stanford Intermediate Paragraph-Meaning Test*, for which the standard error of measurement was estimated in appendix E. It was 6.41, the square root of 41.05. Numerical values for s^2_J and s^2_K may be obtained by the method shown in appendix C. The computations are shown in Table F.1. The variances are 347.96 and 299.21, respectively. Substituting these numerical values in equation F.1, we obtain the reliability coefficients for scores on Forms J and K as follows:

$$r_{JJ'} = 1 - \frac{41.05}{347.96} = .88;$$

$$r_{KK'} = 1 - \frac{41.05}{299.21} = .86.$$

The difference of .02 between .86 and .88 is too small to be considered meaningful when the scores of only ten pupils are used to estimate the reliability coefficients. It arises because the variances of Forms J and K

342

TABLE F.1

Computation of Variances of Grade Scores on Forms J and K of the
Stanford Intermediate Paragraph-Meaning Test in a Fifth Grade Class
of Ten Pupils

Pupil	J	J^2	K	K^2
A	97	9,409	92	8,464
B	81	6,561	79	6,241
C	60	3,600	68	4,624
D	72	5,184	53	2,809
E	58	3,364	53	2,809
F	64	4,096	73	5,329
G	47	2,209	46	2,116
H	51	2,601	64	4,096
I	43	1,849	43	1,849
J	35	1,225	38	1,444
Sum	608	40,098	609	39,781
Mean	60.80	4,009.80	60.90	3,978.10
Variance	347.96		299.21	
Standard Deviation	18.65		17.30	

were not exactly the same in the sample of ten pupils, but the difference between them is so small that it can easily be explained as a chance variation in so tiny a sample.*   In these circumstances, and with data for two test forms available, a better estimate of the reliability coefficient of either form may be obtained by pooling the variances of the errors of measurement and of the obtained scores on both forms.   Then the reliability coefficient of either form may be estimated by equation F.2, which yields the reliability coefficient of parallel forms that have insignificantly different variances.

$$r_{AA'} = r_{BB'} = 1 - \frac{s^2_{(A-B)}}{s^2_A + s^2_B}, \tag{F.2}$$

where A and B = obtained scores on parallel forms of a test that measure the same mental functions and have insignificantly different variances;

$s^2_{(A-B)}$ = the variance of differences between obtained scores A and B for each individual; and

s^2_A and s^2_B = the variances of obtained scores A and B, respectively.

* The statistical significance of a difference between these variances can be estimated if the product-moment correlation coefficient between scores on the parallel test forms (or the parallel half tests) has been computed, as shown in appendix G.   See Q. McNemar, *Psychological Statistics*, third ed. (New York: John Wiley & Sons, Inc., 1962), Equation (14.2), p. 246.

For Forms J and K a reliability coefficient may be estimated by equation F.2 with data already available. The computations are as follows:

$$r_{JJ'} = r_{KK'} = 1 - \frac{82.10}{647.17} = 1 - .13 = .87.$$

If the variances of two parallel forms of a test are significantly different, an estimate of the reliability coefficient of each form separately may be made by a method suggested by William H. Angoff.* If the two parallel forms are represented by A and B, the necessary equations are:

$$r_{AA'} = \frac{(s_A + s_B r_{AB})r_{AB}}{s_B + s_A r_{AB}}, \tag{F.3}$$

$$r_{BB'} = \frac{(s_B + s_A r_{AB})r_{AB}}{s_A + s_B r_{AB}}. \tag{F.4}$$

If these equations are used to estimate the reliability coefficients of Forms J and K of the *Stanford Intermediate Paragraph-Meaning Test*, using the standard deviations given in Table F.1 and their correlation obtained by equation G.1, the results are as follows:

$$r_{JJ'} = \frac{[18.65 + (17.30)(.88)][.88]}{17.30 + (18.65)(.88)} = .88;$$

$$r_{KK'} = \frac{[17.30 + (18.65)(.88)][.88]}{18.65 + (17.30)(.88)} = .88.$$

In this case, the variances of Forms J and K are so much alike that the reliability coefficients estimated separately for the two forms do not differ in the second decimal place.

If the standard error of measurement of a test is not available for computing the reliability coefficient of a set of scores, it may be estimated by either equation E.1 or E.2, whichever is appropriate. For most published tests, the standard error of measurement is given in the manual and may ordinarily be used in equation F.1 along with the variance of scores in a sample to estimate a reliability coefficient appropriate for that sample.

When scores on two parts of an unspeeded test (on which essentially every examinee has had time to consider every item) are available and it is judged that the two parts measure the same properties, the reliability coefficient of the entire test may be obtained by using a variant of the procedure suggested by William H. Angoff. The parts need not be made up of the same number of items. The required equation is:

$$r_{AA'} = \frac{2v_A(v_A - v_{A1} - v_{A2})}{(v_A + v_{A1} - v_{A2})(v_A + v_{A2} - v_{A1})}, \tag{F.5}$$

* W. H. Angoff, "Test Reliability and Effective Test Length," *Psychometrika*, XVIII (1953), 1–14.

where $r_{AA'}$ = the reliability coefficient of test A;

  v_A = the variance of scores on test A;

  v_{A1} = the variance of scores on part 1 of test A;

  v_{A2} = the variance of scores on part 2 of test A.

If test M, made up of forty-eight 4-choice reading-comprehension items, is divided into two parts M1 and M2, made up of 26 and 22 items, respectively; and if these two parts are judged to measure the same mental properties, the reliability coefficient of test M can be estimated if v_M, v_{M1}, and v_{M2} are computed. Suppose that these values turn out to be: $v_M = 322.90$; $v_{M1} = 97.26$; and $v_{M2} = 83.76$. With these data, equation F.5 becomes:

$$r_{MM'} = \frac{2(322.90)(322.90 - 97.26 - 83.76)}{(322.90 + 97.26 - 83.76)(322.90 + 83.76 - 97.26)}$$

$$r_{MM'} = \frac{91,626.1040}{104,082.1600} = .88.$$

Selected References

Angoff, William H., "Test Reliability and Effective Test Length," *Psychometrika*, XVIII (1953), 1–14.

Cureton, Edward E., "The Definition and Estimation of Test Reliability," *Educational and Psychological Measurement*, XVIII (1958), 715–738.

Cureton, Edward E., "Validity," in E. F. Lindquist, ed., *Educational Measurement*. Washington: American Council on Education, 1951, pp. 677–680.

Gulliksen, Harold O., *Theory of Mental Tests*. New York: John Wiley & Sons, Inc., 1950. Chapters 15, 16, and 17.

Kelley, Truman L., *Fundamentals of Statistics*. Cambridge: Harvard University Press, 1947, pp. 419–420.

Kelley, Truman L., "The Reliability Coefficient," *Psychometrika*, VII (1942), 75–83.

Kuder, G. Frederic, and Marion W. Richardson, "The Theory of the Estimation of Test Reliability," *Psychometrika*, II (1937), 151–160.

Lord, Frederic M., "Estimating Test Reliability," *Educational and Psychological Measurement*, XV (1955), 325–336.

Lord, Frederic M., "Test Reliability: A Correction," *Educational and Psychological Measurement*, XXII (1962), 511–512.

Otis, Arthur S., and H. E. Knollin, "The Reliability of the Binet Scale and of Pedagogical Scales," *Journal of Educational Research*, IV (1921), 121–142.

Rulon, Phillip J., "A Simplified Procedure for Determining the Reliability of a Test by Split Halves," *Harvard Educational Review*, IX (1939), 99–103.

Thorndike, Robert L., "Reliability," in E. F. Lindquist, ed., *Educational Measurement*, Chapter 15. Washington: American Council on Education, 1951.

Appendix G

THE CORRELATION COEFFICIENT

PRODUCT-MOMENT CORRELATION

The correlation coefficient indicates the amount of relationship between any two sets of scores. Perfect positive relationship between any two sets of scores is represented by a coefficient of $+1.00$; perfect negative relationship, by a coefficient of -1.00. Lack of any systematic relationship is represented by a coefficient of zero. A high degree of relationship exists if the rank order of examinees in two sets of scores is the same, or nearly the same. Suppose that the pupil who had the highest score on Form J, as shown in Table E.1, had the highest score on Form K, the pupil who had the second-highest score on Form J had the second-highest score on Form K, etc. Then the relationship between scores on Forms J and K would be positive and extremely high. Table G.1 shows the rank order on Form J and on Form K of the scores of the ten pupils whose obtained grade scores are given in Table E.1. The two rank orders are in close agreement, so scores on these two forms will display a high degree of positive correlation.

The type of correlation coefficient that is often most satisfactory for determining the relationships between sets of test scores is the *product-moment correlation coefficient*. It can be computed by equation G.1.

$$r_{AB} = \frac{v_A + v_B - v_{(A-B)}}{2s_A s_B}, \qquad (G.1)$$

where $r_{AB} =$ the product-moment coefficient of correlation between scores on tests A and B;

v_A and $v_B =$ the variances of scores on tests A and B, respectively;

s_A and $s_B =$ the standard deviations of scores on tests A and B, respectively;

$v_{(A-B)} =$ the variance of the $(A - B)$ difference scores.

346

TABLE G.1

Rank Orders of Ten Fifth Grade Pupils on Form J and Form K of the *Stanford Intermediate Paragraph-Meaning Test*

	Rank Orders	
Pupil	*Form J*	*Form K**
A	1	1
B	2	2
C	5	4
D	3	6.5
E	6	6.5
F	4	3
G	8	8
H	7	5
I	9	9
J	10	10

* Pupils D and E have the same score (53) on Form K, so the 6th and 7th positions in rank order on that form are represented by 6.5 (the arithmetic mean of 6 and 7).

These are all the data necessary for computing the product-moment correlation coefficient between the scores on Forms J and K listed in Table E.1. The variance of the $(J - K)$ difference scores is 82.10, as shown in Table E.1. The variances and standard deviations of scores on Forms J and K are shown in Table F.1. Substituting the appropriate numerical values in equation G.1, we obtain:

$$r_{JK} = \frac{347.96 + 299.21 - 82.10}{(2)(18.65)(17.30)} = \frac{565.07}{645.29} = .88.$$

As we expected, the coefficient of .88 is positive and high. As the numerical value of a product-moment correlation coefficient increases from zero toward either -1.00 or $+1.00$, a greater degree of relationship is indicated by each additional hundredth. For example, the amount of increase in relationship required to raise a coefficient from .90 to .95 is about 7.2 times as great as the amount required to raise a coefficient from .05 to .10.

To determine whether any product-moment correlation coefficient can be considered significantly different from zero at a designated level of probability, equation G.2 can be used to compute a t value.

$$t_n = \frac{r_{AB}\sqrt{N - 2}}{\sqrt{1 - r^2_{AB}}}, \tag{G.2}$$

where $n = (N - 2)$;

  N = the number of cases for which scores are available; and

  r_{AB} = the correlation coefficient obtained.

The *t* value may be compared with those given in Table L.1.

For the correlation coefficient of .88 between scores on Forms J and K of the ten fifth grade pupils, equation G.2 yields the following value of *t*:

$$t_{n=8} = \frac{.88\sqrt{10-2}}{\sqrt{1-(.88)^2}} = \frac{2.49}{.47} = 5.30.$$

When *n* equals 8, a *t* value of 5.30 indicates, according to Table L.1, that the correlation coefficient of .88 is significantly different from zero at better than the 1-per-cent level. In other words, it is extremely unlikely that the coefficient of .88 is a chance deviation from a true correlation coefficient of zero.

Interpretation of the product-moment correlation coefficient assumes that the relationship between the two sets of scores can be represented by a straight line and that the scores are expressed in units that measure equivalent increments in the variable tested. With many types of obtained scores, these assumptions are reasonably well satisfied; if they are not, the product-moment correlation coefficient should not be used to express the degree of relationship between the two sets of scores.

One final word should be said regarding the interpretation of product-moment correlation coefficients. Their magnitudes are determined not only by the degree of true relationship existing between the variables correlated, but also by several other factors, such as the reliability coefficients of the scores, the range of talent in the sample used, the shapes of the score distributions, and the amount of curvature (if any) in their regression lines. A discussion of these influences on the magnitudes of correlation coefficients is beyond the scope of this book, but the beginning student should recognize the need for caution in the interpretation of such coefficients.

RANK-ORDER CORRELATION

Rank-order correlation coefficients may be used to express the relationship between two sets of scores if the latter clearly represent unequal increments in the ability measured or if we have no reason to suppose that they represent approximately equal increments. The rank-order coefficient called *rho* is given by equation G.3.

$$rho = 1 - \frac{6\sum D^2}{N(N^2-1)}, \tag{G.3}$$

where N = the number of rank-order pairs; and

$\sum D^2$ = the sum of the squared differences between the rank orders assigned to each individual or object.

TABLE G.2

Rank Orders of Ten Pictures According to Merit, as Judged by Two Art Teachers

Picture	Rank Order		Differences Between Rank Orders	
	Teacher A	Teacher B	D^*	D^2
1	1	3	-2	4
2	2	2	0	0
3	6	4	2	4
4	10	9	1	1
5	4	1	3	9
6	8	6	2	4
7	3	5	-2	4
8	7	7	0	0
9	9	10	-1	1
10	5	8	-3	9
Sum			0	36

* D = the algebraic difference between the ranks given to each picture by Teacher A and by Teacher B.

The use of rank-order correlation coefficients may be illustrated by the data presented in Table G.2. Ten pictures made by eighth grade pupils were displayed on a bulletin board without the names of the pupils who drew them. Two art teachers from another school ranked the pictures in order according to their merit. The rank orders assigned to the pictures by Teacher A and Teacher B are shown in Table G.2 together with the differences between these rankings. To determine the correlation of the two rank orders, we may compute *rho* by means of equation G.3. The computation

$$rho = 1 - \frac{6(36)}{10(100 - 1)} = 1 - \frac{216}{990} = 1 - .22 = .78.$$

This result indicates that the art teachers agreed rather well with respect to the order of merit of the pictures. Whether the obtained *rho* of .78 is significantly greater than zero at any designated level of probability may be estimated by using equation G.2 to compute a *t* value:

$$t_{n=8} = \frac{.78\sqrt{8}}{\sqrt{1 - (.78)^2}} = \frac{2.206}{.626} = 3.52$$

When *n* equals 8, the value of *t* that is significant at the 5-per-cent level is found in Table L.1 to be 2.306. For the *rho* of .78, *t* equals 3.52. Therefore, it is significantly different from zero at the 5-per-cent level. We may conclude that the value of .78 is not likely to have arisen as a chance deviation from a true coefficient of zero.

RATIONALE FOR ESTABLISHING THE CONFIDENCE INTERVAL

As explained in chapter 8, the confidence interval is used to determine a range of scores that, when applied to the obtained scores of successive individuals, will include the individuals' true scores a designated percentage of times. The reasoning that underlies the establishment and interpretation of a confidence interval is as follows: (1) an individual's true score is defined as the arithmetic mean of his obtained scores on an indefinitely large number of equivalent tests given under similar conditions with no change taking place in the individual during the testings; (2) any differences among the indefinitely large number of scores that result from the testing are assumed to represent errors of measurement. Under these circumstances, the individual's scores will distribute themselves normally around their mean, which we have defined as his true score. The standard deviation of these scores is also the standard deviation of errors of measurement—the standard error of measurement. Figure H.1 shows a hypothetical distribution of an indefinitely large number of obtained scores around the true score of Harold Jones on Form W of the *Stanford Advanced Spelling Test.* Since the standard error of measurement of this test is six points, each grade-score point includes one-sixth of a standard error of measurement, or .17 (rounded to the nearest hundredth). Each of the 29 strips from -14 to $+14$ in Figure H.1 is .17 of a standard measure in width. The center strip straddles the mean of the distribution, which represents Harold's true score (the numerical value of which we do not know). This strip is labeled 0 because the identical obtained scores included in it deviate by less than half a point from his true score, which is at the point represented by the dotted line at the center of the distribution. Rounded to the nearest whole number, therefore, scores in the center strip deviate 0 points from Harold's true score. The next strip to the right is labeled $+1$ because the identical scores in it are from .5 up to (but not

FIGURE H.1

Five 85-per-cent Confidence Intervals Placed in Position below a Hypothetical Distribution of Obtained Scores.

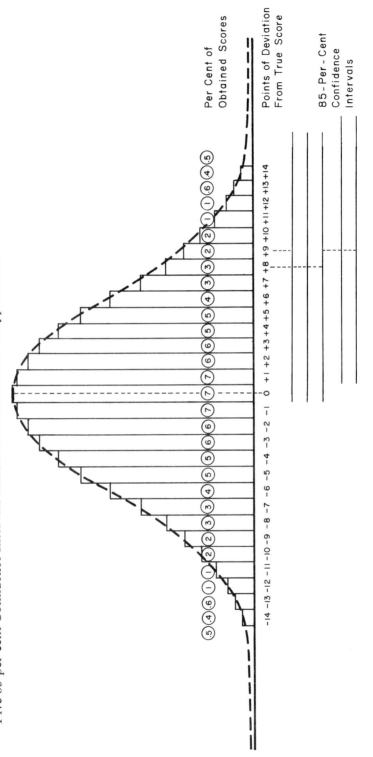

including) 1.5 points above his true score and thus deviate (to the nearest whole number) one point from his true score.   The next strip to the right is labeled $+2$ because the scores in it are from 1.5 to 2.5 points above his true score and thus deviate (to the nearest whole number) two points from his true score.   Strips above $+14$ and below -14 are not drawn under the curve because they include only about one per cent of the indefinitely large number of scores in the distribution.

Using Table K.1, we can determine the percentage of scores included by each of the 29 strips.   These percentages are given as circled numbers superimposed on the distribution in Figure H.1.   They can be summed appropriately to indicate the likelihood that Harold's obtained scores will deviate from his true score by any given amount.   For example, his obtained scores will exceed his true score by more than 8 points about $2 + 2 + 1 + 1 + .6 + .4 + .5 = 7.5$ per cent of the time.   Conversely, his obtained scores will be more than 8 points below his true score about 7.5 per cent of the time.   Therefore, it can be concluded that his obtained scores will deviate by 8 points or less from his true score about 85 per cent of the time.   In other words, a range, or interval, of 17 points centered around his true score will include 85 per cent of the indefinitely large number of scores he obtains.   Similarly, an interval of 29 points centered around his true score will include about 99 per cent of his obtained scores.

Assume that each one of Harold's obtained scores is used as the center of an interval of 17 points.   In the long run, out of every 100 scores, 7 such intervals will be centered around obtained scores less than one-half a point from his true score, 7 will be centered around scores one point above his true score, and so on, as shown by the percentages circled in Figure H.1.   Three out of every 100 intervals would center around obtained scores 8 points above his true score.   They have been drawn below the baseline of the curve in Figure H.1.   Note that they extend far enough to the left to include his true score.   Two out of every 100 intervals would be centered around scores 9 points above his true score.   They are also shown in Figure H.1.   Note that these two intervals do *not* extend far enough to the left to include Harold's true score.

It is at once apparent that intervals 17 points in width will not include Harold's true score if they are centered around obtained scores that deviate more than 8 points above or below his true score.   Since about 15 out of every 100 obtained scores will deviate more than 8 points from his true score, it is apparent that only about 85 out of every 100 intervals of this length applied to successive obtained scores will include Harold's true score.   Thus, if we center intervals 17 points in length around 100 successive obtained scores, each time concluding that the interval includes Harold's true score, we shall be correct about 85 times out of 100.   For this test, an interval 17 points in length is called the 85-per-cent confidence interval.

If we center intervals 23 points in length around successive obtained scores on the *Stanford Advanced Spelling Test*, each time concluding that the interval includes Harold's true score, we shall be correct about 95 times out of 100.   For this test, an interval 23 points in length is called the 95-percent confidence interval.

In practice, confidence intervals for the *Stanford Advanced Spelling Test* and for any other test can be determined very easily.   It is necessary only to multiply the standard error of measurement of the scores by a constant chosen from Table 8.1 to yield the desired level of confidence. Table 8.1 provides multipliers for five different levels of confidence.   For the *Stanford Advanced Spelling Test*, the 85-per-cent confidence interval is equal to 6 times 2.88, or 17.28.   This value, rounded to one decimal point, is given in Table M.11.   It differs slightly from the value of 17 we obtained from Figure H.1 mainly because of rounding errors involved in preparing that figure.   The difference is of no practical consequence.

Each multiplier in Table 8.1 represents simply the length of a confidence interval expressed in standard deviations.   Centered around the mean of a normal distribution, each one of these includes the designated percentage of the scores in the distribution.   For example, the confidence interval that extends from a standard measure of -1.44 to $+1.44$ covers the middle 2.88 standard deviations of a normal distribution and includes about 85 per cent of the scores in the distribution.

Appendix I

RATIONALE FOR DETERMINING AND INTERPRETING THE SIGNIFICANCE OF A DIFFERENCE

Differences between individual obtained scores, between individual obtained scores and averages, and between averages form the basis for most interpretations of test scores. Failure to recognize this fact often results in gross misinterpretations by teachers, counselors, school psychologists, and clinicians. They sometimes take it for granted that all obtained differences are true differences. Actually, differences between obtained scores are merely estimates of *true* differences just as obtained scores are merely estimates of *true* scores.

The first step in the interpretation of a difference is usually to estimate the probability that it deviates from zero only because of errors of measurement. When an obtained difference can readily be attributed to the effect of errors of measurement, it can most safely be treated as a zero difference. To show how an obtained difference should be interpreted, consider the difference between speed-of-comprehension scores on Form 1A of the *Davis Reading Test* obtained by two pupils in grade 12. When tested in September, Eleanor obtained a score of 74 and Robert got a score of 69. The difference between their scores is, therefore, five points.

If Eleanor and Robert could be tested with an indefinitely large number of equivalent forms of the *Davis Reading Test* under identical conditions and without any change in their true scores in speed of comprehension, a difference between their scores would be obtained for each form administered. These differences would vary by chance around the true difference, and the shape of the distribution of differences would approach normality as more and more forms were given to them. The standard deviation of this distribution of differences can easily be computed by using equation 8.3. If Eleanor's score is represented by Xe and Robert's score by Xr, the desired standard deviation, which is called the standard error of measurement of the difference between obtained scores, can be computed as follows:

$$s_{\text{meas}(Xe-Xr)} = \sqrt{s^2_{\text{meas }Xe} + s^2_{\text{meas }Xr}}. \tag{8.3}$$

The standard error of measurement of a speed-of-comprehension score on the *Davis Reading Test* obtained by a twelfth grade pupil is given in the *Manual for the Davis Reading Test* as 2.9 points. Entering this value into the equation above, we obtain:

$$s_{\text{meas}(Xe-Xr)} = \sqrt{(2.9)^2 + (2.9)^2} = \sqrt{16.82} = 4.10.$$

To determine whether the difference of five points between the scores of Eleanor and Robert deviates from zero only because of errors of measurement, construct the distribution shown in Figure I.1. If their true scores were the same (whatever that numerical value), about 10 out of every 100 testings would yield a difference of zero between their obtained scores. This is shown in Figure I.1 by the number 10 superimposed in a circle on the center strip of the distribution. This strip includes all difference scores of zero. Similarly, the number of times out of every 100 that we should expect differences of $+1$, $+2$, $+3$, and so on up to $+9$ to occur is shown on each of these strips in the distribution. Differences of $+10$ or more would be most likely to occur only about once in every 100 testings, so they have been lumped together at the right-hand end of the distribution. The frequencies with which negative differences would be most likely to occur out of every 100 testings have been shown in a similar manner.

How likely are differences of five points or more to occur in this distribution? If the frequencies in the strips corresponding to differences of five points or more in both ends of the distribution are added together, their sum is 28. This means that differences of $+5$, or -5, or more, will occur about 28 times out of every 100 testings. In other words, if the true difference between the speed-of-comprehension abilities of Eleanor and Robert is zero, a difference between their obtained scores of 5 points, or more, would nevertheless occur about 28 times out of every 100 testings as the result of errors of measurement. The difference of 5 points between Eleanor's obtained score of 74 and Robert's score of 69 may very well have occurred on this basis as a deviation from a true difference of zero. Since we lack strong evidence to support the belief that Eleanor's true ability in speed of comprehension is different from Robert's, we adopt the conservative point of view that the pupils have equal ability in this respect.

At this point, the student may reasonably ask, "What constitutes 'strong evidence' that Eleanor's true ability in speed of comprehension is

FIGURE I.1

Hypothetical Distribution of Differences around a True Difference of Zero.

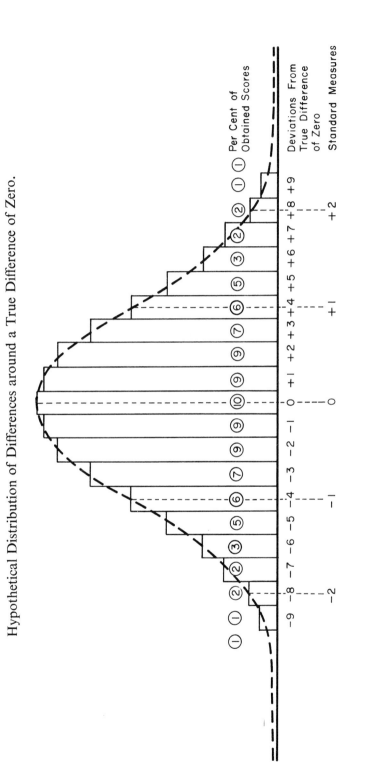

different from Robert's?" A glance at Figure I.1 shows that the greater the difference between obtained scores, the smaller is the probability that a difference of that magnitude would occur as a deviation from a true difference of zero simply because of errors of measurement. In practice, evidence that a difference would occur 15 or fewer times out of 100 is often considered strong enough to warrant concluding that the difference is not attributable merely to errors of measurement. Such a difference is said to be significant at the 15-per-cent level. Sometimes, evidence that a difference would occur either 5 or fewer times out of 100, or 1 or fewer times out of 100 is demanded before concluding that it is not attributable merely to errors of measurement. Evidence that it would occur 5 or fewer times out of 100 because of errors of measurement is usually regarded as "strong." Evidence that it would occur not more than once out of 100 times because of errors of measurement is usually considered to be "very strong."

Table 8.3 provides multipliers for obtaining differences significant at the 1-, 5-, 10-, 15-, and 32-per-cent levels. For example, to find the smallest difference between speed-of-comprehension scores on Series 1 of the *Davis Reading Test* obtained by pupils in grade 12 that is significant at the 15-per-cent level, we multiply the standard error of measurement (found on page 355 to be 4.10) by 1.44 (the appropriate multiplier from Table 8.3). The result is 4.10 times 1.44, or 5.90. In practice, then, differences of 6 points or more would be accepted as significant at the 15-per-cent level.

Since test users should not be expected to compute this for themselves, the result is given in the *Manual for the Davis Reading Test* along with other interpretive information. To understand the basis for this result, the student should count in Figure I.1 the frequency with which differences of six points or more occur in the distribution of differences between the scores of two twelfth grade pupils in speed of comprehension, as measured by the *Davis Reading Test*. Beyond the strips labeled +6 and −6 are frequencies that sum up to 6 on each side of the distribution. A difference of +6 points is halfway through a strip with a frequency of 3. Therefore, about half of this strip (or a frequency of 1½) lies beyond the difference of 6 points. The same is true of the strip corresponding to a difference of −6 points. Summing on each side, therefore, we get a frequency of 7½ lying beyond the difference of +6 or −6 points. Adding the frequency of 7½ on one side to the frequency of 7½ on the other side, we obtain a total frequency of 15 beyond a difference of +6 or −6. Thus, the chances are about 15 out of 100 that differences of 6 points or more (either positive or negative) will occur as chance deviations from a true difference of zero. This agrees with the result we obtained by using the multiplier from Table 8.3 for computing the smallest difference significant at the 15-per-cent level.

A general procedure for determining the significance of any difference between obtained scores is as follows:

1. Postulate that the true difference is zero and decide on the level of significance to be required for rejecting this hypothesis and thus accepting the difference as indicative of a true difference other than zero.

2. Estimate the standard error of measurement of the difference by equation 8.3.

3. Divide the obtained difference by the standard error of measurement of the difference, thus obtaining the standard *measure* corresponding to the difference.

4. Determine from Table K.1 the area in both ends of the normal distribution lying beyond the standard *measure* (not the standard error) corresponding to the difference.

5. Regard the proportion of the area under the normal distribution determined in step 4 as the probability that the obtained difference deviates from a true difference of zero only as a result of errors of measurement.

6. Compare this probability with the level of significance decided upon in step 1.

CHOICE OF A LEVEL OF SIGNIFICANCE

As previously defined, the level of significance of a difference indicates the probability that it deviates from a postulated true difference of zero only as a result of errors of measurement. Thus, if a test interpreter concludes that all differences between obtained scores that are significant at, say, the 15-per-cent level are indicative of differences between true scores, 15 per cent of his conclusions will be wrong and about 85 per cent will be correct. That is, about 15 times out of every 100 he will conclude that differences between obtained scores are caused by differences in true scores when in fact they are *not*. This is called a type-1 error. By adopting the 1-per-cent level of significance, the interpreter could cut his type-1 errors to about 1 in every 100 decisions. Why not, therefore, adopt the 1-per-cent level, the .1-per-cent level, or even more stringent levels of significance? By so doing, the interpreter could reduce his type-1 errors to the vanishing point.

The answer to this question is bound up with the fact that there is a second kind of error that the test interpreter makes when he designates a level of significance and draws conclusions on this basis. The second kind of error consists of concluding that certain differences between obtained scores are entirely the result of errors of measurement when in fact they are *not*, but are actually the result of differences in true scores. An error of this kind is called a type-2 error. It is easy to prove that the chances of making a type-

2 error increase as the chances of making a type-1 error decrease, and vice versa.

The practical import of this fact for the test interpreter is that the more he reduces his chances of paying attention to differences that he ought to ignore, the more he increases his chances of ignoring differences to which he ought to pay attention.   In practice, then, the choice of a level of significance represents a compromise between reducing type-1 and type-2 errors.   What the compromise will be depends on the relative seriousness of making the two kinds of errors.   A guidance counselor may be influenced to a certain extent in discussing the choice of curricula and elective courses with a pupil by the presence or absence of a significant difference between his verbal and nonverbal scores on an aptitude test.   She does not want to pay attention to differences attributable merely to errors of measurement; on the other hand, she does not want to ignore clues provided by test data which she can combine with other information to provide an understanding of the pupil's mental skills and potentialities.

Because individual verbal and nonverbal scores on most aptitude tests are only moderately reliable, if she adopts a stringent level of significance (such as the 1-per-cent level), the scores of very few pupils will be sufficiently different to warrant attention.   This fact implies that a fairly lenient level of significance should be used.   It is reinforced by the fact that aptitude-test data constitute only a part of the information about the pupils' probable performance in various courses and curricula.   In short, the penalty for making type-1 errors in this situation is not likely to be severe.

If the counselor regarded all differences as true differences, the number of her type-1 errors would be maximized, but the number of her type-2 errors would be minimized.   Most counselors are willing to take the risk of interpreting some differences that are merely the result of errors of measurement because, as previously mentioned, test data are not used alone but are combined with other information.   Nevertheless, most counselors and other test interpreters like to feel that differences that reflect nothing more than errors of measurement will not influence their decisions.   Hence, they prefer to limit type-1 errors even at the cost of allowing some type-2 errors to occur.

As a practical compromise, I suggest the 15-per-cent level of significance for interpreting individual scores.   It is essentially the same as the level recommended by the Educational Testing Service for interpreting differences between scores on the *School and College Ability Test*, the *Sequential Test of Educational Progress*, and the *Cooperative Reading Comprehension Test*. Its use steers a middle path between the two types of errors.

It should be noted that the sophisticated test interpreter attaches greater weight to differences between scores that are much larger than the minimum size required by the level of significance that he has adopted for use.   Conversely, he attaches least importance to those close to this minimum size because the chances of his drawing incorrect conclusions are greatest for them. Procedures for estimating the chances of drawing incorrect conclusions at any given score level have been discussed by Cronbach and Gleser.*

A DIFFERENCE BETWEEN MEANS

Interpreting differences between means follows the same line of reasoning as interpreting differences between obtained scores. However, two different procedures may be employed for determining the significance of the difference between means. Sometimes it is desirable to know whether a difference between two means can reasonably be regarded as a chance deviation from a true difference of zero in the particular group or groups tested; and sometimes it is desirable to know whether a difference between two means can reasonably be regarded as a chance deviation from a true difference of zero in the population represented by the group or groups tested.

If it is desired to estimate the probability that a difference can reasonably be attributed to chance in the particular group or groups tested, a t value is computed by dividing the difference by the *standard error of measurement of the difference between means*. An estimate of this (denoted $s_{\text{meas}(\bar{X}_A - \bar{X}_B)}$) may be found by equation I.1.

$$s_{\text{meas}(\bar{X}_A - \bar{X}_B)} = s_{\text{meas } X} \sqrt{\frac{1}{N_A} + \frac{1}{N_B}}, \qquad (I.1)$$

where $s_{\text{meas } X}$ = the standard error of measurement of an obtained score on test X;

N_A and N_B = the number of cases in groups A and B, respectively, for which the means are $\bar{X}_A$ and $\bar{X}_B$.

The t value for estimating the significance of the difference between $\bar{X}_A$ and $\bar{X}_B$ may be computed by equation I.2.

$$t_n = \frac{\bar{X}_A - \bar{X}_B}{s_{\text{meas}(\bar{X}_A - \bar{X}_B)}}, \qquad (I.2)$$

where $n = N_A + N_B - 2$.

* L. J. Cronbach and G. C. Gleser, "Interpretation of Reliability and Validity Coefficients: Remarks on a Paper by Lord," *Journal of Educational Psychology*, L (1959), 230–237.

The value of t is used to enter Table L.1.   If it is desired to estimate the probability that a difference can reasonably be regarded as a chance deviation from zero in the population represented by the group or groups tested, the t value for the obtained difference is computed by dividing that difference by the *standard error of the difference*.   This may be estimated by equation I.3.

$$s_{(\bar{X}_A - \bar{X}_B)} = s_X \sqrt{\frac{1}{N_A} + \frac{1}{N_B}}, \tag{I.3}$$

where $s^2{}_{X_A}$ and $s^2{}_{X_B}$ are not significantly different, and s_X has been computed by equation I.4.

$$s_X = \sqrt{\frac{\sum(X_A - \bar{X}_A)^2 + \sum(X_B - \bar{X}_B)^2}{N_A + N_B - 2}} \tag{I.4}$$

The t value for estimating the significance of the difference $\bar{X}_A - \bar{X}_B$ may be computed by equation I.5.

$$t_n = \frac{\bar{X}_A - \bar{X}_B}{s_{(\bar{X}_A - \bar{X}_B)}}, \tag{I.5}$$

where $n = N_A + N_B - 2$.

As usual, the value of t is used to enter Table L.1 in order to determine the significance of the difference to which it pertains.

A choice between equation I.2 and equation I.5 for computing t values is not difficult to make.   To compare one particular class or grade group with another specific class or grade group with respect to average scores, equation I.2 should be used.   On the other hand, to infer from the results of teaching two different classes with different methods which one, if either, of the two methods would prove to be superior if they were used over and over with classes like the ones actually taught requires the use of equation I.5. Broadly speaking, equation I.2 yields a t value that is pertinent to everyday comparisons of specified groups in schools whereas equation I.5 yields a t value that is pertinent to comparisons of groups involved in some experiment or research study.

Selected References

Davis, Frederick B., "Interpretation of Differences among Averages and Individual Test Scores," *Journal of Educational Psychology*, L (1959), 162–170.

Kelley, Truman L., "A New Method for Determining the Significance of Differences in Intelligence and Achievement Scores," *Journal of Educational Psychology*, XIV (1923), 321–333.

SQUARES AND SQUARE ROOTS OF NUMBERS FROM 1 TO 1,000

N	N²	√N	N	N²	√N	N	N²	√N
1	1	1.0000	26	676	5.0990	51	2601	7.1414
2	4	1.4142	27	729	5.1962	52	2704	7.2111
3	9	1.7321	28	784	5.2915	53	2809	7.2801
4	16	2.0000	29	841	5.3852	54	2916	7.3485
5	25	2.2361	30	900	5.4772	55	3025	7.4162
6	36	2.4495	31	961	5.5678	56	3136	7.4833
7	49	2.6458	32	1024	5.6569	57	3249	7.5498
8	64	2.8284	33	1089	5.7446	58	3364	7.6158
9	81	3.0000	34	1156	5.8310	59	3481	7.6811
10	100	3.1623	35	1225	5.9161	60	3600	7.7460
11	121	3.3166	36	1296	6.0000	61	3721	7.8102
12	144	3.4641	37	1369	6.0828	62	3844	7.8740
13	169	3.6056	38	1444	6.1644	63	3969	7.9373
14	196	3.7417	39	1521	6.2450	64	4096	8.0000
15	225	3.8730	40	1600	6.3246	65	4225	8.0623
16	256	4.0000	41	1681	6.4031	66	4356	8.1240
17	289	4.1231	42	1764	6.4807	67	4489	8.1854
18	324	4.2426	43	1849	6.5574	68	4624	8.2462
19	361	4.3589	44	1936	6.6332	69	4761	8.3066
20	400	4.4721	45	2025	6.7082	70	4900	8.3666
21	441	4.5826	46	2116	6.7823	71	5041	8.4261
22	484	4.6904	47	2209	6.8557	72	5184	8.4853
23	529	4.7958	48	2304	6.9282	73	5329	8.5440
24	576	4.8990	49	2401	7.0000	74	5476	8.6023
25	625	5.0000	50	2500	7.0711	75	5625	8.6603

N	N²	√N	N	N²	√N	N	N²	√N
76	5776	8.7178	116	13456	10.7703	156	24336	12.4900
77	5929	8.7750	117	13689	10.8167	157	24649	12.5300
78	6084	8.8318	118	13924	10.8628	158	24964	12.5698
79	6241	8.8882	119	14161	10.9087	159	25281	12.6095
80	6400	8.9443	120	14400	10.9545	160	25600	12.6491
81	6561	9.0000	121	14641	11.0000	161	25921	12.6886
82	6724	9.0554	122	14884	11.0454	162	26244	12.7279
83	6889	9.1104	123	15129	11.0905	163	26569	12.7671
84	7056	9.1652	124	15376	11.1355	164	26896	12.8062
85	7225	9.2195	125	15625	11.1803	165	27225	12.8452
86	7396	9.2736	126	15876	11.2250	166	27556	12.8841
87	7569	9.3274	127	16129	11.2694	167	27889	12.9228
88	7744	9.3808	128	16384	11.3137	168	28224	12.9615
89	7921	9.4340	129	16641	11.3578	169	28561	13.0000
90	8100	9.4868	130	16900	11.4018	170	28900	13.0384
91	8281	9.5394	131	17161	11.4455	171	29241	13.0767
92	8464	9.5917	132	17424	11.4891	172	29584	13.1149
93	8649	9.6437	133	17689	11.5326	173	29929	13.1529
94	8836	9.6954	134	17956	11.5758	174	30276	13.1909
95	9025	9.7468	135	18225	11.6190	175	30625	13.2288
96	9216	9.7980	136	18496	11.6619	176	30976	13.2665
97	9409	9.8489	137	18769	11.7047	177	31329	13.3041
98	9604	9.8995	138	19044	11.7473	178	31684	13.3417
99	9801	9.9499	139	19321	11.7898	179	32041	13.3791
100	10000	10.0000	140	19600	11.8322	180	32400	13.4164
101	10201	10.0499	141	19881	11.8743	181	32761	13.4536
102	10404	10.0995	142	20164	11.9164	182	33124	13.4907
103	10609	10.1489	143	20449	11.9583	183	33489	13.5277
104	10816	10.1980	144	20736	12.0000	184	33856	13.5647
105	11025	10.2470	145	21025	12.0416	185	34225	13.6015
106	11236	10.2956	146	21316	12.0830	186	34596	13.6382
107	11449	10.3441	147	21609	12.1244	187	34969	13.6748
108	11664	10.3923	148	21904	12.1655	188	35344	13.7113
109	11881	10.4403	149	22201	12.2066	189	35721	13.7477
110	12100	10.4881	150	22500	12.2474	190	36100	13.7840
111	12321	10.5357	151	22801	12.2882	191	36481	13.8203
112	12544	10.5830	152	23104	12.3288	192	36864	13.8564
113	12769	10.6301	153	23409	12.3693	193	37249	13.8924
114	12996	10.6771	154	23716	12.4097	194	37636	13.9284
115	13225	10.7238	155	24025	12.4499	195	38025	13.9642

N	N^2	$\sqrt{N}$	N	N^2	$\sqrt{N}$	N	N^2	$\sqrt{N}$
196	38416	14.0000	236	55696	15.3623	276	76176	16.6132
197	38809	14.0357	237	56169	15.3948	277	76729	16.6433
198	39204	14.0712	238	56644	15.4272	278	77284	16.6733
199	39601	14.1067	239	57121	15.4596	279	77841	16.7033
200	40000	14.1421	240	57600	15.4919	280	78400	16.7332
201	40401	14.1774	241	58081	15.5242	281	78961	16.7631
202	40804	14.2127	242	58564	15.5563	282	79524	16.7929
203	41209	14.2478	243	59049	15.5885	283	80089	16.8226
204	41616	14.2829	244	59536	15.6205	284	80656	16.8523
205	42025	14.3178	245	60025	15.6525	285	81225	16.8819
206	42436	14.3527	246	60516	15.6844	286	81796	16.9115
207	42849	14.3875	247	61009	15.7162	287	82369	16.9411
208	43264	14.4222	248	61504	15.7480	288	82944	16.9706
209	43681	14.4568	249	62001	15.7797	289	83521	17.0000
210	44100	14.4914	250	62500	15.8114	290	84100	17.0294
211	44521	14.5258	251	63001	15.8430	291	84681	17.0587
212	44944	14.5602	252	63504	15.8745	292	85264	17.0880
213	45369	14.5945	253	64009	15.9060	293	85849	17.1172
214	45796	14.6287	254	64516	15.9374	294	86436	17.1464
215	46225	14.6629	255	65025	15.9687	295	87025	17.1756
216	46656	14.6969	256	65536	16.0000	296	87616	17.2047
217	47089	14.7309	257	66049	16.0312	297	88209	17.2337
218	47524	14.7648	258	66564	16.0624	298	88804	17.2627
219	47961	14.7986	259	67081	16.0935	299	89401	17.2916
220	48400	14.8324	260	67600	16.1245	300	90000	17.3205
221	48841	14.8661	261	68121	16.1555	301	90601	17.3494
222	49284	14.8997	262	68644	16.1864	302	91204	17.3781
223	49729	14.9332	263	69169	16.2173	303	91809	17.4069
224	50176	14.9666	264	69696	16.2481	304	92416	17.4356
225	50625	15.0000	265	70225	16.2788	305	93025	17.4642
226	51076	15.0333	266	70756	16.3095	306	93636	17.4929
227	51529	15.0665	267	71289	16.3401	307	94249	17.5214
228	51984	15.0997	268	71824	16.3707	308	94864	17.5499
229	52441	15.1327	269	72361	16.4012	309	95481	17.5784
230	52900	15.1658	270	72900	16.4317	310	96100	17.6068
231	53361	15.1987	271	73441	16.4621	311	96721	17.6352
232	53824	15.2315	272	73984	16.4924	312	97344	17.6635
233	54289	15.2643	273	74529	16.5227	313	97969	17.6918
234	54756	15.2971	274	75076	16.5529	314	98596	17.7200
235	55225	15.3297	275	75625	16.5831	315	99225	17.7482

N	N^2	$\sqrt{N}$	N	N^2	$\sqrt{N}$	N	N^2	$\sqrt{N}$
316	99856	17.7764	356	126736	18.8680	396	156816	19.8997
317	100489	17.8045	357	127449	18.8944	397	157609	19.9249
318	101124	17.8326	358	128164	18.9209	398	158404	19.9499
319	101761	17.8606	359	128881	18.9473	399	159201	19.9750
320	102400	17.8885	360	129600	18.9737	400	160000	20.0000
321	103041	17.9165	361	130321	19.0000	401	160801	20.0250
322	103684	17.9444	362	131044	19.0263	402	161604	20.0499
323	104329	17.9722	363	131769	19.0526	403	162409	20.0749
324	104976	18.0000	364	132496	19.0788	404	163216	20.0998
325	105625	18.0278	365	133225	19.1050	405	164025	20.1246
326	106276	18.0555	366	133956	19.1311	406	164836	20.1494
327	106929	18.0831	367	134689	19.1572	407	165649	20.1742
328	107584	18.1108	368	135424	19.1833	408	166464	20.1990
329	108241	18.1384	369	136161	19.2094	409	167281	20.2237
330	108900	18.1659	370	136900	19.2354	410	168100	20.2485
331	109561	18.1934	371	137641	19.2614	411	168921	20.2731
332	110224	18.2209	372	138384	19.2873	412	169744	20.2978
333	110889	18.2483	373	139129	19.3132	413	170569	20.3224
334	111556	18.2757	374	139876	19.3391	414	171396	20.3470
335	112225	18.3030	375	140625	19.3649	415	172225	20.3715
336	112896	18.3303	376	141376	19.3907	416	173056	20.3961
337	113569	18.3576	377	142129	19.4165	417	173889	20.4206
338	114244	18.3848	378	142884	19.4422	418	174724	20.4450
339	114921	18.4120	379	143641	19.4679	419	175561	20.4695
340	115600	18.4391	380	144400	19.4936	420	176400	20.4939
341	116281	18.4662	381	145161	19.5192	421	177241	20.5183
342	116964	18.4932	382	145924	19.5448	422	178084	20.5426
343	117649	18.5203	383	146689	19.5704	423	178929	20.5670
344	118336	18.5472	384	147456	19.5959	424	179776	20.5913
345	119025	18.5742	385	148225	19.6214	425	180625	20.6155
346	119716	18.6011	386	148996	19.6469	426	181476	20.6398
347	120409	18.6279	387	149769	19.6723	427	182329	20.6640
348	121104	18.6548	388	150544	19.6977	428	183184	20.6882
349	121801	18.6815	389	151321	19.7231	429	184041	20.7123
350	122500	18.7083	390	152100	19.7484	430	184900	20.7364
351	123201	18.7350	391	152881	19.7737	431	185761	20.7605
352	123904	18.7617	392	153664	19.7990	432	186624	20.7846
353	124609	18.7883	393	154449	19.8242	433	187489	20.8087
354	125316	18.8149	394	155236	19.8494	434	188356	20.8327
355	126025	18.8414	395	156025	19.8746	435	189225	20.8567

N	N^2	$\sqrt{N}$	N	N^2	$\sqrt{N}$	N	N^2	$\sqrt{N}$
436	190096	20.8806	476	226576	21.8174	516	266256	22.7156
437	190969	20.9045	477	227529	21.8403	517	267289	22.7376
438	191844	20.9284	478	228484	21.8632	518	268324	22.7596
439	192721	20.9523	479	229441	21.8861	519	269361	22.7816
440	193600	20.9762	480	230400	21.9089	520	270400	22.8035
441	194481	21.0000	481	231361	21.9317	521	271441	22.8254
442	195364	21.0238	482	232324	21.9545	522	272484	22.8473
443	196249	21.0476	483	233289	21.9773	523	273529	22.8692
444	197136	21.0713	484	234256	22.0000	524	274576	22.8910
445	198025	21.0950	485	235225	22.0227	525	275625	22.9129
446	198916	21.1187	486	236196	22.0454	526	276676	22.9347
447	199809	21.1424	487	237169	22.0681	527	277729	22.9565
448	200704	21.1660	488	238144	22.0907	528	278784	22.9783
449	201601	21.1896	489	239121	22.1133	529	279841	23.0000
450	202500	21.2132	490	240100	22.1359	530	280900	23.0217
451	203401	21.2368	491	241081	22.1585	531	281961	23.0434
452	204304	21.2603	492	242064	22.1811	532	283024	23.0651
453	205209	21.2838	493	243049	22.2036	533	284089	23.0868
454	206116	21.3073	494	244036	22.2261	534	285156	23.1084
455	207025	21.3307	495	245025	22.2486	535	286225	23.1301
456	207936	21.3542	496	246016	22.2711	536	287296	23.1517
457	208849	21.3776	497	247009	22.2935	537	288369	23.1733
458	209764	21.4009	498	248004	22.3159	538	289444	23.1948
459	210681	21.4243	499	249001	22.3383	539	290521	23.2164
460	211600	21.4476	500	250000	22.3607	540	291600	23.2379
461	212521	21.4709	501	251001	22.3830	541	292681	23.2594
462	213444	21.4942	502	252004	22.4054	542	293764	23.2809
463	214369	21.5174	503	253009	22.4277	543	294849	23.3024
464	215296	21.5407	504	254016	22.4499	544	295936	23.3238
465	216225	21.5639	505	255025	22.4722	545	297025	23.3452
466	217156	21.5870	506	256036	22.4944	546	298116	23.3666
467	218089	21.6102	507	257049	22.5167	547	299209	23.3880
468	219024	21.6333	508	258064	22.5389	548	300304	23.4094
469	219961	21.6564	509	259081	22.5610	549	301401	23.4307
470	220900	21.6795	510	260100	22.5832	550	302500	23.4521
471	221841	21.7025	511	261121	22.6053	551	303601	23.4734
472	222784	21.7256	512	262144	22.6274	552	304704	23.4947
473	223729	21.7486	513	263169	22.6495	553	305809	23.5160
474	224676	21.7715	514	264196	22.6716	554	306916	23.5372
475	225625	21.7945	515	265225	22.6936	555	308025	23.5584

N	N^2	$\sqrt{N}$	N	N^2	$\sqrt{N}$	N	N^2	$\sqrt{N}$
556	309136	23.5797	596	355216	24.4131	636	404496	25.2190
557	310249	23.6008	597	356409	24.4336	637	405769	25.2389
558	311364	23.6220	598	357604	24.4540	638	407044	25.2587
559	312481	23.6432	599	358801	24.4745	639	408321	25.2784
560	313600	23.6643	600	360000	24.4949	640	409600	25.2982
561	314721	23.6854	601	361201	24.5153	641	410881	25.3180
562	315844	23.7065	602	362404	24.5357	642	412164	25.3377
563	316969	23.7276	603	363609	24.5561	643	413449	25.3574
564	318096	23.7487	604	364816	24.5764	644	414736	25.3772
565	319225	23.7697	605	366025	24.5967	645	416025	25.3969
566	320356	23.7908	606	367236	24.6171	646	417316	25.4165
567	321489	23.8118	607	368449	24.6374	647	418609	25.4362
568	322624	23.8328	608	369664	24.6577	648	419904	25.4558
569	323761	23.8537	609	370881	24.6779	649	421201	25.4755
570	324900	23.8747	610	372100	24.6982	650	422500	25.4951
571	326041	23.8956	611	373321	24.7184	651	423801	25.5147
572	327184	23.9165	612	374544	24.7386	652	425104	25.5343
573	328329	23.9374	613	375769	24.7588	653	426409	25.5539
574	329476	23.9583	614	376996	24.7790	654	427716	25.5734
575	330625	23.9792	615	378225	24.7992	655	429025	25.5930
576	331776	24.0000	616	379456	24.8193	656	430336	25.6125
577	332929	24.0208	617	380689	24.8395	657	431649	25.6320
578	334084	24.0416	618	381924	24.8596	658	432964	25.6515
579	335241	24.0624	619	383161	24.8797	659	434281	25.6710
580	336400	24.0832	620	384400	24.8998	660	435600	25.6905
581	337561	24.1039	621	385641	24.9199	661	436921	25.7099
582	338724	24.1247	622	386884	24.9399	662	438244	25.7294
583	339889	24.1454	623	388129	24.9600	663	439569	25.7488
584	341056	24.1661	624	389376	24.9800	664	440896	25.7682
585	342225	24.1868	625	390625	25.0000	665	442225	25.7876
586	343396	24.2074	626	391876	25.0200	666	443556	25.8070
587	344569	24.2281	627	393129	25.0400	667	444889	25.8263
588	345744	24.2487	628	394384	25.0599	668	446224	25.8457
589	346921	24.2693	629	395641	25.0799	669	447561	25.8650
590	348100	24.2899	630	396900	25.0998	670	448900	25.8844
591	349281	24.3105	631	398161	25.1197	671	450241	25.9037
592	350464	24.3311	632	399424	25.1396	672	451584	25.9230
593	351649	24.3516	633	400689	25.1595	673	452929	25.9422
594	352836	24.3721	634	401956	25.1794	674	454276	25.9615
595	354025	24.3926	635	403225	25.1992	675	455625	25.9808

N	N^2	$\sqrt{N}$	N	N^2	$\sqrt{N}$	N	N^2	$\sqrt{N}$
676	456976	26.0000	716	512656	26.7582	756	571536	27.4955
677	458329	26.0192	717	514089	26.7769	757	573049	27.5136
678	459684	26.0384	718	515524	26.7955	758	574564	27.5318
679	461041	26.0576	719	516961	26.8142	759	576081	25.5500
680	462400	26.0768	720	518400	26.8328	760	577600	27.5681
681	463761	26.0960	721	519841	26.8514	761	579121	27.5862
682	465124	26.1151	722	521284	26.8701	762	580644	27.6043
683	466489	26.1343	723	522729	26.8887	763	582169	27.6225
684	467856	26.1534	724	524176	26.9072	764	583696	27.6405
685	469225	26.1725	725	525625	26.9258	765	585225	27.6586
686	470596	26.1916	726	527076	26.9444	766	586756	27.6767
687	471969	26.2107	727	528529	26.9629	767	588289	27.6948
688	473344	26.2298	728	529984	26.9815	768	589824	27.7128
689	474721	26.2488	729	531441	27.0000	769	591361	27.7308
690	476100	26.2679	730	532900	27.0185	770	592900	27.7489
691	477481	26.2869	731	534361	27.0370	771	594441	27.7669
692	478864	26.3059	732	535824	27.0555	772	595984	27.7849
693	480249	26.3249	733	537289	27.0740	773	597529	27.8029
694	481636	26.3439	734	538756	27.0924	774	599076	27.8209
695	483025	26.3629	735	540225	27.1109	775	600625	27.8388
696	484416	26.3818	736	541696	27.1293	776	602176	27.8568
697	485809	26.4008	737	543169	27.1477	777	603729	27.8747
698	487204	26.4197	738	544644	27.1662	778	605284	27.8927
699	488601	26.4386	739	546121	27.1846	779	606841	27.9106
700	490000	26.4575	740	547600	27.2029	780	608400	27.9285
701	491401	26.4764	741	549081	27.2213	781	609961	27.9464
702	492804	26.4953	742	550564	27.2397	782	611524	27.9643
703	494209	26.5141	743	552049	27.2580	783	613089	27.9821
704	495616	26.5330	744	553536	27.2764	784	614656	28.0000
705	497025	26.5518	745	555025	27.2947	785	616225	28.0179
706	498436	26.5707	746	556516	27.3130	786	617796	28.0357
707	499849	26.5895	747	558009	27.3313	787	619369	28.0535
708	501264	26.6083	748	559504	27.3496	788	620944	28.0713
709	502681	26.6271	749	561001	27.3679	789	622521	28.0891
710	504100	26.6458	750	562500	27.3861	790	624100	28.1069
711	505521	26.6646	751	564001	27.4044	791	625681	28.1247
712	506944	26.6833	752	565504	27.4226	792	627264	28.1425
713	508369	26.7021	753	567009	27.4408	793	628849	28.1603
714	509796	26.7208	754	568516	27.4591	794	630436	28.1780
715	511225	26.7395	755	570025	27.4773	795	632025	28.1957

N	N^2	$\sqrt{N}$	N	N^2	$\sqrt{N}$	N	N^2	$\sqrt{N}$
796	633616	28.2135	836	698896	28.9137	876	767376	29.5973
797	635209	28.2312	837	700569	28.9310	877	769129	29.6142
798	636804	28.2489	838	702244	28.9482	878	770884	29.6311
799	638401	28.2666	839	703921	28.9655	879	772641	29.6479
800	640000	28.2843	840	705600	28.9828	880	774400	29.6648
801	641601	28.3019	841	707281	29.0000	881	776161	29.6816
802	643204	28.3196	842	708964	29.0172	882	777924	29.6985
803	644809	28.3373	843	710649	29.0345	883	779689	29.7153
804	646416	28.3549	844	712336	29.0517	884	781456	29.7321
805	648025	28.3725	845	714025	29.0689	885	783225	29.7489
806	649636	28.3901	846	715716	29.0861	886	784996	29.7658
807	651249	28.4077	847	717409	29.1033	887	786769	29.7825
808	652864	28.4253	848	719104	29.1204	888	788544	29.7993
809	654481	28.4429	849	720801	29.1376	889	790321	29.8161
810	656100	28.4605	850	722500	29.1548	890	792100	29.8329
811	657721	28.4781	851	724201	29.1719	891	793881	29.8496
812	659344	28.4956	852	725904	29.1890	892	795664	29.8664
813	660969	28.5132	853	727609	29.2062	893	797449	29.8831
814	662596	28.5307	854	729316	29.2233	894	799236	29.8998
815	664225	28.5482	855	731025	29.2404	895	801025	29.9166
816	665856	28.5657	856	732736	29.2575	896	802816	29.9333
817	667489	28.5832	857	734449	29.2746	897	804609	29.9500
818	669124	28.6007	858	736164	29.2916	898	806404	29.9666
819	670761	28.6182	859	737881	29.3087	899	808201	29.9833
820	672400	28.6356	860	739600	29.3258	900	810000	30.0000
821	674041	28.6531	861	741321	29.3428	901	811801	30.0167
822	675684	28.6705	862	743044	29.3598	902	813604	30.0333
823	677329	28.6880	863	744769	29.3769	903	815409	30.0500
824	678976	28.7054	864	746496	29.3939	904	817216	30.0666
825	680625	28.7228	865	748225	29.4109	905	819025	30.0832
826	682276	28.7402	866	749956	29.4279	906	820836	30.0998
827	683929	28.7576	867	751689	29.4449	907	822649	30.1164
828	685584	28.7750	868	753424	29.4618	908	824464	30.1330
829	687241	28.7924	869	755161	29.4788	909	826281	30.1496
830	688900	28.8097	870	756900	29.4958	910	828100	30.1662
831	690561	28.8271	871	758641	29.5127	911	829921	30.1828
832	692224	28.8444	872	760384	29.5296	912	831744	30.1993
833	693889	28.8617	873	762129	29.5466	913	833569	30.2159
834	695556	28.8791	874	763876	29.5635	914	835396	30.2324
835	697225	28.8964	875	765625	29.5804	915	837225	30.2490

N	N^2	$\sqrt{N}$	N	N^2	$\sqrt{N}$	N	N^2	$\sqrt{N}$
916	839056	30.2655	946	894916	30.7571	976	952576	31.2410
917	840889	30.2820	947	896809	30.7734	977	954529	31.2570
918	842724	30.2985	948	898704	30.7896	978	956484	31.2730
919	844561	30.3150	949	900601	30.8058	979	958441	31.2890
920	846400	30.3315	950	902500	30.8221	980	960400	31.3050
921	848241	30.3480	951	904401	30.8383	981	962361	31.3209
922	850084	30.3645	952	906304	30.8545	982	964324	31.3369
923	851929	30.3809	953	908209	30.8707	983	966289	31.3528
924	853776	30.3974	954	910116	30.8869	984	968256	31.3688
925	855625	30.4138	955	912025	30.9031	985	970225	31.3847
926	857476	30.4302	956	913936	30.9192	986	972196	31.4006
927	859329	30.4467	957	915849	30.9354	987	974169	31.4166
928	861184	30.4631	958	917764	30.9516	988	976144	31.4325
929	863041	30.4795	959	919681	30.9677	989	978121	31.4484
930	864900	30.4959	960	921600	30.9839	990	980100	31.4643
931	866761	30.5123	961	923521	31.0000	991	982081	31.4802
932	868624	30.5287	962	925444	31.0161	992	984064	31.4960
933	870489	30.5450	963	927369	31.0322	993	986049	31.5119
934	872356	30.5614	964	929296	31.0483	994	988036	31.5278
935	874225	30.5778	965	931225	31.0644	995	990025	31.5436
936	876096	30.5941	966	933156	31.0805	996	992016	31.5595
937	877969	30.6105	967	935089	31.0966	997	994009	31.5753
938	879844	30.6268	968	937024	31.1127	998	996004	31.5911
939	881721	30.6431	969	938961	31.1288	999	998001	31.6070
940	883600	30.6594	970	940900	31.1448	1000	1000000	31.6228
941	885481	30.6757	971	942841	31.1609			
942	887364	30.6920	972	944784	31.1769			
943	889249	30.7083	973	946729	31.1929			
944	891136	30.7246	974	948676	31.2090			
945	893025	30.7409	975	950625	31.2250			

Appendix K

PERCENTAGES OF AREA IN THE NORMAL DISTRIBUTION

To obtain the percentage of the total area of a normal distribution that is between any one of many pairs of lines drawn perpendicular to its baseline is easy if Table K.1 is used. Column 1 consists of standard measures in units of .01 from 0.00 (the mean of a normal distribution expressed in standard measures) to 3.14. As positive values, these mark points on the baseline between the mean and plus infinity, at which unattainable point one end of the normal distribution lies. In Figure K.1, points corresponding to standard measures of +1.00, +2.00, and +3.00 have been labeled.

In appendix D, standard measures were defined as deviations from the mean of a distribution expressed in terms of the standard deviation of the distribution. This definition was put in the form of an equation as:

$$z = \frac{(X - \bar{X})}{S_X}. \tag{D.1}$$

To save space in Table K.1, negative values of standard measures have not been included, but in Figure K.1 points corresponding to standard measures of -1.00, -2.00, and -3.14 have been labeled. Since each half of a normal distribution is a mirrored image of the other, information pertaining to areas in one half of the distribution also applies to the other half.

Each entry in Column 2 of Table K.1 shows the percentage of the total area of the normal distribution between the mean (standard measure of 0.00) and the corresponding z value in Column 1. For example, the percentage of the area of the entire distribution between the mean and a standard measure of 1.00 is 34.13. This is the first entry in Column 2 on page 377. The area is crosshatched in Figure K.1. The percentage of the area in this distribution between the mean and a standard measure of -3.14 is 49.92

371

FIGURE K.1

Selected Segments of the Normal Distribution.

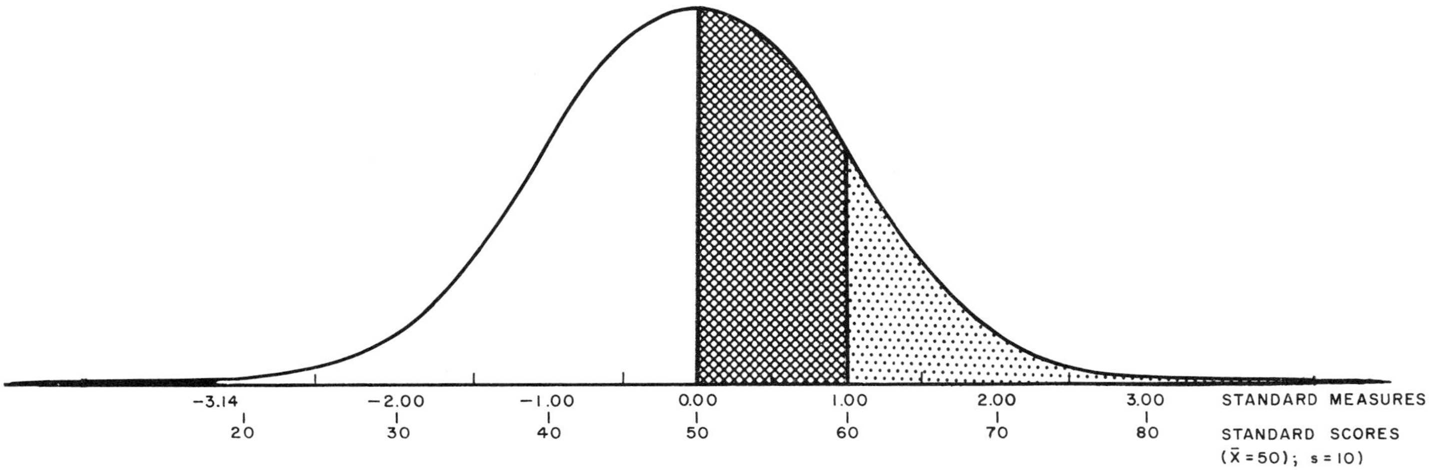

according to the last entry in Column 2 of Table K.1 on page 383.   This area is white in Figure K.1.

Each entry in Column 3 of Table K.1 shows the percentage of the total area of the normal distribution extending outward from the corresponding value in Column 1 to the end of the distribution at infinity.   In Figure K.1, the percentage of the area of the entire distribution in the section extending outward from a standard measure of 1.00 is 15.87.   This area is dotted as far as the distribution extends in the figure.

It should be noted that the diagram of the distribution in Figure K.1 extends only about four and one-half standard measures on either side of the mean.   Column 3 of Table K.1 shows that the percentage of the entire area of the normal distribution extending outward to infinity from a standard measure of −3.14 is 00.08.   This area is black in Figure K.1 as far as the diagram extends.

The percentage of the entire area between many pairs of vertical lines drawn through the baseline of the normal distribution can be obtained by subtraction if the required values from Columns 1, 2, and 3 are used.   For example, the percentage of the total area from the mean to a standard measure of 1.00 is 34.13 (the crosshatched area in Figure K.1).   The percentage of the total area from the mean to a standard measure of 3.00 is 49.87.   Therefore, the percentage of the total area between standard measures of 1.00 and 3.00 must be equal to 49.87 − 34.13, or 15.74.

Entries in Column 4 of Table K.1 are simply double those of corresponding entries in Column 3.   They are provided for convenience in estimating the significance of a difference between a standard measure of 0.00 and any specified standard measure from 0.01 to 3.14 in a normal distribution.*   For example, a difference of 1.96 standard measures (between 0.00 and 1.96) is significant at the 5.00-per-cent level, as indicated by the entry in Column 4 corresponding to a standard measure of 1.96 in Column 1. Put in other words, differences of 1.96 standard measures or more make up 5 per cent of all differences between a standard measure of 0.00 and the infinite number of other points on the baseline of a normal distribution. The rationale for determining the significance of differences is explained in appendix I.

This result also means that differences of 1.96 and all smaller differences between a standard measure of 0.00 and the infinite number of points on the baseline of the normal distribution make up 100.00 − 5.00, or 95.00, per cent of all differences.   Thus, the 95-per-cent confidence interval of a standard measure of 0.00 in a normal distribution is 1.96 + 1.96, or 3.92,

---

* Occasional rounding errors of not more than one one-hundredth of one per cent in Column 4 are not large enough to interfere with practical use of the table.   For more exact values, see T. L. Kelley, *The Kelley Statistical Tables* (Cambridge: Harvard University Press, 1947).

standard measures.   The rationale for establishing confidence intervals is given in appendix H.

TABLE K.1

Condensed Table of Percentages of the Area of the Normal
Distribution*

Standard Measure z	Percentage From Mean to Designated z†	Percentage Extending on 1 Side Beyond Designated z‡	Percentage Extending on Both Sides Beyond Designated z
Column 1	Column 2	Column 3	Column 4
0.00	00.00	50.00	100.00
0.01	00.40	49.60	99.20
0.02	00.80	49.20	98.40
0.03	01.20	48.80	97.60
0.04	01.60	48.40	96.80
0.05	01.99	48.01	96.02
0.06	02.39	47.61	95.22
0.07	02.79	47.21	94.42
0.08	03.19	46.81	93.62
0.09	03.59	46.41	92.82
0.10	03.98	46.02	92.04
0.11	04.38	45.62	91.24
0.12	04.78	45.22	90.44
0.13	05.17	44.83	89.66
0.14	05.57	44.43	88.86
0.15	05.96	44.04	88.08
0.16	06.36	43.64	87.28
0.17	06.75	43.25	86.50
0.18	07.14	42.86	85.72
0.19	07.53	42.47	84.94
0.20	07.93	42.07	84.14
0.21	08.32	41.68	83.36
0.22	08.71	41.29	82.58
0.23	09.10	40.90	81.80
0.24	09.48	40.52	81.04
0.25	09.87	40.13	80.26
0.26	10.26	39.74	79.48
0.27	10.64	39.36	78.72
0.28	11.03	38.97	77.94
0.29	11.41	38.59	77.18

Standard Measure z	Percentage From Mean to Designated z†	Percentage Extending on 1 Side Beyond Designated z‡	Percentage Extending on Both Sides Beyond Designated z
Column 1	Column 2	Column 3	Column 4
0.30	11.79	38.21	76.42
0.31	12.17	37.83	75.66
0.32	12.55	37.45	74.90
0.33	12.93	37.07	74.14
0.34	13.31	36.69	73.38
0.35	13.68	36.32	72.64
0.36	14.06	35.94	71.88
0.37	14.43	35.57	71.14
0.38	14.80	35.20	70.40
0.39	15.17	34.83	69.66
0.40	15.54	34.46	68.92
0.41	15.91	34.09	68.18
0.42	16.28	33.72	67.44
0.43	16.64	33.36	66.72
0.44	17.00	33.00	66.00
0.45	17.36	32.64	65.28
0.46	17.72	32.28	64.56
0.47	18.08	31.92	63.84
0.48	18.44	31.56	63.12
0.49	18.79	31.21	62.42
0.50	19.15	30.85	61.70
0.51	19.50	30.50	61.00
0.52	19.85	30.15	60.30
0.53	20.19	29.81	59.62
0.54	20.54	29.46	58.92
0.55	20.88	29.12	58.24
0.56	21.23	28.77	57.54
0.57	21.57	28.43	56.86
0.58	21.90	28.10	56.20
0.59	22.24	27.76	55.52
0.60	22.57	27.43	54.86
0.61	22.91	27.09	54.18
0.62	23.24	26.76	53.52
0.63	23.57	26.43	52.86
0.64	23.89	26.11	52.22

Standard Measure z	Percentage From Mean to Designated z†	Percentage Extending on 1 Side Beyond Designated z‡	Percentage Extending on Both Sides Beyond Designated z
Column 1	Column 2	Column 3	Column 4
0.65	24.22	25.78	51.56
0.66	24.54	25.46	50.92
0.67	24.86	25.14	50.28
0.68	25.17	24.83	49.66
0.69	25.49	24.51	49.02
0.70	25.80	24.20	48.40
0.71	26.11	23.89	47.78
0.72	26.42	23.58	47.16
0.73	26.73	23.27	46.54
0.74	27.04	22.96	45.92
0.75	27.34	22.66	45.32
0.76	27.64	22.36	44.72
0.77	27.94	22.06	44.12
0.78	28.23	21.77	43.54
0.79	28.52	21.48	42.96
0.80	28.81	21.19	42.38
0.81	29.10	20.90	41.80
0.82	29.39	20.61	41.22
0.83	29.67	20.33	40.66
0.84	29.95	20.05	40.10
0.85	30.23	19.77	39.54
0.86	30.51	19.49	38.98
0.87	30.78	19.22	38.44
0.88	31.06	18.94	37.88
0.89	31.33	18.67	37.34
0.90	31.59	18.41	36.82
0.91	31.86	18.14	36.28
0.92	32.12	17.88	35.76
0.93	32.38	17.62	35.24
0.94	32.64	17.36	34.72
0.95	32.89	17.11	34.22
0.96	33.15	16.85	33.70
0.97	33.40	16.60	33.20
0.98	33.65	16.35	32.70
0.99	33.89	16.11	32.22

Standard Measure z	Percentage From Mean to Designated z†	Percentage Extending on 1 Side Beyond Designated z‡	Percentage Extending on Both Sides Beyond Designated z
Column 1	Column 2	Column 3	Column 4
1.00	34.13	15.87	31.74
1.01	34.38	15.62	31.24
1.02	34.61	15.39	30.78
1.03	34.85	15.15	30.30
1.04	35.08	14.92	29.84
1.05	35.31	14.69	29.38
1.06	35.54	14.46	28.92
1.07	35.77	14.23	28.46
1.08	35.99	14.01	28.02
1.09	36.21	13.79	27.58
1.10	36.43	13.57	27.14
1.11	36.65	13.35	26.70
1.12	36.86	13.14	26.28
1.13	37.08	12.92	25.84
1.14	37.29	12.71	25.42
1.15	37.49	12.51	25.02
1.16	37.70	12.30	24.60
1.17	37.90	12.10	24.20
1.18	38.10	11.90	23.80
1.19	38.30	11.70	23.40
1.20	38.49	11.51	23.02
1.21	38.69	11.31	22.62
1.22	38.88	11.12	22.24
1.23	39.07	10.93	21.86
1.24	39.25	10.75	21.50
1.25	39.44	10.56	21.12
1.26	39.62	10.38	20.76
1.27	39.80	10.20	20.40
1.28	39.97	10.03	20.06
1.29	40.15	09.85	19.70
1.30	40.32	09.68	19.36
1.31	40.49	09.51	19.02
1.32	40.66	09.34	18.68
1.33	40.82	09.18	18.36
1.34	40.99	09.01	18.02

Standard Measure z	Percentage From Mean to Designated z†	Percentage Extending on 1 Side Beyond Designated z‡	Percentage Extending on Both Sides Beyond Designated z
Column 1	Column 2	Column 3	Column 4
1.35	41.15	08.85	17.70
1.36	41.31	08.69	17.38
1.37	41.47	08.53	17.06
1.38	41.62	08.38	16.76
1.39	41.77	08.23	16.46
1.40	41.92	08.08	16.16
1.41	42.07	07.93	15.86
1.42	42.22	07.78	15.56
1.43	42.36	07.64	15.28
1.44	42.51	07.49	14.98
1.45	42.65	07.35	14.70
1.46	42.79	07.21	14.42
1.47	42.92	07.08	14.16
1.48	43.06	06.94	13.88
1.49	43.19	06.81	13.62
1.50	43.32	06.68	13.36
1.51	43.45	06.55	13.10
1.52	43.57	06.43	12.86
1.53	43.70	06.30	12.60
1.54	43.82	06.18	12.36
1.55	43.94	06.06	12.12
1.56	44.06	05.94	11.88
1.57	44.18	05.82	11.64
1.58	44.29	05.71	11.42
1.59	44.41	05.59	11.18
1.60	44.52	05.48	10.96
1.61	44.63	05.37	10.74
1.62	44.74	05.26	10.52
1.63	44.84	05.16	10.32
1.64	44.95	05.05	10.10
1.65	45.05	04.95	09.90
1.66	45.15	04.85	09.70
1.67	45.25	04.75	09.50
1.68	45.35	04.65	09.30
1.69	45.45	04.55	09.10

Standard Measure z	Percentage From Mean to Designated z†	Percentage Extending on 1 Side Beyond Designated z‡	Percentage Extending on Both Sides Beyond Designated z
Column 1	Column 2	Column 3	Column 4
1.70	45.54	04.46	08.92
1.71	45.64	04.36	08.72
1.72	45.73	04.27	08.54
1.73	45.82	04.18	08.36
1.74	45.91	04.09	08.18
1.75	45.99	04.01	08.02
1.76	46.08	03.92	07.84
1.77	46.16	03.84	07.68
1.78	46.25	03.75	07.50
1.79	46.33	03.67	07.34
1.80	46.41	03.59	07.18
1.81	46.49	03.51	07.02
1.82	46.56	03.44	06.88
1.83	46.64	03.36	06.72
1.84	46.71	03.29	06.58
1.85	46.78	03.22	06.44
1.86	46.86	03.14	06.28
1.87	46.93	03.07	06.14
1.88	46.99	03.01	06.02
1.89	47.06	02.94	05.88
1.90	47.13	02.87	05.74
1.91	47.19	02.81	05.62
1.92	47.26	02.74	05.48
1.93	47.32	02.68	05.36
1.94	47.38	02.62	05.24
1.95	47.44	02.56	05.12
1.96	47.50	02.50	05.00
1.97	47.56	02.44	04.88
1.98	47.61	02.39	04.78
1.99	47.67	02.33	04.66
2.00	47.72	02.28	04.56
2.01	47.78	02.22	04.44
2.02	47.83	02.17	04.34
2.03	47.88	02.12	04.24
2.04	47.93	02.07	04.14

Standard Measure z	Percentage From Mean to Designated z†	Percentage Extending on 1 Side Beyond Designated z‡	Percentage Extending on Both Sides Beyond Designated z
Column 1	Column 2	Column 3	Column 4
2.05	47.98	02.02	04.04
2.06	48.03	01.97	03.94
2.07	48.08	01.92	03.84
2.08	48.12	01.88	03.76
2.09	48.17	01.83	03.66
2.10	48.21	01.79	03.58
2.11	48.26	01.74	03.48
2.12	48.30	01.70	03.40
2.13	48.34	01.66	03.32
2.14	48.38	01.62	03.24
2.15	48.42	01.58	03.16
2.16	48.46	01.54	03.08
2.17	48.50	01.50	03.00
2.18	48.54	01.46	02.92
2.19	48.57	01.43	02.86
2.20	48.61	01.39	02.78
2.21	48.64	01.36	02.72
2.22	48.68	01.32	02.64
2.23	48.71	01.29	02.58
2.24	48.75	01.25	02.50
2.25	48.78	01.22	02.44
2.26	48.81	01.19	02.38
2.27	48.84	01.16	02.32
2.28	48.87	01.13	02.26
2.29	48.90	01.10	02.20
2.30	48.93	01.07	02.14
2.31	48.96	01.04	02.08
2.32	48.98	01.02	02.04
2.33	49.01	00.99	01.98
2.34	49.04	00.96	01.92
2.35	49.06	00.94	01.88
2.36	49.09	00.91	01.82
2.37	49.11	00.89	01.78
2.38	49.13	00.87	01.74
2.39	49.16	00.84	01.68

Standard Measure z	Percentage From Mean to Designated z†	Percentage Extending on 1 Side Beyond Designated z‡	Percentage Extending on Both Sides Beyond Designated z
Column 1	Column 2	Column 3	Column 4
2.40	49.18	00.82	01.64
2.41	49.20	00.80	01.60
2.42	49.22	00.78	01.56
2.43	49.25	00.75	01.50
2.44	49.27	00.73	01.46
2.45	49.29	00.71	01.42
2.46	49.31	00.69	01.38
2.47	49.32	00.68	01.36
2.48	49.34	00.66	01.32
2.49	49.36	00.64	01.28
2.50	49.38	00.62	01.24
2.51	49.40	00.60	01.20
2.52	49.41	00.59	01.18
2.53	49.43	00.57	01.14
2.54	49.45	00.55	01.10
2.55	49.46	00.54	01.08
2.56	49.48	00.52	01.04
2.57	49.49	00.51	01.02
2.58	49.51	00.49	00.98
2.59	49.52	00.48	00.96
2.60	49.53	00.47	00.94
2.61	49.55	00.45	00.90
2.62	49.56	00.44	00.88
2.63	49.57	00.43	00.86
2.64	49.59	00.41	00.82
2.65	49.60	00.40	00.80
2.66	49.61	00.39	00.78
2.67	49.62	00.38	00.76
2.68	49.63	00.37	00.74
2.69	49.64	00.36	00.72
2.70	49.65	00.35	00.70
2.71	49.66	00.34	00.68
2.72	49.67	00.33	00.66
2.73	49.68	00.32	00.64
2.74	49.69	00.31	00.62

Standard Measure z	Percentage From Mean to Designated z†	Percentage Extending on 1 Side Beyond Designated z‡	Percentage Extending on Both Sides Beyond Designated z
Column 1	Column 2	Column 3	Column 4
2.75	49.70	00.30	00.60
2.76	49.71	00.29	00.58
2.77	49.72	00.28	00.56
2.78	49.73	00.27	00.54
2.79	49.74	00.26	00.52
2.80	49.74	00.26	00.52
2.81	49.75	00.25	00.50
2.82	49.76	00.24	00.48
2.83	49.77	00.23	00.46
2.84	49.77	00.23	00.46
2.85	49.78	00.22	00.44
2.86	49.79	00.21	00.42
2.87	49.79	00.21	00.42
2.88	49.80	00.20	00.40
2.89	49.81	00.19	00.38
2.90	49.81	00.19	00.38
2.91	49.82	00.18	00.36
2.92	49.82	00.18	00.36
2.93	49.83	00.17	00.34
2.94	49.84	00.16	00.32
2.95	49.84	00.16	00.32
2.96	49.85	00.15	00.30
2.97	49.85	00.15	00.30
2.98	49.86	00.14	00.28
2.99	49.86	00.14	00.28
3.00	49.87	00.13	00.26
3.01	49.87	00.13	00.26
3.02	49.87	00.13	00.26
3.03	49.88	00.12	00.24
3.04	49.88	00.12	00.24
3.05	49.89	00.11	00.22
3.06	49.89	00.11	00.22
3.07	49.89	00.11	00.22
3.08	49.90	00.10	00.20
3.09	49.90	00.10	00.20

Standard Measure z	Percentage From Mean to Designated z†	Percentage Extending on 1 Side Beyond Designated z‡	Percentage Extending on Both Sides Beyond Designated z
Column 1	Column 2	Column 3	Column 4
3.10	49.90	00.10	00.20
3.11	49.91	00.09	00.18
3.12	49.91	00.09	00.18
3.13	49.91	00.09	00.18
3.14	49.92	00.08	00.16

* The values in columns 2 and 3 are based on entries in Table III in Allen L. Edwards, *Statistical Methods for the Behavioral Sciences* (New York: Holt, Rinehart and Winston, Inc., 1954). This source was used by permission of the publisher.

† Shown in Figure K.1 as crosshatched area for $z = 1.00$.

‡ Shown in Figure K.1 as dotted area for $z = 1.00$.

THE *t* DISTRIBUTION

When the number of cases on which computations are based is large, confidence intervals and levels of significance can properly be estimated by using percentages of the area of the normal distribution, as shown in Table K.1. If the number of cases in the distribution is less than 30, there is definite need for employing percentages of the area of the *t* distribution instead. Table L.1 makes this conveniently possible.

Table L.1 is entered with the level of significance desired and the number of degrees of freedom on which the computations are based. In this book, that number is represented by *n*. (In statistics books it is often denoted as *dof* or *df*.) The value in Table L.1 at the junction of the column and row with which it is entered is the smallest *t* value that can be regarded as significantly different from zero.

Use of Table L.1 may be illustrated by the *t* value computed on page 348 to determine whether the correlation coefficient of .88 between scores on Forms J and K of the *Stanford Intermediate Paragraph-Meaning Test* is significantly different from zero. According to the data given,

$$t_{n=8} = \frac{.88\sqrt{10-2}}{\sqrt{1-(.88)^2}} = \frac{2.49}{.47} = 5.30.$$

To determine whether the coefficient of .88 is significantly different from zero at the 10-per-cent level, Table L.1 is entered in the column headed 10 and the row labeled 8. The value at the junction of that column and row is 1.86. This is the minimum value of *t* that can be regarded as significantly different from zero at the 10-per-cent level when $n = 8$. Since the obtained value is 5.30, the correlation coefficient of .88 is highly significant at better than the 10-per-cent level. Further inspection of the entries in the row labeled 8 shows that the obtained value is greater than the *t* value given in the column headed 1. This indicates that the coefficient is significantly different from zero at better than the 1-per-cent level.

TABLE L.1

Condensed Table of the *t* Distribution*

n†	Level of Significance			
	20	10	5	1
1	3.08	6.31	12.71	63.66
2	1.89	2.92	4.30	9.93
3	1.64	2.35	3.18	5.84
4	1.53	2.13	2.78	4.60
5	1.48	2.02	2.57	4.03
6	1.44	1.94	2.45	3.71
7	1.42	1.90	2.37	3.50
8	1.40	1.86	2.31	3.36
9	1.38	1.83	2.26	3.25
10	1.37	1.81	2.23	3.17
11	1.36	1.80	2.20	3.11
12	1.36	1.78	2.18	3.06
13	1.35	1.77	2.16	3.01
14	1.35	1.76	2.15	2.98
15	1.34	1.75	2.13	2.95
16	1.34	1.75	2.12	2.92
17	1.33	1.74	2.11	2.90
18	1.33	1.73	2.10	2.88
19	1.33	1.73	2.09	2.86
20	1.33	1.73	2.09	2.85
21	1.32	1.72	2.08	2.83
22	1.32	1.72	2.07	2.82
23	1.32	1.71	2.07	2.81
24	1.32	1.71	2.06	2.80
25	1.32	1.71	2.06	2.79
26	1.32	1.71	2.06	2.78
27	1.31	1.70	2.05	2.77
28	1.31	1.70	2.05	2.76
29	1.31	1.70	2.05	2.76
30	1.31	1.70	2.04	2.75
40	1.30	1.68	2.02	2.70
60	1.30	1.67	2.00	2.66
120	1.29	1.66	1.98	2.62
∞	1.28	1.65	1.96	2.58

* The *t* distribution is attributable to William Seely Gosset, who wrote under the pseudonym of Student.   See Student, "The Probable Error of a Mean," *Biometrika*, VI (1908), 1–25.

Table L.1 is an abridgement of Table III in R. A. Fisher and F. Yates, *Statistical Tables for Biological, Agricultural, and Medical Research*, published by Oliver & Boyd Ltd., Edinburgh, and used by permission of the authors and publishers.

† *n* equals the number of degrees of freedom.

AIDS FOR INTERPRETING SCORES FROM TESTS IN COMMON USE

The tables in appendix M are so simple to use that an understanding of the principles underlying their construction is not a prerequisite to their use. Yet so fundamental is the information they provide and so indispensable is it to proper interpretation of individual scores that clinical and school psychologists as well as guidance counselors should become thoroughly familiar with them before they attempt to interpret scores derived from the tests for which data are provided.*

Standard error of measurement. Standard errors of measurement are given in each of the tables in appendix M principally because they constitute the basic data used to compute the 85-per-cent confidence intervals and the smallest differences between pairs of scores that are significant at the 15-per-cent level, or better.†

Confidence interval. The 85-per-cent confidence interval is given for each set of scores listed in appendix M. The confidence interval should be centered around the individual score that it is desired to interpret. Out of every 100 times that the confidence interval is used in this way for separate scores it will include the individual's true score 85 times. In effect, then, the practical inference may be made that the 85-per-cent confidence interval identifies a range of scores that is very likely to include an individual's true score. The technically correct meaning of a confidence interval is given in appendix H.

Suppose that a second-grade pupil takes Form B of the *Metropolitan*

* The techniques for making the tables are presented in chapter 8 and may be used to construct similar tables for other tests.

† For a discussion of the standard error of measurement, see chapter 2; for methods of computing it, see appendix E.

Achievement Test, Primary Battery.   On the word-knowledge test he obtains a grade-equivalent score of 2.2.   According to Table M.14, the 85-per-cent confidence interval for this score is .72.   Half of .72 is .36.   If .36 is sub-tracted from and added to 2.2, the resulting range of grade-equivalent scores is 1.84 to 2.56.   In practice, the inference may be made that this pupil's true grade-equivalent score is very likely included in the range of grade-equivalent scores from 1.8 to 2.6.   This inference provides assurance that the pupil's obtained score of 2.2 is likely to be reasonably representative of his true score.

Because scores on various tests differ greatly in accuracy of measure-ment, use of a confidence interval is important in their interpretation.   The 85-per-cent confidence interval is recommended for this purpose.   How-ever, data given in Table 8.1 can be used with the standard errors of measure-ment provided in the tables in appendix M to compute other confidence intervals.

Smallest differences significant at the 15-per-cent level.   The smallest differences significant at the 15-per-cent level, or better, between pairs of scores are given in the tables in appendix M.   Most test users prefer not to make inferences about a pupil if the differences between scores are so small that they can easily be attributed to errors of measurement.   This can be avoided if only differences as great as or greater than those shown in the tables in appendix M are used as a basis for making inferences.*

The data in the tables may be used with reference to four types of differences:

1. differences between scores on different tests administered to the same individual;
2. differences between scores on various forms of the same test administered to the same individual;
3. differences between scores on the same test administered to different individuals;
4. differences between scores on different tests administered to different individuals.

For differences of types 2 and 3, the leftmost entry in each row is used. For example, a test interpreter wishes to know whether a pupil's obtained grade-equivalent scores of 2.2 and 2.5 in word discrimination (test 2) on Forms A and B, respectively, of the *Metropolitan Achievement Test*, Primary Battery I, are significantly different at the 15-per-cent level.   He should look

---

* Whether differences are positive or negative, they are looked up in the tables as though they were positive.   The tables are so constructed that the differences presented all meet the criterion of significance at the 15-per-cent level. Because they have been systematically rounded to the next largest whole number or first decimal place, many of them are significant at better than the 15-per-cent level.

in Table M.14 at the leftmost entry in row 2. It is .4. Since the pupil's two scores in word discrimination differ by only .3 grade-equivalent score, the interpreter concludes that the difference is not significant and may be regarded as a variation attributable to errors of measurement. His best estimate of the pupil's grade-equivalent score in word discrimination is, therefore, the average of 2.2 and 2.5, or 2.35.

Suppose that two ten-year-old pupils, Jack and Frank, obtain full-scale IQ's of 93 and 99, respectively, on the *Wechsler Intelligence Scale for Children* (WISC). Can the teacher safely infer that Frank's IQ is truly higher than Jack's? He should look in Table M.20. The leftmost entry in row 15 is 7. Thus, any difference between full-scale IQ's on the WISC of less than 7 points is not significant at the 15-per-cent level and the difference of 6 points between the full-scale IQ's of Jack and Frank can best be ascribed to errors of measurement.

For differences of types 1 and 4, the entry at the junction of the appropriate row and column of most of the tables in appendix M should be used. Suppose that Charles, a seventh grade pupil, obtained grade scores of 74 in paragraph meaning (test 1) and 60 in arithmetic computation (test 4) on Form W of the *Stanford Achievement Test*, Advanced Battery. To determine whether this difference of 14 grade-score points is significant at the 15-per-cent level, the teacher should look in Table M.11 at the junction of row 1 and column 4. The entry is 13. Since the difference of 14 points is more than the entry of 13 at the junction of row 1 and Column 4, the teacher regards it as significant at the 15-per-cent level, or better, and concludes that Charles is truly better in reading comprehension than in arithmetic computation.

Differences of type 4 are less frequently of interest to psychologists and educators than those of types 1, 2, and 3. Nonetheless, they can be evaluated if the scores from different tests are comparable. If Jack's verbal IQ on the WISC is 91 and Frank's performance IQ on the same test is 100, the significance of the difference between these two IQ's may be determined by reference to Table M.20. The entry at the junction of row 13 (verbal IQ) and column 14 (performance IQ) is 9. Since the difference between Jack's verbal IQ and Frank's performance IQ is 9 points, it can be regarded as significant at the 15-per-cent level, or better, and it is proper to infer that Frank's verbal ability is relatively superior to Jack's performance ability, as these abilities are measured by the WISC.

After a test interpreter becomes familiar with the tables in appendix M, their practical use becomes very easy. For example, Table M.21 presents data pertaining to the *Flanagan Aptitude Classification Tests* (FACT). The smallest differences between pairs of stanines on the nineteen tests that are significant at the 15-per-cent level, or better, are either 2 or 3 when they are rounded to the nearest whole number. As a quick rule of thumb, a counselor might regard differences of three stanine points or more as acceptably reliable and worthy of attention.   In this case, Table M.21 need be consulted only for more careful interpretations of individual patterns of scores.   More detailed directions for using the tables in appendix M are given in chapter 8.

TABLE M.1

Stanford Achievement Test
Primary Battery, Forms J, K, L, M, N
Standard Errors of Measurement and 85-Per-Cent Confidence Intervals
of Grade Scores, and Smallest Differences Between Grade Scores
Significant at the 15-Per-Cent Level, or Better*

Test	Differences Between Grade Scores					85 Per Cent C.I.†	s_{meas}
	1	2	3	4	5		
1. Paragraph Meaning	5	5	4	6	4	5.8	2
2. Word Meaning		5	4	6	4	5.8	2
3. Spelling			3	5	3	2.9	1
4. Arithmetic Reasoning				7	5	8.6	3
5. Arithmetic Computation					3	2.9	1

* To convert these values to grade-equivalent scores, divide by 10.
† 85-per-cent confidence interval.

TABLE M.2

Stanford Achievement Test
Elementary Battery, Forms J, K, L, M, N
Standard Errors of Measurement and 85-Per-Cent Confidence Intervals of Grade
Scores, and Smallest Differences Between Grade Scores Significant at
the 15-Per-Cent Level, or Better*

Test	Differences Between Grade Scores						85 Per Cent C.I.†	s_{meas}
	1	2	3	4	5	6		
1. Paragraph Meaning	8	7	6	12	6	6	10.1	3.5
2. Word Meaning		6	5	11	5	5	7.2	2.5
3. Spelling			5	11	5	4	5.8	2.0
4. Language Usage				15	11	11	20.2	7.0
5. Arithmetic Reasoning					5	4	5.8	2.0
6. Arithmetic Computation						4	4.3	1.5

* To convert these values to grade-equivalent scores, divide by 10.
† 85-per-cent confidence interval.

Stanford Achievement Test

Intermediate Battery, Forms J, K, L, M, N
Standard Errors of Measurement and 85-Per-Cent Confidence Intervals of Grade
Scores, and Smallest Differences Between Grade Scores Significant at
the 15-Per-Cent Level, or Better*

Test	Differences Between Grade Scores									85 Per Cent C.I.†	s_{meas}
	1	2	3	4	5	6	7	8	9		
1. Paragraph Meaning	13	11	11	17	12	10	11	12	13	17.3	6.00
2. Word Meaning		9	9	15	9	8	9	10	11	11.5	4.00
3. Spelling			9	15	9	8	9	10	11	11.5	4.00
4. Language Usage				20	16	15	16	16	17	27.4	9.50
5. Arithmetic Reasoning						10	9	10	11	12	13.7	4.75
6. Arithmetic Computation							7	8	10	11	8.6	3.00
7. Social Studies								10	11	12	13.0	4.50
8. Science									12	13	15.8	5.50
9. Study Skills										27	18.7	6.50

* To convert these values to grade-equivalent scores, divide by 10.
† 85-per-cent confidence interval.

Stanford Achievement Test

Advanced Battery, Forms J, K, L, M, N
Standard Errors of Measurement and 85-Per-Cent Confidence Intervals of Grade
Scores, and Smallest Differences Between Grade Scores Significant at
the 15-Per-Cent Level, or Better*

Test	Differences Between Grade Scores									85 Per Cent C.I.†	s_{meas}
	1	2	3	4	5	6	7	8	9		
1. Paragraph Meaning	24	20	19	23	19	21	23	22	25	33.1	11.50
2. Word Meaning		15	14	20	14	17	20	18	22	20.9	7.35
3. Spelling			12	19	12	15	19	17	21	15.8	5.50
4. Language Usage				24	19	21	23	22	25	33.1	11.50
5. Arithmetic Reasoning						12	15	19	17	21	15.8	5.50
6. Arithmetic Computation							18	21	20	23	25.2	8.75
7. Social Studies								24	22	25	33.1	11.50
8. Science									21	24	28.8	10.00
9. Study Skills										27	37.4	13.00

* To convert these values to grade-equivalent scores, divide by 10.
† 85-per-cent confidence interval.

TABLE M.5

Stanford Achievement Test

Grade 1, Primary Battery I, Forms W, X, Y
Standard Errors of Measurement and 85-Per-Cent Confidence Intervals of Grade
Scores, and Smallest Differences Between Grade Scores Significant at
the 15-Per-Cent Level, or Better*

Test	Differences Between Grade Scores						85 Per Cent C.I.†	s_{meas}
	1	2	3	4	5	6		
1. Word Reading	3	2	3	2	3	2	4.3	1.5
2. Paragraph Meaning		1	3	2	2	2	1.4	.5
3. Vocabulary			4	3	3	3	7.2	2.5
4. Spelling				2	2	2	2.9	1.0
5. Word Study Skills					3	2	4.3	1.5
6. Arithmetic						2	2.9	1.0

* To convert these values to grade-equivalent scores, divide by 10.
† 85-per-cent confidence interval.

TABLE M.6

Stanford Achievement Test

Grade 2, Primary Battery II, Forms W, X, Y
Standard Errors of Measurement and 85-Per-Cent Confidence Intervals of Grade
Scores, and Smallest Differences Between Grade Scores Significant at
the 15-Per-Cent Level, or Better*

Test	Differences Between Grade Scores								85 Per Cent C.I.†	s_{meas}
	1	2	3	4	5	6	7	8		
1. Word Meaning	6	5	8	5	6	6	5	5	7.2	2.5
2. Paragraph Meaning		5	8	5	5	5	5	5	5.8	2.0
3. Science and Social Studies Concepts			10	8	8	8	8	8	13.0	4.5
4. Spelling				5	5	5	5	5	5.8	2.0
5. Word Study Skills					6	6	5	5	7.2	2.5
6. Language						6	5	5	7.2	2.5
7. Arithmetic Computation							5	5	5.8	2.0
8. Arithmetic Concepts								5	5.8	2.0

* To convert these values to grade-equivalent scores, divide by 10.
† 85-per-cent confidence interval.

TABLE M.7

Stanford Achievement Test
Grade 3, Primary Battery II, Forms W, X, Y
Standard Errors of Measurement and 85-Per-Cent Confidence Intervals of Grade Scores, and Smallest Differences Between Grade Scores Significant at the 15-Per-Cent Level, or Better*

Test	Differences Between Grade Scores								85 Per Cent C.I.†	s_{meas}
	1	2	3	4	5	6	7	8		
1. Word Meaning	6	6	10	5	7	7	5	8	7.2	2.5
2. Paragraph Meaning		6	10	5	7	7	5	8	7.2	2.5
3. Science and Social Studies Concepts			12	10	11	11	10	11	17.3	6.0
4. Spelling				5	6	7	5	8	5.8	2.0
5. Word Study Skills					8	8	6	9	10.1	3.5
6. Language						9	7	9	11.5	4.0
7. Arithmetic Computation							5	8	5.8	2.0
8. Arithmetic Concepts								10	13.0	4.5

* To convert these values to grade-equivalent scores, divide by 10.
† 85-per-cent confidence interval.

TABLE M.8

Stanford Achievement Test
Grade 4, Intermediate Battery I, Forms W, X, Y, Z
Standard Errors of Measurement and 85-Per-Cent Confidence Intervals of Grade Scores, and Smallest Differences Between Grade Scores Significant at the 15-Per-Cent Level, or Better*

Test	Differences Between Grade Scores										85 Per Cent C.I.†	s_{meas}
	1	2	3	4	5	6	7	8	9	10		
1. Word Meaning	10	9	8	10	10	8	10	9	9	9	13.0	4.5
2. Paragraph Meaning		9	7	10	9	7	9	8	9	8	11.5	4.0
3. Spelling			6	9	8	6	8	7	7	8	7.2	2.5
4. Word Study Skills				11	10	9	10	9	10	9	14.4	5.0
5. Language					10	8	10	9	9	9	13.0	4.5
6. Arithmetic Computation						6	8	7	7	7	7.2	2.5
7. Arithmetic Concepts							10	9	9	9	13.0	4.5
8. Arithmetic Applications								8	8	8	10.1	3.5
9. Social Studies									9	8	11.5	4.0
10. Science										8	10.1	3.5

* To convert these values to grade-equivalent scores, divide by 10.
† 85-per-cent confidence interval.

TABLE M.9

Stanford Achievement Test

Grade 5, Intermediate Battery II, Forms W, X, Y, Z
Standard Errors of Measurement and 85-Per-Cent Confidence Intervals of Grade
Scores, and Smallest Differences Between Grade Scores Significant at
the 15-Per-Cent Level, or Better*

Test	Differences Between Grade Scores									85 Per Cent C.I.†	s_{meas}
	1	2	3	4	5	6	7	8	9		
1. Word Meaning	10	9	10	10	10	11	11	10	10	13.0	4.5
2. Paragraph Meaning		9	9	9	9	11	11	9	10	11.5	4.0
3. Spelling			10	10	10	11	11	10	10	13.0	4.5
4. Language				10	10	11	11	10	10	13.0	4.5
5. Arithmetic Computation					10	11	11	10	10	13.0	4.5
6. Arithmetic Concepts						13	13	11	12	17.3	6.0
7. Arithmetic Applications							13	11	12	17.3	6.0
8. Social Studies								10	10	13.0	4.5
9. Science									11	14.4	5.0

* To convert these values to grade-equivalent scores, divide by 10.
† 85-per-cent confidence interval.

TABLE M.10

Stanford Achievement Test

Grade 6, Intermediate Battery II, Forms W, X, Y, Z
Standard Errors of Measurement and 85-Per-Cent Confidence Intervals of Grade
Scores, and Smallest Differences Between Grade Scores Significant at
the 15-Per-Cent Level, or Better*

Test	Differences Between Grade Scores									85 Per Cent C.I.†	s_{meas}
	1	2	3	4	5	6	7	8	9		
1. Word Meaning	10	10	9	10	11	10	11	10	11	13.0	4.5
2. Paragraph Meaning		11	10	10	11	10	11	11	12	14.4	5.0
3. Spelling			9	9	10	9	10	10	11	11.5	4.0
4. Language				10	11	10	11	10	11	13.0	4.5
5. Arithmetic Computation					12	11	12	11	12	15.8	5.5
6. Arithmetic Concepts						10	11	10	11	13.0	4.5
7. Arithmetic Applications							12	11	12	15.8	5.5
8. Social Studies								11	12	14.4	5.0
9. Science									13	17.3	6.0

* To convert these values to grade-equivalent scores, divide by 10.
† 85-per-cent confidence interval.

TABLE M.11

Stanford Achievement Test

Grade 7, Advanced Battery, Forms S, W, X, Y, Z*
Standard Errors of Measurement and 85-Per-Cent Confidence Intervals of Grade
Scores, and Smallest Differences Between Grade Scores Significant at
the 15-Per-Cent Level, or Better†

Test	Differences Between Grade Scores								85 Per Cent C.I.‡	s_{meas}
	1	2	3	4	5	6	7	8		
1. Paragraph Meaning	11	12	11	13	14	15	12	15	14.4	5.0
2. Spelling		13	12	14	15	16	13	16	17.3	6.0
3. Language			11	13	14	15	12	15	14.4	5.0
4. Arithmetic Computation				15	16	17	14	17	20.2	7.0
5. Arithmetic Concepts					17	18	15	18	23.0	8.0
6. Arithmetic Applications						19	16	19	25.9	9.0
7. Social Studies							14	16	18.7	6.5
8. Science								19	25.9	9.0

* Form S is reserved for large testing programs by special arrangement with the publisher.

† To convert these values to grade-equivalent scores, divide by 10.

‡ 85-per-cent confidence interval.

TABLE M.12

Stanford Achievement Test

Grade 8, Advanced Battery, Forms S, W, X, Y, Z*
Standard Errors of Measurement and 85-Per-Cent Confidence Intervals of Grade
Scores, and Smallest Differences Between Grade Scores Significant at
the 15-Per-Cent Level, or Better†

Test	Differences Between Grade Scores								85 Per Cent C.I.‡	s_{meas}
	1	2	3	4	5	6	7	8		
1. Paragraph Meaning	17	17	18	17	17	22	19	19	23.0	8.0
2. Spelling		17	18	17	17	22	19	19	23.0	8.0
3. Language			20	18	18	23	21	21	27.4	9.5
4. Arithmetic Computation				17	17	22	19	19	23.0	8.0
5. Arithmetic Concepts					17	22	19	19	23.0	8.0
6. Arithmetic Applications						26	24	24	36.0	12.5
7. Social Studies							22	22	30.2	10.5
8. Science								22	30.2	10.5

* Form S is reserved for large testing programs by special arrangement with the publisher.

† To convert these values to grade-equivalent scores, divide by 10.

‡ 85-per-cent confidence interval.

TABLE M.13

Stanford Achievement Test
Grade 9, Advanced Battery, Forms S, W, X, Y, Z*
Standard Errors of Measurement and 85-Per-Cent Confidence Intervals of Grade
Scores, and Smallest Differences Between Grade Scores Significant at
the 15-Per-Cent Level, or Better†

Test	Differences Between Grade Scores								85 Per Cent C.I.‡	s_{meas}
	1	2	3	4	5	6	7	8		
1. Paragraph Meaning	19	18	18	19	19	23	21	18	25.9	9.0
2. Spelling		17	17	18	18	22	20	17	23.0	8.0
3. Language			17	18	18	22	20	19	23.0	8.0
4. Arithmetic Computation				19	19	23	21	18	25.9	9.0
5. Arithmetic Concepts					20	24	21	20	27.4	9.5
6. Arithmetic Applications						27	25	23	37.4	13.0
7. Social Studies							23	21	31.7	11.0
8. Science								18	24.5	8.5

* Form S is reserved for large testing programs by special arrangement with the publisher.
† To convert these values to grade-equivalent scores, divide by 10.
‡ 85-per-cent confidence interval.

TABLE M.14

Metropolitan Achievement Test
Primary Battery I, Forms A, B, C
Standard Errors of Measurement and 85-Per-Cent Confidence Intervals
of Grade-Equivalent Scores, and Smallest Differences Between
Grade-Equivalent Scores Significant at the 15-Per-Cent Level, or Better

Test	Differences Between Grade-Equivalent Scores				85 Per Cent C.I.*	s_{meas}
	1	2	3	4		
1. Word Knowledge	.6	.5	.4	.5	.72	.25
2. Word Discrimination		.4	.4	.4	.55	.19
3. Reading			.2	.3	.29	.10
4. Arithmetic				.4	.46	.16

* 85-per-cent confidence interval.

TABLE M.15

Metropolitan Achievement Test
Primary Battery II, Forms A, B, C
Standard Errors of Measurement and 85-Per-Cent Confidence Intervals
of Grade-Equivalent Scores, and Smallest Differences Between
Grade-Equivalent Scores Significant at the 15-Per-Cent Level or Better

Test	Differences Between Grade-Equivalent Scores					85 Per Cent C.I.*	s_{meas}
	1	2	3	4	5		
1. Word Knowledge	.5	.7	.5	.6	.4	.60	.21
2. Word Discrimination		.8	.7	.8	.6	1.07	.37
3. Reading			.5	.6	.4	.63	.22
4. Spelling				.7	.6	.95	.33
5. Arithmetic					.4	.52	.18

* 85-per-cent confidence interval.

TABLE M.16

Metropolitan Achievement Test
Elementary Battery, Forms A, B, C, D
Standard Errors of Measurement and 85-Per-Cent Confidence Intervals
of Grade-Equivalent Scores, and Smallest Differences Between
Grade-Equivalent Scores Significant at the 15-Per-Cent Level, or Better

Test	Differences Between Grade-Equivalent Scores							85 Per Cent C.I.*	s_{meas}
	1	2	3	4	5	6	7		
1. Word Knowledge	.8	.8	.8	.7	.9	.7	.7	1.12	.39
2. Word Discrimination		.7	.7	.6	.8	.6	.6	.86	.30
3. Reading			.7	.6	.8	.6	.6	.89	.31
4. Spelling				.6	.8	.5	.5	.75	.26
5. Language					1.0	.8	.8	1.30	.45
6. Arithmetic Computation						.5	.5	.58	.20
7. Arithmetic Problems							.5	.63	.22

* 85-per-cent confidence interval.

TABLE M.17

Metropolitan Achievement Test
Intermediate Battery, Forms A, B, C, D
Standard Errors of Measurement and 85-Per-Cent Confidence Intervals
of Grade-Equivalent Scores, and Smallest Differences Between
Grade-Equivalent Scores Significant at the 15-Per-Cent Level, or Better

Test	Differences Between Grade-Equivalent Scores										85 Per Cent C.I.*	s_{meas}
	1	2	3	4	5	6	7	8	9	10		
1. Word Knowledge	.9	1.0	1.0	.9	1.3	.8	.8	1.2	1.1	.8	1.27	.44
2. Reading		1.1	1.1	1.0	1.4	.9	1.0	1.3	1.2	1.0	1.55	.54
3. Spelling			1.1	1.0	1.4	.9	.9	1.3	1.2	.9	1.44	.50
4. Language				.9	1.3	.8	.8	1.2	1.1	.9	1.27	.44
5. Language Study Skills					1.6	1.2	1.3	1.5	1.5	1.3	2.25	.78
6. Arithmetic Computation						.6	.7	1.1	1.0	.7	.75	.26
7. Arithmetic Problems							.7	1.1	1.1	.8	.98	.34
8. Social Studies Information								1.4	1.4	1.2	1.96	.68
9. Social Studies Study Skills									1.3	1.1	1.78	.62
10. Science										.8	1.09	.38

* 85-per-cent confidence interval.

TABLE M.18

Metropolitan Achievement Test
Advanced Battery, Forms A, B, C, D
Standard Errors of Measurement and 85-Per-Cent Confidence Intervals
of Grade-Equivalent Scores, and Smallest Differences Between
Grade-Equivalent Scores Significant at the 15-Per-Cent Level, or Better

Test	Differences Between Grade-Equivalent Scores										85 Per Cent C.I.*	s_{meas}
	1	2	3	4	5	6	7	8	9	10		
1. Word Knowledge	1.9	1.6	1.5	1.6	2.3	1.5	1.4	1.8	2.9	1.7	2.56	.89
2. Reading		1.4	1.3	1.3	2.1	1.2	1.1	1.6	2.8	1.5	1.93	.67
3. Spelling			1.1	1.1	2.0	1.0	1.0	1.5	2.7	1.4	1.50	.52
4. Language				1.2	2.0	1.1	1.0	1.5	2.7	1.4	1.58	.55
5. Language Study Skills					2.6	2.0	1.9	2.2	3.2	2.2	3.66	1.27
6. Arithmetic Computation						1.0	.9	1.4	2.7	1.3	1.30	.45
7. Arithmetic Problems							.8	1.4	2.6	1.3	1.04	.36
8. Social Studies Information								1.8	2.9	1.7	2.48	.86
9. Social Studies Study Skills									3.6	2.8	5.07	1.76
10. Science										1.6	2.25	.78

* 85-per-cent confidence interval.

TABLE M.19 Wechsler Adult Intelligence Scale

Standard Errors of Measurement and 85-Per-Cent Confidence Intervals of Scaled Scores and IQ's; Smallest Differences Between Scaled Scores and IQ's Significant at the 15-Per-Cent Level, or Better; and Smallest Deviations of Single Scaled Scores from the Average Score of an Individual Significant at the 5-Per-Cent Level, or Better*

Test	Differences Between Scaled Scores														85 Per Cent C.I.†	s_{meas}	Deviation from Average‡	Deviation from Average§
	1	2	3	4	5	6	7	8	9	10	11	12	13	14				
1. Information	2	3	3	3	3	3	2	3	3	3	3				2.53	.88	1.72	1.90
2. Comprehension		3	3	3	4	3	3	3	3	4	4				3.92	1.36	2.53	2.78
3. Arithmetic			3	3	4	3	3	3	3	4	4				3.97	1.38	2.57	2.82
4. Similarities				3	3	3	3	3	3	3	3				3.20	1.11	2.10	2.31
5. Digit Span					4	4	4	4	4	4	4				4.69	1.63	2.98	3.29
6. Vocabulary						2	2	3	3	3	3				1.99	.69	1.45	1.59
7. Digit Symbol							2	3	3	3	3				2.45	.85	1.69	1.84
8. Picture Completion								3	3	3	3				3.40	1.18	2.21	2.45
9. Block Design									3	3	3				3.34	1.16	2.20	2.41
10. Picture Arrangement										4	4				4.92	1.71	3.12	3.43
11. Object Assembly											4				4.75	1.65	3.02	3.31

Differences Between IQ Scores

Test	12	13	14	85 Per Cent C.I.†	s_{meas}
12. Verbal IQ (Tests 1 through 6)	7	8	6	8.64	3.00
13. Performance IQ (Tests 7 through 11)		9	5	11.43	3.97
14. Full-Scale IQ (Tests 1 through 11)			6	7.49	2.60

* Based on data from 200 cases at ages 18–19. Cf., Wechsler, D. *WAIS Manual.* (New York: Psychological Corp., 1955), Table 6, page 13.

† 85-per-cent confidence interval.

‡ Smallest deviation of a single Scaled Score from the average of 11 Scaled Scores significant at the 5-per-cent level.

§ Smallest deviation of a single Scaled Score from the average of 10 other Scaled Scores significant at the 5-per-cent level.

TABLE M.20 Wechsler Intelligence Scale for Children

Standard Errors of Measurement and 85-Per-Cent Confidence Intervals of Scaled Scores and IQ's; Smallest Differences Between Scaled Scores and IQ's Significant at the 15-Per-Cent Level, or Better; and Smallest Deviations of Single Scaled Scores from the Average Score of an Individual Significant at the 5-Per-Cent Level, or Better*

Test	Differences Between Scaled Scores															85 Per Cent C.I.†	s_{meas}	Deviation from Average‡	Deviation from Average§
	1	2	3	4	5	6	7	8	9	10	11	12	13	14	15				
1. Information		3	3	3	3	4	4	4	3	4	4	3				3.86	1.34	2.53	2.80
2. Comprehension			3	3	3	4	4	4	3	4	4	3				4.49	1.56	2.88	3.19
3. Arithmetic				3	3	4	4	3	3	4	4	3				3.45	1.20	2.29	2.55
4. Comparison					3	4	4	3	3	4	4	3				3.77	1.31	3.16	2.74
5. Vocabulary						4	3	3	3	3	4	3				2.59	.90	1.82	2.02
6. Digit Span							4	4	4	4	4	4				5.53	1.92	3.88	3.88
7. Picture Completion								4	3	4	4	4				5.04	1.75	3.19	3.55
8. Picture Arrangement									3	4	4	3				4.66	1.62	2.98	3.31
9. Block Design										4	4	3				3.11	1.08	2.12	2.35
10. Object Assembly											4	4				5.24	1.82	3.31	3.68
11. Coding‖												4				5.47	1.90	3.45	3.84
12. Mazes																3.77	1.31	2.72	2.72
Differences Between IQ's																			
13. Verbal IQ (omitting Digit Span)													7	9	8	8.64	3.00		
14. Performance IQ (omitting Mazes)														12	5	14.34	4.98		
15. Full-Scale IQ (omitting Digit Span and Mazes)															7	9.67	3.36		

* Based on data from 200 cases at age 10½. Cf., Wechsler, D. *Manual for Intelligence Scale for Children.* (New York: Psychological Corp., 1949), Table VII, page 13.

† 85-per-cent confidence interval.

‡ Smallest deviation of a single Scaled Score from the average of 10 tests (excluding Digit Span and Mazes) significant at the 5-per-cent level.

§ Smallest deviation of a single Scaled Score from the average of all *other* tests (except Digit Span and Mazes) significant at the 5-per-cent level.

‖ Standard error of measurement of Coding Test from 200 cases at age 7½ was used in constructing this table.

Flanagan Aptitude Classification Tests

Standard Errors of Measurement and 85-Per-Cent Confidence Intervals of Stanines, and Smallest Differences Between Stanines Significant at the 15-Per-Cent Level, or Better*

Test	Differences Between Stanine Scores																			85 Per Cent C.I.†	s_{meas}
	1	2	3	4	5	6	7	8	9	10	11	12	13	14	15	16	17	18	19		
1. Inspection	3	3	3	3	2	3	3	2	3	2	2	3	2	3	3	2	3	3	3	3.0	1.1
2. Mechanics		3	3	2	3	3	3	3	3	3	3	3	2	3	3	2	3	3	3	3.3	1.1
3. Tables			2	3	2	2	3	2	3	2	2	3	2	3	3	2	2	2	3	2.8	1.0
4. Reasoning				3	2	3	3	2	3	2	2	3	2	2	3	2	3	3	3	2.9	1.0
5. Vocabulary					2	2	2	2	2	2	2	2	2	3	2	2	2	2	3	1.7	.6
6. Assembly						2	3	2	3	2	2	3	2	3	3	2	2	3	3	2.8	1.0
7. Judgment							3	2	3	2	2	3	2	3	3	2	3	3	3	3.0	1.0
8. Components								2	3	3	3	2	2	2	2	2	2	2	3	2.3	.8
9. Planning									3	3	3	3	2	3	3	2	3	3	3	3.4	1.2
10. Arithmetic										2	2	3	2	2	3	2	2	2	3	2.6	.9
11. Ingenuity											2	3	2	2	3	2	2	2	3	2.6	.9
12. Scales												3	2	3	3	2	3	3	3	3.3	1.1
13. Expression													2	2	3	2	3	3	3	1.8	.6
14. Precision														3	3	3	3	3	3	2.9	1.0
15. Alertness															3	3	3	3	3	3.6	1.2
16. Coordination																2	2	2	3	2.2	.7
17. Patterns																	2	2	3	2.8	1.0
18. Coding																		3	3	2.9	1.0
19. Memory																			3	3.9	1.3

* Based on variance errors of measurement in J. C. Flanagan, *Technical Report for the Flanagan Aptitude Classification Tests.* (Chicago: Science Research Associates, 1959), Table 5-4.

† 85-per-cent confidence interval.

TABLE M.22

Differential Aptitude Test

Standard Errors of Measurement and 85-Per-Cent Confidence Intervals
of Standard Scores and Smallest Differences Between Standard
Scores Significant at the 15-Per-Cent Level, or Better*

Test	Differences Between Standard Scores									85 Per Cent C.I.†	s_{meas}
	1	2	3	4	5	6	7	8	9		
1. Verbal	7	7	7	7	8	9	7	7	7	9.1	3.2
2. Numerical		8	7	7	8	10	8	7	8	10.0	3.5
3. Abstract			7	7	8	9	7	7	7	9.1	3.2
4. Space				6	7	9	7	6	7	8.2	2.8
5. Mechanical—Boys					8	10	8	7	8	11.1	3.9
6. Mechanical—Girls						11	10	9	10	15.5	5.4
7. Clerical							8	7	8	10.4	3.6
8. Spelling								6	7	8.2	2.8
9. Sentences									8	10.0	3.5

* Standard scores are shown on the Individual Report Form of the *Differential Aptitude Tests*. The data on which this table is based are in Table 27 of the *Manual for the Differential Aptitude Tests*, page 66. Except for the data pertaining to the Mechanical Reasoning Test, the data for boys and girls have been combined.

† 85-per-cent confidence interval.

TABLE M.23

Iowa Tests of Educational Development

Standard Errors of Measurement and 85-Per-Cent Confidence Intervals
of Standard Scores and Smallest Differences Between Standard
Scores Significant at the 15-Per-Cent Level, or Better*

Test	Differences Between Standard Scores									85 Per Cent C.I.†	s_{meas}
	1	2	3	4	5	6	7	8	9		
1. Social Concepts	7	7	6	8	7	7	7	7	8	9.2	3.2
2. Natural Sciences		8	7	8	7	7	7	7	8	10.4	3.6
3. Expression			6	7	6	6	6	6	8	7.5	2.6
4. Quantitative				8	8	8	8	7	9	11.2	3.9
5. Social Studies Reading					7	7	7	7	8	9.2	3.2
6. Natural Sciences Reading						7	7	7	8	9.2	3.2
7. Literature							7	7	8	9.2	3.2
8. Vocabulary								6	8	8.1	2.8
9. Use of Sources									9	11.8	4.1

* The data in this table are based on reliability coefficients reported in Table 1 of the *Manual for the School Administrator*. (Chicago: Science Research Associates, 1949), p. 33.

† 85-per-cent confidence interval.

TABLE M.24

Kuder Preference Record, Vocational
Forms CH, CM

Standard Errors of Measurement and 85-Per-Cent Confidence Intervals
of Standard Scores,* and Smallest Differences Between Standard
Scores Significant at the 15-Per-Cent Level, or Better†

Test	Differences Between Standard Scores										85 Per Cent C.I.‡	s_{meas}
	0	1	2	3	4	5	6	7	8	9		
0. Outdoor	6	6	7	7	6	7	7	7	7	7	8.2	2.8
1. Mechanical		6	7	7	6	7	7	7	7	7	8.2	2.8
2. Computational			8	8	8	8	8	8	8	8	11.1	3.9
3. Scientific				8	8	8	8	8	8	8	11.1	3.9
4. Persuasive					7	7	7	7	7	7	8.6	3.0
5. Artistic						8	8	8	8	8	10.8	3.7
6. Literary							8	8	8	8	10.8	3.7
7. Musical								8	8	8	10.8	3.7
8. Social Service									7	8	9.6	3.3
9. Clerical										8	10.8	3.7

* Standard scores obtained by using Table D.5 to convert percentiles on the Profile Chart into corresponding standard scores having a mean of 50 and a standard deviation of 10, a normal distribution for all scores being assumed as characteristic of the population.

† Data are based on reliability coefficients for 1,000 men reported in Table 5 in the *Examiner Manual*, Fifth Edition. (Chicago: Science Research Associates, 1953.) In practice, the data may be used for interpreting the scores of males and females properly plotted on any one of the Profile Charts.

‡ 85-per-cent confidence interval.

TABLE M.25

Lorge-Thorndike Intelligence Tests

Standard Errors of Measurement and 85-Per-Cent Confidence Intervals
of Single IQ's, and Smallest Differences Between Verbal and
Nonverbal IQ's Significant at the 15-Per-Cent Level, or Better*

Level	IQ	Differences Between Verbal and Nonverbal IQ's	85 Per Cent Confidence Interval	Standard Error of Measurement
1	Total		18.7	6.5
2	Total		22.5	7.8
3	Verbal	11	17.9	6.2
3	Nonverbal		12.7	4.4
4	Verbal	13	20.4	7.1
4	Nonverbal		13.2	4.6
5	Verbal	12	17.6	6.1
5	Nonverbal		14.7	5.1

* Data are based on over-all standard errors of measurement in Table 5 of the *Technical Manual*. (Boston: Houghton Mifflin, 1957), p. 9.

TABLE M.26

Kuhlmann-Anderson Intelligence Tests*
Seventh Edition, Booklets G and H
Comparable Verbal and Quantitative Scores, and Smallest Differences
Between Them Significant at the 15-Per-Cent Level, or Better†

Raw Score	Comparable Score Booklet G‡ V	Comparable Score Booklet G‡ Q	Booklet H§ V	Booklet H§ Q	Raw Score	Comparable Score Booklet G‡ V	Comparable Score Booklet G‡ Q	Booklet H§ V	Booklet H§ Q
73	80				39	56	53	53	52
72	79				38	56	52	53	51
71	79	80	80	80	37	55	51	52	50
70	78	79	79	79	36	54	51	51	50
					35	53	50	51	49
69	78	79	78	78					
68	77	78	77	77	34	52	49	50	48
67	76	77	76	76	33	52	48	49	47
66	75	76	75	75	32	51	47	49	47
65	75	75	74	74	31	50	47	48	46
					30	49	46	47	45
64	74	74	73	73					
63	73	73	72	72	29	48	45	47	44
62	72	73	71	71	28	47	44	46	44
61	72	71	70	70	27	46	44	45	43
60	72	70	69	69	26	46	43	45	42
					25	45	42	44	42
59	71	70	68	68					
58	70	69	67	67	24	44	41	43	41
57	70	68	66	66	23	44	41	42	40
56	69	67	66	66	22	42	40	42	39
55	68	66	65	65	21	42	39	41	39
					20	41	38	41	38
54	67	65	64	64					
53	67	65	63	63	19	40	37	40	37
52	66	64	63	62	18	39	36	39	36
51	65	63	62	61	17	38	36	38	35
50	64	62	61	60	16	37	35	38	35
					15	36	34	37	34
49	64	61	60	59					
48	63	61	60	59	14	36	33	36	33
47	62	60	59	58	13	35	32	35	32
46	62	59	58	57	12	34	31	34	30
45	61	58	57	57	11	33	30	33	29
					10	32	29	32	27
44	60	57	57	56					
43	60	56	56	55	9	31	27	30	26
42	59	56	55	54	8	29	26	29	23
41	58	55	55	54	7	28	24	27	21
40	57	54	54	53	6	26	22	26	
					5	25	20	24	

* Footnotes on page 404.

* See F. B. Davis, "Kuhlmann-Anderson Test: Measure of Academic Potential. Seventh Edition," *Personnel and Guidance Journal*, 40 (1962), 481-484.

† Estimated graphically by the equi-percentile method from data in Tables 2 and 5 in the *Norms Manual* and reliability coefficients in Table 14 in the *Technical Manual*. These data are not as accurate as if they had been based on all cases in grades 7 through 12, but they are serviceable in estimating the significance of individual differences between V and Q scores in each booklet. They do not provide a basis for the comparison of comparable scores from Booklet G to Booklet H, and vice versa.

‡ The smallest difference between comparable scores significant at the 15-per-cent level is 10 points for Booklet G. (The standard error of measurement of the difference between comparable scores is about 6.8 points.)

§ The smallest difference between comparable scores significant at the 15-per-cent level is 8 points for Booklet H. (The standard error of measurement of the difference between comparable scores is about 5.4 points.)

INDEXES

INDEX OF NAMES

INDEX OF TOPICS

W